BASIC PRIMER for the IBM® PC & XT

This comprehensive, yet exceptionally easy, low-stress introduction to the world of BASIC programming provides detailed instructions on setting up your system, experimenting with BASIC's "direct commands," and writing your first-ever BASIC program. In it you'll find all aspects of BASIC programming thoroughly covered, including monochrome and color graphics, sound and music generation, disk access, floating point, and error-recovery.

Written by experienced computer science teachers, and modeled after the successful Waite Group primers, it's the perfect one-stop book for both beginners and experienced programmers who want to learn about IBM BASIC.

Bernd Enders

Bernd Enders is Professor of Physics and Astronomy at the College of Marin in Kentfield, California. In addition to these subjects, he teaches introductory computer science. Mr. Enders is also a founder of Starsoft, a company specializing in astronomical software. He received his B.S. degree in physics from the University of Chicago, and a Master's in physics from the University of California at Berkeley. Mr. Enders' interests include woodworking, the cello, and painting.

Robert L. Petersen

Robert L. (Bob) Petersen is Professor of Physics and Astronomy at the College of Marin. He received his B.A. and M.Sc., both in physics, from San Francisco University. Having a long-standing interest in computer applications, Mr. Petersen began using computers in education almost twenty years ago. His interests include cabinet-making, travel, and photography. He lives with his wife, Anne, and their two children in Kentfield, California.

BASIC PRIMER

for the

IBM® PC & XT

by
Bernd Enders
and
Bob Petersen

℗

A Plume/Waite Book
New American Library
New York and Scarborough, Ontario

Several trademarks and/or service marks appear in this book. The companies listed below are the owners of the trademarks and/or service marks following their names.

International Business Machines Corporation: IBM, IBM PC, IBM Personal Computer, IBM PC XT, PC-DOS
Microsoft: MS-DOS, MBASIC
Digital Research: CP/M, CP/M-86
MicroPro International Corporation: WordStar
Apple Computer Inc.: Apple
Intel Corporation: Intel
SoftTech Microsystems: UCSD p-System
Epson Corporation: Epson
Atari Inc.: Atari
Lotus: Lotus 1-2-3
Information Unlimited Software: EasyWriter
ATT Corporation: Bell Laboratories, Unix
ComputerLand
KayPro
Osborne
Xerox Corporation

LIBRARY OF CONGRESS CATALOGING IN PUBLICATION DATA

Enders, Bernd, 1947-
BASIC primer for the IBM PC and XT.

   "A Plume/Waite book."
   Includes index.
   1. IBM Personal Computer—Programming.   2. IBM Personal Computer XT—Programming.   3. Basic (Computer program language)   I. Petersen, Bob.   II. Title.
   QA76.8.I2594E53   1984   001.64′2   83-26959
   ISBN 0-452-25495-7

PLUME TRADEMARK REG. U.S. PAT. OFF. AND FOREIGN COUNTRIES
REGISTERED TRADEMARK—MARCA REGISTRADA
HECHO EN WESTFORD, MASS., U.S.A.

SIGNET, SIGNET CLASSIC, MENTOR, PLUME, MERIDIAN and NAL BOOKS are published *in the United States* by New American Library, 1633 Broadway, New York, New York 10019, *in Canada* by The New American Library of Canada Limited, 81 Mack Avenue, Scarborough, Ontario M1L 1M8

Book and cover designed by Dan Cooper

First Printing, May, 1984

   2 3 4 5 6 7 8 9

PRINTED IN THE UNITED STATES OF AMERICA

Contents

ACKNOWLEDGMENTS

The authors would like to thank Mitchell Waite for giving them the opportunity to write this book, and Robert Lafore, our editor, for his many helpful suggestions and his encouragement throughout this project. We'd also like to give thanks to some of our colleagues at the College of Marin, who not only put up with our intense involvement in writing this book, but provided valuable support: Don Martin, Steven Prata, Dick Rodgers, John Hines, Grete Clark, John Foreman, and Tara Flandan. And finally, we owe a great debt to Catheryn Zaro and Anne Petersen for helping us maintain some sense of balance in our lives and for sticking with us despite the fact that they must have felt like computer widows on all too many occasions.

Preface

BASIC is one of the easiest computer languages to learn, and also one of the most popular languages in the computer field. The IBM PC (or XT), with its powerful version of BASIC, and its excellent graphics and sound capabilities, provides an ideal learning tool.

Why Learn BASIC?

Although you may already be using prepackaged commercial programs to handle major jobs like word processing or tracking business finances, you'll find that a new world opens up when you can use BASIC to write programs tailored to your specific needs. You may want to learn BASIC to become a professional programmer. The computer field—specifically programming—is one of the most rapidly expanding areas in today's job market. Or you may simply wish to experience the joy of writing your own programs: it is very satisfying to learn a skill that gives you control of a tool as powerful as the IBM PC.

This book is written for anyone who wants to learn BASIC on the IBM PC or XT, especially the person who *has never done any programming before*. We start at the very beginning, yet by the time you've reached the end of this book you will be able to do some very sophisticated BASIC programming.

The Approach Used in this Book

Our approach is practical and down-to-earth: each new keyword or concept is introduced with actual examples, which you are invited to try out for yourself. And to make the experience of learning BASIC even easier, each chapter lists at the outset those concepts and BASIC instructions that are presented in the body of the chapter. As the chapter proceeds, boxed summaries of important statements, commands, and other elements of BASIC recapitulate in condensed form the material you have just read. In addition, each chapter ends with a summary that gives you an overview of the chapter's contents. Finally, at the end of the chapter, you'll find an exercise that enables you to put together many of the programming techniques you've just learned.

Enjoy Yourself!

We think you'll find this book exceptionally easy to read, informative, and enjoyable—whether you're a computer novice, or a programmer for whom BASIC is a second or even a third language.

1

Getting Started

Concepts
    BASIC as a computer language
    Software vs. hardware
    What you need to get started
    Bringing up BASIC

Welcome to the world of BASIC.

This chapter will give you the background you need to begin learning how to write BASIC programs. We'll discuss BASIC as a computer language, explain the differences between hardware and software, and tell you what kinds of system hardware, standard peripherals, and software you will need to make full use of this book. At the end of the chapter we'll explain how to load BASIC both for those of you who have the regular IBM PC and for those who have an IBM PC XT.

What Is BASIC?

A computer is really nothing more than a large collection of switches — and we do mean *large* — millions of them! These switches are like your light switches in that they are either in an ON or OFF position; this is how information is stored in a computer. All the incredible things that computers do (making complex financial projections, piloting the Space Shuttle) are done by manipulating these millions of switches. Most of us certainly don't want to communicate with computers at that level of ONs and OFFs; that's the job of a relatively few specialists. As users of personal computers, what we want is to be able to "talk" to the PC in a language that is as close as possible to our own way of thinking and communicating. Your IBM PC can't yet understand English, but it does understand BASIC, which is perhaps closer to English than any other computer language. BASIC is a compromise between the natural ON-OFF language of the machine and our own human language.

In addition to being quite a bit like English, BASIC is easy to learn because it gives you immediate feedback. If you're not sure about something, you can just try it and see if it works. BASIC will let you know right away if something is wrong; when this happens it even gives you fairly explicit *error messages*.

You should know, by the way, that not all computer languages are so amenable to this experimental approach. Whether or not a particular language can give you feedback depends, in fact, on how the language is translated into *machine language* — that is, the language of ONs and OFFs. BASIC is what is called an *interpretive language*. This means that whenever a BASIC program is executed by your PC, each of your BASIC instructions is first translated by the PC, one at a time, into machine language before the instruction can be carried out. Other languages, like FORTRAN or Pascal, require that the *whole program* be first translated (or *interpreted*) into machine language before the computer can carry out its instructions. This translation process requires additional steps by the programmer before he or she can test the program. But in BASIC, no such translation process (called *compiling*) is required. All you have to do is to press one key, and your program *runs* immediately; there's no waiting, and you get immediate results.

As convenient as it is, BASIC is also a powerful and extremely versatile language, especially the particular "dialect" written for your IBM PC. You can use BASIC to write business-related programs. For example, such programs might keep track of your business finances, make financial projections or predictions, analyze your investment portfolio, or generate mailing labels. Or you can write BASIC programs for use in your home to keep track of your diet, or to entertain yourself, family, and friends with a clever computer game you just invented!

BASIC on your PC can, of course, also be used for mathematical and scientific applications, ranging from such topics as modeling the motion of a bouncing ball to simulating the motions of the planets. Problems that used to require literally years of hand calculation can be done on your PC in a matter of seconds. Computers are also ideal for teaching certain types of skills, such as arithmetic, spelling, languages, and music.

BASIC for your IBM PC has some special features or extensions built into it that you won't find on many other computers. The most significant of these are the extended graphics capabilities of BASIC on the PC. These allow you to draw points, lines, circles, and ellipses, or complex shapes and patterns with a single BASIC instruction. Your PC and its BASIC are ideally suited for any graphics applications, such as graphing sales or stock performance, or teaching children about geometry.

What You Need To Get Started

Any IBM PC has the familiar keyboard and the box that contains most of the circuitry that makes up the computer. But beyond that, there are many different system configurations and three different versions of BASIC available. Although you can get started learning BASIC with the smallest PC system you can buy (no disk drive, 16K of RAM, and any monitor), you will need more than this minimum configuration to make full use of IBM's sophisticated BASIC. The following sections describe our recommendations as well as the assumptions about equipment we made in writing this book.

Hardware vs. Software

Now is a good time to introduce you to two phrases that are hard to avoid in today's computer world: system *hardware* and system *software*. Hardware refers to the physical system — anything that you can touch. Software, on the other hand, refers to the instructions we give to the hardware; it tells the hardware what to do. Software is information, intelligence. It encompasses all computer programs, including, of course, BASIC. Without software a computer is about as useless as a 747 without a pilot. You might summarize the difference between hardware and software in the following way: If you can kick it, it's hardware; if you can write it, it's software!

Hardware Requirements

Let's discuss one hardware item at a time.

Cassette

Not many PCs are sold without disk drives, but if yours is one of these, then it may be equipped with a cassette interface and a cassette machine, similar to the cassette players used for music and speech. Using cassettes to store programs and data is cheap, but very slow compared with diskette drives. You can use a cassette-based PC with this book, but the sections on using the disk drives and the disk operating system will not be applicable.

Disk Drives

Disk drives and the diskettes that fit in them are convenient devices for storing information more or less permanently — information that you don't want to lose when you turn the power off on your PC. You won't really need to use a disk until you get to Chapter 4, where we'll show you how to save your own BASIC programs on disk. But beginning with Chapter 4, we'll assume that you have at least one disk drive. Chances are, however, that you'll have *two* disk drives, or even a fixed disk. (A fixed disk stores far more data than a diskette, but can not be removed from the drive.)

The Printer

It's advisable to have a printer, but it's not essential. Printers give you a permanent record of your programs and their output. Printers become really important only when your programs start getting much longer than one screen full (which is usually 24 lines); being able to see the whole program at a glance gives you an overview of your programs and keeps you from getting lost in your program listing. Most programs in this book are short enough that a printer is not necessary.

Monitors

Several different types of video display devices can be used with your PC. All of them, of course, work adequately, but you do need to be aware of which one you have in order to relate what happens on your screen with what we describe in this book. Each monitor has its own advantages and limitations. The basic issues revolve around the number of characters your monitor can display, image sharpness and resolution, and whether it is capable of a type of graphics sometimes called *dot graphics*, but also called *all-points-addressable* graphics. ("Graphics" simply means displaying pictures, rather than words).

If you have the IBM Monochrome Display, you've got a sharp and very readable display. It will work perfectly for every chapter except one: Chapter 14, on color graphics. You cannot do true graphics on the IBM Monochrome Display; that is, you can't draw such things as oblique lines or circles. If the IBM Monochrome Display is the only monitor available to you, you won't be able to try out the examples in Chapter 14, but you can still do another form of graphics called *character graphics* which we describe in Chapter 10.

The most versatile — and, of course, the most expensive — display device is a high-quality color monitor, often called an *RGB monitor* (RGB stands for "red-green-blue"). This monitor requires — as do all monitors other than the IBM Monochrome Display — a special circuit board inside your PC called a Color/Graphics Adapter. This display system is able to show fully and dramatically the complete range of text and graphics capabilities of your PC. It works perfectly for every chapter in this book.

A black and white, green or amber monitor (also driven by the Color/Graphics Adapter) gives you somewhat less resolution than the IBM Monochrome Display (meaning that the characters on it won't be quite as sharp and readable as on the Monochrome), but it has the advantage of being able to display true dot graphics. It will work for all the chapters in this book, but of course you won't be able to see the color-graphics displays in color.

Another display option is your home color (or black and white) TV set adapted to your PC with a special little device called an *RF modulator* (and a special switch that allows you to switch between regular TV reception and use of the TV with the computer). Although you can do color graphics on this system, it is the least desirable display system for general purposes because text displayed in the 40-character-width screen mode tends to be a bit fuzzy and hard to read; and in the 80-character-width mode, it is virtually impossible to read. If that is the only display you have, you should go ahead and use it, but be aware that all of the examples in this book are geared to an 80-character-width display, and therefore your display will not look quite like those in the book.

All the various display device options are summarized in Figure 1-1. Notice that there are two basic types of adapters that "drive" the different kinds of video display devices. The Color/Graphics Monitor Adapter drives the three different types of monitors that can do dot graphics; also, this adapter will enable you to display color — provided, of course, that your monitor or TV set is capable of color. The IBM Monochrome Display and Parallel Printer Adapter is designed specifically for the IBM Monochrome Display.

Some people have *two* monitors attached to the two different adapters. For example, you might use the IBM Monochrome Display for all your text display, but do all your graphics on a monitor or TV set driven by the Color/Graphics Adapter. In this case, you'll want to be able to switch back and forth between the two different adapters. Unfortunately, there isn't a single key on your keyboard that does the job, but there are several ways of making the switch. One way is to use a short BASIC program listed in Appendix B. If you are using DOS 2.0, you can use a MODE command also summarized in Appendix B. You won't need to switch between monitors right away, but keep it in mind for later use.

Software Requirements

The word "software" refers to the programs we use to operate our computer, including, of course, BASIC. There are three forms of BASIC available for your PC:

1. Cassette or ROM BASIC is the basic BASIC that comes with every PC except the PC XT. The use of a cassette recorder for permanent information storage is optional.

2. Disk BASIC is a more sophisticated version designed for use with disk storage. If you have a disk, you've got it.

3. Advanced Disk BASIC, also called BASICA, is the same as Disk Basic, but includes a few more sophisticated instructions. If you have

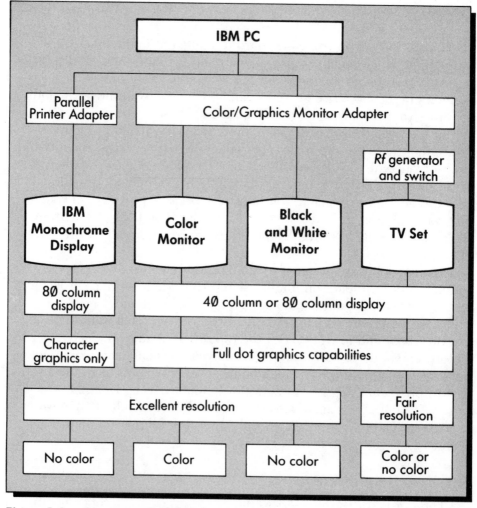

Figure 1-1. Summary of display device options

a disk, you probably have this too.

In case you need to know precisely what the differences are between these three forms of BASIC, see Appendix A. To start out learning BASIC, you'll need only the first of these BASICs, Cassette BASIC. So for those of you who have a PC (rather than the PC XT), we'll start with Cassette BASIC and later, in Chapter 4, show you how to load BASICA into your PC's memory. If you have the PC XT, we'll start you off with BASICA since you don't have Cassette BASIC.

Every PC that has at least one disk drive comes with a Disk Operating System, abbreviated DOS. DOS is a program that helps us to manipulate and control the operation of the disks and the flow of information to and from them.

IBM revises DOS from time to time in an effort to expand DOS's capabilities. At this point in time, IBM has released three versions of DOS. The first version is called DOS 1.0; the next to be released is called DOS 1.1; and the most recent version is DOS 2.0, which is the version generally sold with the PC XT. Each of these different versions of DOS implements BASIC in a slightly different way, but in general the differences are so small that you won't need to concern yourself about them. However, we'll point out whatever differences there are between DOS 1.1 and 2.0 as we come across them.

Loading BASIC

The style of this book is *action oriented* — we don't like to *talk* too much without actually *doing* something. So before we leave this introductory chapter, let's dive right in and turn the machine on and prepare the PC to accept BASIC instructions. If you already know how to do this, you can skip this section and start the next chapter.

If you're working on a PC XT, we'll assume that DOS and BASIC have been loaded onto your hard disk. If this is not the case, the instructions in Chapter 4 of your *IBM Personal Computer Disk Operating System* manual for Version 2.0 tell you how to do this.

Before you turn on your computer, open the doors of your floppy disk drives (you can also take the disks out, but it's not necessary). This prevents unwanted programs from loading themselves into your computer's memory.

Although you probably already know where the ON/OFF switch is, we'll tell you just in case — it's a large, red switch on the right side of your PC, towards the back. To turn the switch on, flip it upwards. After some sounds from your disk drives, and a beeping sound, a mysterious message will appear on your screen. Exactly what appears — and what you should do about it — depends principally on whether you have the regular PC or the PC XT. To avoid any confusion, we'll treat each of these cases separately.

If you have the IBM PC (not the PC XT), then read the following section, section A. If you have the PC XT, then skip section A and read section B entitled "Loading BASIC into an XT."

A. The BASIC Screen on Your IBM PC

Once you've turned on your PC *with the disk drive doors open*, your screen should look something like Figure 1-2. The first two lines on the screen tell you that you just turned on an IBM PC and that BASIC version C1.0 is on the system and ready to go. The letter *C* in "Version C1.0" stands for "Cassette" BASIC. Remember that you don't need a

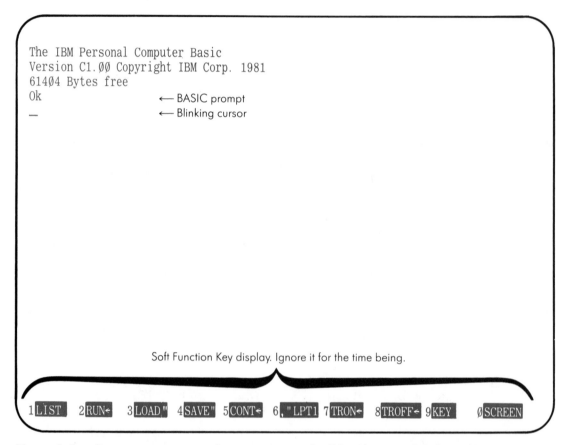

Figure 1-2. Screen appearance when you turn on the PC with open disk drive doors

cassette recorder for Cassette BASIC, nor do you need any disk drives and disks. It's easy to prepare your IBM for this form of BASIC — all you have to do is to turn on your PC with the disk drive doors open. Cassette BASIC is the simplest form of BASIC. We will use it until we get to Chapter 4.

The statement "61404 Bytes free" tells you how much memory is available to you for your BASIC program. The word *byte* refers to a unit of information that is roughly equivalent to one letter or character. The number of free bytes may be quite different on your computer since this number depends on how much memory has been installed in your machine (ours has about 64,000 bytes, usually abbreviated as 64K).

The "Ok" is the BASIC *prompt*. You can think of the prompt as your PC's way of letting you know that it is ready to accept BASIC instructions from you.

The blinking line right underneath the "Ok" is called the *cursor*. It tells you exactly where a character will appear on your screen if you press a key on your keyboard. You will see how the cursor works when we start typing in BASIC instructions in Chapter 2.

All the strange abbreviations at the bottom of your screen, called the *Soft Function Key Display*, are irrelevant to what we'll be doing until we get to Chapter 5. This display line won't be in the way of anything, so for the time being we'll just ignore it.

Now you're ready to try your first BASIC instructions! See you in Chapter 2!

B. Loading BASIC into an IBM PC XT

This section is meant only for people working with an IBM PC XT. Assuming that you have turned on your computer with the door to your floppy disk drive open and that DOS 2.0 resides on your hard disk, something like the following will probably appear on your screen:

```
Current date is Tue 1-01-1980
Enter new date:
```

Respond by entering a new date in the following way. Type the date using the format shown in the first line on your screen, and then press the enter key, which looks like this:

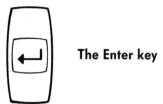 **The Enter key**

(If you don't care whether your computer keeps track of dates, you can omit a date entry and just press the ⏎ key.) Your PC will then request a "Current time" as well.

After you've entered the time by typing the time and then pressing the ⏎ key (again, you can just press the ⏎ key), the following should appear on your screen:

```
The IBM Personal Computer DOS
Version 2.ØØ (C) Copyright IBM Corp 1981, 1982, 1983

C>_
```

The letter *C* (it could also be a *D* instead) with the greater-than symbol (>) after it is what we're looking for. The letter is the name of the disk drive for your hard disk; the > symbol is the DOS prompt, which appears whenever DOS is ready to accept your DOS instructions. (Note that your particular XT may be set up in such a way that you don't have to enter the date and time to get to this point.)

Our next step is to load one of the two versions of BASIC available on the PC XT into the computer's memory. Let's load Advanced Disk BASIC (BASICA) right away, although you won't really need the advanced version until much later.

To load BASICA, type the word BASICA after the DOS prompt and then press the ⏎ key:

```
C>BASICA
```

After some noise from your hard disk drive (it's loading BASICA into the machine's memory), a display similar to Figure 1-3 should appear on your screen. The first two lines here tell you that you just turned on an IBM PC and that BASIC version A2.00 is on the system and ready to go.

The letter *A* in "version A2.00" reflects the fact that we've loaded Advanced Disk BASIC into your computer's memory.

The statement "60429 Bytes free" tells you how much memory is available to you for your BASIC program. The word *byte* refers to a unit of information that is roughly equivalent to one letter or character. The number of free bytes may be quite different on your computer, since this number depends mainly on how much memory has been installed in your machine (ours has about 64,000 bytes, usually abbreviated as 64K).

The "Ok" is the BASICA prompt. You can think of the prompt as your PC's way of letting you know that it is ready to accept BASIC instructions from you.

The blinking line right underneath the "Ok" is called the *cursor*. It tells you exactly where a character will appear on your screen if you press a key on your keyboard. You will have a chance to see how the cursor works in Chapter 2.

The strange abbreviations at the bottom of your screen, called the *Soft function key display*, are irrelevant to what we'll be doing until we get to Chapter 5. This display line won't really be in the way of anything, so for the time being we'll just ignore it.

You're now ready to try your first BASIC instructions! See you in Chapter 2!

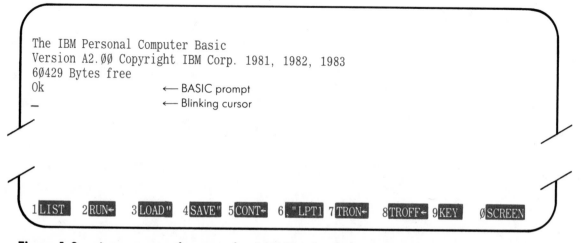

Figure 1-3. Appearance of screen after BASICA is loaded into memory

2

Your First Sight and Sound Program

Concepts
   The (↵) key
   BASIC's vocabulary
   Syntax errors
   Indirect and direct mode
   Simple editing with the *BACKSPACE* Key
   Commands and statements
   Line numbers and programs

Instructions
   PRINT, BEEP, LIST, RUN, CLS, END, NEW

Now let's write a program.

This chapter will give you your first experience in writing and running a simple BASIC program. BASIC is a tool that can be used creatively to solve all kinds of problems and to perform tasks that would otherwise require tremendous labor. What is more, you will experience the great satisfaction that comes from making the computer do what you want it to do.

Let's assume that you've prepared your IBM PC or your PC XT to communicate in BASIC as described in the last chapter. This means that you should find the BASIC prompt — an "Ok" — and the blinking cursor right underneath some introductory IBM BASIC information as shown in Figure 2-1.

To take an experimental approach, type "hello, computer." As you type in the letters, they appear right above the *cursor*. The function of the cursor is to tell you where whatever you are typing is going to appear on the screen. When you're done typing, the text appears on your screen right under the "Ok":

```
Ok
hello, computer _
```

But this is all you will see; nothing more happens.

Now locate what is called the enter key on the right side of your keyboard. The enter key looks like this:

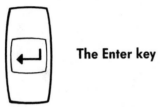

The Enter key

Throughout this book we will depict the Enter key with this keytop symbol: ⏎. It is one of the most important keys on your keyboard. To see what the ⏎ key does, press it. Your computer responds with the rather unappreciative message "Syntax error," as shown below:

```
Ok
hello, computer
Syntax error
Ok
_
```

What has happened? Well, several things. First of all, you didn't break anything! You know everything is all right because the computer says "Ok". In fact, the computer really didn't mind at all and you can

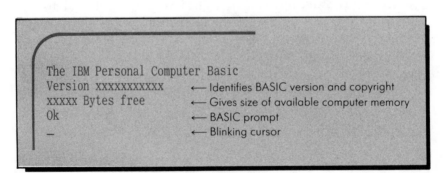

Figure 2-1. The BASIC screen at startup

press (↵) all over again, if you wish.

Second, notice that it is not until you press the (↵) key that the computer really "reads" and responds to what you typed on the screen. This procedure of typing something and then pressing (↵) is called *entering*. So from now on, when we say enter "something" we mean type "something" and press (↵).

Third, your IBM PC evidently did not understand what you said. "Syntax error" is the computer's way of saying "huh?" It's telling you that it didn't understand your words or your *Syntax*. Because people are still smarter than computers, we are the ones who are going to have to make the extra effort to communicate with them — in this case via the computer language BASIC.

Fortunately, however, whereas most human languages have a vocabulary of many tens of thousands of words, advanced IBM PC BASIC has only 159 words. These are called *reserved words* and are listed in Appendix C. Appropriate combinations of these BASIC words, or in many cases the words by themselves, make up BASIC commands and statements that your IBM PC can understand. Chapter 4 of your IBM *BASIC* manual contains a handy summary as well as a complete alphabetical listing with detailed explanations of all the BASIC commands and statements. Don't be alarmed by the size of the list — we're going to introduce you to these commands and statements gradually, one at a time.

Your First Basic Statements — Direct Mode

The simplest way of using BASIC instructions is in what is called the Direct Mode. All you have to do is to enter a legitimate BASIC command.

For example, enter the word "beep." The instant after you press the (↵) key (remember, that's how you enter something), your computer really beeps! The new lines on your screen now look like this:

```
beep
Ok
_
```

The "Ok" prompt signifies that your computer is ready to accept another command. (In the future, you will find the BEEP statement to be very handy as the computer's way of getting your attention.)

Before we get very far into BASIC, we had best tell you how to correct typing errors (a rather crucial concern to some of us!). It is done by means of the BACKSPACE key on the upper right-hand side of your keyboard (not to be confused with the ⏎ key just below it). The BACKSPACE key looks like this:

 The Backspace key

This key does something more than what you would expect from a typewriter. In addition to moving the cursor one space backward, it also *erases* the character right above the cursor. Try this out by typing "bepp" and making the correction by backspacing twice to give you "be" on the screen, and then typing "ep". Incidentally, if you try this after you pressed ⏎, it will be too late. The computer will respond with "Syntax error" and the "Ok", and you will have to start over.

The first words we asked you to enter into your PC were "hello, computer". Now let's write a BASIC statement that will cause your *computer* to print the same message. Enter (type and press ⏎) the following:

```
print "hello, computer"
```

This time you get more than just a "Syntax error". The new lines on your screen should look like this:

```
print "hello, computer"    ← BASIC statement entered.
hello, computer            ← Your PC responds: BASIC command has been executed.
Ok
─
```

As you can see, the PRINT command has the effect of literally printing on the screen the information inside the quotation marks. We'll say much more about this very important and useful BASIC statement in Chapter 3.

To summarize, BASIC instructions in the Direct Mode are executed immediately after the ⏎ key is pressed.

CLS—A BASIC Command for Clearing the Screen

By this time your screen is getting pretty cluttered. In fact, you may even be getting a little anxious about running out of space at the bottom of the screen. You really need not worry about that, however; simply press ⏎ until the cursor gets to the bottom of the screen. If you continue to press ⏎ in an attempt to move the cursor below the screen, the screen will just scroll upward, leaving the cursor at the bottom. (Scroll simply means all the lines on the screen moving upward at once.) So there is no way (at this stage, anyway) to lose your cursor or to get lost outside the screen.

Although you may have scrolled most of your text out of sight, you still have a lot of *Ok's* on your screen. To erase the screen completely, enter the BASIC command

```
cls
```

The effect of *CLS* is to clear the screen and to move the "Ok" prompt and the cursor to the *home* position, which is the upper left-hand corner of your screen. You can use the CLS command whenever the screen gets too messy.

Your First BASIC Program

Using a BASIC statement as a command to perform a single task — as illustrated in the previous examples — has an obvious limitation: you can do only one thing at a time. What if you want the computer to perform many tasks in sequence? Virtually any problem worth buying a computer for involves a *series* of BASIC statements. These statements make up a BASIC *program*, which may involve hundreds of statements arranged in a specified sequence. In contrast to the Direct Mode commands we have used so far, programs operate, by definition, in Indirect or Program Mode.

To illustrate how a BASIC program works, let's write a very simple program using the PRINT and BEEP statements that you are already familiar with. Type the following line. Don't forget the number 10 before "print" — this number is very important, as you will see shortly:

```
10 print "My first BASIC program!"
```

Now press the ⏎ key and type the second line:

```
20 beep
```

Remember to press ⏎. The whole program should now look like this:

```
10 print "My first BASIC program!"
20 beep
```

Although this program may not seem very interesting since the computer didn't do anything, something did happen in the innards of the PC's microelectronic memory: every time you pressed (↵), the computer read and put into its memory the BASIC instructions you had just typed. To make the computer execute this sequence of BASIC statements, all you need to do is enter the command RUN.

Enter "run" now. The result is not totally unexpected: first your computer prints "My first BASIC program!" on your screen, and then it beeps. Your screen now looks like this:

```
Ok
10 print "My first BASIC program!"
20 beep
run
My first BASIC program!
Ok
_
```

Line Numbers and BASIC Statements

Let's take a look at some of the details of the program we have just constructed. Undoubtedly you will have wondered about the numbers at the beginning of each line. These are called *line numbers* and they have two very important functions.

First, line numbers let the computer know that the statements you have entered are part of a program rather than just a series of commands to be executed the instant you press (↵). A program is, in fact, a sequence of BASIC instructions executed by means of the RUN command. This is very different from the way we first used BASIC instructions in what we called the Direct Mode, in which BASIC commands were carried out immediately after (↵) was pressed. We will refer to BASIC instructions used within programs — that is, instructions preceded by line numbers — as BASIC *statements*. Instructions used in the Direct Mode — that is, without line numbers — will be called BASIC *commands*.

The second function of line numbers is to define the *order* in which the computer carries out your BASIC instructions. In a simple program like the one we just wrote, execution always proceeds from the smallest to the largest line number; thus line 10 is executed before line 20. But why did we skip all the numbers between 10 and 20?

The answer is that we could have used 1, 2, and 3, and the program would have worked just as well. Leaving room between line numbers, however, gives you the option of inserting additional BASIC statements between existing numbers later on, in case you want to modify or add to your program. Suppose, for example, that you want to add a beep before your computer prints out "My first BASIC program!" This kind of change is very easy to make in BASIC. Just enter the following new line under the "Ok":

```
5 beep
```

Now run your program again by entering RUN. Your IBM PC does just what it is supposed to do: first it beeps, then it writes "My first BASIC program" onto the screen, and then it beeps again. (You will notice that the beeps blend together into a single, longer beep.)

To summarize, what we have done is to insert a new BASIC statement into an existing program simply by entering a new line with an appropriate line number. Writing programs that have line numbers initially incremented by 10 is a common practice as well as a sensible one because it usually leaves you with plenty of room to insert new statements.

Corrections and Deletions

In addition to inserting lines, you may also make corrections and deletions of lines you have already entered. In order to change a line, you need only reenter the same line and line number with the desired changes.

For example, if you want to change line 10 to say "My first program works!" and to delete the second beep, you would enter

```
10 print "My first program works!"
20        ← That's right, just type 20 and enter it.
Ok
```

Now enter "run" — sure enough, you hear a beep, and then "My first program works!" appears on the screen. Evidently, the computer simply substituted the new contents of lines 10 and 20 for the old contents. The new line 20 with nothing following it simply has the effect of erasing whatever was there before. So an easy way to delete a BASIC line is simply to enter the line number of the line to be deleted without any text.

LIST — A Way To See What You've Done

With all the changes we have made in our original program, it is easy to lose track of what our present program actually looks like. An easy way to find out is to enter "list". The LIST command does exactly what it suggests: it lists the current contents of your program.

Before we try this new command, however, let's clear the screen by entering "cls". You needn't worry that CLS will erase your program; it only clears the screen. The program remains in the computer's memory safe and sound — until you turn the computer off, that is!

Now with the PC's screen cleared, enter "list". Your screen should look like this:

```
list
5 BEEP
10 PRINT "My first program works!"
Ok
_
```

This is your current program. Notice, however, that it is displayed somewhat differently than you entered it: the words BEEP and PRINT are capitalized, whereas you entered them in lowercase. LIST always capitalizes words that are part of the vocabulary of BASIC, regardless of how you entered them. The advantage of this feature is that your program is listed in a clear and transparent way while you are saved the inconvenience of having to use the Shift (SHIFT) key. In this book, we will follow suit and write all BASIC words in capital letters from now on. Realize, however, that you may enter them as lowercase letters.

Another very helpful feature of LIST is that it rearranges your program lines in proper sequence. Notice that line 5 has been properly inserted before line 10. Use the LIST command whenever you want to look at your program, especially if you feel that you are beginning to lose track of what you've been doing.

END — A Good Way To End Your Program

Your previous program as listed above works perfectly well as it stands. When you enter RUN, BASIC starts execution with the lowest line number and finishes with the largest number. When you enter RUN again, BASIC knows that it should start at the beginning — that is with the lowest line number.

In more complex programs, however, there may well be lines *after* the location at which you want the program to end. This is true, for example, in programs containing subroutines which come after the main body of the program and which we will explain in Chapter 12. In such a case, it becomes crucial to define the end of a program with an END statement. END causes the computer to stop execution and to return to the BASIC command level (signified by the "Ok" prompt). In order to develop good habits and to avoid unnecessary problems in the future, you should end all programs with the END statement.

To illustrate the use of the END statement, let's add an END statement to our existing program. Just enter the line

```
20 end
```

and then enter LIST to see if the computer was really listening. This is what should appear on the screen:

```
list
5 BEEP
10 PRINT "My first program works!"
20 END
Ok
_
```

To be sure that END really works the way we said it did, you may wish to add a line after the END statement, like

```
30 PRINT "this statement is past END"
```

If you now run this program, you should get exactly the same output as before: in effect the computer never gets to line 30 because END terminates execution at line 20. Although the execution of a program will always end when it runs out of lines, it's a good idea, for the sake of clarity, to use an END statement to terminate program execution.

NEW — A Way To Start

You have now successfully completed writing, modifying, and running your first BASIC program. You may even be inclined to try some new programs of your own. To begin a new program, it would be very convenient to erase everything that you've done before — like erasing a blackboard before you start writing again. The NEW command does exactly that. NEW simply erases all previous instructions that were in the computer's random access memory (RAM), and gets the computer ready to receive new instructions.

Go ahead and try this command now. Enter

NEW

Now check to see whether the program is gone by entering LIST. You'll find that nothing is listed; the old program has indeed been erased.

Summary

You now know some of the rudiments of BASIC programming. You've learned that a BASIC command is a BASIC instruction that is executed immediately after pressing the ENTER ⏎ key. A BASIC statement, on the other hand, is a BASIC instruction that when entered, is "remembered" by the computer but not executed. BASIC statements are preceded by line numbers, while BASIC commands are not. BASIC statements are executed only after RUN is entered. A BASIC program is made up of a series of BASIC statements that allow the computer to carry out a potentially large set of instructions whenever RUN is entered.

Here is a list of examples of BASIC instructions that we have introduced in this chapter:

BEEP	Causes your computer to "beep."
PRINT "hello"	Causes your PC to PRINT what is inside the quotation marks.
CLS	Clears the screen.
LIST	Causes your PC to "list" the present program.
RUN	Causes your PC to execute the present program.

| END | Terminates program execution. |
| NEW | Erases a program in the computer's memory. |

Exercise

Clear the screen and the computer memory, and then write and run a program that will do the following: (1) print out "My computer can't talk" on the first line; (2) print out "but it can chirp like a bird" on the second line; and (3) make a beep sound. We suggest that you try writing this program *before* you look at our solution.

Solution

Enter CLS and NEW. Enter the program lines shown below, then enter LIST, and finally RUN. This is what your screen should look like when you're all done:

```
Ok
1Ø print "My computer can't talk"
2Ø print "but it can chirp like a bird"
3Ø beep
4Ø end
LIST
1Ø PRINT "My computer can't talk"
2Ø PRINT "but it can chirp like a bird"
3Ø BEEP
4Ø END
Ok
RUN
My computer can't talk
but it can chirp like a bird        ← your PC also "beeps"
Ok
−
```

3

Controlling Your Output— Printing What You Want Where You Want It

Concepts
  Printing strings and numbers
  Centering a title
  Printing columns
  Arithmetic operations
  Screen coordinates
  Error messages

Instructions
  WIDTH, PRINT, TAB, LOCATE

One of the important aspects of programming is being able to generate output to your screen in a format that is both useful and appealing. In this chapter we will investigate in some detail the very powerful PRINT statement. We will explain how it can be used to print text as well as to print the results of simple arithmetic operations. To enhance our ability to print material anywhere on the screen, we will introduce the BASIC statements TAB and LOCATE.

Getting to Know Your Monitor — Screen Size and Width

Before we begin exploring the main topic of this chapter, which is printing (that is, displaying information on the screen), we need to discuss your monitor and its effective screen size.

There are two basically different types of monitors available for the IBM PC: the one you are most likely to have is the IBM Monochrome

Display. The second type of monitor may take various forms: it may be a color or black and white video monitor (or any combination of colors, like green or amber on black) or a regular television. What all the monitors of the second type have in common with each other is that they require some special circuitry inside your computer called the Color/Graphics Monitor Adapter. As we mentioned in Chapter 1, both types of monitors have their advantages and disadvantages: the IBM Monochrome Display is better for text, whereas other monitors run by the Color/Graphics Monitor Adapter can do some pretty fancy graphics not possible with the former. Either of these types of monitors is perfectly suitable for learning BASIC with the help of this book, but you do need to know which of the two types of monitors you have.

Monochrome Display

If you have the IBM Monochrome Display, the situation is relatively simple in that you have a fixed screen size. As Figure 3-1 shows, your screen can display 80 characters in the horizontal direction, and 25 in the vertical direction. The twenty-fifth line, however, is special. For one thing, it normally displays what is called the Soft Function Key Display, which is the line with the rather strange looking messages at the bottom of your screen. (We will explain the meaning of this display line later on in the book.)

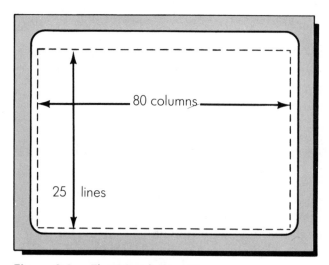

Figure 3-1. The 80-column wide screen

Other Monitors

If you have the other type of a monitor, either color or black and white, that is "driven" by the Color/Graphics Monitor Adapter, you have a choice of two screen sizes for printing text. The first is a 40-column wide display that your IBM PC chooses automatically when the machine is first turned on. The 40-column display is equivalent to the left half of the 80-column display shown in Figure 3-1. (You can see this right away because only the left half of the Soft Function Key Display shows up on the screen.) The second screen size available for monitors other than IBM's Monochrome Display is 80 columns wide — it is identical, in fact, to the display of the IBM Monochrome Display. The 80-column display may, however, be hard to read unless you have a high-quality monitor.

The way to switch back and forth between the 40-column and 80-column modes is to use the WIDTH command. To set the screen to an 80-column width, enter WIDTH 80. To set the screen to a 40-column width, enter WIDTH 40. As you work through the examples in this book, we suggest that you set your monitor to the 80-column width by entering WIDTH 80. All our sample programs will be based on an 80-column screen.

We might note here that WIDTH can also be used as a BASIC statement; that is, if preceded by a line number, WIDTH can be used within a program to switch screen widths.

Printing Strings

In Chapter 2 you became familiar with one of the neat things you can do with the PRINT statement: you can use it to print onto your screen any sequence of characters that are enclosed by quotation marks. For example, the following program

```
1Ø PRINT "BASIC is easy"
2Ø PRINT "*************"
3Ø PRINT "$2.5Ø"
4Ø END
```

will result in the following screen output when you enter RUN:

```
BASIC is easy
*************
$2.5Ø
Ok
```

As you can see, the sequence of characters enclosed by the quotation marks is printed out exactly as written in the PRINT statement. A character can be anything you can find on the typewriter part of your keyboard, including numbers, spaces, dollar signs, and asterisks. Such a sequence of characters bracketed by double quotation marks is called a *string*.

Centering a Title — An Example Using Strings

To illustrate the usefulness of strings, let's write a program to print the centered and underlined title "HOW TO BECOME RICH". Unfortunately, we can't do the underlining as easily as we could on a typewriter (this is one of the very few things that is easier to do on a typewriter!), but the previous example suggests another way to do it: just use the asterisks on the line below the title.

The only thing that is really new in this example, therefore, is centering the phrase, and this is not very hard. All we have to do is to add the right number of spaces in front of the title (but *after* the quotation marks) so that the title appears centered on — let's say — a 65-column wide page. We can do this by trial and error (always acceptable!), or we can do a little arithmetic to find the number of spaces we need: just subtract the number of characters in the title from 65 and divide by 2. We count 18 characters in the title (including spaces, of course), so 65 minus 18 equals 47, and 47 divided by 2 equals approximately 23 (we rounded down). So the following program, in which 23 spaces have been inserted after the opening quotation marks in lines 10 and 20 and before the title and the asterisks, should do the trick:

```
10 PRINT "                       HOW TO BECOME RICH"
20 PRINT "                       ******************"
30 END
        |←——23 spaces——→|
```

Now if we run this program, we get our underlined, centered title as shown in Figure 3-2.

Vertical Formatting

Let's take this example a bit further: how can we produce this title on a cleared screen near the top of the page, for example, on the third line from the top? It's easy, although we'll have to solve a problem we haven't encountered before: namely, how do you print blank lines?

You may have noticed that in the programs we have written so far, two consecutive PRINT statements have always resulted in two printed lines, one above the other. This means, in effect, that the first PRINT statement ends with what on a typewriter would be a carriage return. This suggests the possibility of printing blank lines by means of a PRINT statement with nothing following it. With this idea in mind, let's modify our existing program by entering the following new lines:

```
2 CLS
4 PRINT
6 PRINT
```

Since the line numbers of these statements are less than 10, they should insert themselves before line 10 of our original program.

Let's enter LIST to check that everything is as it should be:

```
LIST
2 CLS
4 PRINT
6 PRINT
1Ø PRINT "                    HOW TO BECOME RICH"
2Ø PRINT "                    *****************"
3Ø END
Ok
```

Voila — just as we expected! What happens here is that line 2 instructs the computer to clear the screen. Lines 4 and 6 say "print nothing but do a carriage return." Then lines 10 and 20 print the actual title and underline it. Note the usefulness of having plenty of room between line numbers here: it makes it easy to insert new lines.

Figure 3-3 shows what your screen will look like if you now run this program.

Now we have a program that prints out a title in a rather nice and useful format (to say nothing about the title itself!) In the process we have learned how to put a phrase anywhere on the screen by the

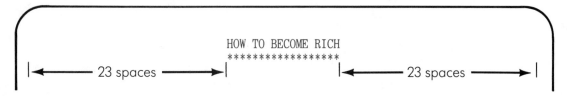

Figure 3-2. Output of centered title program

appropriate use of spaces within a string and by the "empty" PRINT statement — that is, a PRINT statement without anything following it.

Printing Numbers and Doing a Little Arithmetic

Print is really a very versatile and powerful BASIC instruction. Watch what happens when we run the following little program (first erase the previous program by entering NEW):

```
10 PRINT "3+16"
20 PRINT 3+16
30 END
RUN
3+16
 19
Ok
```

Line 10 does what you expected it to do: it just prints the string "3 + 16". The surprise is what line 20 does: instead of printing what you typed, it actually adds 3 plus 16. Evidently that happened because we left off the quotation marks that were previously used to identify a string. This example illustrates the general principle that if you follow PRINT with a simple arithmetic problem, it will print out the *answer* rather than restate the problem.

Subtraction, multiplication, and division are just as easy to do as addition. The following example illustrates the four common arithmetic operations: addition, subtraction, multiplication, and division. To clear the memory and the screen, enter NEW and CLS, and then enter the following program, and run it. Figure 3-4 shows what your screen should look like when you're done.

The symbols used in addition and subtraction are familiar ones. To indicate multiplication, use the asterisk (*), and to show division, use the slash (/). (A word of caution: your keyboard has another slash mark, the

```
            HOW TO BECOME RICH
            ******************
```

Figure 3-3. Output of centered title program with blank lines inserted

backslash (\), which leans the other way. Like the slash, the *backslash* can also be used as a division sign, but it does a different kind of division — called *integer division* — than the division that you are used to.) Table 3-1 summarizes the symbols used for the four common arithmetic operations.

There are several things to notice about the output of the program shown in Figure 3-4. First of all, the results that turned out to be positive numbers have one blank space in front of them. However, when the negative number is printed out, its negative sign (–) occupies the space that was left blank in the case of the positive numbers. The box called "Printing Arithmetic Operations" summarizes this aspect of the use of PRINT to perform arithmetic calculations.

```
Ok
10 PRINT 2+3
20 PRINT 2-3
30 PRINT 2*3
40 PRINT 2/3
55 END
RUN
 5
-1
 6
 .6666667
Ok
```

Figure 3-4. Arithmetic program

The Operation	The BASIC symbol
Addition	+
Subtraction	–
Multiplication	*
Division	/

Table 3-1. The most common arithmetic operations

Printing Arithmetic Operations

PRINT can be used to obtain the results of arithmetic operations (addition, subtraction, multiplication, and division) as shown in the following example:

```
1Ø PRINT 5 - 2
RUN
 3
Ok
```

These numbers are printed out with a space in front of the first digit reserved for the *sign* of the number. The sign is omitted but understood for positive numbers, but the negative sign is shown for negative numbers.

Another thing to notice about the output of the program in Figure 3-4 is that the result of dividing 2 by 3 is .6666667. Although this seven digit number is rather precise for most practical purposes, it isn't exact: an exact answer would have to show an infinite number of 6s! Since that is hardly practical, the people who wrote BASIC for the IBM PC decided to call it quits after seven digits — *unless* you make a special point of representing the number otherwise. This seven-digit precision to which your IBM PC "defaults" is called *single precision*. While the precision of numbers will be discussed in a later chapter, it's important to note here that IBM BASIC returns noninteger numbers to a precision of seven digits unless you instruct BASIC to do otherwise.

The program in Figure 3-4 printed out the results of numeric operations. What if you asked BASIC to print a simple number? No problem: the output will look much like the printed output of the numeric operations in our original program. Try this example:

```
1Ø PRINT "4ØØ9"
2Ø PRINT 4ØØ9
3Ø END
RUN
4ØØ9
 4ØØ9
Ok
```

Again, notice the difference between printing a number within a string and a number *not* within a string: the blank space reserved for the sign of the number that is not part of a string. Numbers not within a string, and numbers that are a result of arithmetic operations, are called *numeric expressions*.

Finally, you can use PRINT to print numeric expressions in the Direct Mode. In this way you can make your not-so-inexpensive IBM PC emulate a $20 calculator! Well, that is a handy feature at times, and it does speak for the versatility of your computer.

Printing with Semicolons and Spaces

So far we have learned how to print either one string or one result of a calculation with each PRINT statement. It turns out, however, that a single PRINT statement can be used to print a series of expressions, be they strings or numbers. Furthermore, you can control the format of the output to some degree by means of the following special characters: the semicolon, the space, and the comma.

The semicolon and the space (generated by pressing the space bar) do pretty much the same thing, so we will look at them together. The following illustrates the use of the semicolon and the space to control output:

```
10 PRINT "watch";"the";"spacing"
20 PRINT "watch" "the" "spacing"
30 END
RUN
watchthespacing
watchthespacing
Ok
```

As this program shows, to print several strings one right after the other with one PRINT statement, simply separate the strings with a semicolon, or a space. Note that the strings are really "stuck" together. In general, semicolons or spaces between strings cause their contents to be printed out in sequence without any spaces between them.

If you do want spaces, however, you have to put them into the strings yourself. For example, let's change line 20 so that it returns something more readable by reentering line 20 to read

```
20 PRINT "watch " "the " "spacing"
```

The output of our program now looks like this:

```
watchthespacing
watch the spacing
```

Since we did not change line 10, the program's output is still what we humans might respond to with "syntax error"!

Printing a Sequence of Numbers

As you probably have already guessed, what we did with strings in the last section we can also do with numbers. If we print numbers as strings separated by semicolons, the numbers will be printed out without spaces just as strings of words would be.

Try the following example. Enter NEW first, and then enter the program as shown below, and finally enter RUN.

```
1Ø PRINT "1";"2";"-3";"-4";"5"
2Ø PRINT 1;2;-3;-4;5
3Ø END
RUN
12-3-45
 1  2 -3 -4  5
Ok
```

The point of this example is to show the difference between printing a sequence of strings and printing a sequence of numbers. Line 10 works pretty much the way we expected; it prints the contents of the strings without any spaces to give "12-3-45." Line 20, on the other hand, has a surprise for us: it returns the proper sequence of numbers all right, but for some reason all those spaces have been added.

It turns out that there are two kinds of spaces involved. The first has to do with something you're already familiar with: BASIC always leaves room for the sign of the number, irrespective of whether it is shown explicitly (as for a negative number) or just implied (as for a positive number). The second kind of space is a space *behind* each number. As a result, each one-digit number takes up three spaces when printed. Figure 3-5 shows the output of line 20 with these spaces clearly marked by

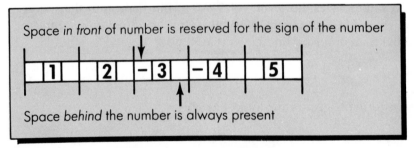

Space *in front* of number is reserved for the sign of the number

Space *behind* the number is always present

Figure 3-5. Output format of printing with semicolons

vertical lines. BASIC inserts this space behind each number so that numbers that really are separate numbers will not be run together. After all, 12 is not the same thing as the number 1 and the number 2. It is important not to have an ambiguous output.

Mixing Strings with Numbers

Strings and numeric expressions may also be mixed in a single PRINT statement. In the following example, we'll use the PRINT statement in the Direct Mode just for the sake of variety and to remind you that, indeed, this can be done. Enter the BASIC command shown below (no line numbers!) Also shown is what BASIC returns immediately after ⏎ has been pressed:

```
PRINT ".Ø6 * 586.24 ="; .Ø6 * 586.24
.Ø6 * 586.24 = 35.1744
Ok
```

First the contents of the string are printed out, and immediately following the string comes the result of the multiplication. Nothing surprising really, but this example does show how you might calculate a 6% interest on a $586.24 purchase and do it using a rather nice format possible with the PRINT statement.

Using PRINT with Semicolons or Spaces

A PRINT statement followed by a sequence of expressions separated either by a semicolon or a space prints out the sequence of expressions one right after the other, without spaces. An expression may be a string or it may have a numeric value. Numeric values returned by PRINT always have spaces reserved for the sign of the number (implicit for positive numbers) and a space after the number in order to keep numeric output unambiguous.

Printing with Commas

Sometimes you may find it desirable to print strings or numbers in well-defined columns, as, for example, in producing a phone list or an inventory. This could be done by means of printing with semicolons and spaces inside strings as discussed in the last section, but it would be, at best, a very tedious way to do it. A very direct and easy way to arrange your output in neat columns is to use the PRINT statement just as in the last section, except that you substitute a comma for the semicolon or the space.

To illustrate this use of the comma, let's enter the following new program (type NEW first) and run it:

```
1Ø PRINT "one","two","minus three","four"
2Ø PRINT 1, 2, -3, 4
3Ø END
RUN
one           two           minus three   four
  1             2             -3             4
Ok
```

The comma is responsible for spreading out the output in this way. If you count the number of spaces between the beginning of each of the words in the output, you will see that there are always 14 of them. In other words, the comma causes the output of PRINT to be dropped into slots or *print zones* 14 characters wide. Furthermore, the output is pushed to the left side of each zone, or *left-justified*. (For a better visual picture of these zones, see Figure 3-6.) Notice that this left-justification works for the numerical output as well, provided that you remember that there is always a space reserved for the sign of the number.

One question you may have at this point is, what happens when the length of what you're printing is *longer* than the zone width of 14

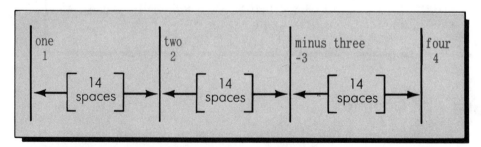

Figure 3-6. Zones created using commas with PRINT

characters? The answer to this question is demonstrated in the following new program (remember to type NEW first to clear away the preceding program):

```
1Ø PRINT "1","2","3"
2Ø PRINT "prestidigitation","has 16 letters"
3Ø PRINT "chocolate cake","has only 14 characters"
4Ø END
RUN
1               2               3
prestidigitation               has 16 letters
chocolate cake                 has only 14 characters
Ok
```

The output of line 10 marks the beginning of each zone. For example, the number 2 marks the beginning of the second zone. We can now see the answer to our question: the word "prestidigitation", which is 16 letters long, just extends into the second zone, pushing the contents of the next string, "has 16 letters", into the third zone. The surprise here, though, is the output of line 30: the phrase "chocolate cake" is exactly 14 characters long (including the space, of course), yet it is printed as if it were too long for a zone of 14 characters; that is, the second string is pushed over to the third zone.

We can interpret this apparent anomaly as BASIC's way of keeping zones from running into each other. After all, if you have columns that are all run together so that you can't distinguish one from the other, what good are the columns? It is clear from this example that you can use PRINT to print out only 13 characters within one zone, even though each zone is really 14 characters wide. The intrusion of text into the fourteenth space is treated by BASIC as a *zone-overflow* situation.

One question about these zones still remains: how many zones are there? We can discover the answer very quickly by running a PRINT statement containing many strings, all separated by commas.

Try the program shown in Figure 3-7. The numbers in the output identify the beginning (the first character) of each zone. You can see that on the first line, there are five complete zones that are 14 characters wide. The sixth zone is cut short by the edge of the screen; if you count the spaces in this zone, you'll see that it is only 10 characters wide. The seventh zone is printed on the next line, but it is indented by four spaces. In effect, the sixth and seventh zones are limited to 10 characters each.

The indentation of the seventh zone is significant because when you write a program, you don't want different zones to appear in the same column in the output. For example, if you wanted to write a program that would produce a table with seven columns, it would obviously be disastrous to have the information that belongs in column seven printed in column one. The moral is that you should keep the rules governing the behavior of print zones in mind, and be careful not to print more on one line than there is room for.

Printing with Commas

A PRINT statement with a sequence of expressions separated by commas prints out the sequence of expressions inside *zones* that have a width of 14 characters. Each expression is left-justified within its zone.

Printing with Tab — Controlling Your Columns

Using commas in your PRINT statement is certainly a convenient way of producing neat columns of information. But not everyone wants columns that are 14 characters wide for all occasions. What is more, there are only five full columns on an 80-column screen. What if you needed larger or smaller zones, or a different number of columns?

This is where the TAB statement comes to the rescue. TAB in BASIC works very much like the tab key on your typewriter: it is a convenient, quick way of writing out something at a specified column position. The required format of the TAB statement is TAB(n), where n stands for the number of the column where you want to start printing.

```
Ok
LIST
10 PRINT "1","2","3","4","5","6","7","8","9","10"
Ok
RUN
1             2             3             4             5             6
     7        8             9             10
Ok
```

Figure 3-7. Program shows how 14-character wide print zones fold over

To get a sense of how TAB works, enter and run the following program:

```
1Ø PRINT TAB(5) "1" TAB(15) "2" TAB(25) "3"
2Ø PRINT TAB(5) "Groucho" TAB(15) "Harpo" TAB(25) "Zeppo"
3Ø END
RUN
     1         2         3
     Groucho   Harpo     Zeppo
Ok
```

What has happened here is that TAB(5) caused the first character of the strings "1" and "Groucho" to be printed in the fifth character position or column of your 80 column screen. TAB(15) caused the contents of the following strings to be printed beginning at position 15. In this way we have produced three columns or zones 10 characters wide, the first one starting at position 5.

Note that TAB only works with PRINT or a statement closely related to PRINT. TAB may not be used alone.

The utility of TAB is obvious: it is a simple way of printing information anywhere on a line. In particular, TAB makes it easy to define the left edge of columns.

Printing with TAB

The BASIC statement

```
2Ø PRINT TAB(5) "Space"
```

means "print the string *Space* so that the first character of the string, *S*, appears at the fifth character (or column) position of your screen." For most practical purposes, the *n* in TAB (*n*) is in the range of 1 to 80.

LOCATE — The Fast Way to Get Around on Your Screen

At this point, we have learned to use PRINT to print whatever you want anywhere on the screen. By means of the TAB function, moreover, you can get to any horizontal position, and by using the appropriate number of blank PRINT statements (PRINT without anything following it), you can get to any vertical position on your screen. But there is one thing you can't do yet: namely, move back up the screen and print once you've printed something at the bottom of the screen. In addition, to get from the middle of the screen to some location near the bottom of the screen, you would have to use a lot of blank PRINT statements.

The LOCATE statement is designed to solve these problems. It's a very handy tool for positioning or for "locating" whatever you want to PRINT anywhere on the screen. Let's find out how it works.

First of all, you need to have a way of assigning a position on the screen. This is done by means of two numbers: the *row* number, which

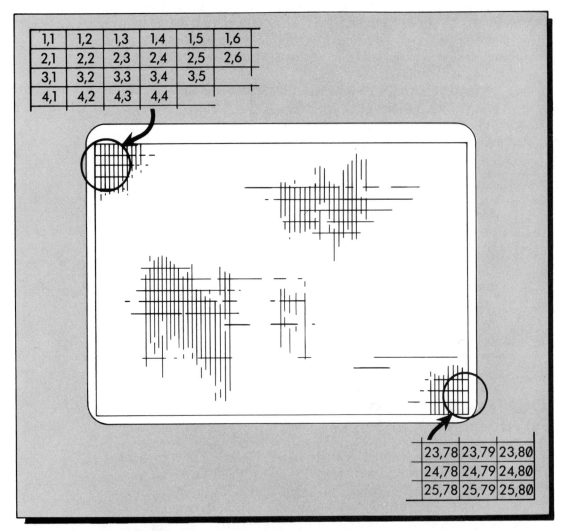

Figure 3-8. Screen coordinates: rows and columns

defines the position vertically, and the *column* number, which defines the position horizontally. The row can be any whole number between 1 and 25, while the column can be any number between 1 and 80. Figure 3-8 shows the location of some screen positions in terms of a pair of numbers written like this: *row,column*.

The format for the LOCATE statement is, in fact, LOCATE (*row, column*), where the row and column parameters define the position on the screen at which printing is to begin. Thus, for example, LOCATE 3, 5 refers to the third row and the fifth column, one of the positions marked in Figure 3-8.

It's time for an example. Let's write a program that uses PRINT and LOCATE to print something at the corners of your screen. Enter the following new program:

```
10 CLS
20 LOCATE 1, 1
30 PRINT "upper left"
40 LOCATE 24, 1
50 PRINT "lower left";
60 LOCATE 24, 80 - 11
70 PRINT "lower right";
80 LOCATE 1, 80 - 11
90 PRINT "upper right"
100 END
```

When you RUN this program, the output will appear in the corners of your screen as shown in Figure 3-9. This program shows quite clearly how LOCATE is used in conjunction with the PRINT statement. Basically, first you tell your IBM PC to start printing *here*, and then you tell it *what* to print. But let's take a closer look at the program now.

The first surprise in this program comes in lines 60 and 80 where we indicate the column position as 80 -11, which the computer evaluates to give 69. As you can see, BASIC will evaluate numeric expressions within statements like LOCATE. In having BASIC calculate the column position here, we ensure that the whole phrase "lower right", which takes up 11 spaces (including the space between words), appears in the lower right corner of the screen. In effect, we are instructing the PC to start printing the letter *l* eleven spaces before the right boundary of the screen.

Another interesting feature of this program is the two semicolons at the *end* of the PRINT statements in lines 50 and 70, in contrast to the semicolons used *between* expressions in a PRINT statement that we discussed earlier. If you try this program without the semicolons at the ends of lines 50 and 70, you'll get an extra blank space at the bottom of the screen, which will in turn cause your screen to scroll up by one line. The culprit here is the PRINT statement: when PRINT is executed, it produces an automatic carriage return. We can suppress this carriage return, however, by ending the PRINT statement with a semicolon.

In the beginning of this chapter, we mentioned the possibility of accessing row 25, which is the very bottom row on your screen and which is usually occupied by some instructions called the Soft Function Key Display. In order to turn this line off, enter the instruction

```
KEY OFF
```

and everything at the bottom of your screen should disappear. If you want to put the Soft Function Key Display back again, enter

```
KEY ON
```

```
upper left                                                    upper right
Ok
```

```
lower left                                                    lower right
1 LIST   2 RUN←   3 LOAD"   4 SAVE"   5 CONT←   6,"LPT1   7 TRON←   8 TROFF←   9 KEY   0 SCREEN
```

Figure 3-9. Output of program with LOCATE

For now, however, let's turn this display line off.

Now, with line 25 free, you can use LOCATE (25, *col*) to print on this line. Let's try this by adding the following three lines to our previous program:

```
100 LOCATE 25, 32
110 PRINT "I'm here to stay!";
120 LOCATE 12, 1
130 END
```

Now run this new version of our program. You'll find the string "I'm here to stay" at the very bottom of your screen (centered, more or less) where the Soft Function Key Display used to be. Now try listing your program — line 25 remains intact! You can also try entering some text near the bottom of your screen; again, row 25 remains intact, while the text above it scrolls as usual. The CLS command, however, will erase the whole screen, including row 25. It is useful to be able to control line 25 so that you can display some permanent (relatively!) instructions of your own there, if you wish.

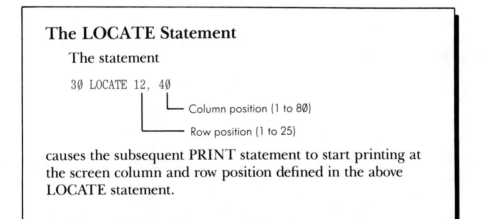

The LOCATE Statement

The statement

```
30 LOCATE 12, 40
```

└── Column position (1 to 80)

└── Row position (1 to 25)

causes the subsequent PRINT statement to start printing at the screen column and row position defined in the above LOCATE statement.

Summary

This chapter has been a fairly thorough exploration of the PRINT statement. We have also seen how TAB and LOCATE add considerable flexibility and power to PRINT.

As a way of reviewing this chapter, we suggest that you reread the boxed summaries of the topics covered. Then you may want to test your newly acquired skills by writing the program suggested below in

"Exercises." This program involves most of the BASIC statements we covered in this chapter.

Up to this point it may not be evident that printing and doing arithmetic with a computer is really any better than doing it via typewriter and calculator. Keep in mind, however, that this chapter was about *output*. We haven't really touched on what computers do best — namely doing manipulations or calculations many times, over and over again — the kind of work that's extremely tedious for us humans. So hang on, you have much to look forward to.

Exercise

Write a program that turns off the Soft Key Display, clears the screen, creates the underlined title "My Shopping List", and prints out a short shopping list of, say, three items, their cost, the tax and the total cost.

Solution

There are a number of ways to write the exercise program. Here is one solution:

```
10 KEY OFF
20 CLS
30 LOCATE 5,1
40 PRINT TAB(25) "My Shopping List"
50 PRINT TAB(25) "****************"
60 PRINT
70 PRINT "Item" TAB(28) " Cost"," TAX(6%)"," total"
80 PRINT "----------------------------------------------------------------"
90 PRINT
100 PRINT "can of sardines" TAB(28) 1.58, .9480001, 1.06*1.58
110 PRINT "a dozen floppies" TAB(28) 35.42, 35.42*.06, 1.06*35.42
120 PRINT "cat litter" TAB(28) 5.86, 5.86*.06, 1.06*5.86
130 LOCATE 23,1
140 END
```

When you RUN this program, the following appears on your screen:

```
          My Shopping List
          ****************

Item                    Cost        TAX(6%)     total
------------------------------------------------------

can of sardines         1.58        .9480001    1.6748
a dozen floppies        35.42       2.1252      37.5452
cat litter              5.86        .3516       6.2116
```

A few brief remarks about this program may be helpful.

First notice that "My Shopping List" isn't centered with respect to the whole screen, but rather with respect to the main body of the output, which ends on column 64.

Second, instead of using four blank PRINT statements to produce the four blank lines at the top of the screen, we used LOCATE 5, 1 to bring us down to line 5.

Third, notice the mixing of TABs and commas in line 70, for example. This turned out to be the easy way to produce a wide (28 characters wide) first column required for names of the items. The rest of the column positions are then determined by the commas.

Fourth, notice that the LOCATE statement in line 130 moves the cursor out of the way, to the bottom of the screen. This is not essential, but the screen seems to look a little better like this.

Finally, you may notice that this output, as neat as it looks, does have some obvious shortcomings: for example, all the columns are left-justified. You might really rather have all the decimal points line up. And look at all those decimal places behind the decimal point — talk about splitting pennies! Well, we can't do *everything* perfectly at the beginning. Later in this book, however, we'll show you some other ways of formatting output that may be more suitable for purposes like making dollar amount lists.

4

BASICA and Other DOS Features

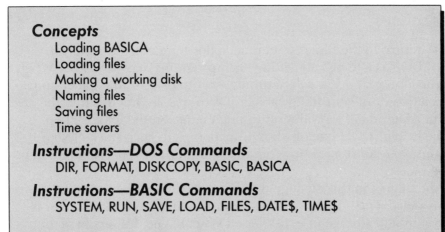

Concepts
Loading BASICA
Loading files
Making a working disk
Naming files
Saving files
Time savers

Instructions—DOS Commands
DIR, FORMAT, DISKCOPY, BASIC, BASICA

Instructions—BASIC Commands
SYSTEM, RUN, SAVE, LOAD, FILES, DATE$, TIME$

Disk Operating Systems are one of the features of computers that have given them the reputation for being great time-savers. This chapter will explain what you need to know about the PC's Disk Operating System, known simply as PC-DOS or DOS.

As a way of visualizing DOS's role in the PC's work, you can imagine DOS as a kind of traffic officer, controlling the flow of information between the PC's components, such as the disk drives, the keyboard, and the printer on the one hand, and the various programs that run on the PC on the other. DOS can also be compared to a sort of filing system, in that it not only controls the flow of information but also organizes and stores that information. For a complete description of DOS, read *DOS Primer for the IBM PC and XT* by Mitchell Waite, John Angermeyer, and Mark Noble (New York: Plume/Waite, New American Library, 1984), another book in this same series.

The second purpose of this chapter is to introduce you formally to two more powerful versions of BASIC than Cassette BASIC, which is the form of BASIC that permanently resides in the plain IBM PC and which also is the form of BASIC we have been using so far. The two new versions of BASIC are Disk BASIC and Advanced BASIC (or BASICA), both of which utilize the Disk Operating System. In this chapter and from this point on in the book, we will focus on BASICA, the most versatile and complete of the three forms of BASIC. Toward the end of the chapter, we will teach you a fast and convenient way to load your BASICA programs into the computer and then to save your programs for future use.

DOS Files

Let's return to the filing system metaphor for a moment. You can think of DOS as a filing cabinet in which programs may be stored. When you write a program, you will naturally want to place it in a folder and then in a drawer of your filing cabinet. Of course, in order to find the folder at a later date, we will want to put a name on the folder. Then, with the help of DOS, one of whose functions is to keep track of your programs, you can store your programs away and retrieve them later any time you want.

If the cabinet in this analogy is DOS, then the folder in computer terms is called a *file*. A file is a collection of similar kinds of data and is the main unit of storage in a disk-based system. The drawers in our analogy may be seen as the diskettes themselves. Finally, the name on the folder is a *file specification* (or *filespec* for short) in computer jargon.

The DOS filing cabinet comes with some files already in the drawers. These programs, which will make life easier for us, fall into two categories:

1. *Utilities*, which are concerned with programming tasks. Examples of these programs are DISKCOPY, DISKCOMP (for "disk compare"), and the disk forms of BASIC, Disk BASIC and BASICA.

2. *Demonstrations*, which give us something to show our friends: for example, the programs MUSIC, DONKEY (a video game), MORTGAGE, and CALENDAR which prints a one-year calendar for any given year.

Different Versions of DOS

The DOS system comes in three different models, as we explained in Chapter 1. The earliest version, called 1.0, was designed for use on single-sided diskettes. The second version, called 1.1, was designed to handle double-sided diskettes as well. The double-sided diskette is an improvement over the single-sided one in that we can store twice as much information on a double-sided diskette. A third version of DOS, called 2.0, supports single- and double-sided diskettes and also a large mass storage system called the *Fixed Disk* or *hard disk*. When you order diskettes, you will want to request single-sided ones if you have DOS version 1.0, or double-sided ones if you have versions 1.1 or 2.0.

There are some differences in the information contained in each version and thus you will need to understand how to use each form. The outside of the manual should tell you which version you have.

Using the Disk Drives and Loading DOS

You may have one or two disk drives. The disk drives are called *drive A*, which is the one on the left, and *drive B*, which is the one on the right if you have two drives (see Figure 4-1). To load DOS, place the DOS diskette (it comes from the back of the DOS manual) in drive A and shut the door of the drive.

If the PC is already turned on, push the following keys: while holding down the (Ctrl) key press the (Alt) key and then add the (Del) key. (This procedure is followed whenever a multikey sequence is used. The first key named should be pressed and then the other keys added in order.)

If, on the other hand, your PC was off, merely turn it on, with the DOS diskette in drive A, and things will begin to happen. First, you will hear that old familiar fan start up inside the PC. Next, some 5 to 40

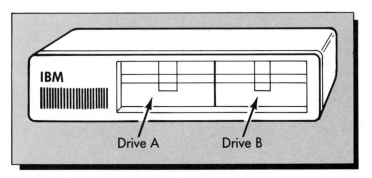

Figure 4-1. Disk drive identification

seconds later, the red light on drive A will come on and the sound of the whirring disk will be heard. The light will go out and the drive will stop temporarily and you will hear a beep. The light will again come on and the drive will again whir.

No, it's not time to take the PC in for repairs. It's simply performing a *self-test*, and reading your DOS diskette. This process is called *booting up*. (The name comes from the expression "pulling yourself up by the boot straps.")

Depending upon which version of DOS you have, your screen will display something like this:

```
Enter today's date (m-d-y):     ←— Version 1.Ø
```

```
Current date is Tue 1-Ø1-198Ø
Enter new date:     ←— Versions 1.1 and 2.Ø
```

In any of the versions, the DOS system is asking for the date in the form "month number-day number-year" (example: 6-23-1983). Next, versions 1.1 and 2.0 will ask for the time in the form "hours:minutes:seconds" (example: 18:13). Only the hours and minutes are necessary, but each *must* be separated by colons. When the (⏎) key is pressed, your screen should look like one of the screens shown in Figure 4-2, Figure 4-3, or Figure 4-4.

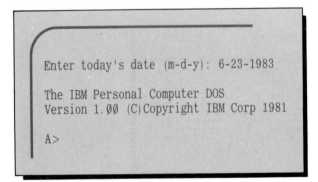

```
Enter today's date (m-d-y): 6-23-1983

The IBM Personal Computer DOS
Version 1.ØØ (C)Copyright IBM Corp 1981

A>
```

Figure 4-2. The initial DOS 1.0 screen

Congratulations! You have just loaded DOS.

Now, how do we find out what goodies are already in our filing cabinet? At this point we are at what is called the *system level*, meaning we are without BASIC and its command set. The DOS system has a set of its own commands. Let's look at a few of these commands.

The DOS Directory and the DIR Command

The DIR command will produce a list of the files in our filing cabinet; that is, DIR will tell you what files are on the DOS diskette. Try entering the command DIR after the system prompt A>:

```
Current date is Tue 1-01-1980
Enter new date: 6-23-1983
Current time is 0:00:15.43
Enter new time: 18:13

The IBM Personal Computer DOS
Version 1.10 (C)Copyright IBM Corp 1981, 1982

A>
```

Figure 4-3. The initial DOS 1.1 screen

```
Current date is Tue 1-01-1980
Enter new date: 6-23-1983
Current time is 0:00:15.43
Enter new time: 18:13

The IBM Personal Computer DOS
Version 2.00 (C)Copyright IBM Corp 1981, 1982, 1983

A>
```

Figure 4-4. The initial DOS 2.0 screen

A>dir ⏎

All the files (programs and other things) on your disk will be listed, as shown in Figures 4-5, 4-6, and 4-7.

COMMAND	COM	3231	08-04-81
FORMAT	COM	2560	08-04-81
CHKDSK	COM	1395	08-04-81
SYS	COM	896	08-04-81
DISKCOPY	COM	1216	08-04-81
DISKCOMP	COM	1124	08-04-81
COMP	COM	1620	08-04-81
DATE	COM	252	08-04-81
TIME	COM	250	08-04-81
MODE	COM	860	08-04-81
EDLIN	COM	2392	08-04-81
DEBUG	COM	6049	08-04-81
LINK	EXE	43264	08-04-81
BASIC	COM	10880	08-04-81
BASICA	COM	16256	08-04-81
ART	BAS	1920	08-04-81
SAMPLES	BAS	2432	08-04-81
MORTGAGE	BAS	6272	08-04-81
COLORBAR	BAS	1536	08-04-81
BUG	BAS	640	08-04-81
CALENDAR	BAS	3840	08-04-81
MUSIC	BAS	4224	08-04-81
DONKEY	BAS	3584	08-04-81
BLUE	BAS	1152	08-04-81
HUMOR	BAS	640	08-04-81
POP	BAS	768	08-04-81
FORTY	BAS	768	08-04-81
DANDY	BAS	640	08-04-81
MARCH	BAS	768	08-04-81
STARS	BAS	768	08-04-81
HAT	BAS	768	08-04-81
SCALES	BAS	640	08-04-81
SAKURA	BAS	512	08-04-81
CIRCLE	BAS	1664	08-04-81
PIECHART	BAS	2304	08-04-81
SPACE	BAS	1920	08-04-81
BALL	BAS	2048	08-04-81
COMM	BAS	4352	08-04-81

Figure 4-5. Directory for DOS 1.0

COMMAND	COM	4959	5-07-82	12:00p
FORMAT	COM	3816	5-07-82	12:00p
CHKDSK	COM	1720	5-07-82	12:00p
SYS	COM	605	5-07-82	12:00p
DISKCOPY	COM	2008	5-07-82	12:00p
DISKCOMP	COM	1640	5-07-82	12:00p
COMP	COM	1649	5-07-82	12:00p
EXE2BIN	EXE	1280	5-07-82	12:00p
MODE	COM	2509	5-07-82	12:00p
EDLIN	COM	2392	5-07-82	12:00p
DEBUG	COM	5999	5-07-82	12:00p
LINK	EXE	41856	5-07-82	12:00p
BASIC	COM	11392	5-07-82	12:00p
BASICA	COM	16768	5-07-82	12:00p
ART	BAS	1920	5-07-82	12:00p
SAMPLES	BAS	2432	5-07-82	12:00p
MORTGAGE	BAS	6272	5-07-82	12:00p
COLORBAR	BAS	1536	5-07-82	12:00p
CALENDAR	BAS	3840	5-07-82	12:00p
MUSIC	BAS	8704	5-07-82	12:00p
DONKEY	BAS	3584	5-07-82	12:00p
CIRCLE	BAS	1664	5-07-82	12:00p
PIECHART	BAS	2304	5-07-82	12:00p
SPACE	BAS	1920	5-07-82	12:00p
BALL	BAS	2048	5-07-82	12:00p
COMM	BAS	4352	5-07-82	12:00p
26 File(s)				

Figure 4-6. Directory for DOS 1.1

Look at the right hand column in the printouts of the directories. The date (in version 1.0) and date-time (in versions 1.1 and 2.0) show when your file was produced or last updated, helping you keep track of which is the most recent version of a program. (This is why the system asks for the date information on start-up.)

If you prefer, in versions 1.1 and 2.0 you may skip the date and time information when asked for it in the booting up process. This may be done by not entering the date or the time but merely pressing the ⏎ key for each entry. However, the directory system will then take 1-01-1980 as the current date.

Copying the DOS Diskette

We would not want to run the risk of losing such a valuable and powerful tool as our DOS diskette, so it is in our best interest to produce

```
Volume in drive A has no label
Directory of A:\
COMMAND  COM    17664    3-08-83 12:00p
ANSI     SYS     1664    3-08-83 12:00p
FORMAT   COM     6016    3-08-83 12:00p
CHKDSK   COM     6400    3-08-83 12:00p
SYS      COM     1408    3-08-83 12:00p
DISKCOPY COM     2444    3-08-83 12:00p
DISKCOMP COM     2074    3-08-83 12:00p
COMP     COM     2523    3-08-83 12:00p
EDLIN    COM     4608    3-08-83 12:00p
MODE     COM     3139    3-08-83 12:00p
FDISK    COM     6177    3-08-83 12:00p
BACKUP   COM     3687    3-08-83 12:00p
RESTORE  COM     4003    3-08-83 12:00p
PRINT    COM     4608    3-08-83 12:00p
RECOVER  COM     2304    3-08-83 12:10p
ASSIGN   COM      896    3-08-83 12:00p
TREE     COM     1513    3-08-83 12:00p
GRAPHICS COM      789    3-08-83 12:00p
SORT     EXE     1280    3-08-83 12:00p
FIND     EXE     5888    3-08-83 12:00p
MORE     COM      384    3-08-83 12:00p
BASIC    COM    16256    3-08-83 12:00p
BASICA   COM    25984    3-08-83 12:00p
     23 File(s)     31232 bytes free
```

Figure 4-7. Directory for DOS 2.0

a copy, called a "working diskette." Not that we *expect* anything to happen to the originals, but a good habit is to keep any original diskettes, like money in the bank, out of harm's way and not employ them for day-to-day use. (Do not put your originals under your mattress, however!)

There are some differences in the copying procedure depending upon whether you have two disk drives or only one, and which version of DOS you're using.

In addition to your DOS diskette, you first need a blank diskette of the proper type (either single or double-sided). Something to be careful of at this point is that this blank diskette *is not write-protected*. A diskette is write-protected when a little adhesive tab is placed over the square notch in the side of the diskette. When this tab is in place, you can't write to the diskette. Thus you must remove this tab, if it's there, before you try to format or use DISKCOPY as described below.

Formatting a Diskette

You only need to use FORMAT if you have DOS version 1.0. If you have version 1.1 or 2.0, you can skip this section and continue with the section called "Using DISKCOPY" below.

Let's return to our filing system analogy. To keep our files in order, it is necessary to establish a *system* for filing, such as using the alphabet or an accession number. The disk system has its own filing system: the formatting processes. You could say this process teaches the PC how to organize its files.

The FORMAT command is used to *initialize* the diskette in the designated drive. For example,

```
FORMAT b:
```

would initialize the diskette in drive B. If your system has more than one disk drive, the PC will look at a particular drive, called the "default" drive, first, for information. The default drive is the master drive and has control (it's usually drive A). If just the command FORMAT were used, without a drive designation, the diskette in the default drive would be initialized. CAUTION! Using the FORMAT command on a diskette wipes out anything already on the diskette.

If you have DOS 1.0, go ahead now and format your blank diskette. You will need to place the copy of your DOS system disk, which has the FORMAT program on it, in drive A, and a blank diskette in drive B. You can then type the command

```
A>format b:
```

The system will ask you again to place the blank diskette in drive B, and then to strike any key when ready. Once you do this, the formatting process will be carried out.

Using DISKCOPY

Now we can proceed to make a working copy of the DOS diskette. At this point, we again have two possible situations: you may either have one disk drive, or you may have two (or more) disk drives. The process of making copies is somewhat different in each instance.

DISKCOPY (Two drives)

As we saw above, to specify a particular drive to read or write from diskette, you use the designation "A:" or "B:" depending on the diskette you wish to access. The command

```
DISKCOPY A: B:
```

will copy the contents of the diskette located in drive A (called the *source*) onto the diskette located in drive B (called the *target*). Something like the following should appear on your screen:

```
A>diskcopy a: b:

Insert source diskette in drive A:

Insert target diskette in drive B:

Strike any key when ready
```

DISKCOPY (One Drive)

With a single drive, the source and target diskettes will have to be alternated in the same drive. In this case your PC's memory will only hold a part of the information contained on your diskette at one time. To copy the entire diskette, the copy command will repeatedly load a *portion* of the diskette into the machine's memory. Then you will remove the source diskette and replace it with the target diskette to transfer the portion in memory to your target diskette. You will then alternate source and target, source and target, until the entire source diskette has been copied onto the target diskette.

Enter the command DISKCOPY. The screen will prompt you as to which diskette — source or target — you are to place in the drive. Your screen will look something like this:

```
A>diskcopy

Insert source diskette in drive A:

Strike any key when ready
```

After a portion of the diskette has been read into memory, you will be asked to put the target diskette in the disk drive. The screen should look like this:

```
A>diskcopy

Insert source diskette in drive A:

Strike any key when ready

X

Copying X side(s)

Insert target diskette in drive A:

Strike any key when ready
```

Finishing Up the DISKCOPY Process

When the copy process has finished, your PC will ask if you wish to make another copy. If you don't, type an *n*.

When you have completed the copying process you should remove the DOS master diskette from drive A and replace it with your newly produced copy. The master should go into a safe place so that it is not damaged and so that you can locate it if you need it at some future point.

With the diskcopy business now out of the way, we will turn our attention to the use of your working diskette. This working copy will be used to call existing utilities and to store and retrieve BASIC programs that you have written, without your having to type them into your PC again.

Using the Disk Versions of BASIC

The commands BASIC and BASICA are used to put the disk forms of BASIC in your machine. From this point on we will use only BASICA (Advanced BASIC). For a comparison of these three forms of BASIC, see Appendix A. To put your PC into this advanced form of BASIC, enter the command

A>basica

Something like Figure 4-8 will appear on your screen telling you that BASICA is loaded. The Ok is our old friend, the BASIC prompt, telling us that it is OK to use BASIC. The appearance of the five digits (or more) in front of the words "Bytes free" tells us how much of the memory is available for our programs after BASICA was loaded. If you want to return to the DOS system, the command within BASIC is SYSTEM, which will return you to the A> prompt, telling you you're back in the DOS.

Running a BASICA Program

Let's now turn our attention to writing a BASIC program and saving it on our working diskette. Although we'll use BASICA, the advanced BASIC, the commands are no different than those we have already used in Cassette BASIC. Try entering a "title page program" in the PC. The program is shown in Figure 4-9.

You'll note that in line 80, there are four PRINT commands

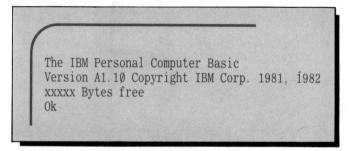

```
The IBM Personal Computer Basic
Version A1.10 Copyright IBM Corp. 1981, 1982
xxxxx Bytes free
Ok
```

Figure 4-8.   The initial BASICA screen

separated by colons. These colons act like individual program lines, but without the line numbers. We could have written

```
8Ø PRINT
9Ø PRINT
1ØØ PRINT
11Ø PRINT
```

When a number of short commands are used together, it is easier to write them on the same line. The colons are used for this purpose.

Let's run the program and see if it works and if so, why it works the way it does. The output of this program should look like this:

```
*********************************
*         TITLE   PROGRAM       *
*    '        BY                *
*         'YOUR NAME HERE'      *
*         Ø6-23-1983    18:34:52 *
*********************************
```

Well, where did the date and time come from? We sneaked in two new commands in this program. DATE$ and TIME$, when used with the

```
1Ø CLS
2Ø PRINT "        ********************************"
3Ø PRINT "        *        TITLE   PROGRAM        *"
4Ø PRINT "        *              BY               *"
5Ø PRINT "        *        'YOUR NAME HERE'       *"
6Ø PRINT "        *    "DATE$;"     "TIME$;"       *"
7Ø PRINT "        ********************************"
8Ø PRINT: PRINT: PRINT: PRINT
9Ø BEEP
1ØØ END
```

Figure 4-9. Title page program

PRINT command, will print the current date and time, which you entered when you "booted up" the DOS diskette some time ago. Try typing these as Direct Mode commands:

```
PRINT DATE$, TIME$

Ø6-23-1983    18:36:12
```

Saving Programs to the Diskette

After you have invested some time writing a program, it would be nice to save it so that it would not be necessary to type in the program again every time you want to use it. The Direct Mode command SAVE is used to record your program on the diskette.

Naming Files

In order to save a program, the DOS filing system needs a *name* to identify the program. A name is used with the SAVE command in the format SAVE *program name* to tell the system what is being saved. You may name your program using any string of characters (the name must have quotation marks around it), but the name is limited to eight characters and a period (.) followed by three more characters, like this: XXXXXXXX.XXX. For example, TITLE.BAS would stand for a program called "TITLE" written in BASIC. The three characters after the period are called the *extension*; the extension identifies the type of data in a file. Your PC will automatically supply the extension .BAS to the file name if you don't use one. However, you can use any three-letter extension you want — .JIM, for example. Together, the file name and the extension make up the *file specification* or *filespec* for short. It's important to note that if the file name you chose already exists, the original file by that name will be written over and therefore lost.

The format of the SAVE command may also specify the drive on which the program is to be saved — for example, SAVE"A:TITLE.BAS", where the "A:" is used to specify that Drive A is the drive on which the program will be stored. So — let's give it a try:

```
SAVE"A:TITLE.BAS"
```

There goes that disk drive, turning its red light on for a second or two so that you know that you've done it right. Your program has been saved on the diskette! You may wish to test whether the program was really saved. Type NEW and then LIST to remove your program from memory. Now how do we get it back?

Loading Programs from the Diskette

Have no fear, the program may be put back in the PC's memory with the LOAD command. The format for the LOAD command is similar to that for SAVE. You type LOAD"TITLE.BAS" using the BASIC command LOAD followed by the filespec.

```
LOAD"title.bas"
```

Now type LIST to see that the program has been restored in memory.

The FILES Command

When the FILES command is entered from BASIC, you will get a list of the files on your diskette (FILES is similar to the DIR command in DOS). Try the FILES command and see if your program TITLES.BAS is in the list of BASIC files.

Soft Function Keys

For your convenience the LIST, RUN, LOAD *filespec*, and SAVE *filespec* may be supplied by the PC without your having to retype these frequently used commands. These commands may be automatically executed through the *soft function keys*, which are labeled (F1) through (F10) on the far left of your keyboard (see Figure 4-10).

The four commands LIST, RUN, LOAD *filespec* and SAVE *filespec* can be given using the following keys:

(F1) — LIST
(F2) — RUN (↵)
(F3) — LOAD"
(F4) — SAVE"

By striking the (F1) key followed by (↵), you get a listing of your TITLE.BAS program. If instead you were to type

$\boxed{F1}$ 20 $\boxed{\hookleftarrow}$,

the PC's response would be a listing of line 20. The $\boxed{F2}$ key does not require the $\boxed{\hookleftarrow}$ key to be struck. For the $\boxed{F3}$ (LOAD *filespec*) and $\boxed{F4}$ (SAVE *filespec*), you supply only the filespec and $\boxed{\hookleftarrow}$. Try this out. Clear the memory of the PC and then load, list, and run the TITLE program using the soft function keys.

What about that twenty-fifth line at the bottom of the screen that never goes away? Well its days are numbered! This line is there to remind you which of the soft function keys (or simply "soft keys") do what. At the beginning this display is most helpful, but after you've gained some experience, it would be nice to be able to turn it off. This may be accomplished by the command KEY OFF. And, as you might have guessed, pressing $\boxed{F9}$ and typing OFF turns off this display, while $\boxed{F9}$ ON puts it back. Remember, of course, to press $\boxed{\hookleftarrow}$ after either KEY ON or KEY OFF.

Summary

In this chapter we have shown you how to use your disk drive(s) for the storage and retrieval of BASIC programs. We introduced you to

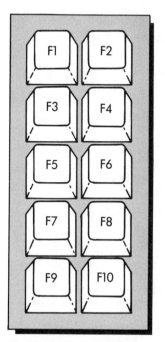

Figure 4-10. Soft keys

formatting and copying diskettes. In teaching you how to load the advanced form of BASIC, called BASICA, we have said good bye to Cassette BASIC. And we have called up the directory (using DIR) containing DOS's program files.

These concepts and the soft function keys will prove to be great time-savers. In the next chapter, we'll introduce you to editing features and additional time-savers that will make your programming much more enjoyable, pleasant and effective.

Here's a recap of the DOS (or system) commands present in this chapter:

DIR — Lists all files on a diskette with the time and date of entry

DISKCOPY A: B: — Copies diskette in drive A: (Source) to diskette in drive B: (Target)

BASIC — Puts PC in extended BASIC (medium level BASIC)

BASICA — Puts PC in to advanced BASIC (highest level BASIC)

FORMAT — Initializes a diskette in the designated drive

These are the BASICA commands and statements we have discussed:

SAVE — Saves a program on the diskette under the name in the form (XXXXXXXX.XXX)

LOAD — Loads a named program from the diskette into PC's memory in the form (XXXXXXXX.XXX)

DATE$ — Gives today's date from internal DOS calendar; used with PRINT (PRINT DATE$)

TIME$ — Gives current time from internal DOS clock; used with PRINT (PRINT TIME$)

FILES — Lists all files on diskette from inside BASIC

SYSTEM — Returns from BASIC or BASICA to DOS

Finally, these are the soft function keys we have worked with:

(F1) — "LIST" shows the lines of program

(F2) — "RUN"ENTER executes program currently in memory from beginning

(F3) — "LOAD" reads named program from diskette into memory

(F4) — "SAVE" stores named program from memory on diskette

(F9) — "KEY" turns on or off key display on line 25

Exercise

Write and store on the diskette a program that will print out the following:

a. Name of program.

b. Written by — "Your name, address, phone number".

c. Date written.

d. Today's date and time.

e. This information centered on the screen within a border.

f. A beep sound of approximately three seconds in length when finished. Hint: use the colons.

Solution

Here is one possible solution:

```
10 CLS
20 PRINT "               ***********************************"
30 PRINT "               *         SOLUTION PROGRAM        *"
40 PRINT "               *              BY                 *"
50 PRINT "               *          I. M. PC  USER         *"
60 PRINT "               *         370 COMPUTER ST.        *"
70 PRINT "               *         HOMETOWN, KANSAS        *"
80 PRINT "               *       PHONE (900) 999-9999      *"
90 PRINT "               *           JULY 4, 1776          *"
100 PRINT "              *     "DATE$;"      "TIME$;" ·    *"
110 PRINT "               ***********************************"
120 PRINT: PRINT: PRINT: PRINT
130 BEEP:BEEP:BEEP:BEEP:BEEP:BEEP:BEEP:BEEP:BEEP:BEEP:BEEP:BEEP
140 END
```

5

Editing Your Programs

Concepts
  Editing keys
  Printing the screen
  Program structuring
  Program comments (remarks)

Instructions
  Insert, DELETE *n-m*, EDIT, LIST *n-m*, RUN *n*, Print Screen, LLIST, REM

Now that you are beginning to write programs of some length, it would be nice to be able to make changes or correct mistakes in your program listings.

This chapter will introduce you to the IBM PC's editing features, which are designed to make editing programs an easy and efficient process.

This chapter will also explain how to access your printer so that you can print hard copies of your programs. A hard copy of a program can facilitate the editing process in two ways: first, by allowing you to mark up the listing on paper if you wish and then enter the changes through the keyboard; and second, by helping you to get an overview of the program you have written in case you want to make changes in its basic design.

Finally, in order to round out your sense of how to make programs clearer, this chapter will suggest some ways in which you can build explanations right into the program. In this final portion of the chapter, we will focus particularly on the BASIC reserved word REM (for "remark"), which you can use to annotate lines in your programs.

The Editing Keys and The Editing Process

In earlier chapters, we explained that you could use the (←) key to delete the character to the left of the cursor. To delete a program line, you simply typed the line number and pressed ENTER. But the IBM PC is actually a much more versatile editing tool than we have so far suggested. In addition to the backspace key, the PC has some special keys that allow you to make changes in the text of your programs as they appear on the screen. These keys are at the right of your keyboard and are known collectively as the *numeric keypad* (see Figure 5-1).

One important thing to note about these keys before we start using them is that they can be in one of two modes: Number Mode or Edit Mode. In Number Mode, the keys are used to enter regular numbers. Thus in Number Mode, the numeric keypad works just like the number keys at the top of the keyboard. The physical arrangement of the keypad just makes it easier to enter numbers. In Edit Mode, the keys in the numeric keypad become *cursor movement keys*, enabling you to move the cursor in the direction indicated by the arrows on keys 2, 4, 6, and 8.

To switch from Number Mode to Edit Mode and back, simply press the (Num Lock) key. The (Num Lock) key works like a toggle switch: press it once, and you are in Number Mode; press (Num Lock) again, and you are

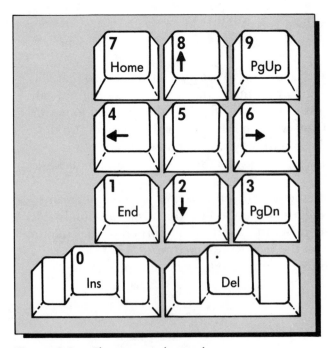

Figure 5-1. The numeric keypad

back in Edit Mode.

To see which mode you are currently in, press the (Home) key (key 7), which is located in the upper left corner of the numeric keypad. If the cursor moves to the upper left corner of the screen (the *home position*), you are in Edit Mode.

In a moment, we will enter a program and use it for our editing practice session. First, however, be sure that BASICA is loaded and that the "Ok" prompt is displayed. Next, in order to be sure the screen is clear, hold down the (Ctrl) key (to the left of the A key) and push the (Home) key. Your screen should now be cleared, and the cursor should be in the home position. It is not always necessary to move the cursor to the home position at the start of an editing session, but it can be useful. It's like starting with a clean slate.

Now type in the following text in the form of a program:

```
10 PRINT "Do not break your bread or roll in your soup."
20 PRINT
30 PRINT "Gentlemen, the time has come to grab the bull by the"
40 PRINT "TAIL and look the matter squarely in the face."
50 PRINT
60 PRINT "Those who will not act"
70 PRINT "Perish in the reason:"
```

Run the program to see what it will do and then save it (with the SAVE command) on your diskette, using "SAMPLE" as the file name. We will use this program and the text that it generates for our editing work. Now, clear the screen once more and place the cursor in the upper left-hand corner of the screen. Finally, list the program, and your screen should look like the preceding program listing.

Editing Characters

Now let's get some practice using the numeric keypad. The only keys on the keypad that we will not discuss here are key 9 (PgUp) and key 3 (PgDn). These keys have no function in BASIC but may be put to use in other programs, such as word processors. Key 5, as you can see from a glance at Figure 5-1 or at your keyboard, has no separate Edit Mode function.

First let's find out about the cursor movement keys: that is, the (→) (right arrow) and (←) (left arrow) keys, which are numbered 6 and 4, and the (↑) (up arrow) and (↓) (down arrow) keys, which are numbered 8 and 2. How would we, for instance, move the cursor to the space in front of the word "or" in line 10?

The cursor may be moved *down* the screen with the ⬇ (2) key and to the right with the → (6) key. Try this now. Notice that if you hold any key down, it will automatically repeat. You can always go back with the ⬆ (8) and ← (4) keys should you overshoot.

By pressing the (Ins) key (insert), we make the cursor change from single blinking underscore (_) to a block (■). The enlarged cursor indicates that we are in the Insert Mode. Now if we push the comma key (,) to insert a comma before the "or," we can change the meaning of the sentence. Also note that the cursor still indicates that we are in Insert Mode. We will remain in this mode until the (Ins) key is again pressed, or until the position of the cursor is changed. Pressing the (Ins) key repeatedly will switch us back and forth between the Insert and the Noninsert Modes, just as pressing (Num Lock) causes an alternation between the Edit and Number Modes.

If we now try running the program, we will find that nothing has changed. Why not? We left out an important step! After all the corrections in the line have been made, you must press the ⏎ key for the change to be made in the program.

Try making the change in line 10 again, but this time, before moving the cursor away from line 10, press ⏎. Now if you list the program, it should look like this:

```
10 PRINT "Do not break your bread, or roll in your soup."
20 PRINT
30 PRINT "Gentlemen, the time has come to grab the bull by the"
40 PRINT "TAIL and look the matter squarely in the face."
50 PRINT
60 PRINT "Those who will not act"
70 PRINT "Perish in the reason:"
```

Move the cursor to the line below the last line of your program and type RUN. Your output should look like this:

```
Do not break your bread, or roll in your soup.

Gentlemen, the time has come to grab the bull by the
TAIL and look the matter squarely in the face.

Those who will not act
Perish in the reason:
```

Now let's work on the problem of the bull's anatomy in line 40. Using the (↑) key, move the cursor to the letter *T* in the word "TAIL" in line 40 of your program, and then press the (Ins) key and insert the word of your choice — say, "horns," for example. Notice that while "horns" was inserted at the beginning of the line, where the word "TAIL" used to be, the word "TAIL" was simply pushed to the right.

How do we get rid of "TAIL"?

Located next to the (Ins) key is the (Del) (for "delete") key. Press the (Del) key once to delete the letter *T* of the word "TAIL." The (Del) key will delete the character at the current cursor position. When a given character is deleted, all the characters to the right move left one place. Proceed with the deleting process by deleting the remaining characters in the word "TAIL." Notice, by the way, that when you press the (Del) key or any of the cursor motion keys, you leave Insert Mode. If you now decide to insert another word or phrase — say, "and ears" — everything at the cursor position as you write will simply be overwritten, thus garbling the rest of the sentence.

After all corrections have been made, be sure to transmit them to the PC by pressing the (⏎) key. Now move the cursor down to the line below the last line on your screen and run the program again. This time your screen should look something like this:

```
Do not break your bread, or roll in your soup.

Gentlemen, the time has come to grab the bull by the
horns and look the matter squarely in the face.

Those who will not act
Perish in the reason:
```

Editing Lines

IBM BASIC allows us to work not only with one character or word at a time, but also with entire lines. For example, let's see how to *duplicate* an entire program line, and in the process, give the text of our program a little complexity. Move the cursor to the beginning of line 60. While the cursor is under the 6 in 60, replace the 6 with an 8 by pressing the 8 key. (Use the 8 on the top row of keys so that you don't have to toggle the (Num Lock) key.) Now move the cursor down to the 7 in line 70, and replace the 7 with a 9. Be sure to press the (⏎) key after changing each line (that is, before you leave the line) so that the changes will be transmitted to the PC. Now list your program and note that there are two pairs of lines that say the same thing: lines 60 and 80 and lines 70 and 90.

```
1Ø PRINT "Do not break your bread, or roll in your soup."
2Ø PRINT
3Ø PRINT "Gentlemen, the time has come to grab the bull by the"
4Ø PRINT "horns and look the matter squarely in the face."
5Ø PRINT
6Ø PRINT "Those who will not act"
7Ø PRINT "Perish in the reason:"
8Ø PRINT "Those who will not act"
9Ø PRINT "Perish in the reason:"
```

Now we can go back to the word "act" in line 60 and replace it with the word "reason." Moving the cursor down to the word "reason" in line 70, replace "reason" with the word "act," and press ⏎. Finally, move the cursor below the last line of your program and run the program. The output should look like this:

```
Do not break your bread, or roll in your soup.

Gentlemen, the time has come to grab the bull by the
horns and look the matter squarely in the face.

Those who will not reason
Perish in the act:
Those who will not act
Perish in the reason:
```

In line 90 let's change the words "in the" to read "for that." Use the ⟮Ins⟯ key so as not to write over the r in "reason." Remember to enter this change into the PC's memory. The program should now look like this:

```
1Ø PRINT "Do not break your bread, or roll in your soup."
2Ø PRINT
3Ø PRINT "Gentlemen, the time has come to grab the bull by the"
4Ø PRINT "horns and look the matter squarely in the face."
5Ø PRINT
6Ø PRINT "Those who will not reason"
7Ø PRINT "Perish in the act:"
8Ø PRINT "Those who will not act"
9Ø PRINT "Perish for that reason:"
```

Deleting a Line with DELETE

From time to time, you may wish to delete a line or even several lines from a BASIC program. For example, we might wish to delete lines 10 through 50 in our little program. Line 10 may be deleted with the command

```
DELETE 1Ø
```

Any line *n* can be deleted by entering DELETE *n*.

You may also delete a range of lines. For example, with the command

```
DELETE 1Ø-5Ø
```

all lines starting with line 10 and ending with line 50 will be deleted. The form of the command is DELETE *n-m*, where *n* is the beginning line number and *m* is the ending line number. Let's give this a try on our program. Delete lines 10 through 50, and then run the program:

```
6Ø PRINT "Those who will not reason"
7Ø PRINT "Perish in the act:"
8Ø PRINT "Those who will not act"
9Ø PRINT "Perish for that reason:"
```

We could also have given the command DELETE -50, which would have removed all lines up to and including line 50. When you do not specify a beginning line number, BASIC assumes that *n* is the first line number in the program.

Note, by the way, that another way to get rid of an unwanted program line is simply to place the cursor anywhere on the line in question and press the $\boxed{\text{Esc}}$ key (for "escape"), which is located near the upper left corner of the keyboard. If you press $\boxed{\leftarrow}$ after you press $\boxed{\text{Esc}}$, the entire line will be erased from memory.

Moving to a Line with EDIT

The EDIT command may be used to make changes in a particular line of a program. This saves moving the cursor to the line in question with the cursor movement keys, which is especially useful for long listings.

For example, in line 90 we might wish to change the punctuation from the colon (:) to a period (.). Give the command

```
EDIT 90
```

to edit line 90, and change the colon to a period. In general, when you would give the command EDIT *n*, BASIC will print on the screen the line of your program that you have requested. The EDIT command is like the LIST in that you use it to display your program on the screen for the purpose of making modifications. But LIST, of course, allows you to list more than a single line of your program at a time.

Now when we run our program in its final form, lines 60 through 90 look like this:

```
Those who will not reason
Perish in the act:
Those who will not act
Perish for that reason.
```

Remember that only the changes have been made to the program in the PC's memory and not to the copy on the diskette, so you must not forget to save the edited version of your program, with the SAVE command, should you prefer the edited version to the original.

Advanced Cursor Commands

There are some advanced cursor movement commands that may prove to be useful to you. You can move the cursor one word to the right at a time by holding down the $\boxed{\text{Ctrl}}$ key and the $\boxed{\rightarrow}$ key at the same time. Similarly, you can move the cursor left one word at a time with $\boxed{\text{Ctrl}}$ $\boxed{\leftarrow}$.

We have not yet mentioned the $\boxed{\text{End}}$ key, which is also key 1 on the keypad. You can use the (End) key to move to the end of the line that the cursor is in. If you press (Ctrl) and (End) simultaneously, all of the line to the right of the cursor position will be erased. Try this now with our SAMPLE.BAS program. List the program and practice using the advanced cursor motion keys.

Advanced Forms of List and Run

For even greater convenience in editing, you can "fine tune" the LIST and RUN instructions by following them with numbers, just as you did with the DELETE and EDIT commands. To list only a *portion* of a program, you may use the command LIST *n-m*, where *n* is the line number of the first line to be printed and *m* is the last line you wish to be printed. For example,

```
LIST 20-40
```

will cause all lines starting with line 20 and ending with line 40 to be printed. This gives you the ability to display only a small portion of a large program for editing.

The same technique may be used with the RUN command. If we typed

```
RUN 20
```

only lines starting with 20 and ending at the end of the program would be run. This execution begins with the specified line *n* instead of the lowest line number. This technique allows you to run only the later portion of a program — something that comes in handy when you debug a program.

Using the Line Printer

If you have a printer, you may have wondered when we would start to use it. Well, now is the time! The line printer (the hard copy printer) can be a great help in the writing of long programs. Let's look at some of the ways you can use it with BASIC.

Using Shift/PrtSc

The printer may be activated in a number of ways. The first method we'll discuss is a way of printing out everything on the video screen.

Whatever is currently displayed on the screen will be sent to the printer if you press ⟨⇧⟩ and the ⟨PrtSc⟩ key, (the asterisk key (*) without ⟨⇧⟩). ⟨PrtSc⟩ is located just below the ⟨↵⟩ key.

Before you try this, be sure that your printer is properly connected to the PC and that it is turned on, loaded with paper, and ready to go. Consult the manual that comes with your printer for instructions.

Go ahead now and press ⟨⇧⟩ ⟨PrtSc⟩. Each line of text shown on your screen will be printed starting from the top of the screen.

Using Ctrl/PrtSc (DOS 2.0 only)

Sometimes it is nice to get a printed copy of material *as it appears* on the screen. ⟨Ctrl⟩ ⟨PrtSc⟩ will do this for you. This technique stands in contrast to ⟨⇧⟩ ⟨PrtSc⟩, which gives you a copy of what has *already* been placed on the screen.

Try using ⟨Ctrl⟩ ⟨PrtSc⟩ now. Your printer will print out everything you type as you type it.

Printing with the LLIST Command

It's often very useful to look at a printed listing of a program rather than a listing on the screen. A printout can be marked up for making revisions, and it's easier to get a feel for long programs when you look at an entire listing rather than pieces of it on the screen.

A printed list of a program which is in the PC's memory is given when the command LLIST is used. You may either press the L key and then the ⟨F1⟩ soft function key (which will automatically activate LIST), or you may type out "LLIST." If you wish to list the entire program currently in memory, simply type LLIST alone. If you wish to list the program lines starting at n and ending at m, type LLIST n-m. Finally, if you want a printout from line n, perhaps somewhere in the middle of the program to the end of the program, then n alone will do the trick.

Try this command now in any of these formats. Remember to press ⟨↵⟩ after you type in the command. You should get a printout of the entire program currently in memory or the lines of the program you specified.

Hints on Program Style

One of the most difficult tasks that a programmer must face is to work through someone else's program to understand what the program does and how it does it. Even your own programs, if you wrote them more than a few weeks ago, may be hard to understand and modify.

For these reasons, we'll now explore some methods that will help to make your program easier to understand. These steps may seem slow and obvious, perhaps even a little silly, but a small amount of time spent now could save you hundreds of hours at some future date.

Using REM Statements

The best way to keep track of why the program was written in a certain way is to explain what the program does at the time you write it. But where do you record these comments on your thinking process at the time you are writing the program?

BASIC has a statement that will allow you to place comments in a program line. The REM statement (for "remark") is used for this purpose. For instance, type the following line:

```
1Ø REM -----This will calculate the interest on my car payment.
```

The REM statement is interpreted by BASIC to mean "do not execute the following characters on this line." You may put anything you want after the REM: no matter what it is, you will not get a "Syntax Error" message. Even bizarre comment lines,

```
1Ø REM xxx!2@
```

will be ignored by your PC but will be listed in any program listing.

Another way to write the REM statement is to use the apostrophe (') in place of the REM — it will mean the same thing. For example

```
1Ø ' xxx!2@
```

is exactly the same as

```
1Ø REM xxx!2@
```

The apostrophe may also be used to give a remark after a line of executable BASIC code. For example:

```
2Ø PRINT DATE$    'This gives today's date.
```

You may make a remark with the apostrophe at the end of any numbered line with one exception: you *may not* make a remark at the end of a line with the command DATA. We will explain this command in a later chapter.

Three Examples Using REM

We have provided three programs that you may want to enter into your PC, or at least study for their use of remarks. Some of the commands and concepts in these programs have not been covered yet, but don't let this bother you: the programs will work anyway. In fact, the programs shown below do exactly the same thing: they make a numbered list of all the characters and symbols available in BASIC. The point of the three different versions of the program is merely to show you the different ways in which the statement may be used to explain and clarify what is going on in a program, and what happens when you don't use remarks.

The first example, shown in Figure 5-2, does not use remarks. You should also notice the use of the colon in this first example. What seems like a three-line program is, in fact, some 7 lines of code. In BASIC, in effect, it is possible to put multiple lines following a single line number, as we mentioned earlier, by placing the colon (:) between each command in a single numbered line. We do not recommend extensive use of this practice, however — at least not for beginning programmers — since it can make editing difficult, and programs hard to understand.

In fact, you would only write a program using colons (like the one in Figure 5-2) to offer someone a challenge. If you were to have the PC list the program, of course, the line numbers would be put in order and a space would appear after the line number and before the command. That would make the program somewhat easier to read, but it would still be confusing since it lacks any annotation as to its overall purposes.

The next two programs (Figure 5-3 and 5-4) show positive examples of ways to write a program. The style in which these programs are written would give the reader a much clearer picture of what the program is doing. The second program differs only in the use of the apostrophe instead of the REM statement. We feel that this *open style* shown in Figure 5-4 gives a less cluttered appearance. From now on in this book, we will try to use the open style of remarks in our programs.

```
666PRINT CHR$ (7)
3CLS: FOR N=Ø TO 255: PRINT N, CHR$ (N)
4FOR L=1 TO 1ØØØ: NEXT: NEXT
```

Figure 5-2. Program using colons

Good Programming Habits

The best way to ensure that your programs are clear and easy to understand is to establish some rules of good programming practice.

Here are some rules to keep in mind when you format and annotate programs. First of all, all programs should have

1. A title

2. The date

3. The author's name

4. An opening statement of purpose

Second, set aside separate sections for comments on or definition of each of the following elements in your program:

- 1. Dimensions (units, for example $, lbs, feet, and so on)

2. References (sources of information)

- 3. Variables (names of items to be changed)

```
100 REM------***************************
110 REM------*        SYMBOLS.BAS          *
120 REM------*             BY               *
130 REM------*    ROBERT L. PETERSEN        *
140 REM------*     SEPTEMBER 12, 1827       *
150 REM------***************************
160 REM
170 REM-----SCREEN PRINTS THE DECIMAL VALUES AND THE SYMBOLS-----
180 REM-----FOR ASCII CHARACTERS--------------------------------
190 REM
200 CLS                          'CLEARS SCREEN
210 REM
220 REM -----SETS UP LOOP TO COUNT THE 256 ASCII CHARACTERS-------
230 REM
240     FOR N=0 TO 255
250         PRINT N, CHR$(N)
260         FOR L=1 TO 1000 'SETS UP DELAY IN DISPLAY
270         NEXT L
280     NEXT N
290 REM
300 REM   ----END OF MAIN PROGRAM ----------------------------------
310 REM
320 PRINT CHR$(7)                    'SOUNDS A BEEP WHEN FINISHED
330 END
```

Figure 5-3. Program using REM statements

- 4. Constants (names and values of unchanged items)

   5. Main Program (where the operations are done)

   6. Subroutines (repeated operations done outside the main program)

   7. Output (the results of the operations)

- 8. Input (sources of information to the program)

- 9. Data (information to be processed)

The terms marked with small circles here will be unfamiliar to you at this point in your study of BASIC. Don't worry about them now; we explain them in upcoming chapters. The main point is that you should explicitly identify every element in your program.

Third, use plenty of spaces and blank lines. This is especially important for longer programs, which can become unreadable otherwise. Avoid putting many statements in a line with the :, unless these statements are very short and clear.

```
100 '------****************************
110 '------*      SYMBOLS.BAS         *
120 '------*           BY             *
130 '------*   ROBERT L. PETERSEN     *
140 '------*    SEPTEMBER 12, 1827    *
150 '------****************************
160 '
170 '-----SCREEN PRINTS THE DECIMAL VALUES AND THE SYMBOLS-------
180 '-----FOR ASCII CHARACTERS-----------------------------------
190 '
200 CLS                         'CLEARS SCREEN
210 '
220 '-----SETS UP LOOP TO COUNT THE 256 ASCII CHARACTERS---------
230 '
240     FOR N=0 TO 255
250         PRINT N, CHR$(N)
260         FOR L=1 TO 1000 'SETS UP DELAY IN DISPLAY
270         NEXT L
280     NEXT N
290 '
300 '-----END OF MAIN PROGRAM -----------------------------------
310 '
320 PRINT CHR$(7)                'SOUNDS A BEEP WHEN FINISHED
330 END
```

Figure 5-4.   Program using the apostrophe for remarks

We'll try to set a good example and help you develop good habits in programming style as we go along.

Summary

We have looked at ways of editing programs using the screen as a window. Within that window we have rearranged a BASIC program. We have explored techniques of insertion, deletion, and printing hard copy of text that appears on the screen and of programs in memory. In addition, we have presented some suggestions for making your programs readable and easy to understand.

These are the keys discussed in this chapter:

(Home) — Cursor to "upper left-hand" corner.

(Ctrl) (Home) — Clears screen and puts cursor in upper-left hand corner.

(←) — Moves cursor left one position.

(→) — Moves cursor right one position.

(↑) — Moves cursor up one position.

(↓) — Moves cursor down one position.

(Ctrl) (→) — Moves cursor right one word.

(Ctrl) (←) — Moves cursor left one word.

(End) — Moves cursor to end of logical line (which ends with (↵)).

(Ctrl) (End) — Erases to the end of logical line, from current position.

(Ins) — Inserts characters at cursor position and moves remaining text to the right.

(Del) — Deletes character at cursor position and text moves left.

(←) — Deletes last character typed.

(Esc) — Erases entire logical line from screen. If (↵) is then pressed will remove from memory.

(PrtSc) — Prints the contents of the text screen on the line printer.

(Ctrl) (PrtSc) — Toggles on/off the printer to duplicate what appears on the screen as you type. (DOS 2.0 only)

These are the BASIC commands that were used in this chapter to edit and annotate programs:

LLIST — Gives LIST on the line printer.

EDIT — Presents a line for editing.

REM — Remark statement for program documentation.

RUN n — Runs a program starting with line n.

LIST $n\text{-}m$ — Lists a program starting with line n and stopping with line m.

Exercise

Write a program of about 10 to 12 lines, and then edit it using as many of the keys and commands discussed in this chapter as possible. When you are through editing, generate a hard copy of your program. This time we'll leave the solution entirely to you!

6

Variables — A First Look

Concepts
Variables
Variable names
Types of variables: integer and string variables
Arithmetic operations with variables
Rules for evaluating arithmetic expressions

This chapter is about one of the most important and useful concepts in programming: the variable. All but the most simple programs have variables in them. Using variables allows you to write programs that give your computer general instructions or "recipes" for performing certain tasks. We already know how to instruct the computer to use PRINT to display the product of 3 and 5, for example; but that product is limited to those specific numbers. We'd like to be able to write a statement like "PRINT the product of number A and number B" — a statement that can be used for *any* numbers A and B. Variables allow us to write such general, flexible instructions. They are one of the tools at our disposal that make the computer such a powerful device.

What are Variables? An Introduction Using Integer Variables

Let's start with the simple task of printing out the length of a room in feet. Let's imagine that the length of the room is 16 ft. Here's the program without variables:

```
1Ø PRINT 16
2Ø END
RUN
 16
Ok
```

There's another way of doing the same thing, however. It's a little more involved, but there is a payoff that will become apparent later. Try this program:

```
1Ø length = 16
2Ø PRINT length
3Ø END
RUN
 16
Ok
```

The output is the same as that produced by the previous program — namely, 16. But this time, we used the *variable* called *"length"*. This is what happened: line 10 instructed the computer to make room in its memory for a quantity called *length* — our variable — and to give it the particular value of 16. In computer-talk, we'd say that the variable *length* *is assigned* the value 16. Line 20 printed the value of the variable *length*, not the name "length" as you might have expected. Remember that *length* in line 20 doesn't have any quotation marks around it, so it is not a string. When your computer encounters letters like *length* that are *not* enclosed by quotation marks, it knows that it is looking at a variable.

To help further define the concept of a variable, add two more lines to the above program so it looks like this:

```
1Ø length = 16
2Ø PRINT length
3Ø length = 16ØØ
4Ø PRINT length
5Ø END
RUN
 16
 16ØØ
Ok
```

The point of this example is to show that there is nothing really permanent about the particular value of a variable — it can easily be changed by a reassignment, like the one in line 30. The PRINT statement in line 40 then prints out the new or most recent value of the variable *length*. The *name* of the variable is a permanent or intrinsic feature of the variable, but its value is not.

Assigning Numeric Variables

Numeric constants can be assigned to variables by means of the equal sign in the following way:

numeric variable name = numeric constant

The following examples illustrate this:

```
4Ø length = 16
5Ø B = 34
6Ø TIME = 3
```

Variable Boxes

The way a computer thinks about a variable is pretty much the way we think about a house: a house is a fairly permanent box (we hope) with a permanent address. The address identifies the house in the same way that a *variable name* (like *length*) identifies the variable. The people living in the house are like the value of a variable: different people can move in and out of a particular house the way that different values can be assigned to the same variable; that is, different occupants can be "assigned" to the same house in the same sense that different values can be assigned to the same variable.

To get a really clear sense of variables, you need to understand how the computer stores variables in its memory. For each variable, a certain amount of memory is allocated for its name, and, associated with the name, is a certain amount of memory reserved for the value of the variable. So if you could look inside your computer, you'd see large stacks of memory boxes that look something like what's shown in Figure 6-1.

This, in a conceptual sense, is how your IBM PC thinks about variables. Figure 6-1 shows how three variables with the names *length*, *A*, and *amt* are assigned the values 16, 5, and −546, respectively.

What if you don't assign a value to a variable? Go ahead and try it with the following program:

```
1Ø PRINT length
3Ø END
RUN
 Ø
Ok
```

No syntax error! All that happened is that BASIC assigned the value 0 to the variable. It is a general rule that if you don't assign a value to a variable then BASIC will do it for you — and it always chooses zero.

Arithmetic with Variables Using PRINT

So far we've just talked about what a variable is, how to introduce it into a program, and how to assign a value to it. At this point we'd like to show you how variables can be used in a simple but rather powerful way.

Consider the following domestic problem: the walls in your living room haven't been painted for 10 years, and since you hate painting, you've decided to cover the walls with wallpaper. Wallpaper is pretty expensive stuff, so you want to buy just the right amount. Since you have a brand-new IBM PC in your study (or at work), you decide to take your machine for a "spin" by writing a program that determines the number of square feet of wall surface to be covered by the wallpaper.

Let's consider just one wall first. (We'll finish the calculations for the other walls at the very end of this chapter.) You measure it and find its length to be 16 ft and its height to be 8 ft. Knowing that the area of the wall is given by the product of its length and height, you *might* be tempted to write a program like this one:

```
1Ø PRINT "Area of wall ="
2Ø PRINT 16 * 12
3Ø END
RUN
Area of wall =
 128
Ok
```

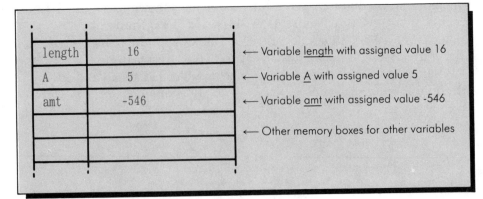

Figure 6-1. Memory "boxes" for storing variables

Well, that does the job. But this program has one serious limitation: it works only for one of your walls. In other words, if you wanted to use this program to find the area of the other wall, which undoubtedly has different dimensions, you'd have to rewrite the whole PRINT statement. Worse yet, if you were a wallpaper contractor and you wanted to generate a table showing the area of walls having 1000 different sizes, you'd really be in trouble!

So, armed with your knowledge of variables, you head off all such problems by writing the following program:

```
1Ø length = 16
2Ø height = 8
3Ø PRINT "Area of wall ="
4Ø PRINT length * height
5Ø END
RUN
Area of wall =
 128
Ok
```

This program really works! Lines 10 and 20 assign values 16 and 8 to the variables *length* and *height*. PRINT in line 40 multiplies the *value* of *length* by the *value* of *height*; it does exactly what it would do if we had asked it to PRINT 16 * 12.

Why is this program involving variables "better" than the previous one that only had numbers in it? For one thing, it's more versatile, more flexible. The PRINT statement in line 40 calculates the product of *any* length and height. This may not seem like much of an advantage to you at this point, since you'd have to change lines 10 and 20 anyway in order to find the area of a wall of different dimensions. But in the next chapter we'll show you how to write some BASIC statements that could, when you run your program, *ask* you for the length and height each time the computer must calculate the area of another surface. Thus if you use variables, you won't have to change your program at all to find the area of *any* wall.

To summarize, using variables allows you to write BASIC statements and whole programs that work for any particular value. It's like a cookbook recipe where you can vary the ingredients so that it works whether you cook just one meal for yourself or a hundred meals for all your friends!

This previous example just involved the product of two variables. But you surely wouldn't be surprised to find out that we can use variables in other arithmetic operations, like addition, subtraction, and division. Try the following example to get a feel for this:

```
10 x = 6
20 y = 3
30 PRINT x + y
40 PRINT x - y
50 PRINT x/y
60 END
RUN
 9
 3
 2
Ok
```

Everything worked as expected. This time, for the sake of variety, we used the rather short variable names *x* and *y*. To many people, these are the "traditional" sort of variables. We'll say more about variable names later.

Printing Numeric Variable Expressions

The print statement will evaluate numeric expressions involving variables and will write the value of the expression to the screen. An example is:

```
50 PRINT x/y
```

which will return a value for the quotient *x/y* using the *present* values of *x* and *y* to do the division.

Integer Variables

So far in our discussion of variables, we have tried to explain what variables are and why we use them. In our examples, we assigned integers to our variables; in effect, we used what are called *integer variables*. Integers are numbers that don't have any decimal points or any fractional parts; they are whole numbers like 3 or 10003. Integer variables are variables that have integer values. One way to "make" an integer variable is simply to assign an integer value to a variable — that's the way we did it.

There is a limit to the size of integer variables on your PC: they can't be larger than 32,767, and they can't be smaller than –32,768. Those are pretty big numbers, but not big enough for many purposes, like counting atoms or national debts!

There are other types of *numeric variables* besides integer variables, but we'll postpone the discussion of variable types and how they are defined until a later chapter.

String Variables

So far in this chapter we have been working with numeric variables; that is, we have assigned numbers — specifically integers — to our variables. The remarkable thing is that we can assign words or whole phrases to a variable as well! Variables whose values consist of words are called *string variables*, and their values are called *string constants*. A "string constant" is really the same thing as what was known as a "string" in previous chapters (see the discussion of PRINT in Chapter 3). Like strings, string constants must be enclosed in quotation marks.

To get started, let's write a simple program and run it:

```
1Ø food$ = "pepperoni pizza"
2Ø PRINT food$
3Ø END
RUN
pepperoni pizza
Ok
```

Let's find out what happened here. Line 10 says "Put the phrase pepperoni pizza in a variable box having the name *food$*". In other words, line 10 assigns the string constant "pepperoni pizza" to the variable called *food$*. The PRINT statement in line 20 then prints the *value* of the string variable.

You can see that both string variables and numeric variables are assigned values in pretty much the same way. We can use the familiar box or house model to visualize how the computer thinks about string variables (see Figure 6-2).

There is, however, one crucial difference between numeric and string variables: it has to do with that dollar sign ($) at the end of the *food$*. No, we didn't put it there because food costs money! Rather, string variable names *must* end with a dollar sign ($), since the $ is the signal to your computer that it is dealing with a string variable. If you forget the dollar sign, and then try to assign a string constant to your variable, you'll get an error message you probably haven't seen before: "Type mismatch." This error message will occur whenever the type of variables — string or numeric (there are others, but we haven't come to them yet) — doesn't match the value assigned them within a given BASIC statement. The reason your computer needs to know which type of variable it is dealing with is that it reserves memory space for the values of variables, and this memory space is different for numeric and string variables.

The Length of Strings and BASIC Program Lines

How long can a string constant be? The answer is 255 characters. That's long enough to put almost a whole menu into one string variable! You may wonder how it's possible for a string constant to be this long since your screen has room for at most 80 characters on one line. The words "on one line" are the key: the string just "folds over" to form the next line. Try it with this program:

```
1Ø longline$="xxxxxxxxxxxxxxxxxxxxxxxxxxxxxxxxxxxxxxxxxxxxxxxxxxxxxxxxxxxxxxxxxx
xxxxxxxxxxxxxxxxxxxxxxxxxxxxxxxxxxxxxxxxxxxxxxxxxxxxxxxxxxxxxxxxxxxxxxxxxxxxxxxxxx
xxxxxxxxxxxxxx"
2Ø PRINT longline$
3Ø END
RUN
xxxxxxxxxxxxxxxxxxxxxxxxxxxxxxxxxxxxxxxxxxxxxxxxxxxxxxxxxxxxxxxxxxxxxxxxxxxxxxxxxx
xxxxxxxxxxxxxxxxxxxxxxxxxxxxxxxxxxxxxxxxxxxxxxxxxxxxxxxxxxxxxxxxxxxxxxxxxxxxxxxxxx
Ok
```

Two whole 80-character lines of *xs* are formed by just one string variable. We could have filled even a *third* line and started a fourth.

Line 10 also demonstrates that you can write BASIC program lines that are longer than 80 characters. What is not at all evident is that this is true for any BASIC statement, not just strings. The maximum length of

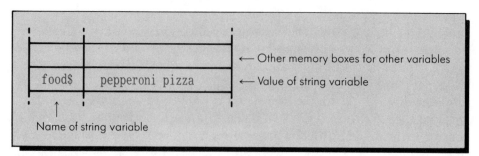

Figure 6-2. Memory boxes for string variables

a BASIC statement is 255 characters, period. However, such long program lines are generally neither very useful nor necessary: long lines that fold over are hard to read, and may be downright incomprehensible. It's better just to break up your BASIC instructions into smaller pieces.

If you do write BASIC statements like line 10 in our program above, though, you need to remember not to press (⏎) until you get to the very end of your BASIC statement — or in computerese, until the end of the *logical line*. So in our example, just keep pressing the X key 160 times (or just hold it down for a while — it's easier!), and, *then* press (⏎). When you get to the end of the screen with your *xs*, they'll continue on the next line all by themselves.

Assigning String Variables

String constants can be assigned to string variables by means of the equal sign, as shown in the following example:

```
cat$ = "siamese"
```

The dollar sign at end of the variable name indicates that this variable is a *string* variable. The string variable name *must* end with a dollar sign ($). A string constant is a sequence of characters enclosed by quotation marks. The length of a string constant can be anywhere from 0 to 255 characters long.

Why Use String Variables? An Example

String variables are very handy when you want your program to print a message or part of a message that needs to be changed (for whatever reason) from time to time. An example would be printing out names of people, phone numbers, or your favorite foods!

Let's try this example:

```
10 food$ = "pepperoni pizza"
20 PRINT "My favorite food is "; food$
30 food$ = "tripe"
40 PRINT "My favorite food is "; food$
50 END
```

```
RUN
My favorite food is pepperoni pizza
My favorite food is tripe
Ok
```

Well, you can take your choice! The point of this example is to
demonstrate how the use of string variables make it possible to make the
same PRINT statement (lines 20 and 40) print *different* results. Both
PRINT statements contain the string constant "My favorite food is" and
the string variable *food$*. But what PRINT returns (that is, what it *does*
when the program runs) depends on the *value* of the variable. In a more
sophisticated program of the kind we'll learn to write in the next chapter,
the value of *food$* might be determined by the program itself or by some
input from the user, so that one PRINT statement would be able to
produce many different outputs.

Notice the use of the semicolon in the PRINT statement: it causes the
variable's value (the string constant) to be printed right after the string
"My favorite food is." In fact, had we left out the space after the word "is"
in "My favorite food is," the two strings would have been run together to
read "My favorite food is tripe."

Concatenation — Adding Strings

It is possible, as we have seen, to perform arithmetic operations on
numeric variables. Are there any similar operations that one can perform
on string variables? It would hardly make much sense to divide two
strings but, amazingly, BASIC does allow you to *add* two string variables
or two string constants. Seeing is believing, so let's try this program:

```
1Ø food1$ = "pepperoni "
2Ø food2$ = "and mushroom pizza"
3Ø PRINT food1$ + food2$
4Ø END
RUN
pepperoni and mushroom pizza
Ok
```

What has happened here is that the values of the variables *food1$* and
food2$ have been printed right next to each other, or joined together. The
plus sign (+) between the string variables stands for "concatenate," which
means to *join* or to *link*. So line 30 prints the linked values of the
variables *food1$* and *food2$*.

Note that we have used numbers within the variable names. That's
permitted, as long as the first character in your variable name isn't a

number. Since both variables represent different foods, the 1 and 2 after *food* is a convenient and meaningful way of making the two variable names different.

Concatenation

Concatenating two string variables (or string constants) by means of a plus sign (+) joins their values without adding any extra spaces. For example, the statement:

```
45 PRINT "hot" + "dog"
```

returns the value

```
hotdog
```

What's in a Variable Name? Some Rules

We have already seen that variable names can contain letters and numbers. But the first character of a name must be a letter. The period (.) is also permitted in a variable name, but again — not as the first character.

Another important "no-no" in the naming of variables is the use of the words that are part of the language of BASIC; these words are called *reserved words*. LIST, RUN, and PRINT, for example, are all reserved words. (Appendix C gives a complete list of all the reserved words in BASIC.) Using any of these reserved words as a variable name will lead to syntax errors or to other errors that may not show up until you run your program. Beware!

Special Characters

We have also seen that string variables must end with the dollar sign. The dollar sign is one of many special characters on your keyboard — that is, characters that aren't letters or numbers.

You may have wondered why numeric variable names, like string variable names, don't end with a special character that tells BASIC what kind of variables it is dealing with. Well, certain special characters *are* permitted at the end of numeric variable names. In fact, sometimes they play a very important role in making sure that the computer understands just exactly what kind of numbers you mean.

So far we've been dealing primarily with *integer numbers* and *integer variables* (integers only have digits, no decimal points or fractions), although occasionally we've tossed in a few decimal numbers of the type called *single-precision*. The way we've used numeric variables hasn't required us to use these special characters; all we needed to do was to assign a value, and whether that value was integer or single-precision, BASIC did the rest. In a later chapter in this book, however, we'll delve more deeply into this whole question of variable types. At this point, you should simply be aware that it is possible to give a complete description of variable names by using special characters.

Length of Variable Names

There is no explicit upper limit on the length of variable names, although only the first 40 characters count; that is, BASIC will simply ignore any of the characters in the name past the fortieth character. So the length of a variable name should never be a problem. (If you're used to some other computers that limit variable names to two characters, you'll really appreciate your PC's generosity!) It's generally a good idea to choose variable names that suggest what they're supposed to represent (for example, the variable *food$* for food); otherwise, it becomes very difficult and confusing to read and write long programs with many variables in them.

People in the past have often argued that variable names should be as short as possible — as short as one or two letters — because long names take up more memory space in your computer and your programs also run more slowly. But with a sophisticated machine like your IBM PC which is fast and has plenty of memory, such concerns about memory and speed really aren't an issue — unless you're writing huge programs and are worried about milliseconds. In general, it's more important to use variable names that are meaningful than to be concerned about the small amount of memory that meaningful names might take up.

Uppercase and Lowercase

Up until now, we have only used lowercase letters for variables, since it's easier to enter them that way. But in fact it doesn't matter whether you enter variables in lowercase or capital letters: BASIC doesn't make any distinction between the two. You can see this for yourself if you write the following program line,

```
10 PRINT length
```

and then use LIST to list it:

```
LIST
10 PRINT LENGTH
Ok
```

LIST *always* writes out variable names in uppercase letters, no matter how you enter them. (List does the same thing with reserved words, by the way, as we saw in Chapter 2.) From now on, we'll always display our example programs as they would be listed — that is, with variable names written in capital letters. However, you may enter variables either in lowercase or uppercase.

Some Examples of Variable Names

Table 6-1 shows some examples of "legal" variable names. We included the last numeric variable name just to show you that long names are permitted, although in this case not terribly meaningful!

Table 6-2 shows some "illegal" variable names, and what's wrong with them. Sometimes it is helpful to see what you *shouldn't* do.

Numeric Variables	String Variables
LENGTH	FOOD$
HEIGHT.3A	NAME.FRIEND$
X1	ADDRESS.A5$
Z.ABCDEFGHIJKLMNOPQRSTUVWXY	F$

Table 6-1. Legal variable names

Variable Name	Reason for Illegality	A Corrected Version
.SLOP	period as 1st character	SLOP
TRUST ME$	space in name	TRUST.ME$
6DOLLARS	number as 1st character	DOLLARS.6
RUN	reserved word	RUNN

Table 6-2. Illegal variable names

Rules for Variable Names

1. Variable names must have the following form:

Letters, numbers, or period (.)

XXX. . .XXX

↑   ↑

First character   Last character may be a special character to indicate variable
must be a letter.   type. The dollar sign ($) is required for string variables.

2. Length of variable name: any length will do, although only the first 40 characters are significant.

3. BASIC's reserved words are not permitted as variable names, although they can be part of a variable name: for example, SHOPPINGLIST$.

4. Special characters used to define variable types (variable type declaration):

$ — Used for string variables.
! — Optional; used for integer variables.
% — Optional; used for single precision variables.
# — Optional; used for double precision variables.

5. IBM PC BASIC does not distinguish between lower- and uppercase letters in variable names. LIST will always return variables in uppercase letters.

Arithmetic with Variables — Arithmetic Expressions

Recall the example program at the beginning of this chapter in which we used the following PRINT statement to calculate the area of a wall:

```
40 PRINT LENGTH * HEIGHT
```

Using PRINT in this way to evaluate expressions is perfectly acceptable, but it is not always the best way, nor is it always possible. More complex problems usually involve a whole sequence of expressions, most of which you may not actually want to print. It is therefore often more convenient or even necessary to define a *new* variable in terms of *old* variables.

Let's rewrite our wall area program in the following way:

```
1Ø LENGTH = 16
2Ø HEIGHT = 8
3Ø AREA = LENGTH * HEIGHT
4Ø PRINT "area of wall ="
5Ø PRINT AREA
6Ø END
RUN
area of wall =
 128
Ok
```

The significant new BASIC statement is line 30. It defines a new variable AREA which is equal to the product of the variables LENGTH and HEIGHT. This makes perfectly good sense, since that's the meaning of area. Your computer interprets line 30 to mean "find the product of the *value* of variable LENGTH and HEIGHT and assign it to a variable called AREA." In terms of our house-like computer memory boxes, we might imagine a new memory box called AREA being added to the previously defined boxes LENGTH and HEIGHT as shown in Figure 6-3. The central computer "brain," called the *Central Processing Unit* (CPU for short), calculates the product of 16 and 12 and puts the result into the value box of the variable AREA. All that PRINT in line 40 now has to do is to print the value of the variable AREA that was already calculated in line 30.

Breaking Down a Problem into Small Pieces

To get a better feel for the power of this technique, let's also ask our computer to find the cost of the required wallpaper. We'll introduce a

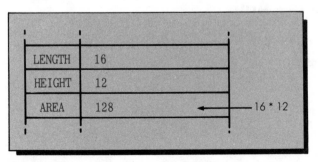

Figure 6-3. A product is stored in a memory box

new variable called PRICE that represents the price of the wallpaper in dollars per square foot. Given that the price is $6 per square foot, we can write our program this way:

```
1Ø LENGTH = 16
2Ø HEIGHT = 8
3Ø PRICE = 6
4Ø AREA = LENGTH * HEIGHT
5Ø COST = PRICE * AREA
6Ø PRINT " Area=", " Cost($)="
7Ø PRINT AREA, COST
8Ø END
Ok
RUN
 Area=         Cost($)=
 128           768
Ok
```

This is pretty neat stuff! The first new line is line 30: it assigns the value 6 (dollars) to the variable PRICE. Line 50 multiplies the value of PRICE with the value of AREA and assigns this product to the variable COST. PRINT in line 70 simply writes out the values of AREA and COST (with the 14-character wide zone spacing produced by the comma — see Chapter 3!).

The main point of this example is to demonstrate how a problem — and the corresponding program — can be broken up into small units. Each unit represents a phase in a process in which variables are defined in terms of each other. The first such unit finds the area by means of line 40; the second, in line 50, finds the cost in terms of price and area. Although this problem of finding the cost of wallpaper is simple enough so that we certainly could have just written one BASIC statement to do the whole job for us, such as:

```
4Ø PRINT LENGTH * HEIGHT * PRICE
```

The program we just wrote is more transparent in the sense that we can more easily see what's going on, and we get the fringe benefit of finding (and printing) the *area* of the wall as well as the cost of wallpapering it.

How New Variables Are Assigned In Terms of Old Variables

New variables can be defined in terms of the operation between other variables by means of the equal (=) sign as in the following example:

AREA = LENGTH * HEIGHT

To the computer this means:

To the variable AREA assign the value obtained by multiplying the value of LENGTH by the value of HEIGHT.

All the arithmetic operations — addition, subtraction, multiplication, and division — may be involved in these operations on variables.

Rules of Order — Evaluating Expressions with Three or More Variables

Suppose that some new friends invite you over for dinner at their place. Since you haven't been to their house before, you are given the following instructions: "Turn left at the fifth stop sign, go another two blocks and turn right, and then find the first pink house on your left." These directions have two important aspects. The first has to do with the individual "operations" you need to perform, like "go another two blocks and turn right." The second has to with the *order* in which you carry out the instructions. If you get either aspect of your directions mixed up, you'll never get the dinner you expected!

The point of this little story about how to follow directions is that in addition to getting the individual operation right, you also have to do these operations in the correct order. Of course, we're not *really* talking about finding your way through town, but rather about rules for evaluating arithmetic expressions involving more than just two operations.

To take the mystery out of this, let's take a look at the following program:

```
10 A = 2
20 B = 3
30 C = 4
```

```
4Ø D = A + B * C
5Ø PRINT D
6Ø END
RUN
 14
Ok
```

Line 40 defines a variable D in terms of two arithmetic operations on variables A, B, and C. Which of these operation did your computer do first? Did it first *add* A to B, and *then* multiply that sum by C? Or did it first do the multiplication and *then* the addition?

We can find out what your computer actually did by plugging in the values for our variables and doing the arithmetic ourselves. If we add first and then multiply, we get 20 — evidently that's *not* what the computer gets! However, if we multiply first and then add, we get 14 — the same answer that the computer gets.

Computers always do all multiplications before any additions, even though, as in this example, the addition appears first in our line of instructions. What about subtraction and division? Subtraction is very similar to addition, and division is similar to multiplication, so the rule is that all multiplications and divisions in an arithmetic expression are evaluated before additions and subtractions. We should note at this stage, however, that there is one way to override this rule: namely, by using parentheses. We'll explain this in the last section of this chapter.

In short, the order in which you do this arithmetic really does matter in the same sense that it matters whether we "turn left at the fifth stop light" first and then "go two blocks and turn left" or vice versa. Take a look at the box that summarizes the rules for the order of arithmetic operations.

Rules for Evaluating Arithmetic Expressions

All

$\begin{Bmatrix} \text{multiplications} \\ \text{and} \\ \text{divisions} \end{Bmatrix}$ are carried out before $\begin{Bmatrix} \text{additions} \\ \text{and} \\ \text{subtractions} \end{Bmatrix}$

provided that no parentheses are used.

Let's add a few more lines to our previous program to include subtraction and division. The result looks like this:

```
1Ø A = 2
2Ø B = 3
4Ø C = 4
5Ø D = A + B*C        ← 2 + 3*4 = 2 + 12 = 14
6Ø E = A/B + C        ← 2/3 + 4 = .6666667 + 4 = 4.666667
7Ø F = A*B - A/C      ← 2*3 − 2/4 = 6 − 5.5 = 5.5
8Ø PRINT D,E,F
9Ø END
RUN
14                4.666667              5.5
Ok
```

We suggest that you evaluate lines 50, 60, and 70 yourself to see if the computer did it right!

Using Parentheses — Overriding the Rules

Using parentheses in arithmetic expressions allows you to override the rules described in the previous section. Consider the following program:

```
1Ø A = 2
2Ø B = 3
3Ø C = 6
4Ø D = A + B*C
5Ø E = (A + B)*C
6Ø PRINT D,E
7Ø END
RUN
14            2Ø
Ok
```

Lines 40 and 50 are identical *except* for the parentheses. The parentheses in line 50 tell the computer to "add A and B first, and *then* multiply that sum by C." In general, parentheses instruct your computer to take care of the business inside the parentheses *first*, and *then* proceed using the rules of order discussed in the previous section. Parentheses are a very useful tool: they give you much flexibility in writing expressions. Also, if you forget the rules of order, you can always use parentheses to be sure to get what you want!

Let's try a more complicated example to really see how this works:

```
10 X = 3* 4 - 5  + 8 / 4 - 2
20 Y = (3*(4 - 5)) + (8 /(4 - 2))
30 PRINT X,Y
40 END
RUN
 7              1
```

Using the rules of order of the previous section results in a value of 7 for X. See if you agree. Line 20 is identical to line 10 *except* for the parentheses, but it results in a value of 1 instead of 7.

Here's how the above example is calculated:

$$(3*(4-5)) \ + \ (8/(4-2))$$
$$(3* \ -1 \ ) \ + \ (8/ \ \ 2 \ \ )$$
$$-3 \ \ + \ \ \ \ 4$$
$$1$$

The first step is to evaluate the expression inside the innermost parentheses: so $(4-5)$ equals -1, and $(4-2)$ equals 2. The next step is to evaluate the next "level" of parentheses: so $(3* -1)$ equals -3 and $(8/2)$ equals 4. The last step is just to add -3 to 4, which equals 1. After a bit of practice, you'll find this easier to do than to explain! The box "Order of Operations with Parentheses" summarizes the rules for evaluating BASIC expressions that use nested parentheses.

Order of Operations with Parentheses

Parentheses in arithmetic expressions are evaluated in the following way. First, expressions inside the innermost parentheses are evaluated; these expressions are then treated as values. Then the next level of parentheses are evaluated. These in turn are treated as values for the next stage in this process. This procedure is continued until a single value results.

Summary

This chapter has focused on a very important programming tool known as the variable. We first explained the basic concept behind variables — the fact that variables allow you to plug different values or pieces of information into the same program line, making the program more general, more flexible, and more transparent in its fundamental workings. The value or constant assigned to a variable may, in effect, be reassigned within the program, or as we will see later, by input from a user interacting with your program. We also explained that because the computer needs to know what type of variable it is dealing with, the dollar sign must always be the last character in a string variable; in this way, string variables — that is, variables that stand for letters or words — are distinguished by the computer from numeric variables. Furthermore, while string variables must always end in a dollar sign, string constants (the "values" of the string variables) must always be enclosed in quotation marks. Finally, in this first portion of the chapter, we discussed the rules for the length of variables and string constants. In addition, certain other specific rules must be followed when you create variable names.

While this chapter did not present any new BASIC instructions, it did explain several kinds of operations that can be performed using variables. We saw how to concatenate or link the values of string variables with the plus sign. And we did quite a few arithmetic operations with variables. In this process, we saw that the order in which arithmetic operations are performed in BASIC is the same as in algebra (multiplication and division come first, followed by addition and subtraction) but that this natural order may be overriden by the use of parentheses. Finally and perhaps most important of all, we saw how to define new variables in terms of old ones. Defining variables in terms of each other in this way allows you to break a problem down into manageable parts.

Exercise

Suppose that we have the job of covering the walls of a room with wallpaper (the ceiling doesn't need any). Write a program that determines the total number of square feet of wallpaper required and the total cost of the wallpaper. Here is the relevant information: the length of the room is 16 ft., the width is 12 ft., the height is 8 ft., and the price of the wallpaper is \$6 per square foot. The program should clear the screen, turn off the Soft Function Key Display, and create a well-formatted output.

Solution

Here's one possible solution:

```
1Ø   REM----NAME: "WALLPAP.B6"--------------------------
12   REM
14   REM----***************************************
2Ø   REM----* Program determines area of walls    *------
25   REM----* and cost of wallpapering a room      *------
28   REM----***************************************
3Ø   REM
4Ø      KEY OFF
5Ø      CLS
6Ø   REM
7Ø   REM----input variables
75   REM
8Ø      LENGTH = 16
9Ø      WID = 12
1ØØ     HEIGHT = 8
11Ø     PRICE = 6
12Ø  REM
13Ø  REM----main program
135  REM
14Ø     AREA.1 = LENGTH * HEIGHT
15Ø     AREA.2 = WID * HEIGHT
16Ø     AREA.TOT = (AREA.1 + AREA.2) * 2
17Ø     COST = PRICE * AREA.TOT
18Ø  REM
19Ø  REM----output of program
195  REM
2ØØ     PRINT
21Ø     PRINT TAB(14) "AREA AND COST OF WALLPAPERING A ROOM"
22Ø     PRINT TAB(14) "***********************************"
23Ø     PRINT
24Ø     PRINT "Size of room (sq. ft.)"
25Ø     PRINT "      length=", LENGTH
26Ø     PRINT "      width=", WID
27Ø     PRINT "      height=",HEIGHT
28Ø     PRINT
29Ø     PRINT "Price of wallpaper ($/sq.ft.)="; PRICE
3ØØ     PRINT
31Ø     PRINT
```

```
32Ø    PRINT "Total area of walls (sq. ft.)=" TAB(32) AREA.TOT
33Ø    PRINT "Total cost of wallpaper ($)=" TAB(32) COST
34Ø    PRINT
35Ø    PRINT
36Ø    END
```

The output of this program looks like this:

```
            AREA AND COST OF WALLPAPERING A ROOM
            ************************************

Size of room (sq. ft.)
      length=   16
      width=    12
      height=   8
Price of wallpaper ($/sq.ft.)= 6


Total area of walls (sq. ft.)=    448
Total cost of wallpaper ($)=      2668


Ok
```

We suggest that you take some time to look over this program to see if everything makes sense to you. There are a few remarks we'd like to make about it.

Notice the use of REM statements and the indentation of the BASIC instructions right after the line numbers. Both of these help to make the program easier to read and to understand. A word about what we called the main program. The variable AREA.1 is the area of one of the walls. AREA.2 is the area of the other wall, which is a different size. The total area of all the walls, which we called AREA.TOT is given by twice the sum of AREA.1 and AREA.2 — that accounts for four walls. Our variable name for the width of the room is WID. Why not use WIDTH? Well, we tried it, but we got the message "Syntax error in 90"! We had forgotten one of the rules for naming variables: reserved words (words belonging to the language of BASIC) can't be used as variable names. And WIDTH happens to be one of those reserved words! Well, we make mistakes too!

7

Input — Your Program Listens

Concepts
    INPUT with numeric and string variables
    INPUT with a prompt
    INPUT with multiple variables
    Default values for variables
    Error message from INPUT
    Interrupting program execution

Instructions
    INPUT, LINE INPUT

Computer programs can be thought of as having three stages. The first stage is the input stage, in which your program gathers the information it needs from the outside world. The second stage is the main program, which does all the manipulating and calculating needed to perform the task or tasks for which the program was written in the first place. The last stage is output, which displays the results obtained by the main program in some way that we can easily understand. We can represent these stages in the following way:

In previous chapters we have learned much about the last two stages: variables and the various operations on them provide us with many of the tools required in a typical main program. PRINT and PRINT-related statements give us very powerful tools for displaying output.

This chapter is an introduction to the first input stage of a program. In case you're wondering why we're covering the first stage last...well, we do have a reason! We didn't do it earlier because we need to know something about variables before discussing input. We also need to know how to PRINT in order to see what information we actually input to our program.

What's an example of input? Recall the wallpaper program at the end of our last chapter. At that time the only way we could provide our program with the dimensions of the room and the price of the wallpaper was by means of direct assignment statements like

```
1Ø LENGTH = 16
```

Of course that works just fine. But there's one problem: if you want to run that program again for a *different* room size or price of wallpaper, you would have to rewrite those particular assignment statements. You'd have to make changes inside your program. Wouldn't it be a lot better and more convenient if your program would *ask* you, the user, a question like "well, what values for room size and wallpaper price do you want me to use this time?" Then we could run the program over and over again with different input information — without making changes inside the program every time.

Input Without Frills — Your First BASIC INPUT Statement

The INPUT statement is exactly what we're looking for. INPUT is BASIC's way of asking the user for information. The following sections will teach you the fundamentals of working with INPUT.

INPUT to Numeric Variables

To see how INPUT can be used with numeric variables, let's dive right in and enter the following program:

```
1Ø PRINT "enter price ($)"
2Ø INPUT PRICE
3Ø PRINT PRICE
4Ø END
```

When you run this program, the following appears on your screen:

```
RUN
enter price ($)
?  _        ← Blinking cursor
```

The blinking cursor right after the question mark means "I'm ready for you now; enter a value." So go ahead, enter a value — say, 15.25. Immediately after pressing ⏎, the following new information appears on the screen:

```
 15.25
Ok
```

The whole program and the result of running it look like this:

```
1Ø PRINT "enter price ($)"
2Ø INPUT PRICE
3Ø PRINT PRICE
4Ø END
RUN
enter price ($)
? 15.25
 15.25
Ok
```

What's new in this program is the INPUT statement in line 20. The INPUT statement is responsible for the question mark (?) and the blinking cursor that request input from you. Your computer will just sit there and wait until you enter something — or until you do something special, like turn the power off! We entered the value 15.25, which is immediately assigned to the variable PRICE — that is, the variable listed right after INPUT in line 20. When it is PRINT's turn to do its job, it returns the value of PRICE, namely 15.25. Pretty straightforward!

Run the program again, but this time enter a different value in response to the question mark:

```
RUN
enter price ($)
? 235ØØ.99
 235ØØ.99
Ok
```

As you can see, whatever you enter in response to the question mark resulting from INPUT really does get assigned to the variable PRICE.

So here we have what we were looking for: a simple method of passing input information from you, the user, to the program *without* having to cast this information in concrete through assignment statements within your program. Your computer talks to you via the

PRINT statement, whereas it *listens* to you via the INPUT statement. You can see why INPUT is one of the most important words in your BASIC vocabulary.

The Simple Form of INPUT for Numeric Variables

The statement

```
3Ø INPUT PRICE
```

results in the following output:

? _ ← Blinking cursor

The cursor waits for the user to enter a numeric value. When entered, this value is assigned to the variable PRICE.

INPUT to String Variables

By now you won't be too surprised to find out that it's also possible to use INPUT with string variables as well! Try this program:

```
1Ø PRINT "enter your name"
2Ø INPUT NAM$
3Ø PRINT NAM$
4Ø END
```

Running this program causes the already familiar question mark and blinking cursor to appear on your screen:

```
RUN
enter your name
? _   ← Blinking cursor
```

As before, the question mark and cursor are your computer's request for input.

Suppose we respond with Dietrich Buxtehude (he can't do it himself — he died in 1707!). The complete output of the program would look like this:

```
RUN
enter your name
? Dietrich Buxtehude
Dietrich Buxtehude
Ok
```

As you can see, inputting values to string variables is very similar to inputting values to numeric variables. The only difference is in the variable type. The dollar sign ($) at the end of the variable NAM$ right after INPUT tells BASIC to expect you to enter a *string* constant rather than a numeric constant. This, of course, is in line with what we already know about assigning variables of different types. What may be somewhat surprising to you is that even though the phrase "Dietrich Buxtehude" is a string constant, we didn't put any quotation marks around it when we input it. It turns out that you *can* bracket your string entry with quotation marks, but this is not required. In the next section, we'll show you a case in which quotation marks do serve a very useful function.

You may also have wondered why we used NAM$ as our variable name and not the more obvious NAME$. Go ahead and try it — if you want to get a "Syntax error in 20"! We have to admit we fell for it too. The key to the mystery is the list of reserved words in Appendix C: NAME is one of them! We can't use reserved words as variable names, even though we include the dollar sign at the end.

INPUT's Error Message — What Can Go Wrong, Wrong, Wrong

Run the previous program once again, but this time enter the name of Mr. Buxtehude in "officialese" – that is, last name first, separated by a comma. This is the result:

```
RUN
enter your name
? Buxtehude, Dietrich
Redo from start
? _
```

Whoa! What's wrong? First of all, "?Redo from start" means "Start over again," or more explicitly, "Something is wrong with what you entered, so try it again but do it right this time!" What could be wrong? We only reversed the names! Well, this is almost all we did. We also added a *comma* — that's our culprit. You can check this by reentering the name of Mr. Buxtehude in exactly the same way as before, but leaving out the comma. (You don't have to enter RUN again: the question mark and the blinking cursor let you know that your computer is ready to listen once again.) This time the program accepts your input.

"?Redo from start" is what your computer says whenever it doesn't like what you entered in response to an INPUT statement. It's INPUT's version of "Syntax error." The reason INPUT doesn't like the comma is that it gets confused. Remember how we separated different variables in PRINT by means of commas (as in PRINT X, Y, Z)? Well, INPUT thinks of commas in the same way — as separators for different variables; that is, with the comma between Buxtehude and Dietrich, INPUT thinks *two* variables are being input, whereas only *one* variable is listed after INPUT (namely, NAM$). You get the error message "?Redo from start" whenever the computer thinks you are trying to enter more values than the number of variable boxes you have provided for them. We'll talk more about inputting multiple variables later on.

But how do we input a string constant that contains a comma? There are several ways. One of them is to use — you guessed it — quotation marks around the string you are entering. Try it:

```
RUN
enter your name
? "Buxtehude, Dietrich"
Buxtehude, Dietrich
Ok
```

Great, that did the trick. Notice that although you entered quotation marks, they didn't get printed. PRINT never shows you the quotation marks that define the boundaries of a string. But whatever is "inside" the quotation marks gets treated literally by both INPUT and PRINT.

Using quotation marks in this way may be rather tedious or even somewhat puzzling to an uninitiated user. A better way to enter strings with commas may be by means of another BASIC statement called LINE INPUT, which we'll discuss later on.

Another way to get a "?Redo from start" response from your computer is from a variable *type mismatch*. For example, enter and run this program:

```
10 INPUT NUMBER
20 PRINT NUMBER
30 END
RUN
? fourteen
```

```
?Redo from start
? 14
   14
Ok
```

Our first response to INPUT's question mark was the string constant "fourteen." But string constants can't be assigned to numeric variables, so the computer's message really isn't surprising. We responded correctly the second time around.

Inputting Zeros the Easy Way — Default Values

What happens when INPUT asks you for a response and you just hit the (←) key? The answer is — the same thing as when you use a variable without assigning a value to it. Run the previous program without entering a number:

```
RUN
? _
   Ø
Ok
```

Since we didn't assign a value to NUMBER, the computer assumed the value to be zero. If the variable named in the INPUT statement is a *string variable* and we respond by just pressing (←), we are, in effect, entering a string of zero length. A string of zero length, called a *null* string, is returned by PRINT as nothing at all.

Interrupting INPUT with CTRL BREAK

There may be times when you really don't want to respond to the INPUT question mark with the usual type of response we've been talking about. For example, if you are dealing with a lengthy program and you realize that you just entered something you didn't really want, you may wish to break out of this particular run of the program and start over again without resetting the computer.

Fortunately, there is a way to do this. When confronted with the beckoning question mark and cursor of INPUT, just press the two keys labeled Ctrl (for "Control") and Break simultaneously. It's best to press (Ctrl) first and hold it down while you press (Break). From now on, we'll refer to this particular combination of keys simply as (Ctrl) (Break).

Let's try it once with the following familiar program. Enter RUN to get the usual question mark:

```
1Ø INPUT NUMBER
2Ø PRINT NUMBER
3Ø END
RUN
? _
```

Now press (Ctrl) (Break) and you'll get this on your screen:

```
Break in 1Ø
Ok
```

This tells you two things. First, the "break" or interruption occurred in line 10; that may be very handy to know in a complex program. Second, BASIC is once again at your service as indicated by the "Ok" prompt.

You can use (Ctrl) (Break) to interrupt your program at *any* stage of its execution. It's a very handy and potent combination of keys — especially when you need to get out of trouble!

INPUT with the Prompt — A Better Way to Communicate

Up until now, we've used a PRINT statement right in front of the INPUT statement to tell the user what information INPUT wants. For example, if we had wanted to INPUT a value for your age, we might have written:

```
1Ø PRINT "how old are you?"
2Ø INPUT AGE
3Ø PRINT AGE
4Ø END
```

Here PRINT has the function of letting you know that when INPUT's question mark appears, you should enter your age and not some other possibly interesting but irrelevant information.

This approach works just fine, of course. But there's a shortcut; namely, the INPUT statement with what is called the *prompt*. The prompt is a string constant within the INPUT statement that takes the place of the initial PRINT statement immediately before INPUT. The following program does exactly the same thing as the previous program, but it does it without the initial PRINT statement:

```
1Ø INPUT "how old are you"; AGE
2Ø PRINT AGE
3Ø END
RUN
how old are you? _
```

As before, the question mark and the cursor invite your response. The prompt is the string "how old are you." It always goes right after the word INPUT. When INPUT is executed, it first prints out the prompt, and then displays the question mark and the cursor.

INPUT with Prompt

The following statement is an example of the syntax of an INPUT statement with a prompt:

```
10 INPUT "how old are you"; AGE
```
        ‿‿‿‿‿‿‿‿‿‿   ↑
          Prompt   Variable

When this line is executed in a program, it requests user input in the following form:

```
how old are you ? _
```
  ← Blinking cursor

Although the variable AGE in the previous example is a numeric variable, the same form of INPUT can be used with string variables as well. We'll give you a problem at the end of the chapter that puts it all together by making use of both types of variables. But first, there's another variation on a theme.

The Prompt with a Comma — Avoiding the Question

Suppose you don't want your prompt to ask a question, but instead you want it to make a statement or direct request like "enter your age, (please!)" Try the line

```
1Ø INPUT "enter your age"; AGE
```

This line will return

```
enter your age? _
```

Maybe we're being just a bit picky, but that question mark after the prompt looks out of place, doesn't it? The phrase "enter your age" is a request, not a question.

BASIC gives us an easy way to remove the question mark that up until now we've learned to associate with INPUT: all you have to do is to substitute a comma (,) for the semicolon (;). So the line

```
10 INPUT "enter your age", AGE
                         ↑
                   Note the comma
```

will return

```
enter your age _      ← blinking cursor without question mark preceding it
```

That's better. Using a comma between the prompt and the variable name suppresses the question mark.

INPUT with Multiple Variables

So far we've entered just one value with each INPUT statement. There are programs, however, which require the INPUT of a lot of data, such as lists of numbers like stock prices, test scores, and the like. Such programs would require as many INPUT statements as the number of values you need to enter. In cases like this, wouldn't it be handy to be able to enter a lot of data with just *one* INPUT statement?

Indeed, the versatile INPUT allows you to do just that. Simply list the variables (separated by commas) to which the user is to assign values, right after the word INPUT. Let's try it out:

```
10 INPUT "enter a word, and a number--", WORD$, NUMBER
20 PRINT WORD$, NUMBER
30 END
RUN
enter a word, and a number--cello, 6500
cello          6500
Ok
```

The first entry "cello" is assigned to the first listed variable WORD$, and the second entry "6500" is assigned to the next listed variable NUMBER. In other words, the order in which values are entered in response to INPUT should be identical to the order in which variables are listed after INPUT. Well, that makes sense. Also, your entries in response to the

INPUT prompt should be separated by commas, just as the variables are.

We only used two variables here, but there's nothing to stop you from using more. The only limitation is the maximum length of the logical BASIC line, which is 255 characters. So if you use short variable names, you'd have room for quite a few variables!

One of the exercise problems at the end of the chapter will ask you to use multiple variables in an INPUT statement.

Pitfalls — How to Avoid Them

There are a few pitfalls to watch out for. What better way to become familiar with them than by falling right in at least once? Let's run the preceding program again with the following entries:

```
RUN
enter a word, then a number--65ØØ,cello    ← Mismatched variable types
?Redo from start
enter a word, then a number--cello,65ØØ,3  ← Too many values
?Redo from start
enter a word, then a number--cello         ← Not enough values
?Redo from start
enter a word, then a number--cello,65ØØ    ← We got it right!
cello         65ØØ
Ok
```

Hopefully, we can avoid all those error messages in the future! The problem with our first entry attempt is a mismatch between the type of value entered and the type of variable to which we tried to assign it; that is, we tried to assign the numeric value 6500 to the *string* variable WORD\$ — a taboo that will *always* result in an error message (computers can be *very* petty and stubborn about things like that!). Our second entry, "cello," is just as unacceptable to our computer since "cello" is a string constant, and we're trying to stuff it into a numeric variable box.

In our second attempt to respond to INPUT, we typed in *three* values, whereas INPUT only has *two* values listed. So we really can't blame our computer for its "?Redo from start" message; there just isn't a third variable box for the third value. Similarly, in our third attempt to satisfy INPUT, we only gave INPUT *one* value, so that our second variable (NUMBER) was left unassigned. BASIC *might* have said to itself, "ok, since they didn't give me a second value for NUMBER, I'll just assume it's zero," but the fact is, BASIC won't do this. The rule is that the number of values entered must match the number of variables listed.

LINE INPUT — For Strings Only

In the beginning of this chapter we ran across the problem of inputting a string constant containing commas; that is, we got a "?Redo from start" message when we responded to INPUT by entering text containing a comma. We solved this problem by asking the user to bracket the string to be entered with quotation marks. Although this is a simple solution, it isn't necessarily the best, since it puts the whole burden on the user. It's inconvenient to have to use quotation marks and they're easy to forget (if this author's experience is any indication). BASIC gives us another option for entering strings as input; the LINE INPUT statement.

LINE INPUT does almost the same thing as INPUT, but its function is more specialized: it can *only* be used to input a *string* constant. It avoids the comma problem of INPUT by allowing only *one* entry for each LINE INPUT statement. Therefore, *all* characters, including the comma, can now be interpreted as characters that are part of the string constant that the user types in. Whole sentences can be entered using LINE INPUT. Also, LINE INPUT doesn't automatically present the user with a question mark. If you want one, you, as the programmer, have to write the question mark explicitly into the prompt.

Let's try the following example illustrating the use of LINE INPUT:

```
10 LINE INPUT "Enter your name and profession--"; NAME.PROF$
20 LINE INPUT "Enter your birth date-----------"; B.DATE$
30 PRINT
40 PRINT NAME.PROF$ ", was born on " B.DATE$
50 END
RUN
Enter your name and profession--Dietrich Buxtehude, composer
Enter your birth date-----------July 8, 1637

Dietrich Buxtehude, composer, was born on July 8, 1637
Ok
```

If you've never heard his wonderful organ music, you've missed something (if you like organ music, that is)! Notice the commas in our responses to the prompts of LINE INPUT: they're reproduced by PRINT exactly as entered, so we know that they are really part of the string value assigned to the two string variables. Notice also the absence of any question marks; we didn't want any anyway. For a summary of what LINE INPUT does, see the box called "LINE INPUT."

LINE INPUT

The syntax of LINE INPUT is identical to that of INPUT *except* for the following differences:

1. LINE INPUT *only* accepts string constants. *All* characters entered in response to the prompt, including commas and quotation marks, are included in the string constant.

2. Only *one* string constant can be entered with each LINE INPUT statement.

3. LINE INPUT does *not* return a question mark as INPUT does.

The variable listed after LINE INPUT has to be a string variable (of course!).

Summary

In this chapter we've learned much about the input stage of a BASIC program. We've learned how to use INPUT and LINE INPUT statements to enable the user to enter values into a program — *without* the user having to fiddle with the program itself. We can now write programs that can be run over and over again with different input values.

We now have at our disposal most of the fundamental tools for programming in BASIC. We know how to use variables, how to input values, how to manipulate variables within the main program, and how to print out the results. But we are still missing one essential tool: the ability to break out of the order of executing program lines as dictated by our line numbers; that is, the ability to *branch*. That is the principal topic of our next chapter. See you there!

Exercises

1. Write a program that estimates the number of meals you've eaten in your lifetime. Make the simplifying assumptions that on the average you've eaten 3 meals a day (that is, we won't count such things as snacks!). Also, in order to keep it simple, ignore the time since your last birthday so that we only have to deal with integer years.

2. As a way of practicing the INPUT statement with multiple variables, write a program that finds the price of your favorite stock averaged over five days. Also, clear the screen and turn the Soft Function Key Display off.

Solutions

1. The main program has to find the number of days you've been alive and then multiply that number by 3 to find the number of meals you've eaten. The number of days you've lived equals your age times the number of days in a year, which equals 365.25 (on the average). The rest is input and output. By having the INPUT statement ask for your name as well as your age, you will get a chance to input both numbers and strings. We suggest that you use prompts with your INPUT statements.

Here is our solution:

```
10 REM----HOW MANY MEALS HAVE YOU EATEN?--------------
20 REM
30 REM----program input-----------------------------
40 REM
50 INPUT "What's your name"; NAM$
60 INPUT "Enter your age (years) ", AGE
70 REM
80 REM----main program------------------------------
90 REM
100 MEALS = 3 * 365.25 * AGE
110 REM
120 REM----program output----------------------------
130 REM
140 PRINT
150 PRINT NAM$ ", you have eaten" MEALS "meals!"
160 PRINT
170 END
```

Running this program results in the following output:

```
RUN
What's your name? Johann Pachelbel
Enter your age (years) 53

Johann Pachelbel, you have eaten 58Ø74.75 meals!

Ok
```

That's a lot of food for Mr. Pachelbel (1653 – 1706)! This program is pretty straightforward, but we suggest that you look it over carefully to make sure that everything makes sense to you. Notice that we've identified the three stages of our program by means of REM statements. The main program stage is the shortest one! That's actually not uncommon; program input and output is often the most time-consuming and challenging part of writing what are known as *user-friendly* programs. ("User- friendly" is computerese for "programs that are easy to use.")

Notice also that we used the semicolon in the INPUT statement of line 50 and the *comma* in line 60 in order to suppress the question mark.

2. Here is the way we solved this problem:

```
1ØØ REM----STOCK AVERAGING PROGRAM----------------------------------
11Ø REM
12Ø    CLS: KEY OFF
13Ø REM
14Ø REM----title------------------------------------------------
15Ø REM
16Ø    LOCATE 3,2Ø
17Ø    PRINT "STOCK AVERAGING PROGRAM"
18Ø    PRINT
19Ø REM
2ØØ REM----program input--------------------------------------
21Ø REM
22Ø    INPUT "Name of company"; COMPANY$
23Ø    INPUT "enter price of stock for 5 days---",PR1,PR2,PR3,PR4,PR5
24Ø REM
25Ø REM----main program--------------------------------------
26Ø REM
27Ø PR.AVERAGE = (PR1 + PR2 + PR3 + PR4 + PR5)/5
28Ø REM
29Ø REM----program output--------------------------------------
3ØØ REM
31Ø PRINT
32Ø PRINT "The price average of your " COMPANY$ " stock is" PR.AVERAGE
33Ø PRINT
34Ø END
```

An example output of this program is the following:

```
                    STOCK AVERAGING PROGRAM

Name of company? IBM
Enter price of stock for 5 days---65,68,66,74,75

The price average of your IBM stock is 69.6
Ok
```

The price average of your IBM stock is 69.6. A good week for IBM! It would have been a good week for you too if you had bought IBM stock on the first day of that week!

The advantage of being able to enter a lot of numbers by means of one INPUT statement is fairly obvious in this example. This sort of program is easily used by the programmer or someone knowledgeable about computers and BASIC, although someone else might have some difficulty; for example, they might not know to put commas between the values to be typed in. Or it might be easy to miscount the number of entries, especially if you have a large number of them. So writing professional programs that are foolproof and user-friendly takes a bit more sophistication — and work! We have come a long way in learning BASIC, but we aren't finished.

8

Branching and Decisions

Concepts
Unconditional and conditional branching
Looping
Relational operators
Logical operators

Instructions
GOTO, CTRL/BREAK, FOR...NEXT, FOR...NEXT...STEP, IF...THEN,
IF...THEN...ELSE, WHILE...WEND

All of the programs we've written so far are executed by the computer in an order dictated by the order of the line numbers. Your computer first reads and executes the first line, then the second, and it continues this linear process until, inexorably, it gets to the last line. Such linear program structures have their limitations, however. In many cases it is desirable to be able to repeat one portion of a program over and over again, each time with different values. That's just the kind of work that we humans like the least (to say nothing about our reliability) and that the computer, in contrast, does with great speed and reliability — and without getting bored! This type of repetition, called *looping*, is one of the very powerful techniques that we'll introduce in this chapter.

In many cases it is also important for a program to be able to *branch* to different parts of a program. Branching is usually based on some sort of decision. Before you leave your house in the morning, you decide what you're going to wear on the basis of the weather outside. If it looks like rain, you'll probably wear your boots and all your other rain paraphernalia, and if the sun is shining, you'll go light. Computer programs frequently need to make decisions too (although not about what to wear).

This chapter is about such nonlinear program execution. Looping, branching, and decision making are some of the important and powerful tools a programmer has at his disposal.

The GOTO Statement — No Two Ways About It

Of all the BASIC statements that have to do with branching and loops, the GOTO statement is the easiest to understand. To see how it works, enter the following program:

```
1Ø GOTO 3Ø
2Ø PRINT "hello, I'm line 2Ø"
3Ø PRINT "hello, I'm line 3Ø -- GOTO made me do it"
4Ø END
RUN
hello, I'm line 3Ø -- GOTO made me do it
Ok
```

There are two PRINT statements here, but only the second one, in line 30, was executed! What happened to line 20?

The responsible party is, of course, the GOTO statement in line 10. GOTO 30 tells your computer "go directly to line 30; do not go to line 20 the way you normally would." Yes, it's just like Monopoly's "go directly to jail, do not pass go...." We can visualize how the program is executed like this:

```
1Ø GOTO 3Ø ⌐
2Ø ...      |  Arrow shows how program
3Ø ... ◄────┘  lines are executed
4Ø ...
```

GOTO 30 causes the program to *branch* to line 30, thereby bypassing line 20. This branching is *unconditional* in the same sense that mother tells little Johnny "wash your hands, and no if's, but's or why's!" — there simply isn't any choice.

> ### The GOTO statement
>
> The statement
>
> ```
> 1Ø GOTO 3Ø
> ```
>
> will cause program execution to branch to the specified line number, which is 30 in this example.

Well, that's really all there is to GOTO. But what good is it? After all, basically all GOTO did in the previous program was to cause the program to skip line 20. If that's all we wanted to do, we needn't have written line 20 — and line 10, for that matter.

However, as you might have guessed, there's more to it. GOTO can be a very valuable statement in conjunction with other programming tools. For example, later in this chapter we'll see how GOTO can be used very effectively in conjunction with what is called an IF statement. It can also be used to return execution from a program branch back to the main program. We'll get to that topic when we discuss subroutines in Chapter 12.

The Endless Loop — Doing Things Over and Over Again

Let's use GOTO to explore the concept of the loop. In our previous program we used GOTO to jump forward in our program. But there's no reason why we can't use GOTO to redirect program execution back to an earlier program line as well. Try the following program:

```
1Ø PRINT "happy birthday, Ludwig"
2Ø BEEP
3Ø GOTO 1Ø
4Ø END
```

Running this program will cause your computer to beep and to PRINT out

```
happy birthday, Ludwig
happy birthday, Ludwig
happy birthday, Ludwig
*     *     *
*     *     *
*     *     *
```

... all the way to the bottom of the screen! And still "happy birthday, Ludwig" keeps coming as indicated by the flicker of the bottom line! Also, your BASIC prompt "Ok" hasn't returned, so you know your computer is still busy running your program.

Is there no end to this? Barring a power-failure, equipment malfunction, or your personal intervention, your program will run forever! We have here what is called an *endless loop*. Have we created a monster? Well, not quite, but such endless loops sometimes happen inadvertently and can cause real headaches to programmers and users alike, not to mention the computers themselves. Computers don't smoke or say "tilt" the way cartoons suggest, but a large system can *crash* — that is, become totally useless to anybody because it's so busy looping.

So how does this loop work? First, line 10 prints "happy birthday,

Ludwig." Then line 20 causes a beep for 1/4 of a second and thus slows down our program sufficiently so that we can see what's going on. The GOTO statement in line 30 now says "go to line 10" — that is, start all over again! So here we go: another "happy birthday, Ludwig," another BEEP, and GOTO to start once again. So 'round and 'round we go — that's our loop. Program execution never gets to the END in line 40. Figure 8-1 will help you to visualize this loop.

Although this particular loop is rather useless, it illustrates the concept of the loop. We can transform such loops into truly powerful and useful tools by doing two things: first, replace the body of the loop — the statements that are executed in one cycle of the loop — by something more interesting than just a PRINT and a BEEP; that is, really make the loop *do* something. Second, we need to *control* the loop so that it does only a specified number of cycles. There are several ways to do this. One of the easiest and most concise methods is by means of the FOR...NEXT statements to be discussed in a moment. But first, we still have our endless loop to deal with!

The CTRL BREAK keys — Interrupting a Program

So how do we escape from this endless loop? We could do it by turning our machine off. The less drastic and more effective method (more effective because we won't lose our program this way) is to use the (Ctrl) (Break) key combination we encountered in the last chapter. Remember that (Ctrl) (Break) means "hold down the (Ctrl) key while hitting the (Break) key." Go ahead and try it now. You'll get a message on your screen similar to:

```
^C
Break in 2Ø
Ok
```

```
1Ø PRINT "..."

2Ø BEEP              Loop

3Ø GOTO 1Ø

4Ø END
```

Figure 8-1. An endless loop

We said *similar* because the number could be different: it could be any one of the line numbers within the loop. The fact that we got "20" means that the instant we hit (Ctrl) (Break), the program was executing line 20. In general, you can use (Ctrl) (Break) whenever you want or need to interrupt a program.

The FOR...NEXT Statements — Controlling Your Loops

Enough of endless loops! Let's take a look at one of BASIC's true gems: a pair of statements that we'll refer to as FOR...NEXT. This combination of statements provides us with a direct and powerful way to produce controlled loops.

Instead of explaining at great length what FOR...NEXT does and how it does it, let's write a simple program that will help to reveal the inner secrets of the FOR...NEXT statements:

```
10 FOR J = 1 TO 5
20    PRINT J
30 NEXT J
40 PRINT "done!"
50 END
Ok
RUN
 1
 2
 3
 4
 5
done!
Ok
```

You can see that the single PRINT statement in line 20 printed all five numbers. This happened because the PRINT statement in line 20 is part of a loop that was executed exactly five times. Only after all the looping was done did line 40 print "done!" The statement FOR J = 1 TO 5 in line 10 defines the beginning of the loop, and the statement NEXT J defines the end of the loop. Whatever is between the FOR statement and the NEXT statement is called the body of the loop — in this example, just the single PRINT statement. We indented the word PRINT to keep the body of the loop visually distinct.

However, the FOR and NEXT statements do more than define the boundaries of the loop: they also control the loop. To see how this works, let's follow the execution of this program. The first statement in line 10 to be executed is FOR J = 1 to 5. This tells the computer to assign a value 1 to a variable J, usually called the *index* or *counter variable*. It also causes the computer to decide whether to proceed with the loop — that is, whether to go on to the PRINT statement in line 20, which is the body of the loop. If the present value of J is less than or equal to 5 (the number listed after TO), then the loop is given the green light. If J has a value greater than 5, the loop is terminated and program execution proceeds with line 50, the line immediately after the NEXT statement. Since the value of J at this stage is 1, which is clearly less than 5, the loop is permitted; that is, execution proceeds with the body of the loop, the PRINT statement in line 20.

Line 20 prints the value of J, which is 1. That's why we wrote PRINT J into the body of our loop: it tells us what the value of J is at the time that statement is executed.

Then the statement NEXT J is executed. It does just what it suggests: it determines the "next value of J," which it does by adding 1 to the value of J passed down through the loop. Since this old value of J is 1, the next value is 2. At this point, NEXT directs program execution back to the FOR statement — and we begin all over again.

FOR J = 1 TO 5 tests the value of J to see if it is equal to or less than 5. Since the present value of J is 2, and 2 is indeed less than 5, execution resumes with PRINT J, which returns 2, the second number in our output. NEXT J again increments J by 1 to get 3, and passes program control back up to FOR J = 1 TO 5. And so it goes.

That is, *until* we get to the fifth cycle of this loop. There, PRINT J returns 5, NEXT J increments the value of J to 6, and FOR J = 1 TO 5 makes its test. This time, however, J fails the test: J has the value 6, which is clearly *larger* than 5, and consequently the loop will *not* be executed again. Instead, execution "drops" through the loop to resume with the first statement *after* NEXT J, which in our example prints "done!" Phew! It takes a lot longer for us to "loop" through these explanations than it takes your IBM PC to execute them!

Figure 8-2 shows how we can visualize this whole looping process. In that figure, the loop proceeds as long as J has a value from 1 to 5. We get one loop for each acceptable value of J – five loops in our example. So it's easy to see how you can change the number of loops to, say, 7: just replace the number 5 with a 7! The FOR...NEXT statements are ideal for controlling the number of times a loop is executed.

The Limits of the Counter Variable

The FOR...NEXT statements are actually much more flexible than you might infer from our example so far. For one thing, the beginning value of J doesn't have to be 1: it can be any integer, positive or negative number; it can even be a single-precision decimal number, although that's generally not very useful. Try this program:

```
1Ø FOR J = 6 TO 1Ø
2Ø    PRINT J;
3Ø NEXT
Ok
RUN
 6  7  8  9  1Ø
Ok
```

This time J starts with a value of 6 and the last loop executed has a counter value of 10. There are five acceptable values of J — 6, 7, 8, 9, and 10 — so five loops will be executed. Later in this chapter, we'll consider an example in which it is useful to start the counter with a value other than 1.

Undoubtedly you've noticed that we sneaked in a few other changes. First, the output is displayed horizontally! That happened because we put a semicolon (;) at the end of PRINT J in line 20. Remember that a semicolon at the end of PRINT statement always suppresses the carriage return so that the *next* PRINT will do its job on the *same* line. The second change is more subtle — can you find it? We left out the J in the NEXT

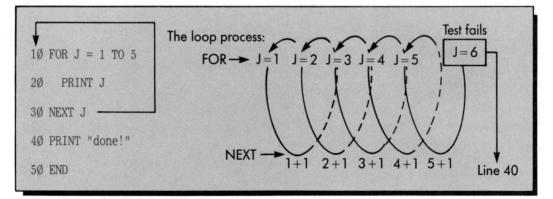

Figure 8-2. The FOR ... NEXT loop

statement! Yes, it is perfectly OK to leave out the counter variable name in a NEXT statement. Some people even prefer it because it speeds up your program — very slightly, to be sure, but perhaps significantly in large programs. However, when you get to what are called *nested* FOR...NEXT loops, it's advisable to use the counter in NEXT. But more of that later.

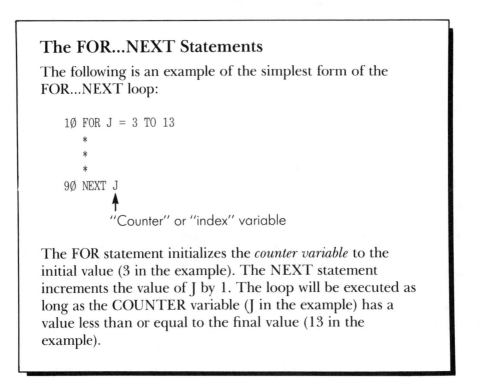

The FOR...NEXT Statements

The following is an example of the simplest form of the FOR...NEXT loop:

```
10 FOR J = 3 TO 13
     *
     *
     *
90 NEXT J
```

"Counter" or "index" variable

The FOR statement initializes the *counter variable* to the initial value (3 in the example). The NEXT statement increments the value of J by 1. The loop will be executed as long as the COUNTER variable (J in the example) has a value less than or equal to the final value (13 in the example).

Variables as Counter Limits

It is also possible to use variables (with values assigned to them) to determine the initial and final values of the counter variable. This feature allows you to INPUT the range of the counter variable as illustrated by the following program:

```
1Ø INPUT "enter the beginning value---", BEGIN
2Ø INPUT "enter the final value-------", FINAL
3Ø FOR J = BEGIN TO FINAL
4Ø   SQUARE = J * J
5Ø   PRINT J, SQUARE
6Ø NEXT
7Ø END
Ok
RUN
enter the beginning value---5
enter the final value-------9
 5              25
 6              36
 7              49
 8              64
 9              81
Ok
```

BEGIN and FINAL determine the smallest and largest values of the counter variable. The fact that these are variables gives this program a flexibility it wouldn't have if we used fixed numbers.

We've done something else in this program to illustrate the use of the FOR...NEXT loop: we've made a table of numbers and their squares! (As you no doubt know, the square of a number is simply the number multiplied by itself.) The FOR...NEXT loop is ideal for generating tables of all kinds. We'll give some more sophisticated examples later in this chapter.

Your First Graph — Putting FOR...NEXT to Good Use

The FOR...NEXT loop opens up an almost infinite number of programming possibilities. It's not yet time to really get into graphing, but we can't resist showing you how you can get a very simple graph of the output of the previous program. We'll use TAB to position an asterisk so that the column position of the asterisk is equal to the square of J, our index. Also, for the sake of simplicity, we won't use INPUT this time. Here's our program:

```
1Ø FOR J = 1 TO 6
2Ø    SQUARE = J * J
3Ø    PRINT TAB(SQUARE)  "*"
4Ø    PRINT
5Ø NEXT
Ok
RUN
*

    *

        *

            *

                *

                    *

Ok
```

Your first graph! Notice the slight curve to the line of asterisks. SQUARE gets large really fast! As you can see from line 20, SQUARE is assigned the value of the product of J times J — the square of J. Line 30 causes the asterisk to be printed in the column equal to the value of SQUARE. So the bigger the value of SQUARE, the further to the right is the asterisk.

Including STEP — Adding More Flexibility to FOR...NEXT

FOR...NEXT, as we've described it so far, is already pretty powerful. But there's one goody we haven't told you about yet: it's possible to change the interval between successive counter values by appending the word STEP to the FOR...NEXT statement and putting the size of the desired increment after STEP. The following program illustrates this expanded version of the FOR... NEXT loop:

```
1Ø FOR L = -4 TO 4 STEP 2
2Ø    PRINT L                   Indicates that L should
3Ø NEXT                         be incremented by 2 with each
4Ø END                          execution of the loop
Ok
RUN
-4 -2  Ø  2  4
```

Line 10 assigns the initial value of − 4 to the counter L (we used L this time so that you wouldn't get the impression that the counter always has to be named J!). The output shows that each time the loop is executed, the number 2 (not 1) is added to the previous value of L. Of course STEP 2 is responsible for this phenomenon. STEP 2 tells the computer to increment the counter by 2 with each execution of the loop.

The number following STEP can be any integer, even a negative one. Try this variation of the preceding program:

```
10 FOR L = 5 TO -8 STEP -2
20    PRINT L
30 NEXT
40 END
Ok
RUN
5  3  1 -1 -3 -5 -7
Ok
```

STEP −2 causes the number −2 to be added to L each time the loop is executed (adding −2 is the same thing as subtracting 2). We start with 5 and add −2 each time NEXT is executed. The last value of L to be printed is −7. The NEXT value of L, −9, is *not* printed because −9 is *smaller* than −8, the final value of the counter. When the program uses STEP to step in the negative direction, the loop continues to be executed as long as the counter is equal to or *larger* than the final counter value — that is, as long as the counter hasn't passed through the final value. The diagram in Figure 8-3 may clarify this stepping procedure:

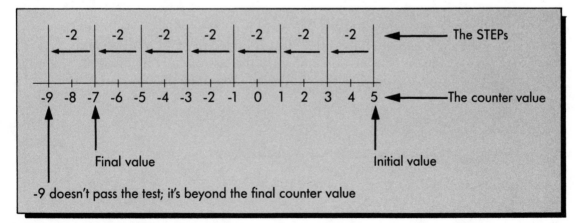

Figure 8-3. Using STEP with − 2

The following program shows how STEP might be used in a somewhat more interesting way. Suppose we want to write a program that tells us the sum of all even numbers between, say, 0 and some final number. Here's how you might do it:

```
1Ø INPUT "enter the last number to be summed---", LAST
2Ø SUM = Ø
3Ø FOR N = 2 TO LAST STEP 2
4Ø    SUM = SUM + N
5Ø NEXT N
6Ø PRINT SUM
7Ø END
RUN
enter the last number to be summed---1ØØ
 255Ø
```

This is what happens: line 10 asks for the value of LAST, the last number to be summed. Line 20 *initializes* the variable SUM to equal zero (actually it isn't essential that we do this, because the default value of a variable is zero, but for the sake of clarity, it is a good practice to be explicit about this sort of thing). Line 30 begins the loop, with N, the counter, initially set to 2. Line 40 finds the sum of the present values of SUM ($=0$) and N ($=2$) to give the value 2, and assigns this value to the variable SUM. Notice that SUM=SUM+N is *not* an algebraic equation (ignore this remark if you're not familiar with algebra!) in that the equal sign here doesn't really mean "equals." Rather, the equal sign is an instruction to the computer to *assign* whatever is to the right of the equal sign to whatever is to the left of it. Line 50 increments N by 2 and the loop starts over again.

This time the value of N is 4, which in line 40 is added to SUM. Each time the loop is executed, the value of N is added to SUM until we add our LAST value of N. Line 60 then prints the last value of SUM. Well, that's just what we wanted — the sum of all even numbers between 0 and LAST.

The FOR...NEXT...STEP Statements

The following example illustrates the complete syntax of the FOR...NEXT...STEP statements:

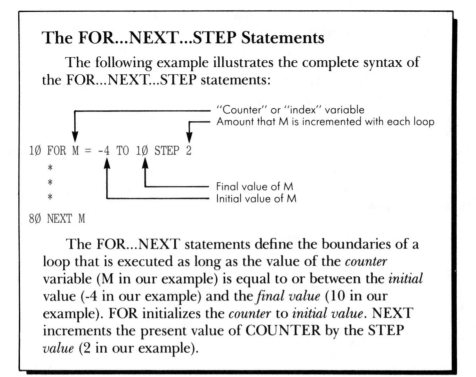

```
10 FOR M = -4 TO 10 STEP 2
   *
   *
   *
80 NEXT M
```

The FOR...NEXT statements define the boundaries of a loop that is executed as long as the value of the *counter* variable (M in our example) is equal to or between the *initial value* (-4 in our example) and the *final value* (10 in our example). FOR initializes the *counter* to *initial value*. NEXT increments the present value of COUNTER by the STEP *value* (2 in our example).

Nested FOR...NEXT Loops

Some programming applications require one FOR...NEXT loop to be placed *inside* another FOR...NEXT loop. To see how such *nested loops* work, try the following program:

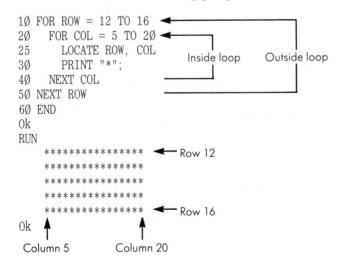

```
10 FOR ROW = 12 TO 16
20    FOR COL = 5 TO 20
25       LOCATE ROW, COL
30       PRINT "*";
40    NEXT COL
50 NEXT ROW
60 END
Ok
RUN
       ****************  ← Row 12
       ****************
       ****************
       ****************
       ****************  ← Row 16
Ok
    ↑              ↑
 Column 5      Column 20
```

Those are a lot of asterisks for such a short program! By changing the final values of our counters ROW and COL, we could easily fill up the whole screen! Let's see how this program works. The inside or *nested* loop causes a single line of asterisks to be printed beginning with column 5 and ending with column 20. Those limits are determined by the initial and final values of COL in the FOR statement on line 20. The *outside* loop defined by lines 10 and 50 are responsible for printing the five rows of asterisks — one for each value of the counter ROW. Not so hard, really!

Let's use nested loops and the above method of drawing asterisks to "fill out" the graph we made earlier which shows the squares of a series of integers. Try this program:

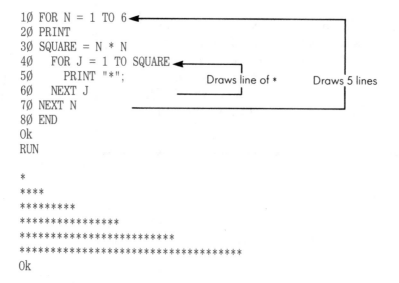

```
10 FOR N = 1 TO 6
20 PRINT
30 SQUARE = N * N
40   FOR J = 1 TO SQUARE
50     PRINT "*";
60   NEXT J
70 NEXT N
80 END
Ok
RUN

*
****
********
****************
*************************
************************************
Ok
```

Pretty fancy stuff! All that the inside loop does is to draw each horizontal line of asterisks. The length of each line is determined by SQUARE, which is equal to the square of the counter N of the *outside* loop. The outside loop evaluates SQUARE and causes the inside loop to be executed six times. That's how we get six lines.

Nested loops may seem a bit complicated at first, but they're really neat once you get used to them. They're also very useful.

Letting Your Computer Make Decisions

Making decisions is often as important in a computer program as it is in your own life. The general form that many of our personal decisions take is *if* a certain thing is true, *then* we are going to do so and so. For example, we might say, "*if* the sun is shining *then* I'll wear my shorts."

BASIC very conveniently provides us with a way to translate such a statement into something your IBM PC can understand:

```
1Ø INPUT "is the sun shining"; ANS$
2Ø IF ANS$ = "yes" THEN PRINT "go ahead and wear your shorts"
3Ø END
RUN
is the sun shining? yes
go ahead and wear your shorts
Ok
```

If we RUN this program again, but answer "no," our program will just ignore us:

```
RUN
is the sun shining? no
Ok
```

The output depends on the decision made by line 20, which says IF "yes" has been assigned to the variable ANS$, THEN go ahead and print "go ahead and wear your shorts." If the string "no" or *any* string other than "yes" has been assigned to ANS$, the IF...THEN statement doesn't do anything. Program execution then continues with the next line.

The general form of IF...THEN looks like this:

IF *expression* THEN *clause*

where the word *expression* refers to some kind of condition on which the decision depends. In our example above, this expression was an equality between a string variable and a string constant. The word *clause* stands for the particular instruction that is to be carried out *if* the expression is true. In our example, the clause was PRINT "go ahead and wear your shorts." Both the expression and the clause can take a vast variety of forms. We'll investigate these in a later part of this chapter.

IF...THEN...ELSE — Clarifying Your Options

In our previous example, IF...THEN caused "go ahead and wear your shorts" to be printed IF ANS$ = "yes" (the sun is shining). There is no response if the answer is anything other than "yes." What if we wanted a response to the answer "no" as well? Does BASIC provide us with a simple way of saying something like, "*if* the sun shines *then* wear your shorts *otherwise* wear your raincoat?"

Yes, it does. All we really need to do to translate such a statement into BASIC is to substitute the word ELSE for the word *otherwise*. Let's modify the preceding program to include this option:

```
10 INPUT "is the sun shining"; ANS$
20 IF ANS$="yes" THEN PRINT "wear shorts" ELSE PRINT "wear your raincoat"
30 END
RUN
is the sun shining? yes
wear shorts
Ok
RUN
is the sun shining? no
wear your raincoat
Ok
```

From the second RUN you can see that when ANS$ is *not* equal to "yes," the PRINT statement following ELSE is executed. In general, the part behind ELSE, which is also called a *clause*, is executed *only* if the condition following IF is *not* true. Not too hard, is it? The IF...THEN...ELSE statement reads just like normal English! Figure 8-4 summarizes how this type of conditional branching is executed.

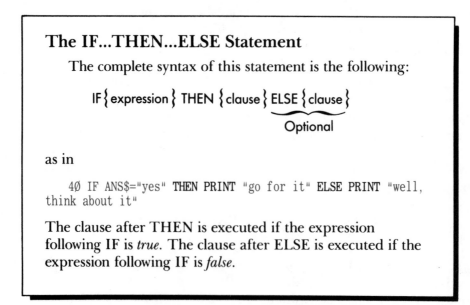

The IF...THEN...ELSE Statement

The complete syntax of this statement is the following:

IF { expression } THEN { clause } ELSE { clause }

Optional

as in

```
40 IF ANS$="yes" THEN PRINT "go for it" ELSE PRINT "well,
think about it"
```

The clause after THEN is executed if the expression following IF is *true*. The clause after ELSE is executed if the expression following IF is *false*.

Relational Operators — Expanding the Conditional Expression

In our previous example, the decision made by the IF...THEN...ELSE statement was based on the equality between a string variable and string constant. However, there are many other types of conditions. For one thing, expressions can involve *numeric* values and variables in addition to *string* values and variables. Also, the equality is just one among many possible conditions that the IF...THEN...ELSE statement can test. The *relational operators* shown in Table 8-1 make it possible to test for five other kinds of situations.

As you can see, all kinds of comparisons are possible. Note the equal sign here really means "equals" (as in $5 = 4 + 1$) and not "assign" (as in "assign" the sum of the value of X and 1 to the variable X, which in BASIC is written as $X = X + 1$). The examples given in Table 8-1 also show that expressions can involve numbers or variables or both.

The following program shows how some of these relational operators might be used:

```
10 INPUT "enter the time (AM) ", TIME
20 IF TIME < 7 THEN PRINT "there's still time to snuggle"
30 IF TIME = 7 THEN PRINT "get up, you lazy bum!"
40 IF TIME > 24 THEN PRINT "your clock is kaput": GOTO 60
50 IF TIME > 7 THEN PRINT "you're LATE, no time for coffee!"
60 END
Ok
RUN
enter the time (AM) 4
there's still time to snuggle
Ok
```

This program is pretty self-explanatory, so we don't need to run through all the possibilities! There's one thing, though, that might have escaped

IF { expression } is ⎡ true → execute THEN clause
                                     ⎣ false → execute ELSE clause

Figure 8-4. Decisions with IF ... THEN ... ELSE

your notice: line 40 has *two* statements in it: first, IF...THEN; and second, separated by a colon (:) from IF...THEN, GOTO 60, which causes END to be executed. The purpose of GOTO 60 here is to cause execution to bypass the next IF...THEN statement in line 50 provided that TIME > 24; that is, we didn't want line 50 to be executed if the expression after IF in line 40 is true. If the expression in line 40 is *not* true, then the second statement, GOTO 60, will not be executed. Such stacked clauses allow one IF...THEN statement to control several functions. One decision can have many consequences.

IF...THEN...ELSE with Logical Operators

It is also possible to write an IF...THEN statement to test for *two* conditions simultaneously. For example, the statement

```
5Ø IF ANS$ = "yes" OR ANS$ = "y" THEN ...
```

will cause THEN to be executed if the value of ANS$ is *either* "yes" or "y." This particular example is useful in cases where you're not sure if the user will respond to an INPUT question with a "yes" or a "y."

Another such *logical* operator is the AND operator. For example, the statement

```
5Ø IF WEATHER$ = "sunny" AND MONEY > 1ØØØØ THEN VACATION$ = "yes"
```

means the following: only if *both* WEATHER$ equals "sunny" AND MONEY is greater than 10,000 is the variable VACATION to be assigned the value "yes"; that is, the whole expression is true only if *both* parts of the expression are true.

BASIC symbol	Meaning	Example
=	equals	a = b + 2
<	is less than	x < 5
>	is greater than	MONTH > 12
< = or = <	is equal to or less than	a * b < = 20
> = or = >	is equal to or greater than	AMOUNT > = SALARY
<> or ><	is not equal to	5 <> 9

Table 8-1. Relational operators

Another logical operator is NOT. Its effect is to negate the adjoining relational operator. For example, =NOT means the same thing as <>.

The Logical Operators

For the following expressions to be true:

- *expression* A OR *expression* B requires A and/or B to be true

- *expression* A AND *expression* B requires *both* A and B to be true

- NOT *expression* negates the expression

Logical Operations on Strings

We now know that numbers can be compared in many different ways, but it may come as a surprise to you to find out that we can compare *strings* just as we compare numbers! Stating that one string equals another makes sense. But what does it mean to say that "a" is less than "m"?

Well, the key idea is that computer people have attached a unique number to each character on your key-board. This particular association between character and number is given by what is called the ASCII code, which is listed in Appendix D. For example, the ASCII code for the letter *a* is 097; for the letter *m*, it is 109. The way that letters, or characters in general, are ordered by your computer is by means of their ASCII code. So it is in this sense that "a" < "m" or that "a" < "b," for that matter. If you look at this code in Appendix D, you'll note that characters follow an order, as shown in Figure 8-5. If strings longer than one character are compared, the rule is that the first character of each string is compared, then the second character, and so forth.

```
Increasing ASCII value ———→

 1 ... 9  A  B ...  Y  Z ...  a  b ...  y  z ... ◄— Character
 |     |  |         |  |      |         |
049   065          090 097             122 ◄— ASCII value
```

Figure 8-5. Ordering characters according to their ASCII value

The following list shows some examples of true statements:

```
"a" > "A"
"a" > "5"
"B" < "a"
"ba" > "bA"
"bb" > "ba"
"mr " > "mr"        ← The space has a value Ø32
```

Comparing strings in this manner is essential to programs that arrange words in alphabetical order.

More about the Clause in IF...THEN

The part that follows THEN (or ELSE) referred to as the *clause*, can be any legitimate BASIC statement. The following are some examples:

```
IF ... THEN PRINT "...."
IF ... THEN GOTO 3ØØ         ← A conditional GOTO!
IF ... THEN 3ØØ              ← Equivalent to the above
IF ... THEN Y = X - 5
IF ... THEN INPUT DAY        ← Asks for user INPUT to assign DAY
IF ... THEN END             ← Terminates program
IF ... THEN X=Y:GOTO 6Ø      ← Assigns Y to X and executes GOTO 6Ø
```

The Conditional Loop — The WHILE...WEND Statement

The FOR...NEXT statements are ideal for repeating BASIC instructions a specified number of times. However, there are occasions when we'll want to repeat a calculation — that is, do a loop — as long as a given condition is true; the number of loops required may vary each time the program is run. Although such a loop can be constructed out of combinations of the FOR...NEXT, IF...THEN, and GOTO statements, BASIC provides us with a set of statements designed specifically for the purpose of executing such conditional loops: the WHILE...WEND statements.

Suppose we want to write a program that prints a descending sequence of integers that stops when we get to a certain value — say, 1. Here's one of several familiar methods we can use to do this job:

```
1Ø INPUT "enter a number: ", X
2Ø PRINT X
3Ø X = X - 1
4Ø IF X >= 1 THEN GOTO 2Ø
5Ø END
RUN
enter a number: 5
 5  4  3  2  1
Ok
```

The key statement here is line 40, which causes the program to branch back to line 20 as long as the value of X is greater than or equal to 1. The result is what we'll call a *conditional loop*; that is, execution of the loop continues as long as a certain condition is true. In this case the condition is that X is greater than or equal to 1.

This program works all right; it does its job. However, it's not the easiest kind of program to read, because you have to get down to the very end of the program — to the IF statement in line 40 — to figure out that there's supposed to be a loop between lines 20 and 40. This really isn't much of a problem in programs as short as this one, but for longer programs, it can get very confusing.

Let's rewrite this program using our new WHILE...WEND statements:

```
1Ø INPUT "enter a number: ", X
2Ø WHILE X >= 1
3Ø    PRINT X
4Ø    X = X - 1
5Ø WEND
6Ø END
RUN
enter a number:   7
 7  6  5  4  3  2  1
Ok
```

As you can see, this program does exactly the same thing as the previous one, although the WHILE...WEND statements take the place of the IF...THEN statement that causes branching to the beginning of the loop as long as X is greater than or equal to one. The WHILE statement says "While (or as long as) the value of X is greater than or equal to 1, execute the statements between WHILE and WEND." The WEND statement sends program execution back up to WHILE; WEND defines the "END" of the WHILE...WEND loop.

By now you're probably thinking "hey, WHILE...WEND is almost identical to FOR...NEXT." True: both generate loops using the same format, in that the FOR and WHILE statements define the beginning of the loop, and the NEXT and WEND statements define the end of the loop. The difference, however, is in the way that looping is controlled: whereas the FOR statement keeps the loop going for a specified number of times, the WHILE statement keeps the loop going as long as or "WHILE" an expression is true.

The previous example shows how WHILE...WEND works by printing out a sequence of descending integers. The real power and usefulness of these statements, however, become apparent only in more complex programs. We'll use them to good advantage in various programs later in this book (particularly in Chapters 17 and 19). We do want to give you one more example right here, though, before we end this chapter.

The following program prints the monthly balance of an account from which you withdraw 1/2 of your present balance every month. When your account gets down to less than $10, calculations are terminated as a reflection of the fact that you've reached the minimum value in your account and the bank will, in its inimitable way, close down your account!

```
110 PRINT "Monthly balance if you withdraw"
120 PRINT "1/2 of balance every month:": PRINT
130 INPUT "Original amount "; BAL
140 PRINT
150 PRINT BAL
160 '
170 WHILE BAL > 10
180    BAL = BAL/2
190    PRINT BAL
200 WEND
210 END
Ok
RUN
Monthly balance if you withdraw
1/2 of balance every month:

Original amount? 1200
```

```
1200
600
300
150
75
37.5
18.75
9.375
Ok
```

Your account (and your spending spree) will last seven months before the bank closes down your account with a final balance of $9.37. You might wish to modify this program to include interest earned on the balance.

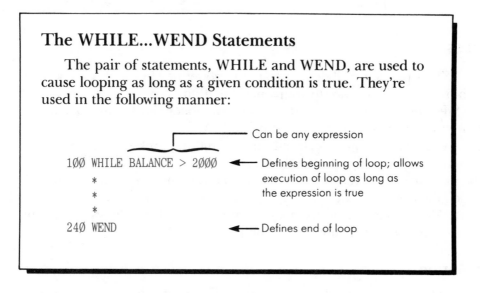

The WHILE...WEND Statements

The pair of statements, WHILE and WEND, are used to cause looping as long as a given condition is true. They're used in the following manner:

```
                                        ┌──── Can be any expression
100  WHILE  BALANCE > 2000  ◄──── Defines beginning of loop; allows
     *                                  execution of loop as long as
     *                                  the expression is true
     *
240  WEND                   ◄──── Defines end of loop
```

Summary

You've just taken a trip through one of the most important programming tools in BASIC. All other computer languages have similar methods of branching, making decisions, and doing something over and over again. These tools really give your computer a chance to show off. We've covered in quite some detail the following BASIC statements:

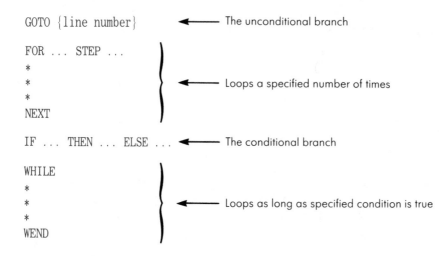

```
GOTO {line number}          ◄────── The unconditional branch

FOR ... STEP ...      ⎞
*                     ⎟
*                     ⎬ ◄────── Loops a specified number of times
*                     ⎟
NEXT                  ⎠

IF ... THEN ... ELSE ...  ◄────── The conditional branch

WHILE                 ⎞
*                     ⎟
*                     ⎬ ◄────── Loops as long as specified condition is true
*                     ⎟
WEND                  ⎠
```

Exercises

1. This problem will demonstrate the power of FOR...NEXT and may also have some relevance to your financial affairs.

Suppose you invest a certain amount of money that earns a given yearly interest but is compounded monthly. Write a program that produces a table showing elapsed months and the present value of the investment. The program should also ask the user to input the amount of the investment, the yearly interest rate, and the number of months for which the present value is to be displayed.

2. Modify the first problem so that the output shows the value of your investment every year, not every month.

Solutions

1. Here is one possible solution to the first problem:

```
100 REM----NAME: "INVEST-M.B8"---------------------------------
110 REM
120 REM----Program Calculates Return on One-time Investment----
130 REM
140 REM----TITLE------------------------------------------------
150 REM
155    KEY OFF: CLS
160    PRINT "VALUE OF INVESTMENT COMPOUNDED MONTHLY"
170    PRINT "------------------------------------"
180    PRINT
190 REM
200 REM----INPUT TO PROGRAM------------------------------------
```

```
21Ø REM
22Ø    INPUT "enter yearly interest rate (%)-----", INTRATE
23Ø    INPUT "enter amount of investment ($)-----", BALANCE
24Ø    INPUT "enter investment period in months--", LAST
25Ø REM
26Ø REM----HEADINGS-----------------------------------------
27Ø REM
28Ø    PRINT: PRINT
29Ø    PRINT "Month", "Balance"
3ØØ    PRINT "-----", "-------"
31Ø REM
32Ø REM----THE MAIN PROGRAM----------------------------------
33Ø REM
34Ø    FOR MONTH = 1 TO LAST
35Ø       BALANCE = BALANCE + BALANCE * INTRATE/12ØØ
36Ø       PRINT MONTH, BALANCE
37Ø    NEXT
38Ø END
```

An example output of this program looks like this:

```
VALUE OF INVESTMENT COMPOUNDED MONTHLY
--------------------------------------

enter yearly interest rate (%)-----18
enter amount of investment (%)-----1ØØØØ
enter investment period in months--12


Month          Balance
-----          -------
  1            1Ø15Ø
  2            1Ø3Ø2.25
  3            1Ø456.78
  4            1Ø613.64
  5            1Ø772.84
  6            1Ø934.43
  7            11Ø98.45
  8            11264.93
  9            11433.9
 1Ø            116Ø5.41
 11            11779.49
 12            11956.18
Ok
```

This is a pretty nice investment! Notice the effect of the monthly compounding: the actual return on your $10,000 after 1 year is $1956, which is 19.56 % (this is sometimes called the *yield*), whereas the interest rate we entered is 18 %.

Most of this program is familiar to us now, but line 340 may need some clarification. It says that the *old* BALANCE of your investment plus the monthly interest earned is to be assigned to the *new* BALANCE of your investment. Ok, that makes sense. It also says that monthly interest earned equals BALANCE * INTRATE/1200. Why is INTRATE divided by 1200? Since interest is entered as a percentage, we first divide INTRATE by 100 to give us the decimal value. Then, since the entered interest represents the *yearly* interest, but we need the equivalent *monthly* rate, we again divide INTRATE, this time by 12. Dividing first by 100 and then by 12 is the same as dividing by 1200 — that's how we get the term INTRATE/1200.

2. Here's how you can solve this problem using nested loops:

```
100 REM----NAME: "INVEST-Y.B8"---------------------------------
110 REM
120 REM----Program Calculates Return on One-time Investment----
130 REM
140 REM----TITLE----------------------------------------------
150 REM
155    KEY OFF: CLS
160    PRINT "VALUE OF INVESTMENT COMPOUNDED MONTHLY"
170    PRINT "------------------------------------"
180    PRINT
190 REM
200 REM----INPUT TO PROGRAM------------------------------------
210 REM
220    INPUT "enter yearly interest rate (%)-----", INTRATE
230    INPUT "enter amount of investment---------", BALANCE
240    INPUT "enter investment period in years---", LAST
250 REM
260 REM----HEADINGS-------------------------------------------
270 REM
280    PRINT: PRINT
290    PRINT "Year", "Balance"
300    PRINT "----", "-------"
310 REM
320 REM----THE MAIN PROGRAM-----------------------------------
330 REM
340    FOR YEAR = 1 TO LAST
```

```
35Ø     FOR MONTH=1 TO 12
36Ø        BALANCE = BALANCE + BALANCE * INTRATE/12ØØ
37Ø     NEXT MONTH
38Ø     PRINT YEAR, BALANCE
39Ø   NEXT YEAR
4ØØ END
```

When this program is run, it yields the following output:

```
VALUE OF INVESTMENT COMPOUNDED MONTHLY
---------------------------------------

enter yearly interest rate (%)-----18
enter amount of interest-----------1ØØØØ
enter investment period in years---6


Year            Balance
----            -------
  1             11956.18
  2             14295.Ø3
  3             17Ø91.4
  4             2Ø434.79
  5             24432.2
  6             29211.59
Ok
```

Basically, our original loop — now the nested loop — is still the same, except that it compounds the interest for exactly 12 months (rather than a variable amount equal to the investment period), and it doesn't contain PRINT BALANCE anymore. The new outside loop now has the job of printing the BALANCE of your account at the end of each year. So the inside loop does all the calculating, and the outside loop prints the result after every 12 executions of the inside loop (one for each month of the year) — that is, at the end of each year.

This is a pretty sophisticated program! It wouldn't be hard to modify it to include monthly contributions, or even the "front end" loading typical of many investment programs. We have a really powerful programming tool at our disposal here!

9

Displaying Numbers

Concepts
  Numbering systems
  Single- and double-precision
  Scientific notation
  Formatted printing

Instructions
  OCT$(n), &O(n), HEX$(n), &H(n), %, !, #, DEFINT, DEFSNG,
  DEFDBL, PRINT USING

There are two parts to this chapter. In the first, we cover numbering systems and the ways the computer handles and represents numbers. In the second we describe PRINT USING, a powerful statement for formatting numeric output.

The first part of the chapter is somewhat theoretical. You don't really need to understand all of this material to program in BASIC or to follow the rest of this book. On the other hand, the first section presents material which, sooner or later in your programs, you will find useful. Our advice is to read the first part of this chapter, but not to worry too much if the concepts are not completely clear to you at this point.

The second part of the chapter describes how to use the PRINT USING statement, which is a refinement of the familiar PRINT statement. PRINT USING makes it possible to produce very clean-looking printouts of tables, and of numbers expressed as dollars-and-cents, which look best in a particular format. This is an important and powerful BASIC statement that everyone who works with BASIC needs to know.

Numbering Systems

Humans use a numbering system that is based upon the number ten

(10), no doubt as a result of the ten fingers on our hands. In our numeric system we start with the number 0 and count up to the number 9.

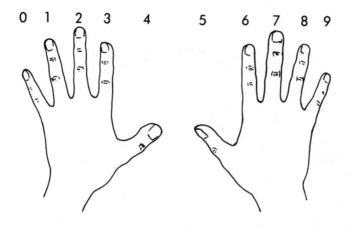

Once we have gone through the ten digits, the next number is represented by 10, the "1" indicating that we have gone through the digits one time and the "0" indicating that we are back at the beginning of our ten digits. This numbering system is called "base ten." Other combinations of numbers are possible. If, for example, two people, each having ten fingers, were to get together, then it would be possible to count to twenty. This numbering system would be called "base twenty." Clearly, there can be many different numbering systems, using different bases.

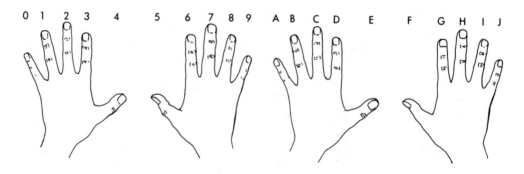

Binary Numbers

Computers come from a land with only two digits ("fingers") and so they count from 0 to 1. That's it — surprising as it may seem, 1 is as high as you can go.

The computer uses a series of electronic switches to store information. The switches may be in either of two states, *on* (1) or *off* (0).

A single switch is called a *bit* of information and is either on or off. In this context, then, if we were to tell you that the light in the living room was "1," you would know that the light was *on*. On the other hand if we told you that the light was "0," then you would know it was *off*. This is an example of the "binary" numbering system.

Just as with other numbering systems, you can represent larger numbers in binary by using more digits. Suppose we were to use three

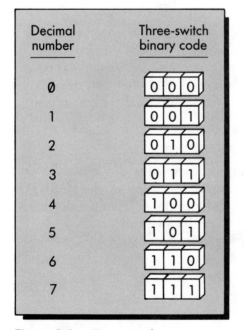

Decimal number	Three-switch binary code
0	0 0 0
1	0 0 1
2	0 1 0
3	0 1 1
4	1 0 0
5	1 0 1
6	1 1 0
7	1 1 1

Figure 9-1. Binary code

switches in our computer, each of which could be either on or off (1 or 0). As long as the order of the switches (bits) was not changed, we could use them to count to eight. Let's say that all were zeros: 000. Then we could say that the number that this stood for was zero. The next number we would want to represent would be the number 1, which would be 001. The number 2 would look like 010, and so on, as shown in Figure 9-1. This binary numbering of switches is called the *binary code*. (See Appendix D for conversion tables.)

Bits and Bytes

We have just seen that eight different numbers (0-7) may be represented by just three switches or bits. What if we were to use, say, eight bits? Then how high could we count? Would you believe two hundred and fifty six? The numbers between 0 and 255 can be encoded in just eight bits of information. In most computers these binary coded numbers represent a letter, number, or symbol in the ASCII code. In Chapter 5 we developed a program to display the ASCII code for all the characters and their corresponding numeric values. These eight bits are called a *byte*. When you hear that brand X computer has 16 kilobytes of memory you know that there are 16,000 bytes of memory in that machine, where each byte is made up of 8 bits.

Octal Numbers

The counting system just described, in which three bits stand for a digit from 0 to 7, is called the *octal* or *base-eight* system. If we were to count in this system, we would not have to carry until we wanted to count the ninth item. Thus 10 (spoken "one zero") is the number 8 in the decimal system, 11 (spoken "one one") is 9 in the decimal system, and so on.

OCT$(n) — Decimal to Octal Conversion

Fortunately, we only have to deal with the complexity of these different numbering systems on rare occasions, but when we do, BASICA has a function that will allow us to make the conversion from the normal base-ten system to the *octal* system. The name for this function is OCT$(n), and it works in the following way:

```
Ok
PRINT OCT$ (3)
3
Ok
PRINT OCT$ (8)
1Ø
Ok
PRINT OCT$ (238)
356
Ok
PRINT OCT$ (-16)
17776Ø
Ok
PRINT OCT$ (3.95)
4
Ok
```

Note that when a noninteger (decimal) is input, the function will round it to an integer and then convert that number to an octal number.

We could write a short program to make these conversions for us with the use of a string variable. Try this one:

```
Ok
1Ø INPUT N
2Ø A$ = OCT$ (N)
3Ø PRINT N "Base ten is " A$ " octal"
RUN
? 3.95
3.95 Base ten is 4 octal
Ok
RUN
? 668
668 Base ten is 1234 octal
```

&O or & — Octal to Decimal Conversion

It is possible to convert back to the decimal from the octal with the use of the ampersand (&) preceding the octal number. We can show this with the following direct commands:

PRINT &01234
   ⌐ The letter O is used for octal

or you can omit the letter *O* as follows:

```
Ok
PRINT &1234
  668
Ok
PRINT &177760
-16
Ok
PRINT &10
  8
Ok
```

Of course, the & can be incorporated into program statements as well as being used as a Direct Mode command. However, & can't be used with a variable: that is, you can't say "&*VAR*". The & must always be followed by a number.

Hexadecimal Numbers

In addition to the binary and octal systems, there is another popular numbering system used in computers. This is the *Hexadecimal* or *base-sixteen* system, which uses *four bits* to represent each digit instead of the three used in Octal. In this system we start with the number 0 and count up to the number F. What's this number F? Well, if you were to avoid carrying until the sixteenth digit, you would need symbols to represent the numbers beyond the number 9. The letters A through F are used for this purpose. (See Appendix D for conversion tables.)

HEX$(n) — Decimal to Hexadecimal Conversion

In BASICA there is a command that will automatically convert a decimal number to hexadecimal: HEX$(*n*). When HEX$(*n*) is used as a command, the PC will give the hexadecimal equivalent of any integer decimal number. If you were to enter a noninteger, the PC would round the number to the nearest integer and then make the conversion to hex. Let's try a couple of numbers:

```
Ok
PRINT HEX$ (3)
3
Ok
PRINT HEX$ (15)
F
Ok
PRINT HEX$ (-593)
FDAF
Ok
PRINT HEX$ (4.98)
5
Ok
PRINT HEX$ (Ø)
Ø
Ok
```

As with octal to decimal conversion, we can use a string variable in a program to give the hex value of any number we input. Run the following program and note the string assignment in line 20:

```
Ok
1Ø INPUT N
2Ø A$ = HEX$ (N)
3Ø PRINT N "Base ten is " A$ " Hexadecimal"
RUN
? 15
 15 Base ten is F Hexadecimal
Ok
RUN
? 623.95
 623.95 Base ten is 27Ø Hexadecimal
```

&H — Hexadecimal to Decimal Conversion

We may convert back to the decimal base from the hexadecimal by preceding the hexadecimal number with &H. The PC will provide the decimal equivalent in the next line. We can demonstrate this with the following Direct Mode Commands:

```
Ok
PRINT &H27Ø
624
Ok
PRINT &HF
15
Ok
PRINT &HFDAF
-593
Ok
```

As with &O, variables can't be used; the "&H" must be followed by a constant.

The table in Appendix D shows the first 256 base-ten (decimal) numbers and their equivalents in the binary, octal, and hexadecimal numbers.

Ways of Expressing Numbers

BASIC gives you a choice of three different ways of representing numbers: *integer*, *single-precision*, and *double-precision*. Let's take a look at each of these.

When possible, integer arithmetic is preferred, since it requires the least memory to represent a number. When a particular program or problem calls for something other than integers, the next step up the scale in memory use is single-precision. The largest amount of memory is used when double-precision is called for.

% — Integer

Some numbers are whole numbers or *integers*. By that we mean that they have no decimal or fractional parts. Whole numbers result from processes such as counting the number of people in the room or the number of letters in this line of type. Here are some examples of integers:

3

21

4,329

0

−65

Some numbers that are *not* integers are

1/3

21.3

0.0000254

1.98

−38.73256

In your PC two bytes (sixteen bits) are set aside to represent each integer number. With the use of two bytes you can represent any integer from 0 to 65535. However, in order to have negative numbers, one bit is used as a sign bit, so the actual range of integers in your PC is from −32768 to +32767, with a zero in the middle. An integer is stored in an assembly of two bytes, as Figure 9-2 shows.

Arithmetic performed on integer numbers uses the least amount of time and smallest amount of memory.

! — Single-precision

When it becomes necessary to do arithmetic with numbers larger than 32767 or smaller than −32768, or if you need to use numbers with decimal points in them (decimal fractions), then more than two bytes must be used to store the number in memory. This method of representing numbers is called *single-precision*. Four bytes are set aside for these numbers.

If you were to type in something like the following, for example, you would probably be surprised by the output on the screen:

```
Ok
print 2351*4559
1.071821E+07
Ok
```

What has happened here? Two things are different from what we might have expected. The first is that the answer is really 10718209. The first six digits of the PC's answer are correct, but there is a difference in the seventh digit. In addition, a decimal point was added by the PC. And what does E+07 mean?

Scientific Notation

The form of expressing a number we have just seen is called *scientific notation*; in computerese, it is also called *floating point notation*. This floating point notation is the form in which the computer keeps track of all noninteger numbers. The E is used to indicate that what follows is the power of 10 multiplied by the number. For example, 1.071821×10^7 is the way the number would be written normally. This means $1.071821 \times 10 \times 10 \times 10 \times 10 \times 10 \times 10 \times 10$; that is, 10 times itself 7 times. (See Figure 9-3.)

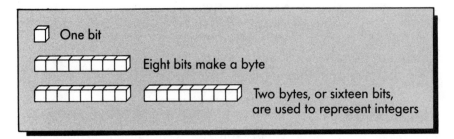

Figure 9-2. Representing integers in binary code

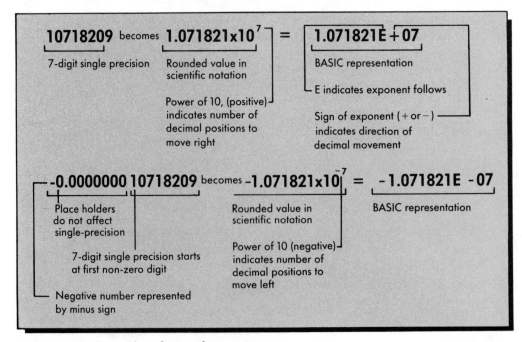

Figure 9-3. Examples of scientific notation

In addition to the floating point format, you should also notice that there are only seven digits shown. In fact, the seventh digit is not correct, because the number has been rounded. When doing arithmetic, your PC will, in fact, support only seven digits of accuracy. (This is generally all that is necessary for ordinary work, unless you're dealing with the national debt.) This level of accuracy — that is, seven digits of accuracy — is single-precision. Unless otherwise specified, calculations will be performed with single-precision. To *ensure* that a variable is to be expressed in single-precision, you may place the exclamation point symbol (!) after the variable name. For example, A! = 27 will make sure that the PC would interpret the value of A! to be 2.700000E + 01 expressed to seven significant digits, and not the integer 27. The largest number in single-precision is $\mp 1.701412E + 38$ and is stored in four bytes (made up of eight bits each). The smallest number in single-precision is $\mp 2.938735E-39$.

— Double-precision

It is sometimes necessary to have a number expressed with more than 7 significant digits. Your PC provides for this with what is called *double-precision*. Double-precision numbers are stored in eight bytes. The form for expressing a double-precision number is A# = 27.37652977, where the number sign (#) is used to specify that A is a double-precision variable. In this mode a number may be expressed with *sixteen* digits of accuracy. For BASIC representation, the D replaces the E to indicate double-precision scientific notation (x.xxxxxxxxxxxxxxxxD + xx) as shown in Figure 9-4. The largest number that may be represented with

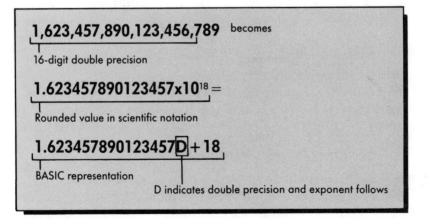

1,623,457,890,123,456,789 becomes

16-digit double precision

$1.623457890123457 \times 10^{18} =$

Rounded value in scientific notation

$1.623457890123457D + 18$

BASIC representation

D indicates double precision and exponent follows

Figure 9-4. Double-precision scientific notation

double precision is $\mp$ 1.701411834604692D + 38. The smallest number in double precision is $\mp$2.938735877055719D − 39.

Variable Type Declaration

It's sometimes necessary to specify what kind of number — integer, single-precision, or double-precision — a variable will be. This can be done by following the variable name with a "type character" as we've shown:

% = type character for integers

! = type character for single-precision

= type character for double-precision

You can also specify the type of a variable with DEF statements.

Why would you want to specify the type of a numeric variable? BASIC assumes variables are single-precision unless told otherwise. But if you knew, for instance, that all the variables in your program were small enough to be integers, you could define them that way with DEFINT A-Z. This would make your program run faster, since BASIC does calculations faster on integers than on floating point numbers. Also, your program would be smaller, since integers take up less space. Needless to say, if you use variable type declaration statements, you should use them at the beginning of your program, before any variables whose type you wish to declare are introduced.

DEFINT — Declaring Integer Variables I

A variable may be declared as a variable *integer type* with the statement DEFINT *T*, which would mean that *T* was an integer. DEFINT *T* may be extended to a range of variables, as in DEFINT A-G, which declares that variables A through G (inclusive) are *integer* variables.

DEFSNG — Declaring Single-Precison Variables

Other variables may be declared as *single-precision* with the DEFSNG *T* statement. An example of DEFSNG is DEFSNG H-K,P. This line would have declared variables H through K and also P as single-precision variables.

DEFDBL — Declaring Double-Precision Variables

Finally, the DEFDBL statement may be used to declare variables as double-precision variables. For example, the statement DEFDBL Q, X-Z would declare the variables Q and all variables X through Z to be double-precision variables.

PRINT USING — Sprucing Up the Output

We have been talking thus far about the number of significant digits used in calculation. However, we may not always want to show all of the digits in our output. Many times the output should have a specific appearance for a report, requiring placement on the page or screen under column headings and/or with the decimal points forming a vertical line, such as might be used in listing dollars-and-cents figures. The PRINT USING statement works well for this purpose. The form of the PRINT USING statement is outlined in Figure 9-5.

Let's try PRINT USING now:

```
PRINT USING "##.#"; 12.3345
```

The output will look like this:

```
12.3
```

A string is used to specify the format of printing. This string can be a variable, as in the following example:

```
10 A$ = "##.#"
20 PRINT USING A$; 12.3
```

Perhaps you would like to put only two digits after the decimal point even though more digits were generated in single-precision as the result of a division:

```
Ok
PRINT 2/3
.6666667
Ok
```

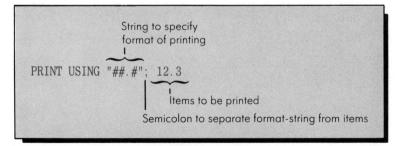

Figure 9-5. Form of PRINT USING statement

If the PRINT USING statement is used, the result is as follows:

```
Ok
PRINT USING ".##";2/3
.67
Ok
```

We may wish to print more than one number using the same format. The following example demonstrates this:

```
Ok
PRINT USING ".##";2/3,1/3
.67.33
Ok
```

By placing characters before and after the format portion, we can produce nice spacing. In the example below we placed one space before and three spaces after, giving us the following output:

```
Ok
PRINT USING " .##   ";2/3,1/3
 .67    .33
Ok
```

This technique is particularly effective when you wish to construct a table of numbers separated from one another. For example:

```
Ok
PRINT USING " ##.##   ";4.2,26.4,1.658,
 4.2    26.4    1.66
Ok
```

One of the especially useful effects of using the PRINT USING statement in this way is that the decimal points will line up automatically, as follows:

```
Ok
10 FOR N = 1 TO 3
20 PRINT USING " ##.##   "; 10*N/3
RUN
  3.33
  6.67
 10.00
Ok
```

Some of these techniques would have been most helpful in the problem in Chapter 8 in which we calculated the value of an investment compounded monthly. Here is the original program without PRINT USING:

```
100 '----NAME: "INVEST-M.B9" ---------------------------------
110 '
120 '----PROGRAM CALCULATES RETURN ON A ONE-TIME INVESTMENT----
130 '
140 '----title----
150 '
155   KEY OFF: CLS
160   PRINT "VALUE OF INVESTMENT COMPOUNDED MONTHLY"
170   PRINT "-------------------------------------"
180   PRINT
190 '
200 '----input to program----
210 '
220   INPUT "enter yearly interest rate (%)-----", INTRATE
230   INPUT "enter amount of investment ($)-----", BALANCE
240   INPUT "enter investment period in months--", LAST
250 '
260 '----headings----
270 '
280   PRINT :PRINT
290   PRINT "Month", "Balance"
300   PRINT "-----", "-------"
310 '
320 '----the main program----
330 '
340   FOR MONTH = 1 TO LAST
350     BALANCE = BALANCE + BALANCE * INTRATE/1200
360     PRINT MONTH, BALANCE
370   NEXT
380 END
```

When we put in numbers other than the very carefully selected example used in the previous chapter, the results look a bit strange, as Figure 9-6 shows. Of course, this isn't how we're used to seeing dollars and cents printed. The months don't line up very well either.

Let's replace line 360 with the following statement:

```
360 PRINT USING "###        $$######.##"; MONTH, BALANCE
```

As Figure 9-7 shows, this small change greatly improves the appearance of the output.

How were these improvements made? The PRINT USING statement sets the format of both the month and the balance columns, as the following diagram shows:

Column spaces | Two dollar signs puts "$" in space before number

360   PRINT USING "### $$######.##"; MONTH, BALANCE

Month form   Balance form

Let's try this approach on a slightly different program. This time let's add a new line 375 as follows:

Single "$" gives a "$" in that column

375 P$ = "### $#######,.##'

Comma here causes a comma to print every third digit to the left of decimal point

```
VALUE OF INVESTMENT COMPOUNDED MONTHLY
----------------------------------------

enter yearly interest rate (%)-----18
enter amount of investment ($)-----8000
enter investment period in months--12


Month        Balance
-----        -------
  1          8120
  2          8241.8
  3          8365.427
  4          8490.908
  5          8618.271
  6          8747.546
  7          8878.759
  8          9011.941
  9          9147.119
 10          9284.326
 11          9423.591
 12          9564.944
Ok
```

Figure 9-6. Program output *without* PRINT USING

```
VALUE OF INVESTMENT COMPOUNDED MONTHLY
----------------------------------------

enter yearly interest rate (%)-----18
enter amount of investment ($)-----8000
enter investment period in months--12


Month        Balance
-----        -------
  1          $8120.00
  2          $8241.80
  3          $8365.43
  4          $8490.91
  5          $8618.27
  6          $8747.55
  7          $8878.76
  8          $9011.94
  9          $9147.12
 10          $9284.33
 11          $9423.59
 12          $9564.94
Ok
```

Figure 9-7. Program output *with* PRINT USING

In addition, let's change the PRINT lines to read as follows:

```
290     PRINT "Year", "Balance"
380     PRINT USING P$; YEAR, BALANCE
```

With these changes, the program will look like this:

```
100 '----NAME: "INVEST-Y.B9" ----------------------------------
110 '
120 '----PROGRAM CALCULATES RETURN ON A ONE-TIME INVESTMENT----
130 '
140 '----title----
150 '
155   KEY OFF: CLS
160   PRINT "VALUE OF INVESTMENT COMPOUNDED MONTHLY"
170   PRINT "-----------------------------------"
180   PRINT
190 '
200 '----input to program----
210 '
220   INPUT "enter yearly interest rate (%)-----", INTRATE
230   INPUT "enter amount of investment ($)-----", BALANCE
240   INPUT "enter investment period in years---", LAST
250 '
260 '----headings----
270 '
280   PRINT :PRINT
290   PRINT "Year", "Balance"
300   PRINT "-----", "-------"
310 '
320 '----the main program----
330 '
340   FOR YEAR = 1 TO LAST
350     FOR MONTH=1 TO 12
360       BALANCE = BALANCE + BALANCE * INTRATE/1200
370     NEXT MONTH
375     P$ = "###        $#######,.##"
380     PRINT USING P$; YEAR, BALANCE
390   NEXT YEAR
400 END
```

The output is shown in Figure 9-8.

You may also use this statement for check protection by printing asterisks in front of the dollar amount. If line 375 were to be modified as shown here,

```
375 P$ = "###      **$#######,.##"
```

then our program output would look like that in Figure 9-9.

If the string in line 375 had too few places for the output to be displayed, an error statement would have appeared in the form of the "%" symbol in front of the number string to indicate that insufficient

```
VALUE OF INVESTMENT COMPOUNDED MONTHLY


enter yearly interest rate (%)------18
enter amount of investment ($)-----6ØØØ
enter investment period in years---6



Year            Balance
----            -------
  1         $   7,173.71
  2         $   8,577.Ø2
  3         $  1Ø,254.84
  4         $  12,26Ø.87
  5         $  14,659.32
  6         $  17,526.95
Ok
```

Figure 9-8. Output of second program with PRINT USING

```
VALUE OF INVESTMENT COMPOUNDED MONTHLY


enter yearly interest rate (%)-----18
enter amount of investment ($)-----8ØØØ
enter investment period in years---6



Year            Balance
----            -------
  1         *****$9,564.94
  2         ****$11,436.Ø2
  3         ****$13,673.11
  4         ****$16,347.83
  5         ****$19,545.76
  6         ****$23,369.26
Ok
```

Figure 9-9. Check protection with PRINT USING

space was specified in the string statement for the display of output numbers. For example, if line 375 were

```
375 P$ = "###          $####,.##"
```

the output would look like that in Figure 9-10.

One technique for dealing with this problem is to insert a REM statement following the string line so that we can measure the number of characters in the PRINT USING statement by actually counting the number of character spaces in the preceding line.

Try this now:

```
375     P$ = "###          $####,.##"
376 '           123456789012345678
```

The REM statement in line 376 constitutes a kind of measuring stick.

On occasion it might be preferable to have the output expressed in floating point notation. This may be accomplished by placing four circumflex marks ($\wedge \wedge \wedge \wedge$) after the position indicators. The four marks reserve the space for the E (in single-precision) or the D (in double-precision), the sign of the exponent ($+$ or $-$), and the exponent itself (two digits). The general format is

```
375 P$ = "###          $##.#######^^^^"
```

```
VALUE OF INVESTMENT COMPOUNDED MONTHLY
-----------------------------------------

enter yearly interest rate (%)-----18
enter amount of investment ($)-----8000
enter investment period in years---6


Year        Balance
----        -------
  1         $9,564.94
  2         $%11,436.02
  3         $%13,673.11
  4         $%16,347.83
  5         $%19,545.76
  6         $%23,369.26
Ok
```

Figure 9-10. Output error detection with PRINT USING

If we enter this new line 375 into our program, we will get the output shown in Figure 9-11.

Summary

In this chapter we learned about the numbering system used by computers in their internal operation: namely, the *binary system* or *binary code* which uses only zeros and ones. We learned how binary numbers may be converted to the decimal numbers that we use in everyday life and also how binary code may be incorporated in the *octal* and *hexadecimal* numbering systems, which are two of the kinds of numbers that BASIC uses and recognizes. In addition, we took a quick look at *floating point* or *scientific notation*, in which numbers are expressed in exponential form. Finally in this first portion of the chapter, we saw that BASIC can represent numbers in three different degrees of accuracy: as *integers* or in *single-precision* or *double-precision*. While BASIC normally represents numbers in single-precision (that is, with seven digits, the seventh possibly the result of rounding), you can specify the way you want numbers to be represented in your programs by using *type declaration* symbols or statements. Table 9-1 summarizes the different precisions or degrees of accuracy that BASIC uses, the way to control

```
VALUE OF INVESTMENT COMPOUNDED MONTHLY
-------------------------------------------

enter yearly interest rate (%)-----18
enter amount of investment ($)-----8000
enter investment period in years---6


Year            Balance
----            -------
  1             $ 9.5649440E+03
  2             $ 1.1436020E+04
  3             $ 1.3673110E+04
  4             $ 1.6347830E+04
  5             $ 1.9545760E+04
  6             $ 2.3369260E+04
Ok
```

Figure 9-11.   Program output with scientific notation

these precisions, and the relative amount of memory that each number type uses.

The second portion of this chapter focused on the PRINT USING statement, a versatile and powerful tool for producing data in tabular output form. If your output is in dollars and cents or in tabular form, you should probably be using PRINT USING.

Exercises

1. Use your PC to rewrite the number 1234567890123 in single-precision scientific notation.

2. Find the octal and hexadecimal values of the following numbers: 107, −23, and 1000.

3. Write a short program that calculates the monthly salary from the yearly salary, and prints out the monthly salary in a format appropriate for writing checks.

Variable Type	Declaration character or statement	Example of variable	Example value	Range of values	Bytes of memory
Integer	% or DEFINT	A%,B% Cans%	9 325	−32768 to 32767	2
Single Precision	! or DEFSNG	A!,B! Intrest!	24.95 4.6E12 -4.3	2.938735 E−39 1.701412 E+38	4
Double Precision	# or DEFDBL	A#,B# Income#	14.95	16 digits D±38	8

Table 9-1. Specifying variable types

Solutions

1. Here's what your screen should look like:

```
PRINT 1234567890123!
 1.2345678E+12
Ok
```

2. Octal values: 153,177751,1750.
Hexadecimal values: 6B, FFE9, 3E8.

3. Here's our solution:

```
10 SALARY = 28690
20 MO.SAL = SALARY/12
30 PRINT USING "**$#######,.##; MO.SAL
RUN
*****$2,390.83
Ok
```

10

Seeing Is Believing — Working with Graphics Characters

CONCEPTS
The ASCII character code
Using the (Alt) key
IBM graphics character set
Drawing boxes and making graphs
Character attributes — underlining, blinking, inverse, high intensity

Instructions
CHR$, ASC, STRING$, COLOR

One of the truly outstanding features of IBM PC BASIC is its ability to produce high-quality graphics with relative ease. By graphics we mean any kind of visually meaningful display of information, such as a picture, a game-related image, a graph, or the use of what are called special characters. This chapter is about a particular kind of graphics called *character graphics* that you can do on either of the two most common display systems available — the IBM Monochrome Display (with the Monochrome Display and Parallel Printer Adapter) and any type of monitor driven by the Color/Graphics Monitor Adapter. *Dot-graphics* or *point-addressable* graphics, which provides higher resolution pictures on the "color" display, is introduced in Chapter 14.

Characters and Pixels — How Images Are Formed on Your Screen

Have you ever looked very closely at a photograph in a newspaper, book, or magazine with a magnifying glass? Nothing but tiny dots! Some of these dots are bigger than others, but they're all black. An area that has lots of "large" black dots appears darker than an area that has "small" black dots. Thousands of these black dots (on a white background) make up a complete, recognizable image.

An image on your screen is produced by a similar matrix (or grid) of dots, although the dots on your monitor screen can only be "on" or "off." (There are actually two levels of being "on," but for simplicity's sake we will not discuss these levels here.) All text or all pictures on your IBM PC are produced by such a matrix of dots or *pixels*, as they are formally called. In the kind of graphics known as *point-addressable* to be discussed in Chapter 14, each such pixel can be separately addressed — that is, turned off or on — by your computer. You can make your IBM PC work in this mode by means of the SCREEN statement, which we explain in Chapter 14.

However, when you first turn on your computer, it *defaults* (goes into a certain mode or state on its own unless you tell it otherwise) to the Text Mode. In the Text Mode, pixels can't be turned on and off independently of each other. Instead, pixels are organized into units called *character spaces*. On your IBM Monochrome Display, each character space requires 14 rows and 9 columns of pixels — a total of 126 pixels! Your whole screen, on the other hand, can have 80 columns and 25 rows of characters. Pressing the A key, for example, causes a specific set of dots to turn on that give the correct appearance of the letter A. Figure 10-1 shows the relationship between your screen, the character spaces, and the letter *A* that is produced by dots within a character space.

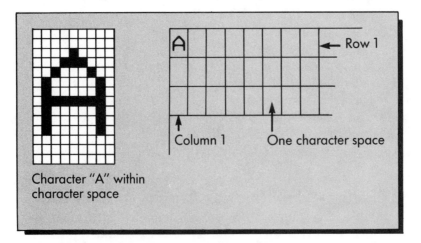

Figure 10-1. Formation of characters on your monochrome screen

In Text Mode, any kind of picture or graph we want to "draw" has to be constructed out of whole characters. For example, in previous chapters we have used the asterisk to draw a box around a title, and to draw a simple graph (the square of a number versus the number). Although your keyboard has a lot of characters (114!), most of them aren't very useful for drawing pictures or graphs. IBM PC BASIC does, however, provide us with an extension of the keyboard that gives us a large variety of special characters, many of which are specifically designed for graphics applications. This keyboard extension is embedded in what is called the ASCII character code.

The ASCII Character Set — Extending Your Keyboard Options

ASCII is an acronym for "American Standard Code of Information Interchange." It's a code that associates a character with a particular number or value. It originated out of the need for different teletyping stations to "talk" to each other. The problem is similar to that faced by a group of people who all speak different languages. The solution to both problems is obvious (even if not so easily accepted by everyone!): agree on a common language or a code. Although today ASCII is primarily used in communications between computers, it is also used frequently to make available a larger selection of symbols or characters than is possible by means of the usual typewriter keyboard. It is this latter use — the keyboard extension — that is of interest to us now.

There are two ways to access or to explore ASCII. The first is by using the (Alt) key, and the second is by means of the special translating function CHR$.

ASCII with the (Alt) Key

The (Alt) (for "alternate") key is on the lower left of your keyboard. Its purpose is to *alter* the usual function of your keyboard keys. If you press it by itself, nothing happens — go ahead and try it. But if you hold it down while you also press another character key, you'll get some interesting results. If you try this with the letter *p* the word PRINT will appear on your screen instead of the letter *p*! Thus the (Alt) key pressed in combination with a letter key returns one of the most commonly used BASIC words. This feature of IBM BASIC is a very handy time-saver.

This time, though, let's hold down (Alt) while pressing a *number*, say 65; more precisely, press and *continue* to hold down the (Alt) key while you press 6 and then 5. Nothing happens as you type the digits 6 and 5, but the instant you release the (Alt) key, the letter *A* appears on your screen! What have you done? You've entered the ASCII code value 65, and the computer returned the corresponding ASCII character, an *A*. In other words,

Holding down ALT
while typing 65
(ASCII code for A), } returns corresponding ASCII character A
and then releasing
the ALT key

IBM has supplied us with a total of 256 ASCII characters having code values of 0 to 255. To get an idea what's in this character set, try a few more code numbers. Table 10-1 shows a selection of some ASCII codes and their corresponding characters. (You can also look up these code values in Appendix D.)

We'd like to make a few remarks about the samples in Table 10-1. Codes 0 to 31 don't return characters on your screen if entered with the (Alt) key. These codes are reserved for special communication instructions between computers and computer peripherals. For example, ASCII code 13 means "do a carriage return."

Codes 32 to 126 include all the standard keyboard characters. Code 127 is another communications instruction meaning "delete." Codes 0 to 127 are considered the really "standard" ASCII codes. Most computers use them internally as well as for communications with other computers and related devices.

All the codes from 127 to 255 are IBM's own embellishment of ASCII. Among them are foreign language characters (like the *a* with an

ASCII Code	ASCII Character	Comments
2	zilch, nothing!	Codes 0-31 don't return visible characters
7	zilch, nothing!	but computer BEEPs
35	#	
53	5	Digits 0-9 have codes 48-57
65	A	Uppercase letters: codes 65-90
107	k	Lowercase letters: codes 97-122
132	a with umlaut	You can write German with it
217	⌋	A corner: one of many graphic characters
251	√	Square root sign

Table 10-1. A selection of ASCII characters and their corresponding code values

umlaut), mathematical symbols (like the square root sign), and a large variety of graphics characters. This chapter is primarily about the use of these graphics characters.

Before we leave this topic of generating ASCII characters by means of the (Alt) key, we'd like to show you how you might use this technique to enter words in a foreign language. Here it goes:

```
1Ø INPUT WORD$
2Ø PRINT WORD$
3Ø END
Ok
RUN
? Hosenträger          ← a with umlaut is entered via [ALT] and 132 combination
Hosenträger
Ok
```

The *a* (with umlaut) was entered by holding down (Alt) and typing 132. This special character is treated just like all the other "normal" characters in the entered string value.

The CHR$ and ASC Functions — the Key to ASCII

A generally more useful way to translate ASCII codes into characters is by means of a BASIC function designed just for this purpose — CHR$. (The word *function* generally refers to a procedure that returns a specific output for a given input.) While CHR$ does almost the same thing as holding down (Alt) and pressing a number, it can be used within a BASIC program. Try this example:

```
1Ø PRINT CHR$ (217)
RUN
⌐
Ok
```

The number 217 inside the parentheses is the ASCII code for a corner graphics character. The function CHR$ translates this code to a character value which is then printed.

Another way CHR$ can be used is illustrated by the following example:

```
1ØX$ = CHR$(217)
2Ø PRINT X$
RUN
⌐
Ok
```

Here the string variable X$ is assigned the value of the CHR$ function, which is the ASCII character corresponding to the ASCII code 217. Note that CHR$ returns a *string* value, so the variable to which you assign it must also be a string variable.

In addition, you should note that CHR$ cannot be used all by itself. You must PRINT it as shown in the first example (or use it with LPRINT to get printer output), or you can assign it to a string variable.

Displaying the Whole ASCII Character Set

Let's use CHR$ to write a program that prints the whole ASCII character set:

```
1Ø '---THE ASCII CHARACTER SET----------
2Ø FOR CODE = Ø TO 255
3Ø   IF CODE >= 9 AND CODE <= 13 GOTO 5Ø
4Ø   PRINT CHR$(CODE) " ";
5Ø NEXT
6Ø END
```

The output is shown in Figure 10-2; there you have it — the whole IBM ASCII character set. But there are a few surprises, both in the program and the output. Let's first look at the program. Line 40 says "first PRINT the character corresponding to the ASCII code number represented by variable CODE and then PRINT a blank." The purpose of the blank is to insert spaces between each of the characters in the output to make it more readable. The FOR...NEXT loop (lines 20 and 50) executes line 40 for all values of CODE from 0 to 255 — *except* values 9 to 13. The IF...THEN statement in line 30 says "if CODE has a value between 9 and 13, then GOTO 50, the end of the loop — that is, bypass line 40." We want to bypass characters 9 to 13 because they wreak havoc with the program output: character 13 for example, causes a carriage return, which we clearly don't want right in the middle of our neat rows of ASCII characters.

The output looks a bit familiar by now: it contains all the characters we generated with the (Alt)-number combination we used previously. Surprisingly, however, it also includes a whole series of new characters corresponding to ASCII codes 0 to 31. These characters — for example, smiling faces, hearts, and musical notes! — weren't available to us using the (Alt)-number method. Again, these are not standard ASCII, but the result of IBM's inventiveness.

ASC — Character to ASCII Code Conversion

CHR$ converts a number to its corresponding ASCII character. But sometimes the inverse function is needed; that is, you may need to convert a character to its ASCII code value. That task is performed by ASC. The following example illustrates one way to use ASC:

```
1Ø PRINT ASC("g")
RUN
 1Ø3
Ok
```

You can easily see what happened here: ASC("g") takes the character g and returns its ASCII code value, which is then printed. As was the case

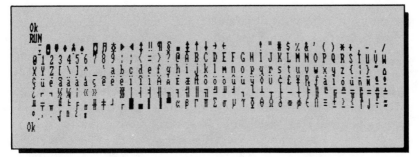

Figure 10-2. ASCII character set as printed out by the program

with CHR$, ASC can't stand all by itself: it has to be used with PRINT or assigned to a variable.

One surprising and interesting feature of ASC is that its argument — the stuff inside the parenthesis after ASC — can be more than just one character, as the following example illustrates:

```
10 PRINT ASC("gamophobia")
RUN
 103
Ok
```

So although the argument of ASC is a whole word ("gamophobia" means fear of marriage), it returns the ASCII code value of just the first character and ignores all the rest.

Translating Functions Between ASCII Code Values and ASCII Characters

CHR$ converts   ASCII code value   to   ASCII character.
ASC   converts   ASCII character   to   ASCII value.

For example

```
PRINT CHR$(36)        ← returns  ASCII character  $
PRINT ASC("fido")     ← returns  ASCII code value  102 (for letter f)
```

Graphics with ASCII Characters

ASCII code values from 176 to 223 define a variety of special characters useful for many graphics applications. Table 10-2 shows a list of these.

There are basically two types of characters in this list. The first includes the box-shaped characters or "fillers" of various intensities. These can be used to construct any kind of solid rectangular shape. The second type includes line segments (single and double), corners (single and double), and a variety of line segment intersections. These can be used to construct horizontal and vertical lines (single and double) and a large variety of boxes and combination of boxes (single and double sides).

In the following sections, we'll show you examples that illustrate how to draw a variety of simple boxes that can be used around a title or as bars for a bar graph.

ASCII value	Character	ASCII value	Character	ASCII value	Character	ASCII value	Character
128	Ç	160	á	192	└	224	α
129	ü	161	í	193	┴	225	β
130	é	162	ó	194	┬	226	γ
131	â	163	ú	195	├	227	π
132	ä	164	ñ	196	─	228	Σ
133	à	165	Ñ	197	+	29	σ
134	å	166	ª	198	╞	230	μ
135	ç	167	º	199	╟	231	τ
136	ê	168	¿	200	╚	232	Φ
137	ë	169	⌐	201	╔	233	⊖
138	è	170	¬	202	╩	234	Ω
139	ï	171	½	203	╦	235	δ
140	î	172	¼	204	╠	236	∞
141	ì	173	¡	205	═	237	Ø
142	Ä	174	«	206	╬	238	ε
143	Å	175	»	207	╧	239	∩
144	É	176	▒	208	╨	240	≡
145	æ	177	▓	209	╤	241	±
146	Æ	178	▓	210	╥	242	≥
147	ô	179	│	211	╙	243	≤
148	ö	180	┤	212	╘	244	⌠
149	ò	181	╡	213	╒	245	⌡
150	û	182	╢	214	╓	246	÷
151	ù	183	╖	215	╫	247	≈
152	ÿ	184	╕	216	╪	248	°
153	Ö	185	╣	217	┘	249	•
154	Ü	186	║	218	┌	250	•
155	¢	187	╗	219	█	251	√
156	£	188	╝	220	▄	252	ⁿ
157	¥	189	╜	221	▌	253	²
158	Pt	190	╛	222	▐	252	■
159	ƒ	191	┐	223	▀	255	(blank 'FF')

Table 10-2. Special graphics characters

Making a Solid Box

The ASCII character of value 219 is a solid box that fills one whole character space. Let's use it to construct a solid box that is 10 columns high by 3 rows wide. We'll do it one step at a time.

First, we need to assemble the character boxes into a line. To do this, we need to PRINT CHR$(219) many times in different locations. One way to do this is to use the FOR...NEXT loop:

```
30 FOR COL = 1 TO 10
40    PRINT CHR$(219)
50 NEXT
60 END
RUN
```

Ok

This is familiar territory. To give our box some height, we can use another (nested) FOR...NEXT loop to draw this line at adjacent row positions. Next, we'll use LOCATE to put our character exactly where we want it. While this is not the only way to accomplish our task, it has the virtue of clarity and ease of use. Modifying the previous program results in the following:

```
10 CLS
20 FOR ROW = 3 TO 6
30    FOR COL = 5 TO 15
40       LOCATE ROW, COL
50       PRINT CHR$(219)
60    NEXT COL
70 NEXT ROW
80 END
```

When run, this program clears the screen and makes a box like this:

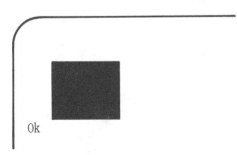

Ok

The counter limits of the two loops determine the position and the dimension of the box. So if we wanted to be able to draw a box of any size anywhere on the screen, we could use variables for the counter limits and let the user assign values to them by means of INPUT statements. Let's try it:

```
100 INPUT "enter row of upper left corner"; TOP
110 INPUT "enter column of upper left corner"; LEFT
120 INPUT "enter width of box"; WIDTZ
130 INPUT "enter height of box"; HEIGHT
140 CLS
150 BOTTOM = TOP + HEIGHT - 1
150 RIGHT =  LEFT + WIDTZ - 1
160 FOR ROW = TOP TO BOTTOM
170   FOR COL = LEFT TO RIGHT
180     LOCATE ROW, COL
190     PRINT CHR$(219)
200   NEXT COL
210 NEXT ROW
220 END
```

If you run this program with the following responses,

```
RUN
enter row of upper left corner----4
enter column of upper left corner-12
enter width of box---------------15
enter height of box--------------5
```

you get a solid box that looks like this:

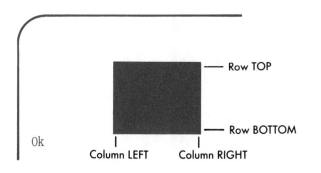

We can make any size of box and put it anywhere we want! Since we used variable names that really reflect the meaning of the variables, the program isn't hard to follow. Note the -1 in line 150: it needs to be there if you interpret a HEIGHT equal to 5 to mean five columns high; if you leave out the − 1, you'll get one too many rows. The same is true for the definition of RIGHT in line 160. Incidentally, our spelling of WIDTZ is not a typo — the more sensible and obvious word WIDTH is one of those infamous reserved words!

Boxes like this have many uses in producing interesting screen displays, backgrounds for titles written in reverse (we'll show you how to do this later), and bar graphs. Our first exercise problem in this chapter will, in fact, illustrate the creation of a bar graph.

Making an Empty Box

Another very useful type of box that can easily be be drawn is an unfilled or empty box. The graphics characters needed are the corners and horizontal and vertical line segments shown in Figure 10-3. The numbers associated with each graphics character are the ASCII codes for that character.

Let's draw a double-walled box. We'll define its location and dimensions in the same way as in a previous filled-box program: the row and column number of its upper left corner as well as its width and height are to be determined by user INPUT. We'll also use the same variable names WIDTZ, HEIGHT, TOP, BOTTOM, LEFT, and RIGHT

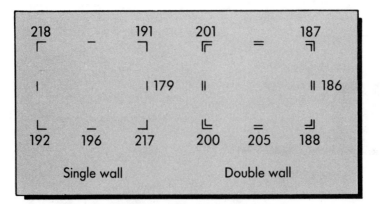

Figure 10-3. ASCII characters needed to make box

to define the dimensions of the box and the row and column positions of its sides. Here's one way to write a box program:

```
8Ø  '----NAME: "DBL-BOX, B1Ø"---------------------------------------
9Ø  '
1ØØ '----DOUBLE-WALLED BOX PROGRAM-----------------------------------
1Ø2 '
1Ø4 CLS
11Ø INPUT "enter row of upper-left corner-----", TOP
12Ø INPUT "enter column of upper-left corner--", LEFT
13Ø INPUT "enter width of box-----------------", WIDTZ
14Ø INPUT "enter height of box----------------", HEIGHT
15Ø CLS
16Ø BOTTOM = TOP + HEIGHT
17Ø RIGHT = LEFT + WIDTZ
18Ø '
19Ø '----LOCATE and PRINT the corners of the box--------------------
2ØØ '
21Ø LOCATE TOP, LEFT
22Ø PRINT CHR$(2Ø1)                        'PRINTs upper left corner
23Ø LOCATE TOP, RIGHT
24Ø PRINT CHR$(187)                        'PRINTs upper right corner
25Ø LOCATE BOTTOM, LEFT
26Ø PRINT CHR$(2ØØ)                        'PRINTs lower left corner
27Ø LOCATE BOTTOM, RIGHT
28Ø PRINT CHR$(188)                        'PRINTs lower right corner
29Ø '
3ØØ '----draw top, bottom and sides of the box using FOR NEXT--------
31Ø '
32Ø FOR COL = (LEFT + 1) TO (RIGHT - 1)    'top and bottom
33Ø    LOCATE TOP, COL
34Ø    PRINT CHR$(2Ø5)
35Ø    LOCATE BOTTOM, COL
36Ø    PRINT CHR$(2Ø5)
37Ø NEXT COL
38Ø FOR ROW = (TOP + 1) TO (BOTTOM - 1)    'left and right sides
39Ø    LOCATE ROW, LEFT
4ØØ    PRINT CHR$(186)
41Ø    LOCATE ROW, RIGHT
42Ø    PRINT CHR$(186)
43Ø NEXT ROW
44Ø END
```

When this program is run with the following input,

```
RUN
enter row of upper-left corner-----3
enter column of upper-left corner--9
enter width of box----------------3Ø
enter height of box---------------4
```

we get the following output on the screen:

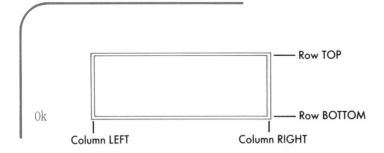

A great box! The program is fairly long, but not, we hope, too difficult to understand. The first part of the program up to line 170 initializes all the required variables (TOP, BOTTOM, LEFT, RIGHT); the second part, from lines 190 to 280, prints the corners of the box; and the last part, from line 300 to the end, draws the sides of box using the the horizontal and vertical line segments defined by ASCII characters 205 and 186.

At this point you may well ask yourself "do I have to go through all this every time I want to draw a box?" The answer has two parts. First, if you need to draw *more* than one box in a program (for several titles, or for a bar graph) all you have to do is to write the program lines for the box *once* (these lines will be what is called a *subroutine*) and *reuse* that part of the program as many times as you need. We'll show you how to do that in Chapter 12, which explains subroutines.

Secondly, there are easier ways to draw a box. By far the easiest way is by means of the single BASIC statement called LINE — a very powerful tool. The use of this statement is limited, however, to the all-points-addressable graphics mode we discussed earlier — and for that you need the Color/Graphics Monitor Adapter. The box program we just presented, on the other hand, is not limited to any particular IBM PC configuration.

The STRING$ Function — Stringing Out ASCII Characters

There is, however, something we can do to simplify our previous box program. BASIC provides us with another function, called STRING$, that is specifically designed to draw horizontal repetitions of an ASCII character. In our box program the STRING$ function enables us to draw the horizontal sides of the box with two statements in place of the six statements needed for the FOR...NEXT loop.

The following example illustrates how the STRING$ function works:

```
1Ø PRINT STRING$(1Ø, CHR$(2Ø5))
RUN
```

========

Ok

As you can see, the ASCII character number 205 (a double horizontal line segment [=]) is printed 10 times. By changing the number 10 inside the parentheses following STRING$, we can change the number of times CHR$(205) is printed. We could have produced the same output using 10 cycles of a FOR...NEXT loop, but using the STRING$ function is clearly the more concise way of producing the same result. Also, your IBM PC executes STRING$ faster than it would execute the corresponding FOR...NEXT loops.

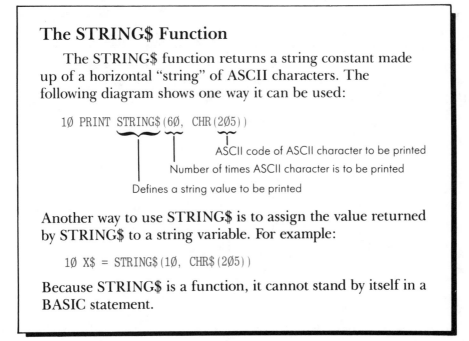

The STRING$ Function

The STRING$ function returns a string constant made up of a horizontal "string" of ASCII characters. The following diagram shows one way it can be used:

```
1Ø PRINT STRING$(6Ø, CHR(2Ø5))
```

ASCII code of ASCII character to be printed
Number of times ASCII character is to be printed
Defines a string value to be printed

Another way to use STRING$ is to assign the value returned by STRING$ to a string variable. For example:

```
1Ø X$ = STRING$(1Ø, CHR$(2Ø5))
```

Because STRING$ is a function, it cannot stand by itself in a BASIC statement.

As is the case with the other functions we've discussed, STRING$ cannot stand by itself in a BASIC statement. STRING$ defines a string constant and so must be either used with PRINT (or with a PRINT-related statement) or assigned to a string variable.

Making a Boxed-In Title Using STRING$

An example that really shows off the power of STRING$ is drawing a box that frames a title. As demonstrated in our previous example, we can use STRING$ to draw the horizontal sides of our box. However, we can also "add" (concatenate) the corners of the box to STRING$ to define a new string that draws both a horizontal side as well as two of the corners. For example, the program

```
10 TOPSIDE$ = CHR$(201) + STRING$(30, CHR$(205)) + CHR$(187)
20 PRINT TOPSIDE$
30 END
```

produces the output

```
╔══════════════════════════════╗
```

which is the TOPSIDE$ of a box (the interior width equals 30 columns) *including* the corners! This technique really cuts down on the number of program lines we need to write in order to make this part of the box (it also saves time — ours and the computer's!).

Let's put all the pieces together in a program that prints out a title with a box around it. The following program puts a double-walled box around the title "THE SECRET LIFE OF THE HUMUHUMUNUKUNUKUAPUAA". The text is centered with respect to a 65 column wide display.

```
100 '----NAME; "BOX.B10"-------------------------------------------
105 '
110 '----******************************
120 '----* WRITES TITLE WITH OPEN BOX *----------------------------
130 '----******************************
140 '
145 CLS
150 TITLE$ = "THE SECRET LIFE OF HUMUHUMUNUKUNUKUAPUAA"
160 LENGTH = 40
170 LEFT = 12
180 '
190 '----defines string which draws topside and bottom of box--------
200 '
```

```
210 TOPSIDE$ = CHR$(201) + STRING$(LENGTH, CHR$(205)) + CHR$(187)
220 BOTTOM$ = CHR$(200) + STRING$(LENGTH, CHR$(205)) + CHR$(188)
230 '
240 '----draws TITLE with box around it----------------------------
250 '
260 PRINT
270 PRINT TAB(LEFT) TOPSIDE$
280 PRINT TAB(LEFT) CHR$(186) TITLE$ CHR$(186)
290 PRINT TAB(LEFT) BOTTOM$
300 END
```

The output looks like this:

```
┌
│     ╔════════════════════════════════════════╗
│     ║ THE  SECRET  LIFE  OF  HUMUHUMUNUKUNUKUAPUAA ║
│     ╚════════════════════════════════════════╝
└
```

As you can see, we didn't use any FOR...NEXT loops this time. Instead, we printed the variables TOPSIDE$ and BOTTOM$, which we obtained by concatenating STRING$ and the string values for the corners of the box. The vertical line segments were printed individually with PRINT. You might find this program or your own modification of it handy in producing the titles for your own programs. Incidentally, that word that's too long for us to repeat once again is the name of a Hawaiian fish!

Color on Your Monochrome Display — Changing Your Character Attributes

Your keyboard and the other "hidden" characters we've been discussing provide us with a large selection of characters. IBM PC BASIC also provides us with a way of changing how these characters are displayed: we can underline them, make them blink, emphasize them by increasing the intensity or brightness, print them black on white instead of the normal white (really green on the IBM Monochrome Display) on black, or combine all of these features, which are called *attributes*.

COLOR is the BASIC instruction that controls these character attributes. The word COLOR does not imply that you need a color monitor to make use of it! COLOR is a very versatile statement: it does, in fact, control the color on a color monitor, but it also controls character attributes on monochrome monitors. In this chapter we'll only deal with the aspects of COLOR relevant to the IBM Monochrome Display.

COLOR controls what is called the *foreground* and the *background* of a character, as defined in Figure 10-4. To use COLOR, you must assign numbers to the background and foreground in the following way:

```
10 COLOR 7, 0
```
|
| This number determines the *background* attribute
|
This number determines the *foreground* attribute.

The number 7 always means "white" (or green) and 0 always means "black" (the way your screen looks when everything is turned off). This particular COLOR statement causes everything following it to be printed as white on black which, of course, is nothing new. When you turn on your computer, it selects this particular COLOR mode automatically because it thinks that that's what most people want most of the time. COLOR 7,0 is the *default* COLOR setting.

Other numbers have different meanings. Try the following example:

```
10 COLOR 1, 0
20 PRINT "what attribute is this?"
30 COLOR 7, 0
40 END
RUN
what attribute is this?      ← Note the underline
Ok
```

So the number 1 assigned to the foreground of the COLOR statement in line 10 causes whatever is printed to be underlined. COLOR 7,0 in line

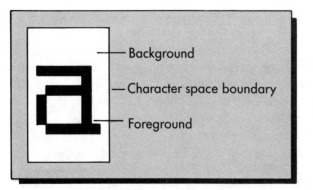

Figure 10-4. Foreground and background of a character

30 returns the computer to printing things without underlining. If you leave it out, *everything* from then on will be underlined, including the "Ok" prompt and whatever you write onto the screen after the program is finished. Your computer will remain in the last COLOR mode set until it encounters a new COLOR statement (or a Direct Mode command), even though the program that set the COLOR mode may have finished running a long time ago.

Now change line 10 in the previous program to read COLOR 0,7. The foreground should now be black (0), while the background should turn white (7); that is, we should get black letters printed on a white (green) background. Sure enough, when you run this program, you'll get

```
RUN
what attribute is this?          ← Inverse: black on white background
Ok
```

Ok, you get the idea. COLOR requires you to translate an effect you want to create into numbers. These numbers don't have any intrinsic meaning to us, so this kind of statement is a bit harder for us to use than the more "user-friendly" statements we've encountered before. However, the COLOR statement has the advantage of being very concise and easy to interpret by your computer.

The Rules for the COLOR Attributes

There are many different combinations of COLOR attributes possible. The rules for finding the foreground and background numeric values that will give you specific effects are summarized in Table 10-3.

Foreground number	Effect (attribute)
0	black
7	white
1	causes underlining
add 8	causes high intensity
add 16	causes blinking
Background number	**Effect (attribute)**
0	black
7	white

Table 10-3. Monochrome COLOR attributes

For example, if we wanted to cause printing with white on black, underlined at high intensity and blinking, all at the same time, we'd use COLOR 25,0 since

1 (for underlining) + 8 (for high intensity) + 16 (for blinking) = 25

In Appendix E you'll find a convenient table giving you most of the possible COLOR statements and their corresponding meanings.

COLOR is a very useful statement whenever you need any special effects on your screen. The following example shows how it can be used to INPUT a secret password:

```
100 CLS
110 PRINT "enter your ";
120 COLOR 9,0                          'high intensity blinking
130 PRINT "PASSWORD";
140 COLOR 0,0                          'black on black, i.e. invisible
150 INPUT PASSWORD$
160 COLOR 7,0                          'back to white on black
170 PRINT "aha! so your secret PASSWORD is ";
180 COLOR 16,7                         'white on black, blinking
190 PRINT PASSWORD$
200 COLOR 7,0                          'back to "normal"
210 END
Ok
```

When this program is run, it produces the following output:

```
RUN
enter your PASSWORD?              ← Entered PASSWORD is invisible
aha! so your secret PASSWORD is dinkelspiel
                                 |
                    The PASSWORD we entered
```

Here you see some of the neat special effects that COLOR can control, including making text invisible! COLOR 0,0 in line 140 says "from now on, make both the foreground and the background black." That way the PASSWORD that you subsequently entered is invisible to snoopy onlookers! (only your computer knows...)

Summary

In this chapter we have explored the ASCII characters available on your IBM PC, and seen how to use the graphics character set to draw various kinds of boxes and also how to produce the special effects of blinking, underlining, emphasizing (high intensity), and inverting (black on white).

This chapter dealt principally with visual screen output. The next chapter will explore the *audio* output of your IBM PC — you'll find it at least as rich in the variety and power as the graphics we've discussed in this chapter.

Exercise

Write a simple program that draws a bar graph. Included should be a centered title making use of some of the special effects possible with COLOR. The program should draw a bar representing a value (stock price, number of sales, inches of rain, or whatever) immediately after the value is entered. It should be possible to enter 12 values, although you should also be able to terminate the program prematurely by entering the value 99.

Solution

```
100 '----NAME; "BAR-GRPH.B10"----------------------------------------
105 '
110 '----*********************
120 '----* MAKING A BAR GRAPH *---------BY B.E.---------------------
130 '----*********************
140 '
150 '----PRINTs the title-------------------------------------------
160 '
165 CLS
170 LOCATE 1, 22
180 COLOR 1,0                      'causes underlining
190 PRINT "MAKING A ";
200 COLOR 9,0                      'causes underlining, high int.
210 PRINT "BARGRAPH";
220 COLOR 1,0                      'back to just underlining
230 PRINT " OF 12 VALUES"
240 COLOR 7,0                      'back to normal
```

```
250 '
260 '----initializes variables-----------------------------------------
270 '
280 WIDTZ = 4                              'defines width of bar
290 BARNUMBER = 12                         'defines number of bars
300 LOCATE 3,1
310 PRINT "enter value (0-22)"
320 '
330 '----draws BARNUMBER of bars------------------------------------
340 '
350 FOR I = 1 TO BARNUMBER
360   LOCATE (I + 3), 1                    'LOCATES posit. of INPUT of VALUE
370   INPUT VALUE                          'INPUT's VALUE to be graphed
380   IF VALUE = 99 THEN END               'means for prgm termination
390   LEFT = 8 + (WIDTZ + 1)*I             'defines LEFT side of bar
400   TOP = 23 - VALUE                     'defines row equal to TOP of bar
410   REM
420   REM----draws one bar---------------------------------------------
430   REM
440   FOR ROW = TOP TO 22                  'controls height of bar
450     LOCATE ROW, LEFT
460     PRINT STRING$(4, CHR$(177));       'PRINTs row of ASCII char. 177
```

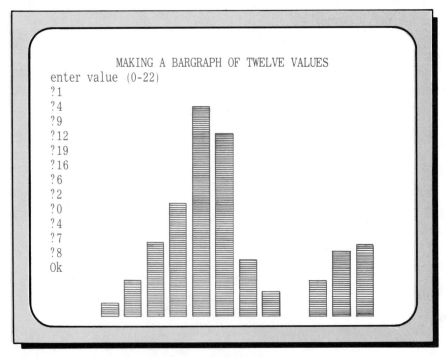

Figure 10-5. Output of program "BAR-GRPH.B10"

```
47Ø    NEXT ROW
475    BEEP
48Ø    REM
49Ø    REM----end of drawing one bar-------------------------------------
5ØØ    REM
51Ø NEXT I
52Ø END
```

Figure 10-5 shows the output of this program. It is fairly self-explanantory. The bars are assembled out of the solid-block ASCII character 177 (it totally fills a character space at medium intensity). The PRINT STRING$ statement in line 460 prints a single row of the bar, and the FOR...NEXT loop defined by lines 440 and 470 stacks these rows on top of each other to draw the whole bar. The FOR...NEXT loop defined by lines 350 and 510 is responsible for drawing a bar each time a new VALUE is entered in response to INPUT.

11

The Sound of Music

Concepts
> Sound effects
> Music with sound
> Special effects
> Music scales
> Octaves
> Foreground
> Background
> Tempo, Legato, Staccato, Pause

Instructions
> SOUND, PLAY

Your PC is equipped with a versatile system for producing musical sounds. The musical sounds played by a musician are encoded in one language (musical notation) that must be converted to another language (BASIC) to be used by the computer. This chapter will give you a short course in music fundamentals, taking you from conventional sheet-music notation to the BASIC commands that will allow you to play this music on your IBM PC.

Music will add interest and variety to your programs. It is also helpful to put sound in a program to get the operator's attention. Music can be used to indicate when an error has occurred (see Chapter 19, Error Trapping), or to alert the operator that it is time to change diskettes or to turn on the printer, or simply to indicate that all is going well in a long computing process. This last use of sound gives the operator the freedom to move about in the room and not have his eyes riveted to the screen.

There are two BASIC statements that give the PC the ability to make sounds. The first of these is the SOUND statement.

The SOUND Statement

The SOUND statement has two arguments or modifiers. They are the *frequency* and the *duration* arguments. Let's look at an example:

```
SOUND 1000, 10
```

Duration (in clock ticks, 18.2 ticks per second)

Frequency in Hertz (cycles per second),
an integer between 32 and 32767

Try the following on your PC and listen to the "Music of the Spheres":

```
Ok
SOUND 1000, 10
Ok
SOUND 1000, 20
Ok
SOUND 2000, 20
Ok
SOUND 4000, 10
Ok
```

If the paint is still on the walls, you will have noticed that the first sound at 1000 hertz was just half as long as the second. The sound will last approximately one second when a duration number of 18 is given. These duration numbers are the internal clock ticks, which are used by the system to update the clock, and for various other functions. The internal clock ticks 18.2 times per second. So the duration of 10 is 10/18.2 seconds, a little more than 1/2 second. The duration of 20 is twice as long as a duration of 10 and is a tad longer than a second.

In the third and fourth sound statements, the frequencies were doubled. The range of frequencies that may be programmed is from 37 vibrations per second (hertz) up to 32,767 hertz.

Sound in general is produced by the vibration of some object at a rate that the ear can detect. Most human ears work between the range of 20 to 20,000 hertz, although the ability to hear different frequencies varies from one individual to another. In addition, the loudness of the sound largely determines whether we hear it or not. Inside the PC there is a small speaker located just behind the IBM Personal Computer label on the main computer box. The loudness of this speaker is fixed and may not be adjusted. Because of the limited size of this speaker and the quality and loudness of the sounds it produces, you will find that not all sounds between 20 and 20,000 hertz may be heard. In short, you should not expect hi-fidelity sound from your PC.

We can still make a number of sounds that have a familiar ring to them, though. The following examples are presented for your amusement:

```
1Ø '------ AAA -----------
2Ø FOR X=1 TO 3            'repeats three times
3Ø    SOUND 44Ø,1Ø         'makes SOUND 44Ø Hertz for 1Ø ticks
4Ø       FOR K=1 TO 12ØØ   'produces delay between sound
5Ø       NEXT K
6Ø NEXT X
```

```
1Ø '------ SIREN ------------
2Ø FOR X=1 TO 4
3Ø    FOR L=7ØØ TO -7ØØ STEP -1Ø    'sets range for L
4Ø       SOUND 85Ø-ABS(L),.3         'frequency — L made positive
5Ø       L=L-2/7ØØ
6Ø    NEXT L
7Ø NEXT X
```

```
1Ø '------ SCOTLAND YARD -------
2Ø FOR X=1 TO 3            'makes sound combination 3 times
3Ø    SOUND 9ØØ,3
4Ø    SOUND 7ØØ,4
5Ø       FOR K=1 TO 16ØØ   'produces delay between sounds
6Ø       NEXT K
7Ø NEXT X
```

```
1Ø '------ TIMER ------------
2Ø FOR X=1 TO 1Ø
3Ø    SOUND 7ØØ,4
4Ø    SOUND 1ØØ,Ø                 'turns sound off
5Ø       FOR K=1 TO 12ØØ:NEXT     'produces delay between sounds
6Ø NEXT X
7Ø SOUND 4ØØØ,1                   'elapsed time signal
```

```
1Ø '------ CAR -----------
2Ø FOR M=6Ø TO 7Ø STEP 1Ø    'switches between two frequencies
3Ø    SOUND M,.Ø1             'makes sound with short duration
4Ø NEXT
```

```
10 '------ DROPPING -----------
20 FOR K=3000 TO 600 STEP -5   'sweeps frequencies
30   SOUND K,K/5000            'variable frequency with variable duration
40 NEXT K
50 SOUND 3000,2                'striking sound
```

We hope that you will load and run each of these little programs and that you will find them not only amusing but also illustrative of the ways in which the SOUND statement may be used. In BASICA it is possible to run the SOUND statement in a background buffer, thus allowing a program to continue without interruption. This approach will be discussed in some detail in the following discussion of the PLAY statement.

Music and the PLAY Statement

IBM BASIC contains a very powerful sound-producing statement called PLAY. This statement, as the name implies, is used to generate music. Since some knowledge of musical scales and musical notation is necessary in order to understand how PLAY is used, we will need to review some of the elements of music.

Try entering the following program and see if the sound it produces is familiar:

```
10 SOUND 262,8     'C4
20 SOUND 294,8     'D4
30 SOUND 233,8     'B3-
40 SOUND 117,8     'B2-
50 SOUND 175,16    'F3
```

Just as computer instructions are written in code, so are the instructions to a musician. This coded form of instructions we call a musical *score*. The five lines of BASIC written above combine both computers and music. We will spend a few moments looking at this code and learning how to convert musical notation into computer commands.

Some Basics of Musical Notation

Modern music uses a set of symbols to show the different tones that are to be played. The symbols are placed on a musical *staff*, which is composed of five lines and four spaces. The location of a symbol on a line or space gives the note the name of that line or space. The treble clef staff is shown in schematic form in Figure 11-1.

The *spaces* spell out the word "F A C E," starting with the lowest space and moving up the staff. The *lines* take on the letters "E G B D F" (E-very G-ood B-oy D-oes F-ine). Again we start with the lowest line and move up the staff. The higher up the staff, the higher the *frequency*, or tone, of the sound that the note represents.

You'll also note the letters are in alphabetical order as we move up the scale; the notes proceed from A to G and then the sequence is repeated. In western music there are eight notes before we begin to repeat. These eight notes comprise a unit called an octave. The eight notes are not equally spaced in frequency, but have whole and half steps as we go up the scale.

Figure 11-1. The treble clef

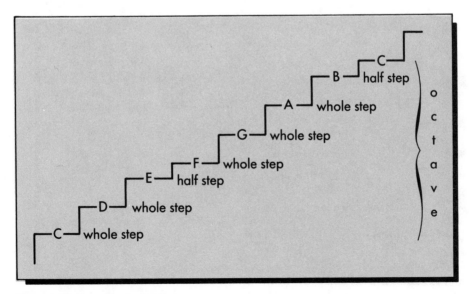

Figure 11-2. Musical octave

Figure 11-2 shows the positions of the whole and half steps in the *diatonic* scale, which is a scale divided into eight tones whose frequencies are in the ratios of small integer numbers.

As we move up the scale, the pitch becomes higher. The diagram in Figure 11-3 shows the numeric frequencies of the middle octave portion of the diatonic scale. These frequencies may be used in the SOUND statement to give the pitch of a note – that is, to specify what tone you want the PC to make.

In the interest of developing more complex cords and larger combinations of instruments, many other musical scales have been developed. One such scale, known as the equal-tempered scale, was developed in the eighteenth century. This scale is based upon twelve equally spaced tones. While there are still eight notes to the scale, the sharps and flats have been added to make all possible half steps. The sharps are one half step higher than the "natural" notes. Thus, the note F has a neighboring note one half step higher called "F sharp." The flats are located one half step lower than the *natural* notes, so the note G has a note one half step lower called "G flat." Yes, G flat and F sharp are different names for the same note in this scale. There are no sharps (or flats) between E and F or between B and C, because they are already one half step apart from each other. In Figure 11-4, all half steps are shown with the two names for what become the black keys on a modern piano.

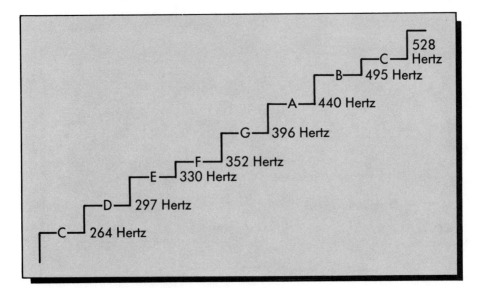

Figure 11-3. Diatonic scale frequencies

The note A sharp may be written as A#. In the BASIC PLAY statement, either A# or A+ may be used to indicate A sharp. Similarly, while musical convention uses B♭ to indicate the half step below B called "B flat," in the PLAY statement we use the symbol B-. With most musical instruments, it is possible to play more than one octave. In order to keep track of which octave the note is located in, it is necessary to have a system of nomenclature. One such system is called the "USA Standard"; it uses a number located after the letter of the note. For example, middle C on the piano is C4, the C in the fourth octave. A2# would be the note A♯ in the second octave.

Other systems for declaring the octave, such as the Helmholtz have been developed. The Helmholtz system uses a system of uppercase letters, lowercase letters, and apostrophes. Table 11-1 shows this system of notation along with the frequencies of the notes in each of the two scales (the diatonic and the tempered) we have talked about.

The IBM PC uses a system called *Octave Number* to denote the octave location. The letter O (not the number 0) is used followed by the number of the octave. Thus O3, for example, would be the octave in which the middle C (C4) on the piano is located. In Table 11-1, the column labeled "Octave Number IBM" gives the values for each of the octaves O0 through O6 (seven octaves).

We need to make one further point about musical notation in order to make full use of Table 11-1. In order to indicate a wider range of

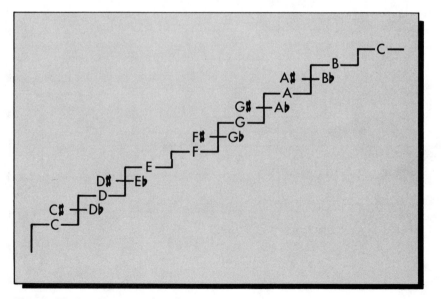

Figure 11-4. Tempered scale

notes covering more octaves, a system of two staffs is used in the written musical scores. The upper staff is called the *treble* and the lower is called the *bass*. Each is given a symbol to indicate its location. More than one octave may be shown on a single staff, extending beyond the range of the staff. The treble clef and the bass clef are shown in the diagram in Figure 11-5.

The symbol 𝄞 is used to denote the treble portion, while the symbol 𝄢 is used for the bass portion of the musical scales. The use of a sharp ♯ or flat ♭ symbol next to the clef symbols means that *all* notes on that line or space are to be made sharp when the ♯ is present and made flat when the ♭ is present. If the note is to be made natural (that is, neither flat or sharp), the symbol ♮ before the note means all such notes will remain natural for the remainder of that measure. In addition

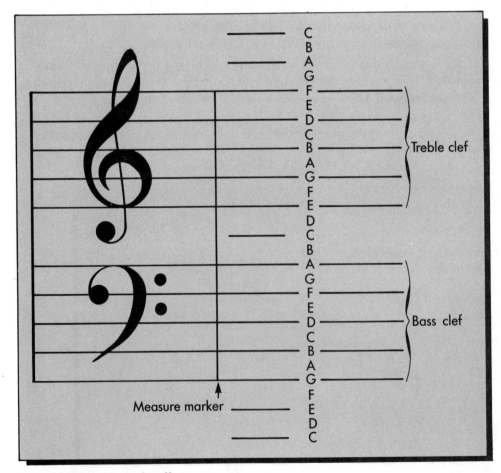

Figure 11-5. Musical staff

to these prefix-like notations, there will be some indication of the duration of a note (timing).

Table 11-1 shows the octaves and their various musical notations for the audible range of musical instruments. The first column (Note) shows the USA Standard notation for the musical octaves (including sharps and flats). The second and third columns give the frequencies of each note in the tempered and diatonic scales. The fourth column is the Helmholtz notation, with which many musicians are familiar. The IBM octave code is given for use in the PLAY statement. Next is the IBM note code, which you may use instead of specifying the octave and the notes (C D E F G A B C). Finally, the seventh column, Staff Location, shows the location of C in that particular octave.

Table 11-1 Notes and octaves

Note	Equal-tempered frequency	Pythagorean diatonic frequency	Helmholtz notation	IBM octave number	IBM note number	Staff location
C0	16.352	17				
C0#, D0 −	17.324					
D0	18.354	19				
D0#, E0 −	19.445					
E0	20.602	21				
F0	21.827	22				
F0#, G0 −	23.125					
G0	24.5	25				
G0#, A0 −	25.957					
A0	27.5	28				
A0#, B0 −	29.135					
B0	30.868	31				
C1	32.703	33	CC	00	N1	
C1#, D1 −	34.648				N2	
D1	36.708	37			N3	
D1#, E1 −	38.891				N4	
E1	41.203	41			N5	
F1	43.654	44			N6	
F1#, G1 −	46.249				N7	
G1	48.999	50			N8	
G1#, A1 −	51.913				N9	
A1	55.000	55			N10	
A1#, B1 −	58.27				N11	
B1	61.735	62			N12	

Note	Equal-tempered frequency	Pythagorean diatonic frequency	Helmholtz notation	IBM octave number	IBM note number	Staff location
C2	65.406	66	C	01	N13	
C2#, D2–	69.296				N14	g
D2	73.416	74			N15	e
D2#, E2–	77.782				N16	c
E2	82.4107	83			N17	a
F2	87.307	88			N18	f
F2#, G2–	92.4999				N19	
G2	97.999	99			N20	
G2#, A2–	103.83				N21	
A2	110.00	11			N22	
A2#, B2–	116.54				N23	
B2	123.47	124			N24	
C3	130.81	132	c	02	N25	
C3#, D3–	138.59				N26	g
D3	146.83	148			N27	e
D3#, E3–	155.56				N28	c
E3	164.81	165			N29	a
F3	174.61	176			N30	f
F3#, G3–	185.00				N31	
G3	196.00	198			N32	
G3#, A3–	207.65				N33	
A3	220.00	220			N34	
A3#, B3–	233.08				N35	
B3	246.94	247			N36	
C4	261.63	264	c'	03	N37	
C4#, D4–	277.18				N38	e
D4	293.66	297			N39	c
D4#, E4–	311.13				N40	a
E4	329.63	333			N41	f
F4	349.23	352			N42	d
F4#, G4–	369.99				N43	b
G4	392.00	396			N44	g
G4#, A4–	415.30				N45	e
A4	440.00	440			N46	c
A4#, B4–	446.16				N47	a
B4	493.88	495			N48	
C5	523.25	528	c''	04	N49	
C5#, D5–	554.37				N50	e
D5	587.33	594			N51	c
D5#, E5–	622.25				N52	a
E5	659.26	666			N53	f
F5	698.46	704			N54	d
F5#, G5–	739.99				N55	b
G5	783.99	792			N56	g
G5#, A5–	830.61				N57	e
A5	880.00	880			N58	c
A5#, B5–	932.33				N59	a
B5	987.77	990			N60	

Note	Equal-tempered frequency	Pythagorean diatonic frequency	Helmholtz notation	IBM octave number	IBM note number	Staff location
C6	1046.5	1056	c'''	05	N61	
C6#, D6−	1108.7				N62	
D6	1174.7	1188			N63	
D6#, E6−	1244.5				N64	
E6	1318.5	1332			N65	
F6	1396.9	1408			N66	b
F6#, G6−	1480.0				N67	g
G6	1568.0	1584			N68	e
G6#, A6−	1661.2				N69	c
A6	1760.0	1760			N70	a
A6#, B6−	1864.7				N71	f
B6	1975.5	1980			N72	
C7	2093.0	2112	c''''	06	N73	
C7#, D7−	2217.5				N74	
D7	2349.3	2372			N75	8
D7#, E7−	2489.0				N76	
E7	2637.0	2664			N77	
F7	2793.8	2816			N78	b
F7#, G7−	2960.0				N79	g
G7	3136.0	3168			N80	e
G7#, A7−	3322.4				N81	c
A7	3520.0	3520			N82	a
A7#, B7−	3729.3				N83	f
B7	3951.1	3960			N84	
C8	4186.0	4224	c^v	NA	NA	
C8#, D8−	4434.9					
D8	4698.6	4744				
D8#, E8−	4978.0					
E8	5274.0	5328				
F8	5587.7	5632				
F8#, G8−	5919.9					
G8	6271.9	6240				
G8#, A8−	6644.9					
A8	7040.0	7040				
A8#, B8−	7458.6					
B8	7902.1	7920				
C9	8372.0	8448	NA	NA	NA	
C9#, D9−	8869.8					
D9	9397.3	9488				
D9#, E9−	9956.1					
E9	10548.1	10656				
F9	11175.3	11264				
F9#, G9−	11839.8					
G9	12541.9	12480				
G9#, A9−	13289.7					
A9	14080	14080				
A9#, B9−	14917.2					
B9	15804.3	15840				
C10	16744.0	16896	NA	NA	NA	

The diatonic scale is old and has been used for music written for small groups of instruments. The tempered scale is newer and is used because a larger number of acceptable combinations of notes is possible when played by many instruments. PLAY is written with the tempered scale; should you prefer to use the diatonic scale, you will need to rewrite your program using the SOUND statement and the frequencies given above. For most purposes the tempered scale will do quite nicely.

The Play Statement

Now let's take a look at PLAY, the second BASIC sound statement and the easiest way to play music on the PC. Here's an example of the PLAY statement:

```
100 PLAY "B B C D D C B A"
```

Here the notes to be played are expressed by letter name. When a note is to be made sharp, it's followed by either + or #. When it's to be made flat, it's followed by −.

For example, if the A in the example above is to be made sharp, you would enter

```
100 PLAY "B B C D D C B A#"
```

or

```
100 PLAY "B B C D D C B A+"
```

To make the A flat you would enter

```
100 PLAY "B B C D D C B A-"
```

The octave notation must be added before the note that is to be played in the new octave:

```
100 PLAY "O3 B B O4 C D D C O3 B A"
```

All notes will be played in octave 3 until a new octave is specified (here octave 4). We have purposely separated the notes with spaces for ease of reading. However, this is not necessary, and the notes may be written in lowercase. (Remember that the letter O is used, not the number 0, to denote the octaves.)

```
100 PLAY "o3bbo4cddco3ba"
```

Note that the default octave is octave 4. If you do not specify an octave, PLAY will assume that the notes you designate are in octave 4.

The PLAY Statement in DOS 2.0

Under DOS 2.0, the PLAY statement may use the < and > symbols to change octaves where < signifies "move down one octave" and > signifies "move up one octave." If we try using these symbols in the preceding example, we get the following:

```
1ØØ PLAY "o3bb>cddc<ba"
              |        |
         up one octave  down one octave
```

Notes and Timing

In conventional musical notation, the duration of a musical note is given by an oval shape; the shape may be with or without stems or flags and may be solid or open. (Whether the stem points up or down has no significance.) Figure 11-6 gives some examples of this system of representing notes and rests. A rest, by the way, may be defined as an absence of sound for a specified period.

When two or more notes are the same in duration, it is customary to link or connect their flags together, as shown in Figure 11-7.

Occasionally it is desirable to make a note longer or shorter than it is

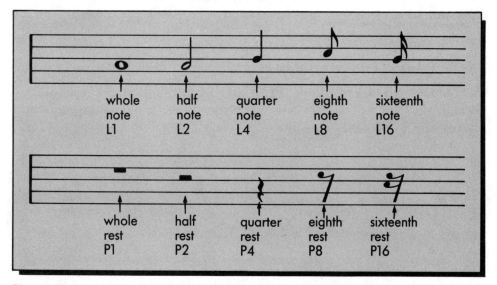

Figure 11-6. Conventional representation of note lengths and rests

normally played. When the note is to be lengthened (played legato) a dot (.) is placed after the note. When a note is played normally, the duration is about 7/8 of the time specified, with a break of 1/8 between notes. When legato is specified, the note is extended to the full period of time. If the note is to be shortened (played staccato), the dot symbol (.) is placed over the note. Where staccato is specified, the note is shortened to 3/4 of the normal time specified, thus decreasing the duration by 1/8.

The PLAY statement provides a number of single-letter and double-letter commands that let you control the tempo of your music and the duration of individual notes.

The letter L is used to specify the duration of a note. Following the L, a number from 1 to 64 will give the length of note. L1 is a whole note, while L4 is a quarter note, and L16 is a sixteenth note, and so on.

The letter T is used to specify the tempo. T100 means 100 quarter notes in one minute. The Tempo may range from 32 to 255. Tempo has a default value of 120; that is, if no tempo is specified through the T command, the tempo will be 120 quarter notes per minute.

The letters ML are used to increase the duration of a note. ML stands for "music legato."

The letters MS are used to decrease the duration of the notes that follow. MS stands for "music staccato."

Finally, the letters MN instruct the PLAY statement to return to the normal duration of note, which is 7/8 of the interval between notes. See Figure 11-8 for a visual representation of the various note durations. Figure 11-9 shows an example of a line of music translated from musical notation to BASIC.

Specifying Rests (Pauses)

The length of a rest in the PLAY statement is indicated in the same way as the length of a note. Just as you specify the length of subsequent notes with L followed by a number, so you can use P followed by the rest

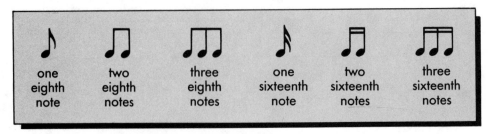

Figure 11-7. Linking notes of the same length

length to specify the length of a rest: P1 for a whole rest, P8 for an eighth rest, and so on (see Figure 11-6).

Specifying Tempo

The tempo of music is widely referred to in the Italian terms for tempo: for example, *largo* for "very slow" or *allegro* for "fast." In Table 11-2 the typical ranges of both beats per minute and IBM clock ticks are given. The clock ticks are useful when using the SOUND statement, while the beats per minute are more useful in the PLAY statement.

To set the tempo, use the T command in a PLAY string. Follow T with a number for the number of quarter notes in a second. You may select a number from 32 to 255, with 120 being the default value. In our

Musical term	Musical notation	IBM code	Duration of note
Normal	♩	MN	break 1/8 — 7/8
Legato	⌒	ML	no break — 8/8
Staccato	♩̇	MN	break 2/8 — 6/8

Figure 11-8. The duration of notes

Figure 11-9. A line of music translated into BASIC

little illustration above, if we wanted to make the tempo *andante*, then we'd change line 100 to the following

```
100 PLAY "T80L403BB04CDDC03BAGGABMLBL8AL2A"
         |
         Tempo
```

Table 11-2 gives a range of values for the various tempo notations.

Background or Foreground

There are two modes in which you can use the PLAY statement: music foreground mode and music background mode. In the music foreground mode (specified by **MF**), each note being produced on the speaker must reach conclusion before the next note will start, and no other processes will take place. To interrupt a process, the (Ctrl) (Keytop) key combination may be used. The foreground command is the default state for both the **PLAY** and **SOUND** statements.

On occasion you may wish other processes to continue while some sounds are generated. One such occasion might be to indicate that all is proceeding "well" in a long computing procedure. Under these circumstances, you can put a short combination of notes — up to 32 notes and pauses — into music background mode. Use the command MB, which stands for music background, and computational processes will proceed while the music is played. Try this example:

```
10 FOR X = 1 TO 10
20   PLAY "mbmnl16t120"
30   PLAY "o2egbgegbgeg-bg-eg-bg-fa#o3do2a#fa#o3do2a#fao3do2afao3do2a"
40   PRINT X, 2*X, 3*X, 4*X
50 NEXT X
```

String Variables with PLAY

You can use a string variable to contain the sequence of commands that the PLAY statement is to use. This procedure allows you to repeat a sequence, perhaps even in another octave, without repeating the code for it (see line 180 in the example below). String variables used in the PLAY statement are defined in the usual way, just as we described in Chapter 6. The only difference is that when you construct the PLAY statement, you

should use an X preceding the string to denote the string variable. For
example:

```
1Ø A$ = "o3bbo4cddco3baggabb.msamna2"
2Ø PLAY "P1 XA$;
```

The "." acts as a dotted note; extends duration by 3/2

Be sure to close the quote

Using the A$ string variable

Tempos			Beats per Minute (Tn) (PLAY)	Clock Ticks (SOUND)
LARGO	♩	=	42 to 66	26 to 17
	♪	=	48 to 92	23 to 12
LENTO	♩	=	50 to 66	22 to 17
	♩.	=	50 to 69	22 to 16
	♩	=	52 to 108	21 to 10
ADAGIO	♩	=	50 to 76	22 to 14
	♪	=	58 to 96	19 to 11
ANDANTE	♩.	=	40 to 72	27 to 15
	♩	=	56 to 88	19 to 12
	♪	=	80 to 126	14 to 9
MODERATO	♩	=	60 to 80	18 to 14
	♩	=	60 to 126	18 to 9
ALLEGRO	♩.	=	63 to 96	17 to 11
	♩	=	69 to 112	16 to 10
	♩.	=	72 to 132	15 to 8
	♩	=	84 to 144	13 to 8
VIVACE	♩.	=	60 to 84	18 to 13
	♩	=	72 to 92	15 to 12
	♪	=	76 to 112	22 to 10
	♩	=	80 to 160	14 to 7
PRESTO	♩.	=	69 to 120	16 to 9
	♩	=	88 to 132	12 to 9
	♩.	=	96 to 144	17 to 8
	♩	=	100 to 152	11 to 7

Table 11-2. Tempos and note durations

Here's a more ambitious piece of music, coded into strings. Try it out!

```
98 '------OP#1.B11---------
99 '----- Amy Petersen's OP #1 ---------------------
100 A$ = "cececececce-ce-ce-ce-dg-dg-dg-dg-dfdfdfdf"
110 B$ = "cegecegece-ge-ce-ge-dg-ag-dg-ag-dfafdfaf"
120 C$ = "cecececececececececececececece"
121 '      123456789012345678901234567890 12345
130 D$ = "egegegegeg-eg-eg-eg-fa#fa#fa#fa#fa#fafafa"
140 E$ = "egbgegbgeg-bg-eg-bg-fa#o3do2a#fa#o3do2afao3do2afao3do2a"
150 F$ = "egegegegegegegegegegegegegegeg"
160 G$ = "cececececce-ce-ce-ce-dg-dg-dg-dg-dfdfdfdf"
170 H$ = "cececececce-ce-ce-ce-dg-dg-dg-dg-dfdfdfe4d4c2"
180 PLAY "MFMNL16T1200O4XA$;O3XA$;O2XA$;XA$;XB$;XC$;XD$;XD$;XE$;XF$;"
190 PLAY "XG$;XH$;"
```

As you can see, by using strings and the PLAY statement, you can create some rather sophisticated pieces of music without using too much BASIC code. Try adding some music to your existing programs. You — and anyone else using your program — will love the results!

PLAY modifier	Meaning
A - G	Notes with # or + for sharp, − for flats
Ln	Length of note n = 1 for whole, n = 4 for quarter etc.
MF	Music Foreground
MB	Music Background
MN	Music note length Normal
ML	Music note length Legato
MS	Music note length Staccato
Nn	Play note number n (0 to 84) piano notation 0 → rest
On	Octave number (0 to 6)
Pn	Pause length n, n = 1 whole rest, n = 4 quarter rest
Tn	Tempo where n is from 32 to 255
Xstring	Execute string
	Same as dotted note duration of note by factor 3/2

Table 11-3. The PLAY statement in music

Summary

We have seen how the SOUND statement may be used to specify a note's frequency and duration. This statement permits the production of nonmusical sounds, or notes not located on the *tempered* musical scale. The format of the SOUND statement is:

SOUND *frequency,duration*

The PLAY statement is the most convenient way to represent the standard musical notes. Table 11-3 is a summary of commands used to modify the PLAY statement.

Exercise

Take the following well-known musical passage and encode it with the PLAY statement. We suggest a tempo of approximately 160 for best definition.

Sonate No. 14 in C-Sharp Minor
Op. 27 No. 2 ("Moonlight")

Solution

Here is our solution:

```
98  '------SONATA.B11-----------
99  '------BEETHOVEN'S MOONLIGHT-------
100 PLAY "MFMNL16T160P1P1"
110 PLAY "O1P16G+O2C+EG+C+EG+O3C+O2EG+O3C+EO2G+O3C+E"
120 PLAY "O3G+C+EG+O4C+O3EG+O4C+EO3MLG+O4C+EMSG+8G+8MN"
130 PLAY "O1P16G+O2CD+G+CD+G+O3CO2D+G+O3CD+O2G+CD+"
140 PLAY "O3G+CD+G+O4CO3D+G+O4CD+O3MLG+O4CD+MSG+8G+8MN"
150 PLAY "O2C+FG+O3C+O2FG+O3C+FO2G+O3C+FG+C+FG+"
160 PLAY "O4C+O3FG+O4C+FO3G+O4C+FG+MLC+FG+O5MSC+8C+8MN"
170 PLAY "O2P16MLC+F+AO3MSC+MLC+F+AO4MSC+MLC+F+AO5MSC+8C+8MN"
180 PLAY "O2P16MLC+EGO3MSC+MLC+EGO4MSC+MLC+EGO5MSC+8C+8MN"
```

Subroutines — Organizing Your Program

All of the programs we have written so far have been quite short — less than a page long. As your programs get longer, it becomes increasingly difficult and also increasingly important to maintain a logical order and structure within your program. Writing a long and complex program is in some ways like building a house: both may be rather overwhelming projects unless they are broken down into smaller, more manageable tasks. This chapter is about one of the principal methods for defining such smaller subunits of a program — the subroutine.

A subroutine is a program within a program. It is a set of instructions that is performed whenever it is "called" by the main program. A subroutine might, for example, use PRINT to print a title page, use PLAY to play a song, or graph the data calculated by the main program. In our house analogy, a subroutine is like subcontracting for the windows of the house: they are ordered, built, and delivered ready-made when "called" for.

Aside from helping to divide your program into smaller, more manageable units, subroutines are also very useful when your program needs to perform a series of instructions several times throughout the program. Suppose your program needs to draw 10 boxes to frame various text lines of your program input and output. Instead of writing the box program each time it's needed, you can write a single subroutine that does the job of drawing a box. Then, every time your program needs to draw a box, it can simply call the same subroutine. Instead of writing 10 box programs (each of which can be a page long as you saw in Chapter 8, "Branching and Decisions"), you only have to write the box program once if you treat it as a subroutine.

If you're beginning to sense that we're really trying to impress you with the importance and utility of subroutines, you're right! In addition to making programming easier, sophisticated statements such as ON KEY GOSUB have an effect that would be difficult or impossible to create in any other way. But let's take care of the basics first.

GOSUB and RETURN — The Dynamic Duo of Subroutines

The easiest way to call a subroutine is by means of the GOSUB statement. Like the GOTO statement, GOSUB results in branching to the specified line number. However, there is an important difference that makes the GOSUB statement particularly useful in calling subroutines and keeping order in your programs. See if you spot the difference in the following program:

```
10 PRINT "hello, the following composition is ";
20 PRINT "brought to you by a SUBROUTINE!"
30 GOSUB 1000
40 PRINT "back to the main program -- did you recognize it?"
50 END
60 '
1000 PLAY "P1 O4 E12 E12 E12 C1 P4 D12 D12 D12 O3 B1"
1010 RETURN
```

When run, the screen output is

```
RUN
hello, the following composition is brought to you by a SUBROUTINE!
back to the main program -- did you recognize it?
Ok
```

and your computer plays the first few notes of a popular symphony right after the first statement "hello, the following composition ..."

It's easy to see what happens here. GOSUB 1000 tells your computer "go to the subroutine that starts at line 1000." So execution of your program branches to line 1000 which causes your computer to play the specified string. So far, that's exactly the same thing that GOTO 1000 would have done.

The next statement to be executed is RETURN in line 1010 which causes program execution to return to the original branch point, line 40, which, in turn, now prints "back to the main program...". RETURN always causes program execution to branch back to the line *immediately following the most recent GOSUB statement*. GOSUB and RETURN usually appear as a pair.

Although it is permitted to have a GOSUB without a RETURN statement, it is the *combination* of the two statements that make them particularly well-suited to define and call a subroutine: GOSUB 1000 causes branching to line 1000, which we can interpret as the *beginning* of a subroutine; RETURN defines the *end* of the subroutine and returns program execution to the original branch point. If your program has to branch to another part of the program to do a given job, it is generally a good idea to come back to the original branching point, since doing so helps to keep your program organized and also makes it easier to read and debug (that is, remove the errors or "bugs" from your program). Using GOSUB and RETURN helps you to do that.

Now the difference between GOTO and GOSUB is evident: GOSUB, like GOTO, causes branching, but unlike GOTO, it also *remembers* where to branch back to when RETURN is executed. Most programmers prefer to use GOSUB statements in place of GOTO statements wherever possible in order to avoid the kind of messy convolutions (pretzels?) in program flow that become all too prevalent if too many GOTOs are used.

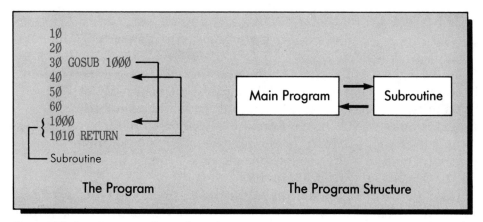

Figure 12-1. Program flow of a subroutine

Returning to our previous example, we can illustrate the flow of our program by means of Figure 12-1.

It is also possible for a subroutine to call another subroutine. The second subroutine is said to be "nested" within the first. Realize, however, that the subroutines themselves aren't nested one inside the other; only the GOSUB statements that call them are nested. You'll find an example of such a nested subroutine in the menu program presented later in this chapter.

We can generalize what we've learned from this example in the box on GOSUB and RETURN:

GOSUB and RETURN

The statement

```
100 GOSUB 1000
```

causes program execution to branch to line 1000, which is the beginning of a subroutine. A GOSUB statement must be accompanied by a RETURN statement in the form

```
1500 RETURN
```

which causes program execution to return to the statement immediately following the GOSUB statement. RETURN defines the end of the subroutine.

Organizing Your Program — The Bar Graph Program Using GOSUB and RETURN

Our previous example of using a subroutine to play the beginning of a symphony illustrated the use of GOSUB and RETURN, but it did little to illustrate the usefulness of subroutines. Since the subroutine consisted basically of just one statement (PLAY plus the mandatory RETURN), we could just as well have included that statement in the main body of the program. Since one of the most important uses of subroutines is to help you organize your program by allowing you to break it down into smaller pieces, we need to look at a more complex and a longer program to really see the benefits of using a subroutine.

Let's rewrite the program BAR-GRPH.BIO presented in the exercises at the end of Chapter 10, but this time using subroutines. Because we are already familiar with this bar graph program, we will be free to ignore the details and to look at the overall structure of the program instead.

Before actually writing down any program lines, it's a good idea to plan your program, to design its overall structure. Long programs are not nearly as forgiving of impulsiveness and "stream of consciousness programming" as programs just a few lines long. When faced with building a house, it's a good idea to have an overall plan that tells you a sequence of jobs to perform, like "build the foundation, put up the frame, put in the plumbing, install the wiring," and so on. Writing programs, reading them, and often the speed with which they are executed all benefit from a similar approach to planning.

So what is it that we want our bar graph program to do? Here's a list of jobs to be performed in their proper sequence:

1. Title of program and program explanations

2. Preliminaries: clear screen, turn KEY OFF

3. Program title to be displayed — — — — — subroutine, line 5000

4. Initialize fixed variables

5. Draw and label axes (that's new) — — — — subroutine, line 6000

6. Draw bars using FOR NEXT

    a. LOCATE bar

    b. INPUT value to be graphed

    c. draw one bar   — — — — — — — — — subroutine, line 7000

This is certainly not the only way to organize this program, but it's a reasonable, fairly logical way to proceed. We've identified three jobs that we'd like to be done by a subroutine. Each of these jobs is a self-contained, logical unit. As subroutines, they can be tucked away at the end of your program (or anywhere you like, although the end is usually the best place) so that their contents don't clutter up your main program. Some subroutines, like the last one which draws a bar, can be used in other programs. You might even build up a library of frequently used subroutines from which you can "check out" an appropriate subroutine whenever needed. For example, a general "title" subroutine might be very useful; the title subroutine for this particular program, however, is a bit specialized for general use (it has all those COLOR statements in it that emphasize parts of the title and cause underlining). We'll show you how to write a general title subroutine when we learn more about string functions in a later chapter.

The next step in planning a program is a familiar one: define your variables; that is, identify what variables you need, and give them meaningful BASIC names. In this bar graph program, for example, we need variables to define the position of each box-like graphics character. We chose the variable names ROW and COL so that we can locate (with the LOCATE statement) the graphics character at a given row and column position. Sometimes it is desirable to list and identify all your variables within your program in REM statements.

Now that we know what we want each part of the program to do and what variables we're going to use, we can proceed with the actual "code" (jargon for program). We usually find it easiest first to write and test the subroutines, and then to assemble the main program. (To be really honest, though, impulse and intuition do play an important role; that is, the program ends up structured and organized, but we don't necessarily get there in a linear, structured way!)

The following is our new version of the bar graph program using subroutines to "structure" the program:

```
100 '----NAME: "BAR-GRPH.B12"-------------------------------------
110 '
114 '----*********************
116 '----* MAKING A BAR GRAPH *------by B.E.---------------------
120 '----*********************
130 '
140 CLS: KEY OFF
150 '=================
160 GOSUB 5000                     'SUBROUTINE PRINTs title
170 '=================
180 WIDTZ = 4                      'defines width of bar
190 BARNUMBER = 12                 'defines number of bars
200 '=================
210 GOSUB 7000                     'SUBROUTINE draws and labels axes
220 '=================
230 LOCATE 3,1
240 PRINT "enter value (0-22)"
250 '
260 '----draws BARNUMBER of bars-------------------------------
270 '
280 FOR I = 1 TO BARNUMBER
290     LOCATE (I + 3), 1         'LOCATEs posit. of INPUT of VALUE
300     INPUT VALUE                'INPUTs VALUE to be graphed
310     IF VALUE = 99 THEN END     'means for prgm termination
320     LEFT = 8 + (WIDTZ + 1)*I   'defines LEFT side of bar
330     TOP = 23 - VALUE           'defines row equal to TOP of bar
340     '=================
350     GOSUB 6000                 'SUBROUTINE draws one bar
```

```
36Ø        '==================
37Ø NEXT I
38Ø END
5ØØØ '
5Ø1Ø '====SUBROUTINE PRINTs the title===============================
5Ø2Ø '
5Ø3Ø LOCATE 1, 22
5Ø4Ø COLOR 1,Ø                      'causes underlining
5Ø5Ø PRINT "MAKING A ";
5Ø6Ø COLOR 9,Ø                      'causes underlining, high int.
5Ø7Ø PRINT "BARGRAPH";
5Ø8Ø COLOR 1,Ø                      'back to just underlining
5Ø9Ø PRINT " OF 12 VALUES"
51ØØ COLOR 7,Ø                      'back to normal
511Ø RETURN                        'RETURNs to 17Ø
6ØØØ '
6Ø1Ø '====SUBROUTINE draws one bar=================================
6Ø2Ø '
6Ø3Ø FOR ROW = TOP TO 22           'controls height of bar
6Ø4Ø    LOCATE ROW, LEFT
6Ø5Ø    PRINT STRING$(4, CHR$(177)); 'PRINTs row of ASCII char. 177
6Ø6Ø NEXT ROW
6Ø7Ø RETURN                        'RETURNs to 36Ø
7ØØØ '
7Ø1Ø '====SUBROUTINE draws and labels axes=========================
7Ø2Ø '
7Ø3Ø '----left for reader as an exercise----
7Ø4Ø '
7Ø5Ø RETURN                        'RETURNs to 22Ø
```

Since the output of this program is the same as that of our original program at the end of Chapter 10, we won't show it again here.

This program can be divided into two major parts: the main program which ends at line 380, and the three subroutines beginning with line 5000. Looking over the main program, you can see that it follows our previous outline or list of jobs to be performed: it takes care of the preliminaries, calls the subroutine 5000 to display the title, initializes some variables, and calls subroutine 7000 to draw and label axes (which it doesn't actually do yet, since we want to leave something for you to do, but don't worry — the program will run fine without the subroutine beginning with line 7000). Finally, the program executes the FOR...NEXT loop beginning with line 280, requests input of the variable VALUE, and calls subroutine 6000 to draw the bar for each VALUE entered.

The statements within the subroutines are identical to the corresponding statements in our original bar graph program. The only aspect of this program that is new is the organization. In effect, with the use of GOSUB and RETURN, we've been able to group many BASIC statements into functional, logical units — our subroutines. By putting these subroutines at the end of the program, we are left with a main program that is relatively short and easy to follow. This organization also makes it easy to change many aspects of the program without affecting its overall organization. For example, if we wanted to change the bars from solid boxes, as they are in this program, to empty boxes, all we would have to do is to change the subroutine — an easy change since we already know how to program such a box (see Chapter 10). Or if the reader wanted to include labeled axes, this could also be easily accomplished through the subroutine.

ON GOSUB — Indexed Branching

The ON GOSUB statement is similar to the GOSUB statement in that both call subroutines. However, whereas GOSUB calls only the one subroutine specified by the line number following GOSUB, ON GOSUB chooses any one of a number of specified subroutines according to the value of an index. ON GOSUB is useful whenever a program needs to branch to one of several different subroutines.

The following program demonstrates how the ON GOSUB statement works:

```
10 INPUT INDEX
20 ON INDEX GOSUB 2000, 1000, 3000
30 END
40 '
1000 PRINT "Subroutine 1000 called by INDEX = 2"
1010 PLAY "02 C"
1020 RETURN
1030 '
2000 PRINT "Subroutine 2000 called by INDEX = 1"
2010 PLAY "03 C"
2020 RETURN
2030 '
3000 PRINT "Subroutine 3000 called by INDEX = 3"
3010 PLAY "04 C"
3020 RETURN
RUN
? 2
Subroutine 1000 called by index = 2    ← (the note "C" in octave #3 plays)
Ok
```

In this particular run, our response to the INPUT question mark assigned the value 2 to the variable INDEX. The output of this program demonstrates that the called subroutine begins with line 1000. In addition, it suggests that this particular subroutine (rather than one of the other two) is "chosen" by the value of the variable INDEX, which in this case is 2. Note that this subroutine is the second one listed right after GOSUB. Aha! So that's how ON GOSUB works: the INDEX value of 2 causes the program to select the *second* subroutine listed after GOSUB. If INDEX has the value 1, the program should branch to the *first* subroutine listed, which begins with line 2000, and similarly, if INDEX equals 3, the program should branch to the *third* subroutine listed. Note that the line numbers listed after GOSUB don't have to be in an ascending order.

The following diagram summarizes how ON GOSUB made its selection in the previous sample run:

```
2Ø ON 2 GOSUB 2ØØØ, 1ØØØ, 3ØØØ
         |            |
     index = 2    Calls 2nd subroutine
                  listed
```

The way ON GOSUB works for other index values is shown by this diagram:

```
2Ø ON {index} GOSUB 1ØØØ, 2ØØØ, 3ØØØ
              └ = 1 ──────┘      |     |
              └ = 2 ─────────────┘     |
              └ = 3 ───────────────────┘
```

Let's try a few more runs of our program to explore some of the fine points of ON GOSUB:

```
RUN
? 1.4
Subroutine 2ØØØ called by INDEX = 1
Ok
RUN
? Ø
Ok
```

The first RUN demonstrates that the value of INDEX is *rounded off*: the value of INDEX that is entered is 1.4, but that value is rounded off to 1 when used by ON GOSUB. If we had entered 1.6, ON GOSUB would have rounded off the 1.6 to 2 and caused branching to the second subroutine.

The second RUN shows what happens when there is no match between the index and the listed subroutines: the index we entered is 0, but there is no 0th subroutine listing (there's a 1st, a 2nd, and a 3rd, but no 0th). The result is that the program ignores the ON GOSUB statement and proceeds to the next line, the END statement. The same thing happens when an index larger than 3 (3.499999 to be precise!) is entered. An index equal to 0 or greater than the number of subroutines (or line numbers) listed after ON GOSUB causes program execution to "fall through" to the next line.

The ON GOSUB Statement

The ON GOSUB statement causes indexed branching. The statement

```
100 ON {index} GOSUB 1000,  5000,  2000, ....

Calls the listed              |      |      |
subroutine via the index:  index=1 index=2 index=3
```

That is,

an index value = 1 causes branching to the 1st listed line number (1000)

an index value = 2 causes branching to the 2nd listed line number (5000)

an index value = 3 causes branching to the 3rd listed line number (2000)

```
        *                                    *


        *                                    *
```

and so forth...

If the index has a rounded off value greater than the number of line numbers listed or if the index equals 0, then program execution falls through to the next line.

Writing a Menu Program — an Example Using ON GOSUB

When you go to a restaurant to eat dinner, you look at the menu, make a choice (you might *want* everything, but few of us can manage it!), and place your order with the waiter. You certainly don't want to go into the kitchen, wash the lettuce, scrub the potatoes, or clean the escargots. You go to restaurants precisely because you don't want to get involved in the details of cooking and in the mess of cleaning up afterwards.

Most people feel pretty much the same way about using computers: unless you're really "into" computers and computer languages, you probably wouldn't want to get involved in the details of operating and programming a computer in order to run a program. You want to see what programs are available and run them without having to know how to list, load, and run programs on that particular machine. What you'd like is a *menu* of programs or subprograms from which you can choose as easily as telling a waiter what you want.

A menu is a list of programs or subroutines from which the user can make a choice by following a set of instructions clearly visible somewhere on the menu. No knowledge of the computer system should be required to make your way through the set of listed programs.

To illustrate how such a menu might be written, we'll write a program that does the following:

1. Displays a menu that includes

   a. a title
   b. a list of selections, including an "exit menu" option
   c. an explanation of how to make the selection

2. Branches to the selected subroutine using an ON GOSUB statement.

3. Displays something on the screen with each subroutine for a short time. The length of the display time is controlled by another subroutine that causes a time delay.

4. Executes a RETURN at the end of each subroutine to return the user to the menu.

A serious set of programs having to do with such topics as finances, growth models, or learning math would most likely be very long. We've chosen an example that is fairly short (the main program is only 26 lines long) and uses some of the graphics techniques you learned in Chapter 10. What is more, the program has the virtue of not being terribly serious.

Here's what our program looks like:

```
100 '----NAME: "MENU.B12"----------------------------------------
101 '
102 '----*********************************************************
103 '----* PRGM DISPLAYS MENU; BRANCHES TO SUBR. FOR SELECTIONS *
104 '----*********************************************************
106 '
107 '----displays MENU---------------------------------------------
108 '
109 CLS
110 PRINT
120 PRINT TAB(20) "MENU OF DESIRABLE ITEMS"
130 PRINT: PRINT
140 PRINT TAB(10) "1. Sunshine"
150 PRINT TAB(10) "2. Happiness"
160 PRINT TAB(10) "3. A little love"
170 PRINT TAB(10) "4. Exit MENU"
180 PRINT
190 PRINT "To make a selection, ENTER number of selection (1-4)"
200 '
210 '----makes SELECTION-------------------------------------------
220 '
230 INPUT SELECTION
240 ON SELECTION GOSUB 1000, 2000, 3000, 260
250 GOTO 100
260 END
270 '
1000 '
1010 '====SUBROUTINE 1000 for sunshine=========================
1020 CLS
1030 FOR J = 1 TO 800                'prints screenful of suns
1040     PRINT CHR$(15) " ";
1050 NEXT
1060 '=============
1070 GOSUB 5000                      'calls subroutine for pause
1080 '=============
1090 RETURN
2000 '
2010 '====SUBROUTINE 2000 for happiness=========================
2020 CLS
2030 LOCATE 12,30
2040 PRINT STRING$(20, CHR$(1))      'prints row of faces
2050 '=============
2060 GOSUB 5000                      'calls subroutine for pause
2070 '=============
2080 RETURN
3000 '
```

```
3010 '====SUBROUTINE 3000 for a little love=====================
3020 CLS
3030 LOCATE 12, 40
3040 COLOR 16,7                    'blinking and reverse image
3050 PRINT CHR$(3)                 'prints throbbing heart
3060 '=============
3070 GOSUB 5000                    'calls subroutine for pause
3080 '=============
3090 COLOR 7,0
3100 RETURN
5000 '
5010 '====SUBROUTINE for pause=================================
5020 '
5030 FOR T = 1 TO 5000
5040 NEXT
5050 RETURN
```

When run, this program presents the following menu:

```
              MENU OF DESIRABLE ITEMS


         1. Sunshine
         2. Happiness
         3. A little love
         4. Exit MENU

To make a selection, ENTER number of selection (1-4)
? _
```

The above menu is straightforward and unambiguous, if not a bit questionable in content! We did assume that the user knows what ENTER means — a safe assumption in this case since you couldn't have gotten this far in the book without knowing that. For a general use program, however, even that has to be explained.

How does this program work? Don't be overwhelmed by its length: the main program is very simple and short. Most of the program is taken up by subroutines that are called by the main program.

The main program (which ends at line 260) has two parts. The first part (lines 100 to 190) simply prints the menu. The second part is responsible for the selection of the subroutines. Line 230 asks the user for input to the variable SELECTION, which then is used as the index in the following ON GOSUB statement to control branching to the chosen subroutine. For example, if SELECTION is assigned the value 2 (by user response to INPUT), then the second listed subroutine beginning with line 2000 is chosen. If the user inputs the number 4, then the fourth listed subroutine is called — the END statement in line 260. Notice that this particular "subroutine" doesn't end with the customary RETURN. Generally, all subroutines should end with a RETURN (you won't get an error message if you don't include one, but you run the risk of confusing and messing up the internal workings of BASIC). One exception to this rule is the special case in which the subroutine executes an END statement.

The remainder of the program consists of four subroutines. The first three print something on the screen; they can be called by the main program. However, the fourth subroutine beginning with line 5000 is called by the other three subroutines. This is an example of *nested subroutines* — that is, a subroutine calling another subroutine.

This nested subroutine (line 5000) is used to produce a delay in program execution. It's called by the other subroutines in order to delay the return to the menu so that the user has time to investigate and enjoy the (graphic) output of each subroutine. If we didn't include this pause, the output would just be a flash on the screen!

The three main subroutines (1000, 2000, 3000) consist of graphics statements with which you're already familiar, so we won't go into any details about them. Even though you can easily figure out what they do, go ahead and run this program — you'll enjoy it!

KEY(*n*) ON and ON KEY(*n*) GOSUB — Calling a Subroutine Anytime, Anywhere

The ON KEY(*n*) GOSUB statement available in Advanced BASIC (BASICA) allows us to call a subroutine at any time during program execution by pressing a key that has been "activated" by the KEY(*n*) ON statement. This pair of powerful statements makes it possible for the user to interact with the computer any time while the program is running.

The following example shows how this pair of statements works:

```
10 KEY(1) ON
20 ON KEY(1) GOSUB 500
30 GOTO 30
40 '
```

```
500 PRINT "hello, this is your subroutine 500; you called?"
510 RETURN
RUN
hello, this is your subroutine 500; you called?        ← result of pressing key ( F1 )
hello, this is your subroutine 500; you called?
```

In the above example, we pressed key (F1) twice. Key (F1) refers to the *function key* (F1) at the upper left corner of your keyboard. If we press it again, the same phrase will be printed again — we can keep doing this forever *unless* we press (Ctrl) (Break) to get us out of the endless loop caused by line 30!

Activating a Function Key

Let's see how this program works. The first statement is KEY(1) ON. It tells your IBM PC to turn on or "activate" function key (F1). This means that, while the program is running, the following ON KEY(1) GOSUB 500 statement will respond to key F1. If we don't activate key (F1) in this way, ON KEY(1) GOSUB 500 simply won't work. That is, if we throw out line 10 in our program, pressing key (F1) wouldn't have any effect in the same sense that pushing your car's gas pedal doesn't do anything unless you first turn on the ignition key to start the engine. With the exception of a few keys like (Ctrl) (Break), the "special" keys on your keyboard don't have any effect if pressed while a program is being executed unless you take definite steps to change that. The KEY(1) ON statement activates the specific key F1 so that it will have an effect on the subsequent ON KEY(1) GOSUB 500 statement. KEY(1) ON is not to be confused with the look-alike KEY ON we've met before. KEY ON turns on the Soft Function Key Display; it has nothing to do with activating a particular function key for a very special purpose.

ON KEY(1) GOSUB 500 — Calling Subroutine 500 Whenever You Want

The second line of our program — ON KEY(1) GOSUB 500 — tells your IBM PC "whenever the user presses function key (F1), call the subroutine beginning with line 500." The way this works is that after executing a program line, your computer checks to see if function key (F1) has been pressed. If it hasn't, program execution resumes with the next statement; if it has, program execution branches to the subroutine beginning with line 500.

What's the purpose of the endless loop in line 30? If it wasn't there, you'd have to press function key (F1) awfully fast in order to call the subroutine before execution reaches the end of the program! (We didn't put in an END, though, since there really isn't any end in this program.) What happens when this program is run is that your computer very quickly *reads* the first two statements of the program and then literally gets stuck looping (going to line 30) — until function key (F1) is pressed. At that point, it temporarily steps out of this loop to do the job that you requested, which is to execute subroutine 500. After that job is done, the program returns to its looping, *waiting* for the next time function key (F1) is pressed.

One of the special features of ON KEY GOSUB is that, once it has been *read* by the computer, it can make its presence felt throughout the remainder of the program execution. Most BASIC statements have to await their turn to be executed. ON KEY GOSUB, on the other hand, can interrupt the program and be executed at any point within the program *whenever* the appropriate key (function key (F1) in our example) is pressed. Your IBM BASIC manual refers to this process as *key trapping*.

Also note that we've been talking about *pressing* key (F1), not entering it. After both KEY ON and ON KEY GOSUB have been *read* by your computer, the listed subroutine will be called whenever you *press* the activated key.

Keys that Can Be Activated

Which keys can be activated to call subroutines? It depends on the particular version of your operating system.

If you have DOS 1.1, the keys that can be activated are:

1. Soft function keys (F1) through (F10), having key numbers 1 through 10.

2. The cursor control keys on your numeric keypad designated by key numbers

11 for the (↑) key
12 for the (←) key
13 for the (→) key
14 for the (↓) key.

If you have DOS 2.0, the keys that can be activated are:

1. The soft function keys (F1) through (F10), having key numbers 1 through 10.

2. The cursor control keys on your numeric keypad designated by key numbers

11 for the ↑ key
12 for the ← key
13 for the → key
14 for the ↓ key
15 to 20 for any other key on your keypad (see your IBM *BASIC*
manual for details on how to activate these keys).

The particular key that is activated appears in the parenthesis in KEY(*n*)
ON. For example,

```
5Ø KEY(13) ON
```

activates the right cursor control ((→)) key. Similarly, the number inside the
parenthesis of ON KEY(*n*) GOSUB defines the key that will cause
branching to the listed subroutine. For example,

```
6Ø ON KEY(13) GOSUB 1ØØØ
```

will cause the subroutine 1000 to be called whenever the → key is
pressed. Note that subroutine 1000 may have nothing whatsoever to do
with cursor control; the result of pressing that key is completely up to
you, the programmer.

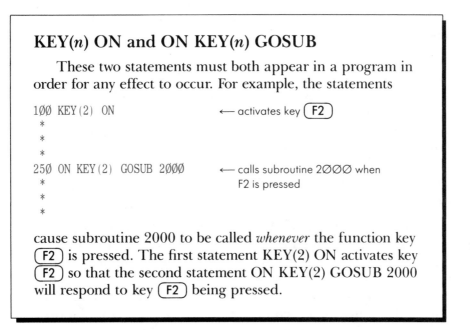

KEY(*n*) ON and ON KEY(*n*) GOSUB

These two statements must both appear in a program in
order for any effect to occur. For example, the statements

```
1ØØ KEY(2) ON
   *
   *
   *
25Ø ON KEY(2) GOSUB 2ØØØ
   *
   *
   *
```

← activates key F2

← calls subroutine 2ØØØ when
   F2 is pressed

cause subroutine 2000 to be called *whenever* the function key
F2 is pressed. The first statement KEY(2) ON activates key
F2 so that the second statement ON KEY(2) GOSUB 2000
will respond to key F2 being pressed.

KEY(*n*) OFF and KEY(*n*) STOP — Deactivating Your Keys

Whenever a program ends (via the END statement) or is terminated with (Ctrl) (Break) (as was the case in our example), all the previously activated keys are automatically restored to their normal function. Soft Function Key (F1) will once more print LIST on your screen.

There may be occasions when you need to deactivate previously activated keys while your program is still running. One way to do this is by means of the KEY(*n*) OFF statement, where the number in the parenthesis indicates which key is being deactivated. For example,

```
120 KEY(1) OFF
```

has the effect of deactivating key (F1).

Another way to deactivate a key is by means of the KEY(*n*) STOP statement. It differs from KEY(*n*) OFF in that it "remembers" if the key has been pressed; when the key is reactivated with KEY(*n*) ON, the subroutine associated with the "remembered" key is then called. For example,

```
120 KEY(1) STOP
```

will deactivate key (F1). If you press key (F1), no program interruption and subroutine call takes place. However, if later in the program the statement

```
200 KEY(1) ON
```

appears, the subroutine associated with key (F1) (through a statement like ON KEY(1) GOSUB 500) is immediately called. Use KEY(*n*) STOP whenever your program needs to shield itself temporarily from key interruptions.

An Example Using ON KEY(*n*) GOSUB — Moving Your Cursor

We'd like to show you how ON KEY(*n*) GOSUB can be used very effectively in an interactive graphics program. We'll start with a very simple program and work our way up to the last program in this chapter which is presented as an exercise problem and which will allow us to place musical notes on a staff that will then be played by your IBM PC.

One of the things we'll need for this final program is the ability to move the cursor while the program is in progress. You probably realize that normally while a program is running your cursor is invisible, and even if it weren't, the cursor control keys wouldn't work. The following example shows how we can make the $\rightarrow$ key work as such during program execution:

```
10 LOCATE 12,1,1          'positions cursor and makes it visible
20 KEY(13) ON
30 ON KEY(13) GOSUB 100
40 GOTO 40
50 '
100 PRINT CHR$(28);       'SUBROUTINE moves cursor to the RIGHT
110 RETURN
```

Go ahead and run this program. Whenever you press the $\rightarrow$ key (number 13), the cursor moves to the right! As with the previous program, you have to press Ctrl Break to terminate the program.

How does it work? Line 10 uses LOCATE to locate the cursor to row 12 and column 1 so that it will be out of the way of the program listing (we've talked about this use of LOCATE in Chapter 3). However, the last 1 in LOCATE 12,1,1 is a feature we haven't discussed before. It causes the cursor to be visible. A 0 in the third position (the last one here) in place of the 1 would make the cursor invisible; that's the default state of LOCATE. See Figure 12-2 for a summary of this more complete form of LOCATE. Incidentally, there's even more to LOCATE (although we won't explain it here): it controls the vertical size and position of the cursor within the character space as well.

The next two statements are familiar. The KEY(13) ON statement in line 20 activates key number 13, the $\rightarrow$ key. ON KEY(13) GOSUB 100 calls subroutine 100 whenever the $\rightarrow$ key is pressed. Line 100, however, does something surprising: it makes use of the IBM ASCII character number 28, which causes the cursor to move right when it is printed. Note that it's the subroutine that moves the cursor, not the cursor control

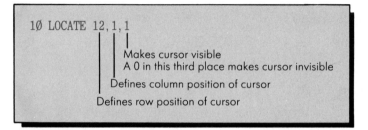

Figure 12-2. Cursor visibility control with LOCATE

key; all that key does is to call the subroutine. Line 40 causes the usual endless loop which keeps the program going.

Let's take the next step and write a program that allows you to move the cursor anywhere on the screen (while the program is running) and to place an ASCII character at the cursor position. Using the previous example as a building block, we've come up with the following program:

```
100 '----NAME: "CURSMOVE.B12"-------------------------------------
101 '
102 '----*****************************************************
103 '----* PRGM LETS USER MOVE CURSOR & PRINT CHARACTER ANYWHERE *
104 '----*****************************************************
105 '
109 CLS
110 KEY(1) ON                   'activates keys
120 FOR KEYNUMBER = 11 TO 14
130     KEY(KEYNUMBER) ON
140 NEXT
150 '
160 LOCATE ,,1                  'makes cursor visible
170 '
180 ON KEY(11) GOSUB 1000       'traps keys and branches to sub.
190 ON KEY(12) GOSUB 1100
200 ON KEY(13) GOSUB 1200
210 ON KEY(14) GOSUB 1300
220 ON KEY(1)  GOSUB 1500
230 '
240 GOTO 240                    'keeps program RUNing
250 '
1000 PRINT CHR$(30);            'SUBROUTINE moves cursor UP
1010 RETURN
1020 '
1100 PRINT CHR$(29);            'SUBROUTINE moves cursor LEFT
1110 RETURN
1120 '
1200 PRINT CHR$(28);            'SUBROUTINE moves cursor RIGHT
1210 RETURN
1220 '
1300 PRINT CHR$(31);            'SUBROUTINE moves cursor DOWN
1310 RETURN
1320 '
1500 PRINT CHR$(2);             'SUBROUTINE prints smiling face
1510 RETURN
```

The first part of the program (lines 100 to 140) activates the cursor control keys. They are convenient keys to use for this purpose since we're already used to moving the cursor that way. LOCATE ,,1 makes the cursor visible. The commas tell the computer that the 1 is in the third position; leaving out row, and column positions causes LOCATE to leave row and column positions unaltered. That's fine, since we're using LOCATE only to make the cursor visible, not to position it.

The ON KEY(*n*) GOSUB statements on lines 180 to 220 cause the *key trapping* and the subsequent calling of the various subroutines. There are five subroutines: the first four cause cursor movement. The last one (line 1500) prints the ASCII character "2" (we just happen to like this one).

This whole program itself can be used as a subroutine within another program that requires this sort of screen input from the user. For example, we could use this technique to write a menu program in which the selection is made by moving the cursor to the line of your choice and then pressing, say, key 1. This is a way to make a more exciting and visually oriented menu.

Summary

In this chapter, you have learned how to use most of the major statements that allow you to create sophisticated subroutines and also to manipulate them. The combination of the GOSUB and RETURN statements allows you to call a subroutine that will branch back to the main program. ON GOSUB gives you the added flexibility of having the program choose a particular subroutine according to the value of an index variable. With ON GOSUB, your programs become responsive to a range of user inputs.

Even more sophisticated are the KEY(*n*) ON and ON KEY(*n*) statements, which make it possible for the user to interact with the program at any time during the program's execution; the user of your program, whether it is you or someone else, may call a subroutine at any time simply by pressing a particular key. Finally, the KEY(*n*) OFF and KEY(*n*) STOP statements allow you to deactivate these same keys used to call various subroutines while the program is running. (Ctrl) (Break) can always be used to interrupt the entire program in mid-stream.

The practice problem presented below gathers together most of these concepts and statements as well as some of the techniques we studied in earlier chapters. Be sure to take a look at this problem and the program we wrote in response to it. We think you'll enjoy it!

Exercise

Write a program that draws a musical staff on your screen; allows the user to manipulate the (visible) cursor by means of the usual cursor control keys; lets the user place a note (no sharps or flats — for a start, anyway) on the staff via key (F1); then uses PLAY to play the note so placed; and finally, when you're ready to quit, the program should terminate when you press function key (F10).

Solution

Here's how we solved this problem:

```
100 '----NAME: "NOTES.B12"--by BE-------------------------------
101 '
102 '----*****************************************************
103 '----* PGRM PLAYS NOTE THAT USER PLACES ON MUSICAL STAFF *---
104 '----*****************************************************
105 '
109 CLS: KEY OFF
110 '=============
120 GOSUB 2000                    'draws staff
130 '=============
140 ROW = 15
150 COL = 1
160 LOCATE ROW,COL,1             'locates and makes cursor visible
170 '
180 '----activates keys 1, 11-14---------------------------------
190 '
200 KEY(1) ON
210 FOR KEYNUM% = 10 TO 14
220     KEY(KEYNUM%) ON
230 NEXT
250 '
260 '----traps keys and branches to subroutines-----------------
270 '
280 ON KEY(11) GOSUB 1000        'moves cursor up
300 ON KEY(13) GOSUB 1200        'moves cursor right
310 ON KEY(14) GOSUB 1300        'moves cursor down
320 ON KEY(1)  GOSUB 1500        'prints and plays notes
330 ON KEY(10) GOSUB 350         'terminates program
340 GOTO 340                     'keeps program running
350 END
360 '
```

```
1000 PRINT CHR$(30);   '==========SUBROUTINE moves cursor UP=====
1010 ROW = ROW - 1                'updates ROW
1020 RETURN
1030 '
1200 PRINT CHR$(28);   '==========SUBROUTINE moves cursor RIGHT===
1210 RETURN
1220 '
1300 PRINT CHR$(31);   '==========SUBROUTINE moves cursor DOWN====
1310 ROW = ROW + 1                'updates ROW
1320 RETURN
1330 '
1500 PRINT CHR$(219); '==========SUBROUTINE prints and plays note
1510 '
1520 IF ROW = 15 THEN PLAY "O3 C"
1530 IF ROW = 14 THEN PLAY "O3 D"
1540 IF ROW = 13 THEN PLAY "O3 E"
1550 IF ROW = 12 THEN PLAY "O3 F"
1560 IF ROW = 11 THEN PLAY "O3 G"
1570 IF ROW = 10 THEN PLAY "O3 A"
1580 IF ROW = 9  THEN PLAY "O3 B"
1590 IF ROW = 8  THEN PLAY "O4 C"
1600 IF ROW = 7  THEN PLAY "O4 D"
1610 IF ROW = 6  THEN PLAY "O4 E"
1620 RETURN
1630 '
2000 LOCATE 5,1    '===============SUBROUTINE draws staff=========
2010 FOR ROW = 1 TO 5
2020      STAFFLINE$ = STRING$(70, CHR$(196))
2030      PRINT STAFFLINE$
2040      PRINT
2050 NEXT
2060 LOCATE 20,1                    'instructions to user
2070 PRINT "Use Cursor Control Keys to move cursor"
2080 PRINT "Use key F1 to place and PLAY a note"
2090 PRINT "Use key F10 to end program";
3000 LOCATE 18,1
3010 RETURN
```

The following is an example of what your screen might look like while you're running this program:

If you can read music, then you'll know what this sounds like! We've come a long way! You may wish to embellish this program with the options for different length notes, and include sharps and flats. Also, after we learn about *arrays* in a later chapter in the book, you could make the program *remember* the notes you entered — and then play them back all at once! The possibilities are virtually endless.

Data and Arrays — Organizing Information

In Chapter 5 we learned about variables; we saw both how to use variables and how to assign values to them. A variable is a symbolic representation of one piece or unit of information, like a number or a phrase (that is, a string). Many programming problems, however, require the handling of large bodies of information: values have to be assigned to a large number of variables, and large blocks of these variables have to be manipulated in some way. This chapter is about the efficient storage of data by means of DATA and READ statements, and the powerful method of organizing and manipulating information by means of what are called *arrays*.

DATA and READ Statements — Storing and Reading Large Amounts of Information

Suppose we are writing a program that requires us to assign the number of a month to a variable having the name of that month. We could fulfill our objective by using 12 statements, of which the first few look like this:

```
1Ø JAN = 1
2Ø FEB = 2
3Ø MAR = 3
    *
    *
    *
```

That's fine, although these statements take up 12 lines in our program. What if we needed to assign calories to 1000 different food variables? We'd need to write 1000 program lines! There has *got* to be a better way to do this!

BASIC comes to the rescue with the DATA and the READ statements. The following program makes the same assignments as the previous statements, except it uses DATA and READ:

```
1Ø DATA 1,2,3,4,5,6
2Ø READ  JAN, FEB, MAR, APR, MAY, JUN
3Ø PRINT JAN; FEB; MAR; APR; MAY; JUN
4Ø END
RUN
 1  2  3  4  5  6
Ok
```

From this output you can see that indeed JAN has the value 1, FEB the value 2, and so forth. It's easy to see how these assignments were made: the numbers following DATA in line 10 are values, and these values are assigned to the variables listed after READ (in line 20) in their proper order. For example, the third variable listed after READ is MAR, and it is assigned the third value listed after DATA. We can visualize this assignment process like this:

```
1Ø DATA  1,      2,      3,      4,      5,      6
         ↓       ↓       ↓       ↓       ↓       ↓
2Ø READ JAN;    FEB;    MAR;    APR,    MAY;    JUN
```

Notice that the DATA statement doesn't really "do" anything; it's an example of what is called a *nonexecutable statement*. In other words, your computer simply stores the information listed after DATA. It is the READ statement that actually does the job of reading the values listed after DATA and assigning these values, in order, to the variables listed after READ.

The previous example is straightforward. But there are many different ways to use DATA and READ, and a corresponding number of do's and don'ts.

Match between the DATA List and Variable List

What if we don't use READ to read the whole list of values after DATA? That's no more of a problem than going to the grocery store and buying only a part of the items on your grocery list; if you really do want all the items, you can always go back for the rest.

Try this with the previous program by eliminating the last variable in the READ statement — JUN — and running the program. The output will be the same as before, except that the last number printed out will be a 0, the value of JUN. Since no value was explicitly assigned to the variable JUN, BASIC, as usual, assigns the default value of 0.

However, what if we run out of DATA values; that is, what happens if the number of variables listed after READ exceeds the number of values listed after DATA? Let's try it:

```
1Ø DATA 1, 2, 3, 4, 5,
2Ø READ  JAN, FEB, MAR, APR, MAY, JUN
3Ø PRINT JAN; FEB; MAR; APR; MAY; JUN
4Ø END
RUN
Out of DATA in 2Ø
Ok
```

The message is clear: we ran out of DATA because the sixth variable JUN listed after READ has no corresponding sixth value in DATA. Some error messages may seem a bit ambiguous, but this one is right to the point.

There is a second requirement associated with the READ and DATA statements: namely, that the variable type match the value type. Since using READ and DATA is basically a process of assigning values to variables, all the rules for assigning variables apply — including the requirement of type matching.

Consider the following example in which READ assigns string variables:

```
1Ø DATA grapes, parsley, tripe, "apple pie"
2Ø READ  food1$, food2$, food3$, food4$
3Ø PRINT food1$, food2$, food3$, food4$
4Ø END
RUN
grapes         parsley        tripe          apple pie
Ok
```

There's nothing really surprising here except that we used quotation
marks around "apple pie" — or rather, that we *didn't* use quotation marks
to identify all the other string values! In the past, when we assigned a
string constant to a string variable (by means of an equal sign), we always
had to bracket the string constant with quotation marks. This
requirement is relaxed in the DATA statement: if the variables listed after
READ are string variables, READ "knows" that it should interpret the
values listed after DATA as string constants.

Thus, for one-word string constants such as the first three foods in
our example, quotation marks are optional. However, quotation marks *are*
required for the last string constant listed ("apple pie") because it
contains a space. The general rule is that quotation marks around string
constants are optional *unless* that string constant contains spaces or
punctuation that BASIC would otherwise confuse with its own
vocabulary of characters, such as commas and semicolons.

DATA Can Be Anywhere

Because DATA is a nonexecutable statement, it can be located
anywhere in your program. When READ is executed, it will look for the
DATA statement — and find it, wherever it is. We needn't point out,
however, that in a well-organized program, you wouldn't put your DATA
statements just *anywhere*. Among the preferred locations are the
beginning of a program, near the end of a program, or adjacent to the
READ statements.

Furthermore, you can have more than one DATA statement. The
important thing to note here is that READ will "read" a series of DATA
statements as *one* list. To illustrate this, let's break up the DATA statement
in our example program into two separate statements:

```
1Ø DATA 1, 2, 3
2Ø READ  JAN, FEB, MAR, APR, MAY, JUN
3Ø PRINT JAN; FEB; MAR; APR; MAY; JUN
4Ø DATA 4, 5, 6
5Ø END
RUN
 1  2  3  4  5  6
Ok
```

This works just fine! In addition to splitting up our original DATA statement into two DATA statements (lines 10 and 40), we put the second DATA statement *after* the READ statement to illustrate that it doesn't matter where DATA is located. READ always interprets the values listed after DATA *as a single list*, even though this list may be split up into several different DATA statements in different locations. Every time READ assigns a value from a DATA list, it moves an imaginary pointer to the next value in the DATA list that is to be assigned, wherever the next value in the DATA list is located in the program as a whole. Figure 13-1 illustrates the way DATA is read in the previous program:

Multiple READ Statements

Just as DATA statements can be split up, so can READ statements. Several READ statements may be used to read a DATA list. Let's split up the READ statement in the program we used in the beginning of this chapter:

```
1Ø DATA 1, 2, 3, 4, 5, 6
2Ø READ JAN, FEB, MAR
3Ø READ APR, MAY, JUN
4Ø PRINT JAN FEB MAR APR MAY JUN
5Ø END
RUN
 1  2  3  4  5  6
Ok
```

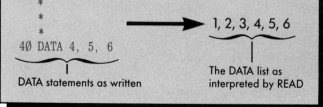

Figure 13-1. Successive DATA statements form a single list

No problem: after the first READ statement in line 20 is finished reading JAN, FEB, and MAR, the second READ statement on line 30 takes over where the first one left off and reads APR, MAY, and JUN. The second READ statement gets in line after the first one, and keeps the pointer moving as if all the variables were listed after one READ statement.

The DATA and READ Statements

DATA and READ appear in a program in the following way:

```
100 DATA 1, 2, 3
110 DATA 4, 5, 6
       *
       *
       *
230 READ A, B, C, D
```

DATA statements are nonexecutable statements that form a single list of DATA that can be read by the READ statement.

READ assigns values from the DATA list to the corresponding variables listed after READ. In the example above, the variables A,B,C,D are assigned the values 1,2,3,4 in that order. Multiple READ statements have the same effect as a single READ statement that contains the combined list of variables.

RESTORE — Going Back to the Beginning

Sometimes it is necessary to be able to read a DATA list more than once. For example, if our previous program were part of a subroutine that is called more than once, the READ statement would try to read the DATA list as many times as the subroutine is called.

But there's a hitch. Remember that every time *any* READ statement reads a value from a DATA list, it reads the value after the last value that was read (the pointer just keeps on going down the list). When READ is executed for a second time, all the data has already been read, and, as you might expect, you'll get an "Out of DATA in xx" response from your computer.

The way out of this difficulty is to use the RESTORE statement before you use READ again to read a DATA list. The following example shows how to read the variables JAN, FEB, and MAR three times:

```
1Ø DATA 1, 2, 3, 4, 5, 6
2Ø FOR J = 1 TO 3
3Ø    READ JAN, FEB, MAR
4Ø    PRINT JAN FEB MAR
5Ø    RESTORE        ←— Restores pointer to beginning of DATA list
6Ø NEXT
7Ø END
RUN
 1 2 3
 1 2 3
 1 2 3
Ok
```

That's the output we want: no matter how many times READ assigns values to JAN, FEB and MAR, we always want those values to be 1, 2, and 3. The function of the RESTORE statement is to restore the DATA pointer to the first value in the DATA list so that the second (and third) time the READ statement is executed (in the second and third loop), it again begins reading the DATA list from the beginning: JAN again is assigned the first value in the DATA list, FEB, the second, and so forth.

It might help you to see what would happen if we neglected to include the RESTORE statement. The following is the output of our previous program with the RESTORE statement in line 50 deleted:

```
RUN
 1 2 3
 4 5 6
Out of DATA in 5Ø
Ok
```

That makes sense, doesn't it? The DATA is read sequentially until we run out of DATA.

An Example — The Number of Days Elapsed Since January 1

If you want to calculate the amount of interest earned since you invested your money, one of the things you'll need to know is the number of days that your money has been invested. Many business calculations (and scientific calculations as well) require that you know the number of days that have elapsed between two given days. We won't give a general solution to this problem, but we will give you a building block by showing you how to find the number of days that have elapsed since January 1.

Let's begin by writing a program that finds the number of days that have elapsed between January 1 and the first day of a given month. We'll use a DATA statement to list the number of days in each month:

```
100 DATA 31, 28, 31, 30, 31, 30, 31, 31, 30, 31, 30, 31
110 INPUT "enter month (1-12)--", MONTH
120 DAYS = 0
130 FOR M = 1 TO (MONTH - 1)
140     READ DAYS.MO
150     DAYS = DAYS + DAYS.MO
160 NEXT
170 PRINT DAYS "days have elapsed since Jan. 1"
180 END
RUN
enter month (1-12)--3
 59 days have elapsed since Jan. 1
Ok
```

This is how the program works. First, the DATA statement lists the number of days in each month. Then INPUT asks the user to enter the number of the MONTH — the program determines the number of days between January 1 and the first of the month the user enters. The rest of the program is best explained by following the particular example run shown. Our response of 3 to INPUT causes the value 3 to be assigned to MONTH, so that the FOR...NEXT loop is executed two times. The first time the loop is executed, the READ statement in line 140 reads the first number in the DATA list — the number of days in January — and the following statement (line 150) adds that number to the existing value of DAYS, which is zero. So the new value of DAYS is 31, the number of days in January. The second time the loop is executed, line 140 reads the second number in the DATA list — the number of days in February — and line 150 adds that value to the existing value of DAYS. The new value of DAYS now is 31 + 28, which equals 59 — the number of days up to March 1! In general, every time the loop is executed, it causes the number of days in the next month to be added to the existing total of DAYS. We want this process to continue until we get to the final result we're looking for.

Now we're ready to tackle the following problem: write a program that determines the number of days between a date entered and January first of the same year. Assume that we are not dealing with a leap year. The following is our solution:

```
100 '----NAME: "DAYSELAP.B13"--------------------------------------
102 '
110 '----****************************************
120 '----* PRGM FINDS DAYS ELAPSED SINCE JAN 1 *-------------------
130 '----****************************************
140 '
145 KEY OFF: CLS
150 DATA "MB 04 C16 E16 G16 05 C10 P16 04 G16 05 C"
160 READ NOTES$
170 '
180 DATA 31, 28, 31, 30, 31, 30, 31, 31, 30, 31, 30, 31
190 '
200 '----INPUT AND INPUT INSTRUCTIONS-----------------------------
210 '
220 PRINT TAB(18) "DAYS ELAPSED SINCE JANUARY 1"
230 PRINT: PRINT
240 PRINT "To determine the number of days elapsed since Jan 1"
250 PRINT
260 INPUT "     enter month (1 - 12)-----", FINAL.MO
270 INPUT "     enter the day (1 - 31)---", DAY.FINAL
280 PRINT
290 '
300 '----MAIN PROGRAM: finds elapsed days------------------------
310 '
320 FOR MO = 1 TO FINAL.MO - 1
330     READ DAY.MO                      'READs DATA from 180
340     DAYS = DAYS + DAY.MO
350 NEXT
360 DAYS.TOT = DAY.FINAL + DAYS - 1
370 '
380 '----PRGRM OUTPUT----------------------------------------------
390 '
400 PLAY NOTES$
410 PRINT "====" DAYS.TOT " days have elapsed since Jan. 1 ===="
420 PRINT
430 END
```

An example output looks like this:

```
                    DAYS ELAPSED SINCE JANUARY 1

      enter month (1 - 12)-----6
      enter the day (1 - 31)---2

==== 152 days have elapsed since Jan. 1 ====        ← music PLAYS

Ok
```

Having gone through the previous example, you'll have no problem understanding this program. It is a good example of how DATA and READ statements can be used to store and read a fixed body of information.

Arrays, Subscripts, and Dimensions — Of Lists and Checkerboards

Different variables represent different quantities. So far, we've done something that seems perfectly obvious: we've used different variable names to represent these different variables (or quantities). For example, the statements

```
1Ø DATA DO, RE, MI
2Ø READ TONE1$, TONE2$, TONE3$
```

assign values DO, RE, MI to the variables TONE1$, TONE2$ TONE3$, which clearly have different names. We chose very similar names, however, (differing only in the numbers 1, 2, and 3) to indicate that all three variables represent similar quantities: namely, musical notes. In applications like this one, in which you need to assign and manipulate related groups of variables, it is often convenient and sometimes essential to use a similar but much more powerful approach called *arrays*.

An array is a group of variables that all have the same array name. The different members within the group (that is, the variables) are called *array elements*, which are identified by a number called the *subscript*. An example of an array element is

where NOTE$ is the array name and the 2 in parentheses is the subscript. Note that the subscript in an array is *always* bracketed by parentheses, and that other array elements have the *same name* but *different subscripts*. For example, the next element in the array NOTE$ is

NOTE$ (3)

Arrays can be assigned values in the same way that "normal" variables are assigned values. For example, the values DO, RE, MI can be assigned to an array using the familiar DATA and READ statements:

```
1Ø DATA DO, RE, MI
2Ø READ NOTE$(1), NOTE$(2), NOTE$(3)
3Ø PRINT NOTE$(1), NOTE$(2), NOTE$(3)
RUN
DO           RE           MI
Ok
```

The output verifies that elements of the array NOTE$ defined by subscripts 1, 2, and 3 are assigned the values DO, RE, MI. Going back to our idea of variable boxes, we can represent this array as shown in Figure 13-2. We placed the array element boxes in a neat, ordered row to suggest that array elements do form an ordered unit or block of information. Your IBM PC actually stores array values in adjacent memory locations.

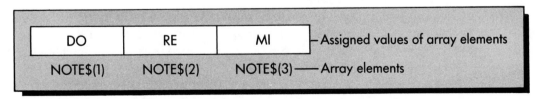

Figure 13-2. Array elements in memory

The power of arrays lies in our ability to refer to the elements in the array by their subscripts. Let's rewrite the previous program using a more sophisticated approach that takes advantage of this feature:

```
1Ø DATA DO, RE, MI
2Ø FOR J = 1 TO 3
3Ø    READ NOTE$(J)
4Ø NEXT
5Ø '
6Ø FOR J = 1 TO 3
7Ø    PRINT NOTE$(J)
8Ø NEXT
9Ø END
RUN
DO              RE             MI
Ok
```

Line 30 reads successive array elements with each execution of the FOR...NEXT loop between lines 20 and 40. That's possible only because each array element is identified by its subscript. Similarly, the loop in lines 60 to 80 prints successive array elements.

If you only have three notes to READ and to PRINT (or PLAY), arrays don't offer any overwhelming advantage over any other method. But what if you wanted to READ and PRINT 40 notes? — or a 150? Now it's beginning to make sense! We'll explore the uses of arrays further in a later section, but first we need to take a look at a few rules.

Array Names and Subscripts — A Few Rules

The rules for naming arrays are identical to the rules for naming variables. Our array NOTE$ ends with a dollar sign ($) since the values we assign to it are string constants. Integer or single-precision floating point arrays don't need to end in any special characters, although memory will be allocated more efficiently for integer arrays if you do type-declare them in this way. Since the array name is the same for all the array elements, all values assigned to an array must be of the same type: you can't mix integer with string values, for example, unless you have an appetite for error messages!

Default values for array elements are also assigned the same way as default values for "normal" variables. This means that if you PRINT STOCKVAL(5) without having explicitly assigned a value to the element, you'll get a 0.

What are the rules for subscripts? Subscripts themselves can be variables, although subscript values must be integers. The smallest subscript in our example is 1, and that agrees with our sense of the "first" array element or value. But run the following BASIC line:

```
10 PRINT MONEY(0)
RUN
 0
Ok
```

No error message — just a 0! We get a 0 because although we didn't assign a value to this "zeroth" element defined by the subscript 0 here, it does exist. Zero is always the lowest array element unless you make a special declaration through the OPTION statement (to be discussed later). In many applications, you can simply ignore this zeroth element if you wish.

What's the largest subscript value you can use? The answer has two parts: if you make what is called a *dimension* declaration by means of the DIM statement, the largest subscript allowed is 32767. If you don't make such a declaration (we haven't made one so far), the largest subscript allowed is 10.

The DIM Statement — Defining Your Arrays

An array represents an ordered group of values that are stored in your computer in adjacent memory locations. In order to keep other values that don't belong to the array from "butting" in, your computer needs to reserve a space in its memory for the whole array.

It does this in a way similar to the way a director of a theater might reserve seating space for the VIPs: he or she might assume 10 or fewer such VIPs will be coming, and accordingly stretch a ribbon across 10 seats before the theater doors open. On the other hand, if you as a theatre-goer wish to have a specified number of seats less than or greater than 10 saved for you, you'd have to make a special request. Like the director, your IBM PC will assume that any array you start using will have subscripts ranging from 0 to 10, unless you indicate otherwise, and it will reserve 11 adjacent memory locations. On the other hand, you can make an explicit request to reserve a specified amount of memory space (often *more* than what the computer would "assume" for subscripts up to 10 rather than *less*) by means of the DIM statement.

The following example shows how this is done. The statement

```
10 DIM NOTE$(12)
```

notifies your computer that you're going to use a string array called

NOTE$, and that it should reserve a block of memory for array elements having 12 as the largest subscript — that is, for 13 elements if zero is included. This DIM statement should be executed before the array is initialized or manipulated (it's usually placed near the beginning of a program) for the same reason that the theater seats have to be reserved before they get filled up by the general public.

A DIM statement for a particular array can only be executed once within a program. "Of course," you say, "why would I write it twice?" Well, chances are you wouldn't, but sometimes a program tries to execute it for a second time inadvertently via some kind of loop and you'll get the error message

Duplicate Definition in 1Ø

in the inimitable style of your IBM PC.

IBM PC BASIC's upper limit of the subscript is 32767 (a huge number), although your computer's memory capacity and your patience to initialize and manipulate such a huge array is more likely to be a limiting factor.

Aside from informing your computer of the name, type, and upper limit of the subscript, the DIM statement has another very important function: namely, to declare the *number* of subscripts that an array has. The number of subscripts an array has determines the array's *dimension*. All arrays we've discussed so far have just one subscript; hence all have been one-dimensional arrays. You can visualize a one-dimensional array as a list of elements (and corresponding values) that can be laid out in one dimension — that is, on a line. In that sense, a shopping list is a one-dimensional list or array.

The previous DIM NOTE$(12) statement defines the dimension of the array NOTE$ to be one because only one subscript is present. However, the statement

1Ø DIM CHESS$(8,8)

defines a two-dimensional array called CHESS$ because it lists the upper value of *two* subscripts (eight for both). Each element of this array is identified by two subscripts as in the element CHESS$(2,7). Such a two-dimensional array can be imagined as a surface or grid, in this case a chessboard (see Figure 13-3.)

Each square on this chessboard corresponds to an element of the array CHESS$, while each row number corresponds to a particular value of the *first* subscript, and each column number corresponds to a particular value of the *second* subscript. The *value* of an array element might be the name of the chess piece standing on the particular square. For example, the assignment

```
2Ø CHESS$(3,2) = "king"
```

could represent the king standing on the square defined by row 3 and column 2. We'll write some programs using two-dimensional arrays later in this chapter. At the moment we simply want to introduce the concept of dimension and the method for defining the dimension of an array.

It is possible and often quite useful to define arrays of more than two dimensions. A total of 255 dimensions are, in fact, permitted by BASIC, although arrays of more than three dimensions are relatively rare.

Now that we've gotten the basics out of the way, let's take a look at some examples that show how arrays are used to store and manipulate blocks of information.

Examples Using One-Dimensional Arrays

The fact that array elements can be referred to by their subscripts (and their array name, of course) is the key to their usefulness in handling large volumes of related information. Consider the following

Array CHESS$(8,8)

1,1	1,2	1,3	1,4	1,5	1,6	1,7	1,8
2,1	2,2	2,3	2,4	2,5	2,6	2,7	2,8
3,1	3,2	3,3	3,4	3,5	3,6	3,7	3,8
4,1	4,2	4,3	4,4	4,5	4,6	4,7	4,8
5,1	5,2	5,3	5,4	5,5	5,6	5,7	5,8
6,1	6,2	6,3	6,4	6,5	6,6	6,7	6,8
7,1	7,2	7,3	7,4	7,5	7,6	7,7	7,8
8,1	8,2	8,3	8,4	8,5	8,6	8,7	8,8

Array element CHESS$(3,2)

Figure 13-3. The chessboard: a two-dimensional array

program that prints the name of a musical note in response to the user's input of the note number (1 to 8):

```
1Ø DIM NOTE$(8)
2Ø DATA DO, RE, MI, FA, SO, LA, TI, DO
3Ø FOR J = 1 TO 8
4Ø    READ NOTES$(J)
5Ø NEXT
6Ø '
7Ø INPUT;"enter note number (1-8)--", J
8Ø PRINT "    the note is " NOTE$(J)
9Ø GOTO 5Ø
1ØØ END
RUN
enter note number (1-8)--3    the note is MI
enter note number (1-8)--6    the note is LA
Break in 7Ø
Ok
```

Notice the efficient way the array is "initialized" (that is, how values are assigned to the array elements) by means of the DATA and READ statements and a FOR...NEXT loop. For J = 1, READ assigns DO to the element NOTE$(1); for J = 2, READ assigns RE to element NOTE$(2), and so forth. This procedure is possible only because we can refer to each array element by its subscript; therein lies the power of arrays.

Arrays are also ideal vehicles for storing a large body of "flexible" or nonpermanent information. For example, consider the following program that plays a sequence of notes entered by the user:

```
1ØØ INPUT "enter number of notes to be played--", NUMBER
11Ø DIM NOTE$(NUMBER)
12Ø PRINT "enter any note accepted by PLAY: "
13Ø '
14Ø FOR J = 1 TO NUMBER        'initializes array NOTE$
15Ø    LINE INPUT NOTE$(J)
16Ø NEXT
17Ø '
18Ø FOR J = 1 TO NUMBER        'PLAYs back notes in array
19Ø    PLAY NOTE$(J)
2ØØ NEXT
21Ø END
RUN
enter number of notes to be played--5
enter any note accepted by PLAY:
```

```
C
E
D
F#
O2 A   ←— IBM PC now plays these 5 notes in given order
Ok
```

The statement DIM NOTE$(100) limits the number of array entries to 100, although the user can set the NUMBER of entries (notes, in this case) to any number less than or equal to 100 (we set it to 5 keep the example on this page!) The array is initialized by repetitions of a LINE INPUT statement (line 150), which is well suited for entering string constants that might have spaces in them, such as our last entry (O2 A refers to the A in the second octave). The last part of the program plays back the notes entered into the array NOTE$ all at once. We suspect that most children would enjoy playing with this program as much as we did!

The Heart of a Sort Routine — Finding the Smallest Number

The ability to refer to particular array elements by their subscripts makes possible some kinds of programming procedures that otherwise would be extremely cumbersome, if not impossible. Consider the apparently simple task of taking a list of numbers and rearranging them in order from the smallest to the largest. Such a sort routine is also related to alphabetizing a sequence of words and is therefore a commonly used type of program (lists of names, purchase order numbers, dates, and so on). We won't take on the whole task of writing such a program, but we will show you one essential building block of all sort routines: namely, a program that finds the smallest number in a series of numbers. Here it goes:

```
100 DIM NUMBER(10)
110 DATA 5,6,4,9,14,3,7,14,9,10
120 '
130 FOR J = 1 TO 10
140     READ NUMBER(J)
150     PRINT NUMBER(J)
160 NEXT
170 '
180 TEST = 1000
190 FOR J = 1 to 5
200     IF NUMBER(J) < THEN TEST = NUMBER(J)
```

```
210 NEXT
220 PRINT
230 PRINT "the smallest number =" TEST
240 END
RUN
 5  6  4  9  14  3  7  14  9  10
the smallest number = 3
Ok
```

Sure enough, 3 *is* the smallest number in this list! The first part of this program is old hat by now: the array NUMBER is defined and is initialized with the given DATA, and the values of the array's elements (the values in DATA) are printed. Line 180 begins the routine that tests for the smallest number in the array. It assigns a value 1000 to the variable TEST, which will later be used as a yardstick to which the elements in the array will be compared. The size of this number doesn't really matter as long as it is larger than any of the numbers in the array.

Line 200 is the key statement in this program: it checks to see whether the array element NUMBER(J) is smaller than TEST. If it is not, program execution drops right through to NEXT, and another loop will begin (if J isn't bigger than 10). If NUMBER(J) *is* less than TEST, then that particular value of NUMBER(J) is assigned to variable TEST. This causes TEST to have a value equal to the smallest value of NUMBER(J) encountered up to this point. By the time all elements of the array NUMBER have been checked in this manner (this happens with the last loop when J = 5) TEST will have a value equal to the smallest member of the list of numbers in the array. Voila!

Examples Using Two-Dimensional Arrays

Sometimes it is necessary to be able to refer to an array element by *two* subscripts. Such two-dimensional arrays can be visualized as a two-dimensional grid having a certain number of squares or elements in one direction (the horizontal), and another number of elements in the perpendicular direction (the vertical). As we mentioned earlier, a chessboard is a good example of an 8 by 8-element array: eight squares in the horizontal direction, and eight squares in the vertical. Other examples of two-dimensional arrays are shown in Table 13-1.

We'll develop the multiplication table array because it is simple and yet it demonstrates some of the powerful things you can do with arrays.

The Multiplication Table — Numbers in Two Dimensions

A multiplication table is a chessboard-like table filled with numbers that are the products of the row and the column numbers of the various squares. Let's write a program that initializes or loads an array N with the product of the row and column of the particular array element and that prints the multiplication table — that is, the array N. Enter the following program:

```
100 CLS
110 MAX = 5
120 DIM N(MAX,MAX)
130 '
140 FOR ROW = 1 TO MAX        'loads array N with product ROW*COL
150     FOR COL = 1 TO MAX
160         N(ROW,COL) = ROW * COL
170     NEXT
180 NEXT
190 '
200 FOR ROW = 1 TO MAX        'PRINTs array
210     FOR COL = 1 TO MAX
220         LOCATE ROW, COL*4
230         PRINT N(ROW,COL)
240     NEXT
250 NEXT
```

Subject	Description	BASIC Array
Seating chart	Name of person as a function of seat row and column	NAME$(ROW,COL)
Stock value	Price of stock at month's close as a function of company and month	STOCK(CO,MO)
Rainfall	Inches of rain as a function of month and year	RAIN(MO,YEAR)
Grocery price comparison	Price is entered as a function of item and market	PRICE(ITEM,MARKET)
A color picture	Color as a function of row and column	COLOR$(ROW,COL)
Multiplication table	Product of row and column as a function of row and column	N(ROW,COL)

Table 13-1.   Examples of two-dimensional arrays

When this program is run, your computer displays the following multiplication table:

```
1   2   3   4   5
2   4   6   8   1Ø
3   6   9   12  15
4   8   12  16  2Ø
5   1Ø  15  2Ø  25
Ok
```

Each number in this table is the product of its row and column number. For example, the number 15 in the fifth row and third column is the product of 5 (the row number) and 3 (the column number).

This program is easy to understand. The DIM statement in line 120 defines or "declares" a two-dimensional array (there are two subscripts) having a maximum subscript value of MAX, which is a variable set to the value 5 by the previous statement (line 110). The value of MAX determines the size of the array and, consequently, the multiplication table. If you want a 10 element by 10 element multiplication table, all you need to do is to assign the value 10 to MAX.

The next part of the program beginning with line 140 initializes the array N by means of two nested FOR...NEXT loops, one for each dimension. Line 160 finds the product ROW * COL and assigns its value to the array element N(ROW,COL); that's how we get each number in the multiplication table to equal the product of the row and column positions.

The last part of this program, beginning with line 200, prints the array. Once again, we use two nested FOR...NEXT loops: the first to print different rows, and the second to print different columns. The location of each printed element is controlled by LOCATE ROW, COL*4 in line 220; in effect, we multiplied COL by 4 in order to give each number in the multiplication table plenty of room in the horizontal direction.

OK, that's how you can initialize and print a two-dimensional array. Is there anything else we can do with it? Of course! As with one-dimensional arrays, the ability to refer to array elements by their subscript gives us some very powerful ways of manipulating array elements. For example, we might want to display just the *diagonal* of the multiplication table, which corresponds to the squares of the row (or column) numbers.

To do this, let's add the following program lines to the previous program:

```
260 '
270 PRINT: PRINT
280 PRINT "Diagonal elements of array (=squares of numbers):"
290 PRINT
300 FOR DIAG = 1 TO MAX
310    LOCATE , DIAG * 4
320    PRINT N(DIAG, DIAG)
330 NEXT
```

Running the "concatenated" program results in the multiplication table shown previously and in the following new output:

```
Diagonal elements of array (=squares of numbers):

   1   4   9   16  25
Ok
```

Great! The fifth is indeed equal to 5 * 5, or to the square of 5. We only need one FOR...NEXT loop to PRINT this series of numbers because the ROW number equals the COL number, which we now call DIAG for "diagonal." The statement LOCATE , DIAG * 4 in line 310 only controls (or locates) the column position: the blank before the comma causes LOCATE to leave the row position unaltered. This has the advantage that if you decide to change MAX to some value other than 5, this part of the output (the diagonal elements of the array) would always be positioned three lines below the multiplication table.

Another very useful and common type of manipulation of two-dimensional arrays is finding the sum of a given column or row. The final program in this chapter illustrates such summing to solve a realistic and relevant problem. To show you the principle of finding such sums, let's append to our most recent program some code that finds the sum of the diagonal elements of the array — that is, the sum of the squares displayed above:

```
34Ø '
35Ø SUM = Ø
36Ø FOR DIAG = 1 TO MAX
37Ø     SUM = SUM + N(DIAG,DIAG)
38Ø NEXT
39Ø PRINT: PRINT
4ØØ PRINT "The sum of diagonal elements = " SUM
5ØØ END
```

When the combined program is run, the multiplication table and the diagonal elements are printed as well as the new statement:

```
The sum of diagonal elements =  55
Ok
```

Although this particular sum has no world-shaking implications, it does illustrate how array elements are summed. The basic method is similar to the one you use when you add a series of numbers with a calculator. Before you enter any numbers, the calculator displays a zero — that's the initial sum or total. Each time you enter a number and press the right buttons to make it add, your calculator adds the new number to the old subtotal, and then displays the new subtotal.

This is exactly how the above program finds the SUM of the diagonal array elements. Line 350 initializes this SUM to be equal to 0 — that's like the 0 displayed on the calculator before you start entering and adding numbers. Line 370 adds an array element N(DIAG,DIAG) to the old value of SUM and assigns this value to the new SUM — that's like your calculator adding entered numbers to the old subtotal to find and display the new subtotal. Every time the FOR...NEXT loop is executed, another diagonal element N is added to the subtotal SUM until the index DIAG is bigger than MAX. At that point, execution drops through the loop and prints the last value of SUM which is our grand total.

For a summary of arrays, take a look at the box called "Arrays and the DIM Statement."

Arrays and the DIM Statement

An array is group of variables having the *same* variable name. Members of the array, called elements, are differentiated and identified by one or more subscripts. The *dimension* of an array is equal to the number of subscripts in its elements. For example,

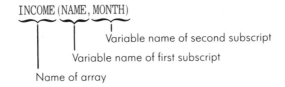

INCOME (NAME, MONTH)

Variable name of second subscript

Variable name of first subscript

Name of array

is an element in the array INCOME having the subscripts equal to the value of NAME and MONTH. Since two subscripts are present, this element belongs to a two-dimensional array.

Before using an array, it is a good practice and, if the largest subscript is to be larger than 10, it is imperative to define or dimension an array by means of a DIM statement like the following:

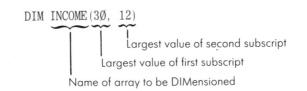

DIM INCOME (3Ø, 12)

Largest value of second subscript

Largest value of first subscript

Name of array to be DIMensioned

This DIM declaration reserves memory space for a two-dimensional array having 30 and 12 as the maximum values for its two subscripts.

Before ending this chapter, we'd like to give you a brief explanation of two array-related BASIC statements that you are likely to use only occasionally.

OPTION BASE — Setting the Lowest Array Index

For many applications it is more natural to count array subscripts starting with 1, not 0. The lowest subscript in all our examples has been 1. However, as we have already pointed out, your computer reserves memory space for the zeroth element as well, although you don't have to make use of it. When arrays get very large and you are short of memory space, you can instruct your computer to use 1 as the lowest subscript of an array by means of the following statement:

```
10 OPTION BASE 1      ← causes lowest subscript value to be 1
```

This OPTION BASE statement must be executed before *any* array name is used in *any* way, or else you'll get the error message "Duplicate Definition". This means, for example, that OPTION BASE should come before the DIM statement. If you do not include the above OPTION BASE statement, BASIC will automatically set the lowest array element subscript to 0.

You don't *have* to use OPTION BASE 1 if your lowest subscript is set to 1; all that happens is that you waste some memory space by not using the zeroth element. Your PC has enough memory so that a few wasted bytes of memory are irrelevant. However, large multidimensional arrays may have many zeroth elements. Consider, for instance, a three-dimensional array with subscripts ranging from 0 to 20 — such an array has 1141 zeroth elements! Now we're starting to talk about memory!

ERASE — Starting Over

The ERASE statement "erases" an array in the sense of removing its contents and freeing the memory space initially reserved by the DIM statement. The statement consists of the word ERASE followed by a list of one or more array names, as in this example:

```
1000 ERASE MONEY(100), ANIMALS$(25,12)
```

This line erases the two listed arrays.

There are several reasons why you may need to use ERASE. First, if you no longer need a large array that takes up needed memory, you can "reclaim" the memory space initially reserved by a DIM statement by means of the ERASE statement. That's like removing the ribbons across the theater seats that initially reserved spaces for your friends.

A second reason for using ERASE is to redimension an array. You cannot (without getting an error message) do this simply by executing another DIM statement. Instead, you must first use ERASE to eliminate the memory space created by the first DIM statement.

Summary

We've covered basically two techniques of handling large amounts of information. The first allows us to store and READ a collection of DATA in a compact and efficient manner. DATA and READ statements are especially useful for initializing variables or arrays with large blocks of fixed information.

The second technique involves arrays, the elements of which are referred to by array name and subscript(s). Arrays are ideal for storing blocks of temporary information and for manipulating (rearranging, adding, etc.) information of the same type.

Exercise

The solution to the following problem serves as both a reminder and summary of the most important concepts and statements covered in this chapter. It can also serve as a model or starting point for your own program!

Write a program that displays a table showing quarterly dividends you have received from five different companies in one year. Also include quarterly totals for all dividends and a grand sum of dividends for the year.

Solution

Here is how we solved this problem.

```
100 '----NAME: "DIVIDEND.B13"-----------------------------------------
105 '
110 '----*********************************
120 '----* 2-DIM ARRAY -- PORTFOLIO DIVIDENDS *
130 '----*********************************
135 KEY OFF: CLS
140 '
150 DIM DIV(4, 6)                    'dimensions array DIVidends
160 '
170 DATA IBM, TIMID, HITECH, BRAZEN, TANDEX, Qtrl totals
180 DATA "1st qtr", "2nd qtr", "3rd qtr", "4th qtr"
190 '============
200 GOSUB 610                        'title, row and column headings
210 '============
```

```
22Ø '
23Ø '---DATA: dividends; rows=quarters; columns=dif. companies--------
24Ø '
25Ø DATA 1ØØ, 15,15Ø, 4Ø, 5Ø, Ø
26Ø DATA 12Ø, 35,142, 54, 63, Ø
27Ø DATA 186, 32,127, 61, 38, Ø
28Ø DATA 234, 25,162, 31, 35, Ø
29Ø '
3ØØ '----loads array DIV with DATA and calculated qtrly totals--------
31Ø '
32Ø FOR ROW = 1 TO 4                         'loads array DIV
33Ø    FOR COL = 1 TO 6
34Ø       READ DIV(ROW,COL)                  'READs DATA from 19Ø to 22Ø
35Ø    NEXT
36Ø NEXT
37Ø '===========
38Ø GOSUB 81Ø               'finds qtrly totals & loads into DIV( ,6)
39Ø '===========
4ØØ '
41Ø '----PRINTS DIV array and YEARTOT---------------------------------
42Ø '
43Ø FOR ROW = 1 TO 4
44Ø    FOR COL = 1 TO 6
45Ø       LOCATE ROW*2 + 1Ø, COL*1Ø + 4
46Ø       PRINT DIV(ROW,COL)                 'PRINTs elements of DIV
47Ø    NEXT
48Ø NEXT
49Ø LOCATE 22, 37
5ØØ PRINT "THE TOTAL FOR THE YEAR =    " YEARTOT
51Ø END
6ØØ '
61Ø '====SUBROUTINE: title, row and column headings, and grid=========
62Ø '
63Ø PRINT: PRINT
64Ø PRINT TAB(2Ø) "SUMMARY OF PORTFOLIO DIVIDENDS FOR 1991"
65Ø PRINT TAB(2Ø) "========================================"
66Ø FOR COL = 1 TO 6                         'PRINTs company headings
67Ø       READ CO$
68Ø       LOCATE 9, COL*1Ø + 4
69Ø       PRINT CO$
7ØØ NEXT
71Ø '
72Ø FOR ROW = 1 TO 4                         'PRINTS quarter headings
73Ø       READ QRT$
74Ø       LOCATE ROW*2 + 1Ø, 1
75Ø       PRINT QRT$
76Ø NEXT
77Ø RETURN
8ØØ '
```

```
810 '====SUB finds qtrly totals (QTOT) and grand total (YEARTOT)=====
820 '
830 FOR ROW = 1 TO 4
840     QTOT = Ø
850     FOR COL = 1 TO 5                 'finds qtrly totals QTOT
860         QTOT = QTOT + DIV(ROW, COL)
870     NEXT
880     DIV(ROW, 6) = QTOT
890     YEARTOT = YEARTOT + QTOT         'finds grand total YEARTOT
900 NEXT
910 RETURN
```

Here's the output of this program.

```
                    SUMMARY OF PORTFOLIO DIVIDENDS FOR 1991
                    ==========================================


                  IBM      TIMID    HITECH   BRAZEN   TANDEX   Qtrl totals

1st qtr          1ØØ        15       15Ø       4Ø       5Ø        355

2nd qtr          12Ø        35       142       54       63        414

3rd qtr          186        32       127       61       38        444

4th qtr          234        25       162       31       35        487



                          THE TOTAL FOR THE YEAR =    17ØØ
Ok
```

This program is similar in some ways (but much simpler!) to many of the commercially available spreadsheet programs that manipulate tables of information. A nice feature of this program is that if you change any of the numbers in the table and rerun the program, it will automatically present the correct totals! You might wish to replace the DATA and READ statements with INPUT statements that would make it more convenient to enter your own data. The drawback is that you'd loose all your INPUT when your program ends. Using a feature of BASIC known as *files*, however, will solve that problem! We will be discussing files in chapter 19.

Color Graphics

Concepts
    Medium- and high-resolution screens
    Drawing points, lines
    Graphs
    Color graphics

Instructions
    SCREEN, PSET, LINE, COLOR, CIRCLE

The graphics capabilities of your IBM PC are very sophisticated, yet easy to use. They are also a lot of fun, especially if you have a playful turn of mind! This chapter is an introduction to some of the graphics capabilities available to you if you have the Color/Graphics Monitor Adapter and an appropriate monitor to go with it.

If the only monitor you have is the IBM Monochrome Display, you won't be able to try out the examples in this chapter (you might read this chapter anyway and decide to go out and buy a color monitor!) On the other hand, if you only have a monitor driven by the Color/Graphics Adapter, you've got exactly what you need and you can go right ahead with this chapter. And there's a third possibility: you may have both types of monitors. In that case, you'll need to switch to the Color/Graphics Monitor by one of the methods given in Appendix B.

The character graphics we discussed in chapter 10 allowed us to assemble images out of special graphics characters available from the ASCII character set. The graphics we'll discuss in this chapter are much more versatile: you can make use of all the pixels (points on your screen that form all the images you see on your screen, including letters) individually, which enable you to draw points, lines, circles, ellipses, and arcs — all in color. With one-line statements, you can draw empty or filled boxes and complex shapes. You can even take an image from part of the screen and move it around to other parts of the screen; this is one of the tools used for animation.

DOS 2.0, the new version of your disk operating system, adds even more to the already powerful arsenal of graphics statements. For example, special scaling functions make it easy to place graphs on any part of your screen and facilitate such special effects as zooming.

This type of *all-points-addressable* graphics is certainly exciting, but it is also a huge topic that would warrant a whole book by itself! So it is with some reluctance that we'll limit ourselves to just a few of the more basic graphics statements and concepts — enough to enable you to get your feet wet, and to pursue a more detailed and complete study with the help of another book on the IBM PC, called *Graphics Primer for the IBM PC* by Christopher L. Morgan and Mitchell Waite (Berkeley: Osborne/McGraw-Hill, 1983).

The SCREEN Statement — Choosing Your Screen Mode

With the Color/Graphics Adapter, three screen modes are available to you: one text mode and two graphics modes. The text mode can be operated with a 40-column or 80-column wide screen; the 80-column mode is very similar to the display of the IBM Monochrome Display with which you are already familiar. The two graphics modes are very similar to each other, but differ in their capability to show color, and their *resolution* — that is, their ability to show detail. The medium-resolution graphics screen consists of a rectangle of dots, 320 dots wide by 200 dots high. Each of these dots or pixels can be turned off or on individually. The high-resolution graphics screen consists of a rectangle of dots 640 wide by 200 dots high, which is twice as many dots in the horizontal direction as for the medium-resolution mode.

Each of the three screen modes has different color options. The text mode gives you the option of a total of 15 colors. The medium-resolution graphics mode also allows for 15 colors, although not all at the same time, but the high-resolution graphics mode is capable only of black and white. That's the price you pay for high-resolution!

The SCREEN statement is used to set the screen mode:

SCREEN Ø   ← Sets screen to TEXT mode, which is the default mode
SCREEN 1   ← Sets screen to medium-resolution graphics mode
SCREEN 2   ← Sets screen to high resolution graphics mode

These statements can be used either in the Direct Mode (just enter the command without a line number) or as program lines (used with line number, of course). SCREEN also erases the screen and sets the color to the usual (default) black and white.

Figure 14-1 summarizes all the screen options and the BASIC statements that set them.

A very convenient feature of the graphics mode is that it also displays text: you can use PRINT to print all of the 255 ASCII characters, and use all the standard PRINT-related statements, including LOCATE. However, be aware that the medium-resolution screen (SCREEN 1) displays text in the 40-column mode, and the high-resolution screen (SCREEN 2) displays text in the 80-column mode.

PSET and Your Graphics Screen — Putting Points on Your Screen

PSET is the simplest of all the graphics statements. It is also an ideal tool with which to explore your graphics screen. PSET is an abbreviation for "Point-SET": it places or sets a point on your graphics screen at any given location.

Before we can use PSET, however, we need to set the screen to one of the two graphics modes (otherwise, you'll get a "syntax error" message). Enter the command

SCREEN 1

to set your screen to the medium-resolution mode. It will remain in this

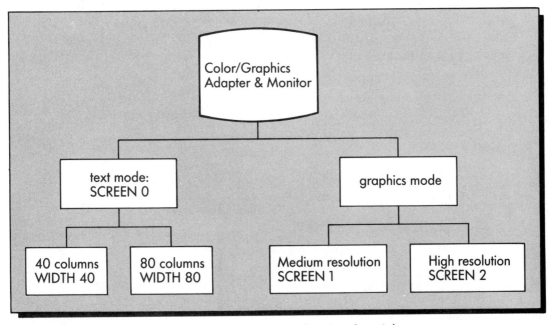

Figure 14-1. Screen options for a monitor with Color/Graphics Adapter

mode until you change it by means of another SCREEN command (or statement within a program) or until you turn your PC off and on again. (When you turn the PC on, it is always in the text (SCREEN 0) mode.)

Now we're ready to try our first graphics command. Enter the Direct Mode command

PSET (16Ø, 1ØØ)

A small dot appears in the middle of the screen! This command says "set a point at the location given by the two numbers in the parentheses."

To find out what these numbers, which are called *coordinates*, have to do with location of the spot, try changing the first of the numbers. For example, you might try

PSET (17Ø, 1ØØ)

The result will be a point to the right of the original one. So the first number determines the *horizontal* position of the point; the bigger this first number, the further to the right is the location of the point. This horizontal coordinate is frequently referred to as the *x-coordinate*. A similar experiment will reveal that the second number, usually called the *y-coordinate*, defines the vertical location of the point; a larger *y*-coordinate results in a *lower* screen position. This may seem a bit peculiar to anyone who has had some experience with making graphs since a larger *y*-coordinate usually means a *higher* position, but it does agree with our sense of row numbers increasing as we go down the page. Figure 14-2 summarizes how coordinates are specified.

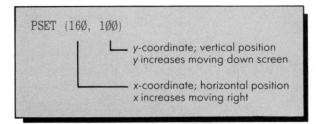

Figure 14-2. The PSET statement

Now enter the following program, which is designed to show you the extent of your screen in terms of the screen coordinates *x* and *y*:

```
1Ø PSET (Ø, Ø)
2Ø PSET (Ø, 199)
3Ø PSET (319, Ø)
4Ø PSET (319, 199)
5Ø END
```

When you run this program, you'll see four small dots appearing near the corners of your screen. These dots define the limits of your graphics screen. The coordinates of these points (the corners) are shown in Figure 14-3.

The numbers in the parentheses in Figure 14-3 are the *x*- and *y*-coordinates of the corner points of your medium-resolution graphics screen; they are the same numbers that appear in the PSET statements. The upper left corner, defined by both *x* and *y*, equal to zero [written as (0,0)] and is called the *origin*; it's the place from which you start counting. The largest *x* value is 319, which means that your screen has a total of 320 horizontal or *x* positions (319 plus 1 for the zero position). Similarly, the largest value of *y* is 199, so we have a total of 200 vertical positions. Contrast these numbers with the 80-column by 25-row display of the character graphics (in 80-column text mode) that we discussed earlier, and you'll see why we can produce much sharper pictures and graphs in this medium-resolution graphics mode!

There is one aspect of defining coordinates that may be confusing later: in the graphics modes, the horizontal position is given first, then

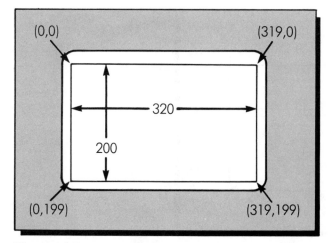

Figure 14-3. Coordinates of the medium-resolution screen

the vertical. This is just the opposite of the way we used LOCATE to locate PRINT statements in the text mode. LOCATE, as you will recall, interprets the first number as the row number (vertical) and the second as the column number (horizontal). You have to be on your toes when you switch back and forth between using LOCATE to locate text and PSET to plot points on a graphics screen!

Your high-resolution (SCREEN 2) screen has the same number of vertical (*y*) divisions but *twice* as many in the horizontal (*x*) direction. In this high-resolution mode, you can place 640 dots on one line in the *x* direction! The screen coordinates of the corners are shown in Figure 14-4.

A Few Examples Using PSET

PSET is perhaps the most versatile of all the graphics statements since any image can theoretically be constructed out of dots made by PSET statements. Working only with PSET, however, might get to be a bit tedious if you have to write a separate PSET statement for each dot, as there are a total of 64,000 dot positions in medium-resolution! The FOR...NEXT loop, however, makes it easy to draw a sequence of points.

For example, let's draw a more or less diagonal line across the screen:

```
10 CLS
15 SCREEN 1
20 FOR J = 0 TO 199
30    PSET (J,J)
40 NEXT
50 END
```

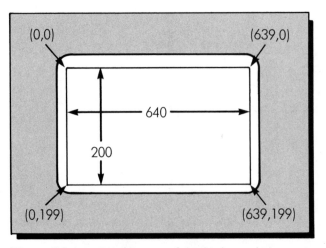

Figure 14-4. Coordinates of the high-resolution screen

The SCREEN statement in line 15 isn't necessary if we're already in the SCREEN 1 mode (SCREEN 1 needs to be executed just once), but it's a good idea to put it there just to make sure. It's easy to see that this program draws 200 points along a diagonal starting with coordinates (0,0) and ending up at (199,199), although the line is not really a diagonal because it doesn't end up at the lower right corner (319,199). To make a diagonal, try substituting the following statement for line 30 in the preceding program:

```
30    PSET (J*1.603, J)
```

Your program will now draw a true diagonal ending up at coordinates (319,199) because 1.603 x 199 equals 319. The point of this modification of our line program is to show you that the numbers in the parentheses can be expressions. What's more, these expressions don't even have to return integers because BASIC will automatically round off the coordinate values to integers (as is true for LOCATE).

Once we know how to use PSET to draw a line, it's easy, and a lot of fun, to invent programs that do all sorts of interesting things. The following is a simple example that draws a zigzag line that looks like the track of a billiard ball bouncing off the sides of an endless billiard table:

```
80   '----NAME: "BILLIARD.B14"---------------------
85   '
90   '----Prgm simulates bouncing billiard ball----
95   '
100 SCREEN 1
110 XMAX =  80
120 YMAX = 120
130 XCHANGE = 2
140 YCHANGE = 2
150 X = 10
160 Y = YMAX
170 FOR J = 0 TO 320
180    IF Y>YMAX OR Y<YMIN THEN YCHANGE = -YCHANGE
190    PSET (X, Y)
200    X = X + XCHANGE
210    Y = Y + YCHANGE
220 NEXT
230 END
```

The output is shown in Figure 14-5.

When you run this program yourself, you'll notice that when the zigzag line gets to the right border of your screen, it suddenly appears on the left side! PSET "wraps around" like this when the coordinates are larger than the maximum 319 and 199 for *x* and *y*, respectively. In this case it gives an interesting effect, although we wouldn't recommend counting on this behavior in all situations.

A few remarks about the program are in order. Lines 190 and 200 update the old values of X and Y by adding the values of XCHANGE and YCHANGE. XCHANGE has a constant value of 2 throughout the whole program, whereas YCHANGE switches back and forth between 2 and -2 as directed by the IF...THEN statement in line 180. That's how we get the line to zigzag.

It would be easy to modify this program so that the "ball" bounces off four sides rather than just the two used in this program. As you can probably guess, all it takes is another IF...THEN statement that limits X in the same way as the existing IF...THEN in line 180 statement limits Y.

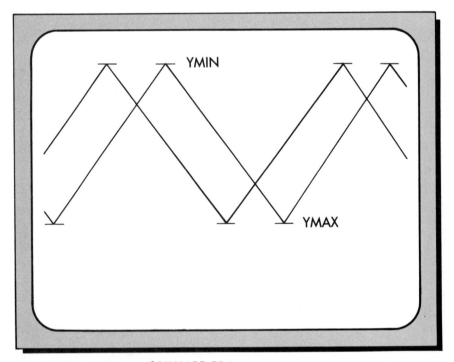

Figure 14-5. Output of BILLIARD.B14

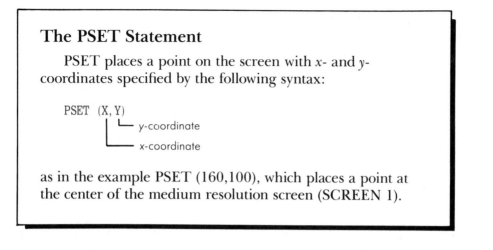

The PSET Statement

PSET places a point on the screen with *x*- and *y*-coordinates specified by the following syntax:

```
PSET (X, Y)
```

as in the example PSET (160,100), which places a point at the center of the medium resolution screen (SCREEN 1).

Of Lines and Boxes

Although you can construct lines out of individual points using PSET, IBM PC BASIC provides us with a single instruction designed just for this purpose: the LINE statement. It's a sophisticated statement that can be used in many different ways to perform a large variety of tasks.

As a way of getting acquainted with LINE, enter the command

```
LINE (Ø,199) - (319,Ø)
```

A diagonal line will appear on your screen from the lower left corner to the upper right corner, as shown in Figure 14-6. Notice how much faster this line is drawn than when you use PSET. This happens because the program that draws a LINE is written in machine language, whereas a line drawn with PSET (as in our examples in the last section) requires the execution of many separate BASIC statements, and that takes much longer than an equivalent machine language program.

The corner points in Figure 14-6 are specified by the two sets of coordinates listed within the parentheses after LINE. In general, LINE draws a line from one set of *x*- and *y*-coordinates to another. These coordinates are specified in the following manner:

```
LINE (Ø,199) — (319,Ø)
```
— x- and y-coordinates of second end point
— x- and y-coordinates of first end point

As you can see, the way the coordinates are specified in LINE is identical to the way they are specified in PSET, except, of course, that LINE requires two sets of coordinates to define the two end points of the line instead of just one. Incidentally, we've written the preceding LINE statement with spaces at various points to make it easier to read the statement, but BASIC really doesn't care about these spaces. In fact, you can write the whole line without any spaces at all or you can add more.

The following example uses LINE to draw an interesting pattern of lines:

```
5   '---NAME: "LINES1.B14"----------
7   '
10 SCREEN 2
20 FOR J = Ø TO 20
30     X = 8Ø + J*2Ø
40     Y = 2Ø + J*7
50     LINE (8Ø,Y) - (X,16Ø)
60 NEXT
70 END
```

The output of this program is shown in Figure 14-7. The program draws 20 lines that make a pattern similar to what you might see in the familiar pin and string pictures.

Notice that this time we used SCREEN 2 mainly to give you some experience in using the high-resolution mode. You might try to rewrite this program for the medium-resolution screen to become more familiar

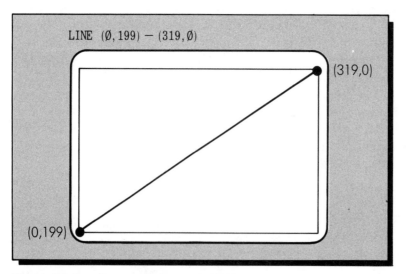

Figure 14-6.   Drawing a line with LINE

with the difference. Aside from using SCREEN 1, you'd have to divide all X values by 2 in order to keep the same horizontal dimensions of the picture. (Remember that the high-resolution screen has twice as many pixels in the horizontal direction as the medium-resolution screen.)

Drawing Boxes with LINE Statements

One of the shapes most frequently used is the rectangle. The rectangle can be used, for example, as a frame for something, as a bar for a bar graph, or as a building block for more complex shapes.

Since a rectangle has four sides, it obviously takes four LINE statements to construct a rectangle, right? Well, yes, if you want to do it the long way! But BASIC does provide us with a shortcut. All you have to do is append the LINE statement with a B in the proper location, and specify the coordinates of two opposite corners of the box as shown in Figure 14-8.

A pretty compact statement! The LINE statement in Figure 14-8 draws the box shown in Figure 14-9 in the medium-resolution mode.

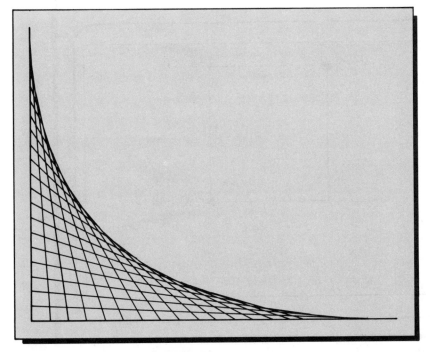

Figure 14-7. Output of LINES1.B14

Notice the two commas between the last parenthesis and the B in that LINE statement. They have the function of reserving space for an optional number that specifies the color of the box. We'll explain how to include such a color code in the next section.

For some applications, like bar graphs, in which you may want solid or filled boxes, BASIC again supplies us with an easy solution: just

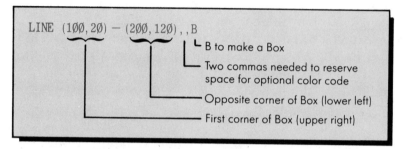

Figure 14-8. The LINE statement with Box option

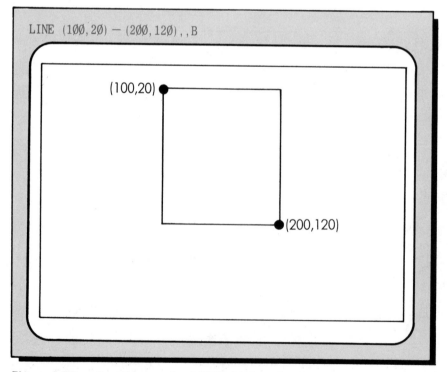

Figure 14-9. Box drawn using LINE with Box Option

append to the letter B (for box) at the end of the LINE statement, the letter F (for filled). For example, the statement

```
LINE (100,20) — (200,120),,BF
```
            └─ Causes LINE to make a Filled Box

produces a solid or filled box having the same corner positions as the previous box. In the next section we'll present an example that uses boxes filled with different colors.

The LINE Statement

The following LINE statement

```
100 LINE (20,40) - (200,160)
```

draws a line from the *x*- and *y*-coordinates (from [20,40] to [200,160]).

The following LINE statement draws a box

```
100 LINE (20,40) — (200,160),,B
```
            └─ Or use BF for a Filled Box

where the letter B specifies a box; the numbers listed in parentheses specify the *x*- and *y*-coordinates of the opposite corners of the box. The letters BF in place of the B result in a filled box.

Including Color in Your Graphics

The ability to create images in color is one of the really outstanding features of the medium-resolution graphics mode of your IBM PC. Color is not available in the high-resolution graphics mode, however. The reason for this limitation is that the memory space used for color in the medium-resolution mode is needed for the additional 64,000 pixels required in the high-resolution mode. Color is also available in the text mode, but since its implementation is quite different in the graphics mode, we'll limit our discussion to color in the medium- resolution graphics mode.

BASIC makes a distinction between foreground and background colors. The term *foreground colors* refers to the colors of the object being drawn on the screen; it might, for example, refer to the color of a point produced by PSET, or the color of a line produced by LINE. The term *background colors* refers to the color of the rest of the screen — literally, of the background. Let's first take a look at how to make background colors.

Background Colors

Background colors are determined by the COLOR statement, as in the following example:

```
1Ø COLOR 2
```

The number 2 represents one of 16 colors coded by numbers in the range from 0 to 15. Background color number 2 happens to be green. Table 14-1 gives the color codes for all the available background colors. Notice that colors 8 to 15 are basically lighter versions of colors 0 to 7.

To get an idea of what these colors really look like, run the following program which displays all the background colors in sequence:

```
1Ø SCREEN 1
15 CLS
2Ø PRINT "background color is now number "
3Ø FOR COL = 15 to Ø STEP -1
4Ø     COLOR COL              'sets the background color
5Ø     LOCATE 1,31
```

Color Code	Color	Color Code	Color
0	black	8	dark grey
1	blue	9	light blue
2	green	10	light green
3	cyan	11	light cyan
4	red	12	light green
5	magenta	13	light magenta
6	gold or brown	14	yellow
7	white or grey	15	bright white

Table 14-1. Color codes for background color

```
6Ø      PRINT COL           'PRINTs color code number
7Ø      FOR J = 1 TO 1ØØØ    'causes pause
8Ø      NEXT
9Ø NEXT
1ØØ END
```

The length of time each color is displayed is determined by the number of loops in the FOR...NEXT statements in lines 70 and 80; you change that display time by changing the final counter value in line 70. Also notice that we started with color 15 and end up with color 0 because we didn't want to end up with a white screen (color 15).

Foreground Colors

The foreground color is determined by a two-stage process. The first step is to select what is called the *palette*. A palette is a particular selection of colors (as in the colors on an artist's palette). For color graphics, there are two such palettes. These are specified by either a 0 or a 1 placed after the background color code in the COLOR statement, as shown below:

```
2Ø COLOR 3,1
```
└─ Specify the palette (0, or 1)

The COLOR statement, then, selects both the background color (number 3, cyan, in our example) and the palette (number 1, blue, in our example).

Each of the two palettes has four colors: the background color, and three other colors. Figure 14-10 shows the colors available within each palette.

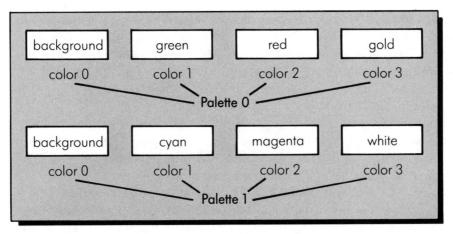

Figure 14-10.   Foreground colors in medium resolution

A particular foreground color is chosen by specifying the color code (1 through 4) in the appropriate place within a particular graphics command. For example, the command

```
PSET (1ØØ,1ØØ),2    ← the number 2 specifies the foregound color
```

draws a point having the color that corresponds to foreground color number 2 in Table 14-1. This color is either red or magenta: if the palette specified by COLOR is 0, then this color is red; if the palette is 1, then this color is magenta.

The color number 0 causes the foreground color to be the same as the background color — that's how you make whatever you're drawing invisible!

Color can be added to a line in a similar way. For example,

```
LINE (1Ø,1ØØ) — (12Ø,4Ø),1
            └── Colors line with color #1 of given palette
```

draws a line having the color green or cyan, depending on whether the existing palette is 0 or 1.

Let's pull all the aspects of setting colors in the graphics mode into a single example:

```
1Ø SCREEN 1                 'sets medium resolution mode
2Ø COLOR 1,Ø                'blue backgnd and palette Ø
3Ø LINE (1Ø,1Ø) - (2ØØ,1ØØ),2  'red line on blue background
4Ø END
```

This program draws a red line on a blue background. If instead you wanted a green line, you'd look at the foreground color table and notice that all you'd have to do is to change the color number at the end of the LINE statement to a 1. If, however, you wanted a magenta line, you would need to change the palette from 0 to 1 because magenta appears only within palette number 1. So you would need to change the COLOR statement to COLOR 1,0. Changing the background color would be easy: just change the first number after COLOR.

If you've actually tried some of the previous examples using PSET and LINE, you may have noticed some unexpected and strange color effects: a colored point may not actually have the expected color at all, and a line may change colors along its length! Be assured that nothing is wrong with your PC nor with your understanding of COLOR. The culprit is your monitor, unless you happen to have a top-of-the-line color monitor designed to cope with this anomaly. The reason for these strange effects is this: if you look at your color screen with a magnifying lens, you'll see tiny rectangles or dots of different colors — specifically, the three primary colors red, green, and blue. All colors are produced by different combinations of these three colors. The problem is that when you plot a point on your screen using PSET, it's so small that it probably won't include all three color dots. For example, if you want magenta, you may "miss" the blue color dot, leaving only the red dot; or the converse may be true, leaving you with only blue.

To see the "true" foreground colors, it is necessary to fill a whole area with color so that the three primary colors will be represented fairly. The following is a program that shows all the foreground colors of palette 1 by means of filled boxes:

```
80   '---NAME: "COLBOXES.B14-----------------
90   '
100  CLS
110  SCREEN 1               'med. res. screen
120  COLOR 0,1              'blck bckgrnd, palette 1
130  COL = 0
140  FOR J = 1 TO 10        'draws 10 filled boxes
150      HEIGHT = 10*J      'finds HEIGHT of box
160      WIDTZ  = 20*(10 - J)   'finds WIDTh of box
170      X1 = 160 - WIDTZ/2     'upper left corner x value
180      Y1 = 100 - HEIGHT/2    'upper left corner y value
185      X2 = 160 + WIDTZ/2     'lower right corner x value
190      Y2 = 100 + HEIGHT/2    'lower right corner y value
200      COL = COL + 1          'changes COLor with each loop
210      IF COL>3 THEN COL = COL - 3   'resets COL to 1 if COL>3
220      LINE (X1,Y1) - (X2,Y2),COL,BF   'colored, filled box
230      FOR I = 1 TO 200      'pause
240      NEXT
250  NEXT
260  END
```

This program makes an interesting pattern and clearly shows off all the colors of palette number 1. Figure 14-11 shows what the output looks like. You might enjoy experimenting with this program, trying palette 0 and some other background colors. The FOR...NEXT loop of lines 230 and 240 purposely slows down the program so you can more easily see how the final pattern is actually constructed. You might wish to change the duration of this delay, or eliminate it altogether.

Color Related Statements

There are two different categories of colors in the medium-resolution graphics mode (only black and white are available in the high-resolution mode): foreground colors and background colors. Background colors are determined by the COLOR statement alone, whereas foreground colors are determined by (a) COLOR, which chooses the palette; and (b) the color number listed in the graphics statement being used (such as PSET or LINE).

For example, the following program

```
10 SCREEN 1
20 COLOR 5,1    ← Chooses background color 5 (magenta), palette 1
30 LINE (10,20) - (80,40),1    ← Chooses foreground color 1 (cyan)
```

draws a cyan-colored line on a magenta background.

Graphing the Growth of Your Investment — An Example

You can use the graphics capabilities on your PC for many different purposes. One of these is to produce graphs that show visual relationships between two changing quantities. For example, you might be interested in charting the growth of an investment as a function of

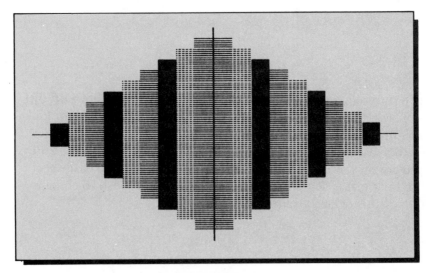

Figure 14-11. Output of COLBOXES.B14

time. The following example illustrates the use of PC graphics to give you a visual picture of the exponential growth of an investment (or of a population) — that is, growth at a fixed rate of return.

Enter the following program which graphs the value of a $100 investment over a period of 10 years. The interest is compounded quarterly, and the interest rate is determined by user input. The program also makes it possible to display many graphs at different interest rates simultaneously so that the user can compare the long-term effects of changing the interest rate.

```
100 '----NAME: "INVESTGR.B14"-----------------------------------------
102 '
108 '----**********************************************************
110 '----* Prgm graphs balance of investment for period of 10 years *
120 '----* Starting balance is $100; interest is entered by user;   *
130 '----* Interest is compounded quarterly                         *
140 '----**********************************************************
150 '
160 CLS
170 SCREEN 1                        'medium resolution screen
180 COLOR 0,1                       'blk backgrd, pallete 1
190 '
200 XCHANGE = (300 - 40)/40         'scaling const. for x axis
210 YCHANGE = (180 - 20)/1000       'scaling const. for y axis
220 '==============
230 GOSUB 440                       'SUBR for axes and tick marks
240 '==============
250 INPUT "enter interest rate in %--"; INTRATE
260 BALANCE = 100                   'initializes BALANCE
270 '
280 COL = COL + 1                   'changes color of graph
290 IF COL>3 THEN COL = COL - 3
300 '
310 '----MAIN PRGM finds BALANCE and graphs result--------------------
320 '
330 FOR MONTH = 1 TO 40
340     BALANCE = BALANCE +BALANCE*INTRATE/400
350     IF BALANCE>1000 THEN 410
360     X = 40 + XCHANGE*MONTH      'converts MONTH to screen x
370     Y = 180 - YCHANGE*BALANCE   'converts MONTH to screen y
380     PSET (X,Y), COL
390 NEXT
400 '
410 INPUT "another graph (y,n)--"; ANS$  'provision for another graph
420 IF ANS$ = "y" THEN GOTO 250
430 END
440 '
```

```
6ØØ  '====SUBROUTINE draws axes and tick marks========================
61Ø  '
62Ø  LINE (4Ø,2Ø) - (3ØØ,18Ø),3,B          'boundary and axes
63Ø  FOR J = Ø TO 1Ø
64Ø      Y = 16*J + 2Ø
65Ø      LINE (4Ø-2,Y) - (4Ø+2,Y)          'tick marks on vertical axis
66Ø      X = 26*J + 4Ø
67Ø      LINE (X,18Ø-1) - (X,18Ø+1)        'tick marks on horiz. axis
68Ø  NEXT
69Ø  RETURN
```

With this program you can answer questions like, "How long would it take to double my money at a 15% interest rate?" or "What interest rate would I require to multiply my investment by a factor of 10 in ten years?" — questions that may have some relevance to your financial affairs! Figure 14-12 shows an example of the output.

This is a bare-bones program used to illustrate graphics concepts and statements, so we've tried to keep it as short as possible. You may find it useful to add some features, like labels for the axes, and perhaps a title page.

The only aspect of this program that needs an explanation has to do with converting time (MONTH) and the value of the investment (BALANCE) to the screen coordinates *x* and *y*. Figure 14-13, which shows the screen locations of the axes of the graph, will help make sense of the numbers in lines 200, 210, 360, and 370, all of which have to do with scaling.

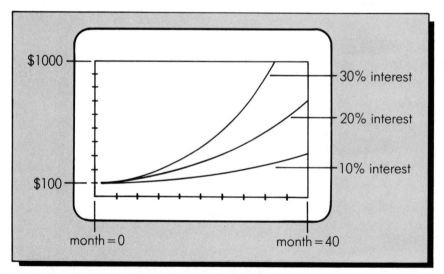

Figure 14-12. Output of INVESTGR.B14

Specifically, line 200 finds the difference between the maximum screen x-coordinate (300) and the minimum screen x-coordinate (40) and then divides this difference by the maximum number of months (40). The resulting value is assigned to the variable XCHANGE, which is used in line 360 to convert from the present value of MONTH to the screen coordinate x. A similar set of statements (lines 210 and 370) converts the present value of BALANCE to the screen coordinate y. If this seems a bit messy — well, we agree. But once you've gone through this scaling problem once or twice, you can apply this technique to all of your other graphics problems.

If you're the lucky owner of the version of BASIC that comes with DOS 2.0, you have an easy way to deal with the problem of scaling to screen coordinates. BASICA includes a new statement called WINDOW that allows you to redefine your screen coordinates to suit the requirements of your particular problem. In effect, WINDOW can automatically make the translation from the variables you are using in your problem (MONTH and BALANCE in our example) to screen coordinates (x and y). We can't cover all the wonderful graphics statements in just one chapter, so we'll leave this one to you to explore on your own.

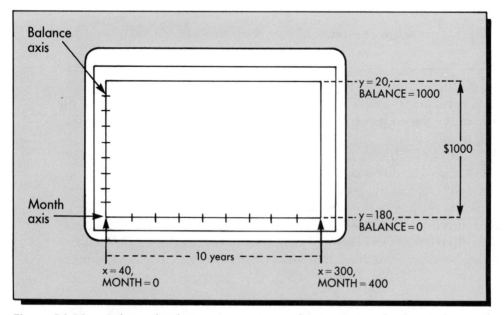

Figure 14-13.   Relationship between screen coordinates (x,y) and values to be graphed in INVESTGR.B14

The CIRCLE Statement

We can do a lot of interesting graphics with PSET and LINE. But not everything in this world is made up of straight lines, and neither would you want all your computer graphics to consist of nothing but straight lines. The CIRCLE statement, available only in Advanced BASIC (BASICA), provides us with a versatile and powerful instruction to draw circles, ellipses, arcs, and even pie-shapes.

The Basic Circle

To draw your first circle, get into the medium-resolution graphics mode by entering

```
SCREEN 1
```

Now enter the command

```
CIRCLE (16Ø, 1ØØ), 5Ø
```

A circle should appear immediately on your screen — well, nearly a circle. Different monitors will produce slightly different shapes, depending on exactly how they're adjusted.

The preceding circle command has the following meaning:

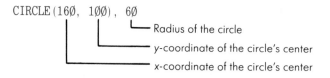

```
CIRCLE (16Ø, 1ØØ), 6Ø
```
— Radius of the circle
— y-coordinate of the circle's center
— x-coordinate of the circle's center

For this particular example, we've chosen the center of the circle to be the middle of the screen ($x = 160$ and $y = 100$). The radius of our circle is 60. But 60 what?

The answer is 60 dots in the horizontal or x direction. The reason we have to specify the direction is that, in terms of pixels on the screen, the radius is different in the horizontal and the vertical directions. In our example, it's 60 dots in the horizontal direction but only 50 dots in the vertical direction. That's not really surprising, though, since dots in the vertical direction are less crowded than dots in the horizontal direction; therefore, to draw something that looks close to a true circle, you want the radius in the vertical direction to be slightly less than in the horizontal. We'll come back to the question of different radii in different directions later in this chapter.

In the CIRCLE command above, we used definite values for the center coordinates and the radius of the circle. But as with most BASIC instructions, you can use variables or even expressions. The following program illustrates the use of the simple CIRCLE statement to draw a series of expanding and moving circles:

```
80   '----NAME: "CIRCLES1.B14"-------------------------------------
85   '
90   '----prgm draws series of expanding, moving circles-----------
95   '
100 CLS
110 SCREEN 1
120 X = 50                          'X-coord. of first circle
125 Y = 100                         'Y-coord. of first circle
130 RADIUS = 4                      'radius of first circle
140 R.CHANGE = 4                    'increment of radius
150 INPUT "enter a number, 0 to 50: ", X.CHANGE
160 '
170 FOR J = 1 TO 20
180    CIRCLE (X,Y),RADIUS
190    RADIUS = RADIUS + R.CHANGE   'new radius
200    X = X + X.CHANGE             'new X of circle center
210    IF X > 320 THEN END          'ends prgm when X is off screen
220 NEXT
230 END
```

Figure 14-14 shows the output of this program. We entered the number 7 in response to the INPUT question. Try it yourself, though; you can get a variety of interesting patterns with different input values.

The Aspect Ratio — Controlling the Shape of Your Ellipses

One of the really fascinating aspects of the CIRCLE statement is that you can change the shape of the "circle." Of course, we should really talk about ellipses here, and not circles. You can draw a very narrow, "squashed" ellipse or a very round one, even an actual circle! This is done by adding another modifier, called the *aspect ratio*, to the CIRCLE statement.

Before we give you the definition of the aspect ratio, try running the following program, which will give you an intuitive sense of its meaning:

```
10 SCREEN 1
20 PRINT "enter ASPECT RATIO (say 0 to 100):
30 INPUT ASPECT
40 CIRCLE(160, 100), 60,,,,ASPECT
50 GOTO 30
```

Aspect ratio

Use four commas

Try a whole range of input values, such as .1, .5, 1, 2, 4, and 10. Figure 14-15 shows several different ellipses drawn with this program. You can see that small aspect ratios produce ellipses that look as if someone sat on a circle while large aspect ratios result in a very "tall" ellipse, and values near 1 produce shapes that are close to circular. By trial and error you'll find that you'll get a nearly perfect circle with an aspect ratio of about .8.

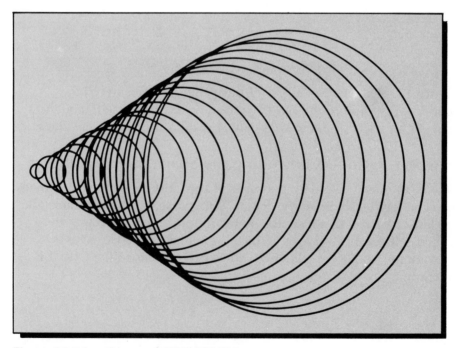

Figure 14-14. Output of CIRCLES1.B14

In the CIRCLE statement in line 40, notice the four commas between the value for the radius and ASPECT. They really have to be there in order for your PC to interpret ASPECT as the aspect ratio, and not some other modifier. CIRCLE can have up to 7 variables in it, which must be separated by commas, whether you use all the variables or not.

Exactly what does "aspect ratio" mean? It is the ratio, in terms of pixels, of the radius in the y direction to the radius in the x direction. That is, given the ellipse shown below,

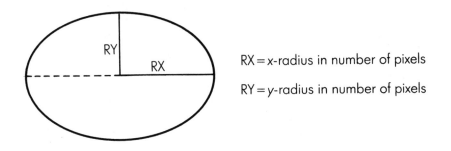

RX = x-radius in number of pixels

RY = y-radius in number of pixels

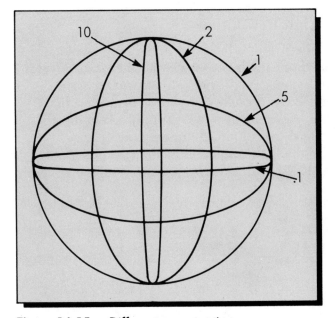

Figure 14-15. Different aspect ratios

the aspect ratio is defined by the following ratio:

$$\text{Aspect ratio} = \frac{RY}{RX}$$

For example, when $RX = 60$ and $RY = 50$, the aspect ratio equals 5/6 or .83. That happens to be equal to the default value of the aspect ratio — that is, the value your PC assumes if you don't specify a value. It is also, by the way, the value of the aspect ratio that results in nearly circular shapes on most monitors.

When we talked about the radius of the circle earlier in this section, we said that the radius specified in the CIRCLE statement is the radius in the horizontal or x direction. That's true if you don't specify the aspect ratio (that is, if you're using the default value 5/6), but it's not necessarily true if you do specify the aspect ratio — it all depends on the particular value of the aspect ratio. The general rule is that the radius indicated in CIRCLE is always equal to the largest radius of the ellipse (in terms of pixels). This largest radius is called the *major axis* and can be either in the x direction or in the y direction, depending on the actual value of the aspect ratio. If the aspect ratio is *less* than 1, the radius indicated in the CIRCLE statement is equal to the *horizontal* or x radius, RX. If, on the other hand, the aspect ratio is *greater than* 1, the radius indicated in the CIRCLE statement is equal to the *vertical* or y radius, RY. The summary in the box entitled "Aspect Ratio" might help to clarify this situation.

The Aspect Ratio in High Resolution

The definition of the aspect ratio is the same in the high-resolution graphics mode as in the medium-resolution mode, but the visual effect is different. The high-resolution mode has twice as many pixels in the horizontal direction as the medium-resolution mode. This means that pixels in the high-resolution mode are also twice as crowded in the x direction as they would be in the medium-resolution mode. Hence, a given CIRCLE statement in the high-resolution mode will appear only half as wide as the same CIRCLE statement in medium resolution.

The Aspect Ratio

The variable RADIUS of an ellipse in the statement

```
CIRCLE(16Ø,1ØØ),RADIUS,,,,ASPECT
```

has the following meaning:

1. If ASPECT < 1, then RADIUS = RX

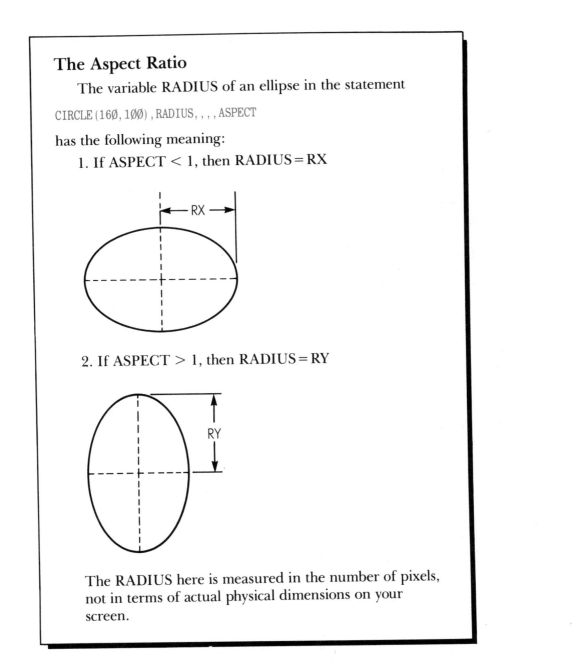

2. If ASPECT > 1, then RADIUS = RY

The RADIUS here is measured in the number of pixels, not in terms of actual physical dimensions on your screen.

To get a feeling for the aspect ratio in the high-resolution mode, substitute for the statement SCREEN 1 in line 10 of our previous program the statement

```
1Ø SCREEN 2
```

and run the program to see the effect of using different aspect ratios. Notice that you need to use a value for the aspect ratio close to .4 to get a circular shape (compared to .8 for medium-resolution). This value is close to the default value in high-resolution of 5/12 (equal to .416). Of course, that's no accident: the default value was chosen to give you something close to a true circle.

Adding Color to Your Circles

Circles can be drawn in a given color in a manner very similar to the way we've drawn colored points and lines. The following program draws a green circle on a black background:

```
1Ø SCREEN 1
2Ø COLOR Ø, 1      'black background, palette #1
3Ø CIRCLE(16Ø, 1ØØ), 6Ø, 1,,,.6   ← color #1 in palette #1 is cyan
```

The indicated color code (number 1) is, of course, the foreground color. The background color is, as usual, specified by the COLOR statement. The color code must be placed in the position shown — that is, right after the radius of the circle.

You'll notice the three adjacent commas in the preceding CIRCLE statement. These commas reserve space for two more modifiers related to the beginning and ending angles of arcs and to pie-shaped pieces of a circle. If you need to draw pie-graphs, this is the way to go. With the knowledge you now have under your belt, you'll find it easy to pursue this variation of CIRCLE on your own.

Summary

Doing color graphics is one of the most enjoyable aspects of programming. We've really just scratched the surface of the graphics capabilities of your PC, although this introduction is a good springboard for a more complete exploration of this topic.

In this chapter we've described the medium- and high-resolution graphics modes that are set by SCREEN 1 and SCREEN 2, respectively; the two graphics statements PSET, which places a point on the screen, and LINE, which draws a line; the procedures for putting color on your

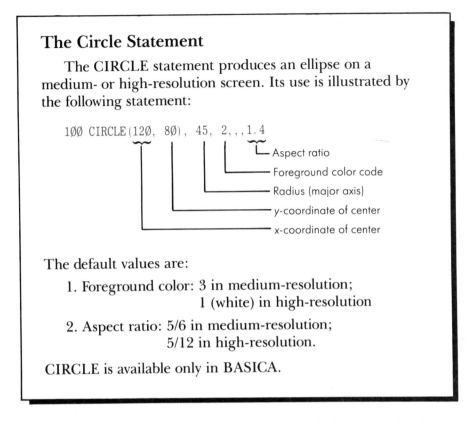

The Circle Statement

The CIRCLE statement produces an ellipse on a medium- or high-resolution screen. Its use is illustrated by the following statement:

```
100 CIRCLE(120, 80), 45, 2,,,1.4
```

- Aspect ratio
- Foreground color code
- Radius (major axis)
- y-coordinate of center
- x-coordinate of center

The default values are:

1. Foreground color: 3 in medium-resolution;
   1 (white) in high-resolution

2. Aspect ratio: 5/6 in medium-resolution;
   5/12 in high-resolution.

CIRCLE is available only in BASICA.

screen by means of color codes that specify both foreground and background colors; and finally, the CIRCLE statement, which draws ellipses (and of course, the circle, as a special case of an ellipse) of any shape and size within the screen's boundaries.

Exercise

This problem serves as a review. It's in a light vein, designed to use most of the statements we've learned in this chapter and to show some neat graphics effects.

Write a program that uses most of the statements we've introduced in this chapter to produce a visually interesting output. (These are pretty vague instructions, we admit, but they give you room to exercise your imagination!)

Solution

Here's our solution:

```
100  '----NAME: "GRAPHICS.B14"-----------------------------------------
110  '
120  '----*********************************************
130  '----* prgrm draws a series of graphic displays *----------------
140  '----*********************************************
150  '
160  '----draws a family of LINEs--------------------------------------
170  '
180  SCREEN 1                            'med. resol. graphics
190  CLS
200  COLOR Ø,1                           'blck backgrnd, pallete 1
210  FOR VISIBILITY = 1 TO Ø STEP -1     'draws, then erases lines
220     FOR J = Ø TO 20                  'draws 2Ø sets of lines
230        ASPECT = .Ø2 *J *J
240        DX = J*12                     'x-increment
250        DY = J*8                      'y-increment
260        IF VISIBILITY = 1 THEN COL = J MOD 3 + 1 ELSE COL = Ø
270        LINE(4Ø, 2Ø + DY) - (4Ø + DX, 18Ø),COL
280        LINE(4Ø + DX,18Ø) - (28Ø, 18Ø - DY), COL
290        LINE(28Ø, 18Ø - DY) - (28Ø - DX, 2Ø), COL
300        LINE(28Ø - DX, 2Ø) - (4Ø, 2Ø + DY),COL
310     NEXT
320  NEXT
330  '
340  '----draws 2 families of closely spaced circles --------------
350  '
360  FOR J = 1 TO 5Ø                     'draws 5Ø pairs of circles
370     RADIUS = J * 3
380     COL = J*8 MOD 3 + 1              'sets COLor to 1,2,or 3
390     CIRCLE(15Ø, 1ØØ), RADIUS, COL
400     CIRCLE(17Ø, 1ØØ), RADIUS, COL
410  NEXT
420  '
430  '----makes a filled box-------------------------------------------
440  '
450  LINE (5Ø, 3Ø)-(27Ø, 17Ø),1,BF
460  '
470  '----uses CIRCLE to draw family of ellipses------------------
480  '
```

```
49Ø ASPECT = .1
5ØØ RADIUS = 5Ø
51Ø FOR J = 1 TO 2Ø                       'draws 2Ø ellipses
52Ø    ASPECT = .Ø2 * J*J
53Ø    RADIUS = .8*((J - 12)*(J - 12)) + 1Ø
54Ø    CIRCLE(16Ø, 1ØØ), RADIUS,,,,ASPECT
55Ø NEXT
56Ø END
```

You might enjoy experimenting with this program by changing some of the constants, such as the "x" and "y" increments in lines 240 and 250, for example. We have to admit that we did sneak in one new BASIC instruction in line 260 — the expression right after THEN, which reads

```
COL = J MOD 3 + 1
```

This expression determines the foreground color code, COL, of the next LINE to be drawn. As the loop index J advances from 0 to 20, COL cycles through the integers between 1 and 3. That is, COL assumes values 1, 2, 3, 1, 2, 3, etc. — the whole selection of visible foreground color codes available to us. The key to this expression is the operator MOD: its effect in "J MOD 3" is to return the *remainder* of the quotient J divided by 3, which has the value 0, 1, or 2. To get the desired foreground color, all we have to do is to add 1. Pretty neat, yes? Previously we've produced the same effect with two statements — see lines 200 and 210 in program "COLBOXES.B14".

Line 260 produces another interesting effect. The expression after ELSE assigns 0 to the variable COL, which causes the foreground color to equal the background color. So a LINE drawn with this color value will be invisible — that's how we make lines disappear!

Arithmetic Functions — Number Crunching

We've seen how to program your PC to perform a vast variety of tasks, from making decisions to graphing colored pictures and investment returns. Many programs we've written involve the basic arithmetic operations of addition, subtraction, multiplication, and division. Your computer, however, has mathematical abilities far beyond these four operations. Some of these mathematical "talents" are used primarily for scientific applications, although many of them are of a much more general interest as well, particularly in business and graphics applications. In this chapter we'll explore the different ways your PC can manipulate numbers by means of numeric *functions*. It's interesting to note that computers were really invented to do just this type of "number crunching," and this is still one of the things that computers can do best.

Don't be concerned that you need to be a mathematician to read this chapter. Far from it! While it certainly helps if at some time in your life you've been exposed to a little algebra and trigonometry, this background is not necessary in order to learn from this chapter and enjoy it! In fact, the computer is a wonderful tool for teaching (and reviewing) many basic mathematical concepts.

If you really just can't stand mathematics, however, it's all right to skip this chapter. None of the information in this chapter is absolutely essential to the remaining chapters.

Arithmetic Functions — An Introduction Using ABS and SGN

We'd like to introduce the concept of numeric functions by showing you a specific example. The ABS function is ideal for this purpose because it's very simple. Enter the following commands:

```
ABS(5.68)
 5.68
Ok
ABS(-2.5)
 2.5
Ok
```

As you can see, the output is the same number as that inside the parentheses after ABS, except that the negative sign is gone. ABS is an abbreviation for "absolute value"; it is the name of a function that takes any number and returns the same number, but drops the negative sign if there was one. The absolute value of any number is always positive. The number inside the parentheses after ABS is called the *operand* — it's the number that the function ABS "operates" on to produce the value of the function. We can summarize the various aspects of this function in the following way:

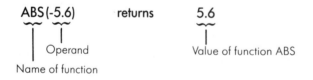

Most BASIC functions have a similar syntax: they have a name, followed by an operand enclosed by parentheses. The operand can, in general, be a variable or an expression. The value of a function can also be assigned to a variable, like this:

```
10 INPUT N
20 MAGNITUDE = ABS(N)
30 PRINT N, MAGNITUDE
```

Line 20 assigns the value of ABS(N) to the variable MAGNITUDE.

The ABS is typical of most numeric functions: a numeric function takes a number — the operand — and returns another number — the value of the function, which is determined by rules dictated by the particular function. In the case of the ABS function, the rule is simply "drop all negative signs." If you're not offended by loose analogies, you might think of a function as a meat grinder: you put some stuff (numbers) in the top, and different stuff (other numbers — the value of the function) comes out the bottom.

The SGN Function — Another Sign-Related Function

Before we leave this introduction to functions, let's take a look at another sign-related function: the SGN function. SGN is an abbreviation for "sign"; it's a function that tells you what the sign of a number is. As an example, run the following program:

```
1Ø FOR N = -3 TO 3
2Ø     PRINT N, SGN(N)
3Ø NEXT
Ok
RUN
-3                -1
-2                -1
-1                -1
 Ø                 Ø
 1                 1
 2                 1
 3                 1
Ok
```

As you can see, SGN(N) returns a +1 when N is positive, 0 when N is 0, and -1 when N is negative. Figure 15-1 summarizes the way SGN works.

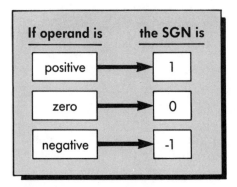

Figure 15-1. The SGN function

Sign-related Functions

One of the sign-related functions is ABS, which returns the absolute value of its operand. The example

ABS (-24)   operand

returns 24, the operand without the negative sign. The following is the equivalent statement in standard mathematical notation:

$|-25| = 25$

The other sign-related function returns the sign of a number (the operand) in the following manner:

SGN(-5) returns -1

SGN(0) returns 0

SGN(5) returns 1

Playing with Digits and Number Types

In the following sections, we'll look at some easy ways to turn noninteger numbers into integers and also to turn single-precision numbers into double-precision numbers and vice versa.

CINT, FIX, and INT — Three Different Ways to Make Integers

Everyone is familiar with rounding off a decimal number to an integer: for example, 5.4 can be rounded off to 5, 5.8 to 6, and 3.5 to 4. You do this whenever you round off a dollar-and-cents amount to a dollar amount. In PC BASIC, the function that does that job is CINT. For example,

```
PRINT CINT(3.45)
```

returns the integer 3. CINT stands for "convert to integer": this function takes a single- or double-precision number and converts it to an integer value by rounding off. This means that the value of CINT must be in the usual range of integer values: namely, between -32768 and 32767.

You'd probably expect that a language like BASIC has a function like CINT, but you may be surprised to learn that there are two other functions that have a similar job: the FIX and INT functions. For positive operands, these two functions do exactly the same thing: they simply remove the decimal part of the number so that it looks like an integer.

For example, enter the following:

```
PRINT FIX(5.9); INT(5.9)
 5  5
Ok
```

Both FIX and INT simply drop or "truncate" the operand 5.9 to give 5. Notice that rounding with CINT would have given 6 rather than 5. Another difference between CINT and the two functions FIX and INT is that whereas CINT returns a true integer, both FIX and INT return single-precision numbers that have a 0 decimal part. That means that FIX and INT aren't limited to the value range of integers.

The difference between FIX and INT shows up only with negative operands. FIX simply truncates all digits after the decimal point. For example, enter

```
PRINT FIX(-4.6)
-4
Ok
```

FIX drops the 6 after the decimal point to return the value -4. However, contrast this result with the value of INT(-4.6):

```
PRINT INT(-4.6)
-5
Ok
```

INT returns -5 instead of the -4 that FIX returned. For negative operands, INT returns an integer that is less than (more negative) or equal to its operand. At the risk of rattling your neurons, we summarize the effect of INT on both positive and negative numbers this way: INT returns the largest integer that is less than or equal to its operand.

To help you (and us!) keep all these differences straight, we've come up with the visual summary of the three functions presented in Figure 15-2. CINT, FIX, and INT all take a number N and return values as shown in the figure. As you can see, CINT rounds off to return a true integer value. FIX drops all digits after the decimal point. INT returns the largest number that is less than or equal to its operand.

An Example Using FIX, CINT, and ABS

All right, that's what these functions do, but what good are they? Consider the problem of finding the number of hours and minutes, if you're given the hours in decimal form. The following program makes this conversion:

```
1Ø INPUT "enter time in decimal hours:    ", TIME
2Ø HOURS = FIX(TIME)
3Ø MINUTES = CINT(ABS(TIME - HOURS)*6Ø)
4Ø PRINT "the time is " HOURS "hours and" MINUTES "minutes."
5Ø END
RUN
enter the time in decimal hours:    3.253
the time is  3 hours and 15 minutes
Ok
RUN
enter the time in decimal hours:    -3.253
the time is -3 hours and 15 minutes
Ok
```

We've run this program twice to show you that even a negative decimal hour will give a sensible output. For positive times, we could have used INT in place of FIX in line 20; but for a negative time (as in the second RUN), we would have gotten the hours wrong. Line 30 has two functions, one within the other: ABS makes sure that the minutes always come out positive, and CINT rounds off the minutes to the nearest integer. You might wish to extend this program to include a calculation of seconds!

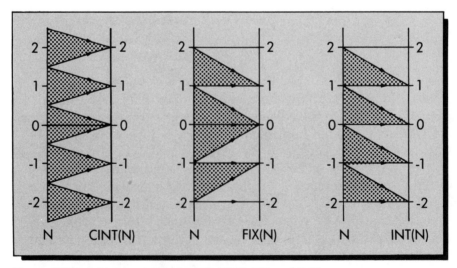

Figure 15-2. Making integers with CINT, FIX and INT

The Functions CSNG and CDBL — Converting to Single- and Double-Precision

Sometimes it is important to be able to convert from a double-precision number to a single-precision number. For example, you may be short on memory space, or you may simply want to round off a 14-digit number to the more usual seven-digit (single-precision) number. The function that does this job is called CSNG, which stands for "convert to single-precision." Try this example:

```
10 N# = 1.123456789#
20 PRINT N#, CSNG(N#)
RUN
 1.123456789    1.123457     ← Single-precision number rounded off
Ok                             from double-precision number N#
```

You can see that CSNG(N#) rounded off the double-precision number N# to the seventh digit, the standard length of a single-precision number.

It is sometimes also useful to convert from a single-precision number to a double-precision number by means of the CDBL function. CDBL stands for "convert to double-precision." Consider the following example:

```
10 N = 1.1
20 PRINT N, CDBL(N)
RUN
 1.1             1.10000002384185B
Ok
```

The value of CDBL(N) has 16 digits, which is true to the form of a double-precision number. Notice, however, all the nonzero digits in the second half of the double-precision number: these are arbitrary digits added in the conversion process and have nothing to do with the original number N. This may seem a bit odd and perhaps even distressing to you, but you should realize that these extra digits added in the conversion process don't make the number any less accurate, since the original number N = 1.1 is known to your PC only to six or seven significant digits. There is no real reason for your PC to assume that the original number N was "meant" to be exactly 1.100000000000000, even though such a tidy number might *look* better.

One reason you might want to use the CDBL function is illustrated in the following example:

```
10 A = 45632.5
20 B = 78564.5
30 PRINT A * B
40 PRINT CDBL(A) * CDBL(B)
RUN
 3.585095E+09         ← A * B
 3585094546.25        ← CDBL(A) * CDBL(B)
Ok
```

The product A * B is rounded off to seven digits (single-precision default). However, the product CDBL(A) * CDBL(B) has 12 digits, and it's exact. In general, the CDBL function is useful whenever you multiply (or divide) single-precision (or integer) numbers and you need more accuracy than possible with a seven digit or single-precision number.

Trigonometry on Your PC — The TAN, SIN, COS, and ATN Functions

We'll now take a look at a really interesting group of functions — the trigonometric functions. They are extremely useful whenever you're dealing with triangles and angles. The tangent function, for example, gives you a tool with which to answer the following type of question: "Suppose you are out on a safari and see a giraffe. If the giraffe is standing at a known distance away from you (say, at a riverbank), and you've measured the visual angle between the giraffe's feet and its head (you happen to have a protractor in your pocket), how tall is the giraffe?" We'll come back to this problem later after we've dealt with some of the basics.

The three basic trigonometric functions are the tangent, sine, and cosine. The names of these functions in BASIC are TAN, SIN, and COS, which are identical to their names as they usually appear in mathematics texts.

Let's find the tangent of an arbitrary operand, say 1, by using the command

```
PRINT TAN(1)
 1.557408
Ok
```

This tells you that the tangent of 1 is 1.557408. Great, but what do these numbers mean?

Measuring Angles: Degrees and Radians

First of all, the operand — the number 1 in our example — represents an angle. That's simple enough, except there's one small hitch. Most of us think of angles in terms of degrees; there are 360 degrees in one whole circle, 180 degrees in half a circle, and 90 degrees in a right angle. Your IBM PC, however, (as well as people who work with calculus), uses the *radian* measure instead of degrees.

What is a radian? If you look at Figure 15-3, you will see that an angle *A* measured in radians is equal to the arc length *s* divided by the radius *r* of the circle. For example, given the arc length equal to 6 units and a radius equal to 5 units as shown in the diagram, the angle *A* equals 6/5 radians, or 1.2 radians.

Since we will usually want to find the TAN (or SIN, or COS) of some angle in *degrees*, we'll need to find a way of converting degrees to radians. That's not hard: simply apply the first formula shown in Table 15-1. We also included a conversion from radians to degrees that will come in handy later in this section. (These formulas result from a comparison between radians and degrees; see any elementary trigonometry text for a derivation, if you're interested.)

At this point, although we now know what degrees and radians are, and how to convert from one to the other, and that the angles in the

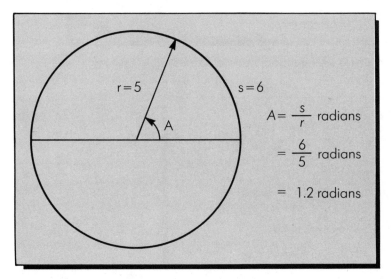

Figure 15-3. Finding a radian angle

TAN, SIN, and COS functions have to be given in radians, we still need to describe the meaning of the functions themselves.

The Meaning of TAN, SIN, and COS

To get an understanding of the meaning of these functions, let's draw a right triangle (a right triangle has one right angle in it) having sides with lengths 3, 4, and 5 units, as shown in Figure 15-4. The letter A represents the angle between the adjacent side (adjacent to A) and the hypotenuse (which is always opposite to the right angle). Using a protractor, you can measure angle A to be equal to approximately 36.9 degrees which equals .0237 radians.

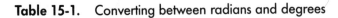

Conversion	Conversion Formula
Degrees to Radians	$radians = degrees * \dfrac{pi}{180}$ $= angle\ in\ degrees * 1.745329E\text{-}2$
Radians to Degrees	$degrees = radians * \dfrac{180}{pi}$ $= radians * 57.29578$

$$pi = 3.141593$$

Table 15-1. Converting between radians and degrees

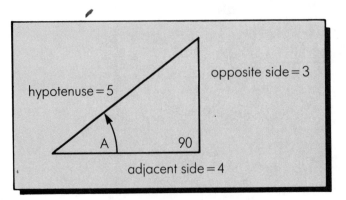

hypotenuse = 5

opposite side = 3

adjacent side = 4

A

90

Figure 15-4. A right triangle with sides of 3, 4 and 5 units

Based on this diagram, we can define the tangent, sine, and cosine of the angle *A* in the manner shown in Table 15-2. From these definitions, you can see that these trigonometric functions are simply ratios of the lengths of different sides of a right triangle. The values of these ratios are uniquely related to the particular angle involved.

Notice that we were able to find the value of any one of the trigonometric functions for the angle of .0237 radians (36.9 degrees) by measuring the length of the sides of a triangle having this angle, and calculating the appropriate ratio. Nothing hard about that. But who wants to draw a triangle, take measurements, and calculate ratios every time you need the value for a tangent, sine, or cosine? That's a great way to learn about trigonometric functions, but not something you want to do too often, especially if you have a PC around that can do it in a fraction of a second!

The following program puts your computer to work (finally!) to find the value for TAN, SIN, and COS, given any angle in degrees:

```
1Ø PI = 3.141593
2Ø INPUT "enter angle in degrees: ", DEGREES
3Ø RADIANS = DEGREES*PI/18Ø
4Ø PRINT TAN(RADIANS), SIN(RADIANS), COS(RADIANS)
5Ø END
RUN
enter angle in degrees: 45
 1              .7Ø71Ø68       .7Ø71Ø68
Ok
RUN
enter angle in degrees  6Ø
 1.732Ø51       .866Ø254       .5ØØØØØ1
Ok
RUN
enter angle in degrees: 9Ø
 -267Ø177       1              -3.745Ø7E-7
Ok
```

If you've ever had to look in mathematical handbooks or use a slide rule to find these functions (the only choice you would have had only about 10 years ago), you'll be impressed by the speed and accuracy of your PC.

A Word About Precision

We chose the last two runs of the preceding program to illustrate just how accurately the trigonometric functions are calculated. Whereas the

cosine of 60 degrees ought to be exactly .5, we obtained the value
.5000001; the difference of .000001 corresponds to the usual accuracy of
single-precision calculations. When we tried 90 degrees in the third run,
we got some interesting results: the tangent of 90 degrees is $\mp$ infinity,
but our PC calculated it to be -2670177 — a very large negative number,
but not equal to -infinity, which is a number more negative than any
number that we can think of! Also, the cosine of 90 degrees should equal
zero, but the PC got -3.74507E-7 — very close to zero.

If the kind of precision illustrated above isn't good enough for you
(maybe you're planning to launch your own planetary space probes), you
can't use anything older than DOS 2.0. While DOS 1.1 only does single-
precision trigonometric calculations, DOS 2.0 provides you with the
option of doing double-precision trigonometric calculations with 16-digit
display!

Using Trigonometric Functions — Some Examples

Now is a good time to fulfill our promise to return to the problem
posed in the beginning of this section: finding the height of a giraffe if
we know its distance and the visual angle between its feet and its head. If
you look at Figure 15-5, you'll notice that the triangle has one of its
corners as the position of your eye, and its opposite side as the giraffe.

The trigonometric function	The BASIC function	Example from Figure 15-4
$\tan(A) = \dfrac{\text{opposite side}}{\text{adjacent side}}$	TAN(A)	$\text{TAN}(.0237\,\text{rad}) = \dfrac{3}{4} = .75$
$\sin(A) = \dfrac{\text{opposite side}}{\text{hypotenuse}}$	SIN(A)	$\text{SIN}(.0237\,\text{rad}) = \dfrac{3}{5} = .6$
$\cos(A) = \dfrac{\text{adjacent side}}{\text{hypotenuse}}$	COS(A)	$\text{COS}(.0237\,\text{rad}) = \dfrac{4}{5} = .8$

Table 15-2. Definitions of TAN, SIN and COS

Notice that only the opposite and the adjacent side to the angle are involved; hence the tangent function should do the trick. Since

$$TAN(A) = \frac{\text{opposite side}}{\text{adjacent side}} = \frac{\text{height of giraffe}}{\text{distance to giraffe}}$$

then height of giraffe = distance of giraffe * TAN(A).

Translating the "then" clause in this formula into a BASIC program, we get the following:

```
10 CRAD = 1.745329E-2
20 INPUT "enter distance of giraffe in feet-------- ", DIST
30 INPUT "enter visual angle of giraffe in degrees- ", DEG
40 HEIGHT = CINT(DIST*TAN(CRAD*DEG))
50 PRINT "the giraffe is" HEIGHT "feet tall"
60 END
RUN
enter distance of giraffe in feet-------- 120
enter visual angle of giraffe in degrees- 12.5
the giraffe is 26 feet tall
Ok
```

Giraffes are very tall! Line 10 defines the constant CRAD that we'll use later in line 40 to convert from degrees to radians. Notice that we rounded off the HEIGHT by using the CINT function (we assumed you weren't interested in fractional feet).

Trigonometric functions can be used very effectively to produce

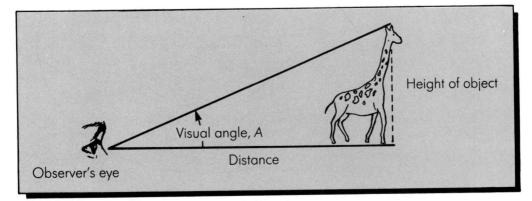

Figure 15-5. Observing objects with a protractor

interesting graphics. The following example uses the SIN and COS functions to draw a spiral:

```
80   '---NAME: "SPIRAL.B15"--------------------------------------------------
90   '
100  CLS
110  PI2 = 6.283185                 'sets the value of pi*2
120  SCREEN 1                       'medium resol. graphics screen
130  COLOR Ø, 1                     'black bckgnd, palette 1
140  NREV = 2.5                     'sets the number of rev. of spiral
150  NDOTS = 100                    'sets the number of dots in spiral
160  FOR DOT = Ø TO NDOTS           'draw NDOT number of dots
170      RAD = DOT*PI2*NREV/NDOTS   'defines angle in RADians of a dot
180      RADIUS = DOT*80/NDOTS      'defines radius of dot position
190      X = 160 + COS(RAD)*RADIUS*1.6  'x coordinate of dot
200      Y = 100 - SIN(RAD)*RADIUS  'y coordinate of dot
210      COL = COL + 1              'increments forgnd COLor by 1
220      IF COL>3 THEN COL = COL - 3  'restarts COLor cycle
240      PSET(X,Y), COL             'plots point at x,y with COLor
250  NEXT
260  END
```

This program is designed for use with a *color* display; a black-and-white monitor driven by the Color/Graphics Adapter will do, but not the IBM

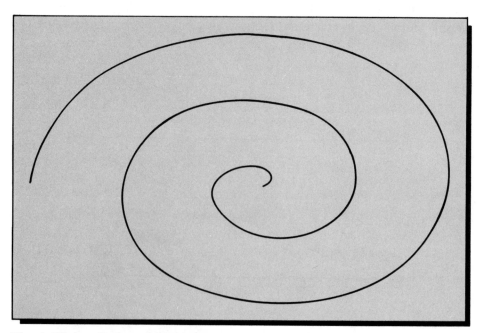

Figure 15-6. Output of SPIRAL.B15

Monochrome Display. The output of this program is shown in Figure 15-6.

The program is reasonably self-explanatory, although we'd like to make a a few comments about its basic concepts. Each dot of the spiral is placed on the screen at coordinates x and y by the PSET statement in line 230. The diagram in Figure 15-7 shows how these x and y coordinates are obtained.

The statement defining x in line 190 also includes a multiplying factor of 1.6 to stretch the spiral in the x direction. The angle RAD, defined by line 170, starts out at 0 and is incremented upwards with each execution of the loop. If the RADIUS were a constant, we'd get a circle. The way to make a spiral is by increasing the RADIUS as the angle RAD increases — that's the job of line 170.

One of the interesting features of a program like this is that you can play and experiment with different variations. For example, you can try running this program with different values for NREV (controls the number of turns in the spiral) or NDOT (controls the number of dots in the spiral). You can also experiment with different color schemes through the COLOR statement. We'll use this program again as a building block in the final program of this chapter.

The Inverse Tangent Function ATN

In the previous discussion, we showed you how to use your PC to find the length of a given side of a right triangle if you know one other side

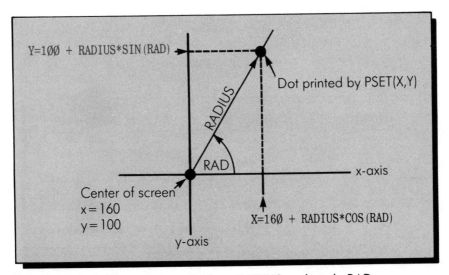

Figure 15-7. Obtaining x and y from RADIUS and angle RAD

and one of the angles (other than the 90 degree angle!) In many situations, however, we need to *find* an angle given the lengths of at least two sides of the triangle. The basic function that allows you to do this job is the ATN function, called the *inverse tangent*.

The inverse tangent does the opposite or "inverse" of the tangent function. The ATN function returns the angle (in radians) whose tangent is given by its operand. That is,

ATN(X) = angle in radians whose tangent equals X

We can contrast the TAN and ATN functions by means of the diagram shown in Figure 15-8. For example, enter the command

```
PRINT ATN(1)
 .7853983            ← Angle in radians whose tangent equals 1
Ok
```

This tells you that the inverse tangent of 1 radian equals .7853983.

Frequently we'll want the angle returned by ATN to be in degrees rather than in radians. That's easy — we can simply multiply the radian angle by the number 180/pi = 57.29578 to obtain degrees. The following program calculates the inverse tangent in both radians and degrees given any input (operand) value:

```
1Ø INPUT "enter value of tangent", TANGENT
2Ø RAD = ATN(TANGENT)
3Ø DEG = 57.29578*RAD
4Ø PRINT RAD, DEG
5Ø END
RUN
```

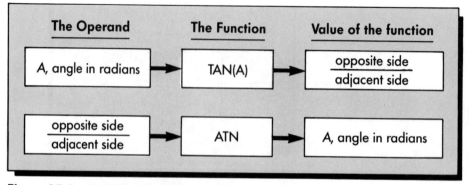

Figure 15-8. Relationship between TAN and ATN

```
enter value of tangent  1
 .7853983       45
Ok
RUN
enter value of tangent  10000
 1.570696       89.99426
Ok
```

The first run says that the inverse tangent of 1 is 45 degrees — that makes sense, right? Remember that in a 45 degree triangle, which has two 45 degree angles and one right angle, the opposite side and the adjacent sides have the same length, so that their ratio equals 1. Thus, 45 degrees is the angle whose tangent equals 1. The second run suggests that as the tangent gets very large — 10,000 in this case — the corresponding angle returned by ATN approaches 90 degrees. You can really do some "experimental" mathematics with your computer!

By this time you are probably waiting for us to show you the inverse functions of the sine and the cosine. Of course, these exist. They return the angle whose sine or cosine equals the operand:

inverse sine $\quad = \arcsin(x) =$ angle whose sine equals x

inverse cosine $= \arccos(x) =$ angle whose cosine equals x

You should note, however, these functions are not part of BASIC's repertoire, although you can easily "construct" them yourself using the formulas given in the mathematical appendix of your BASIC manual.

The BASIC Trigonometric Functions

The four trigonometric functions and their syntax in BASIC are

$\quad$ tan(*angle*) $\quad \rightarrow \quad$ TAN(*angle* in radians)
$\quad$ sin(*angle*) $\quad \rightarrow \quad$ SIN(*angle* in radians)
$\quad$ cos(*angle*) $\quad \rightarrow \quad$ COS(*angle* in radians)
$\quad$ arctan(*value*) $\quad \rightarrow \quad$ ATN(*value*) returns *angle* in radians

Notice that all angles in BASIC are interpreted as radians. The conversion factors between degrees and radians are

$\quad$ radians $=$ degrees $*$ pi/180 $=$ degrees $*$ 1.745329E-2
$\quad$ degrees $=$ radians $*$ 180/pi $=$ radians $*$ 57.29578

Powers, Roots, and Logs

The following sections show you how to use some of BASIC's special functions that relate to the power or exponent of a number.

Exponentiation — Raising Numbers to a Power

Mathematical calculations frequently require a number to be raised to a given power. For example, to find the area of a circle, we need to multiply pi times the radius raised to the second power (also referred to as squaring the radius, which is equivalent to multiplying the radius by itself). We can write a BASIC statement for the area of a circle having a radius of 5 in two different ways:

```
AREA = 3.14 * 5 * 5
```

or

```
AREA = 3.14 * 5 ^ 2
```

where 5 ^ 2 means "raise 5 to the 2nd power," or equivalently, "find the product of 5 * 5." The number 2 is also called the *exponent* of 5. We can write similar statements for different powers or exponents:

```
      5 = 5^1 = 5          exponent = 1
    5*5 = 5^2 = 25         exponent = 2
  5*5*5 = 5^3 = 125        exponent = 3
5*5*5*5 = 5^4 = 625        exponent = 4
    *      *     *            *      *
    *      *     *            *      *
    *      *     *            *      *
```

The following expression

$$5 \wedge 4$$

      | Exponent or power of 5
BASIC exponentiation symbol

summarizes the general way a number (5 in this example) is raised to a given power (4) in BASIC.

All right, so much for the basics. Your PC is really adept at exponentiation or "raising a number to a given power." Try the following program:

```
10 FOR EXPONENT = -3 TO 3
20     Y = 2^EXPONENT
30        PRINT EXPONENT, Y
40 NEXT
50 END
RUN
-3             .125
-2             .25
-1             .5
 0             1
 1             2
 2             4
 3             8
Ok
```

If you've never worked with exponents (or powers), you'll find these results interesting. A negative exponent means the same thing as the reciprocal (1/number) of a number (in this case 2) raised to the positive exponent. Also, 2^0 equals 1, a result which is not at all obvious!

SQR — Taking the Square Root

Exponents don't have to be integers; they can be fractions or decimals. A very common fractional exponent is .5 or 1/2; it has the same effect as taking the *square root* of a number. In fact, taking square roots is such an important and frequently used procedure that BASIC has a special function, called SQR, just for this purpose. Here is an example of how SQR can be used:

```
PRINT SQR(25)
 5
Ok
```

Well, we already knew that the square root of 25 is 5 (because 5 * 5 equals 25, right?).

Let's use the SQR function to solve the frequently very practical problem of finding the length of the hypotenuse of a right triangle, given the lengths of the other two sides:

```
1Ø INPUT "enter base of triangle--- ", BASE
2Ø INPUT "enter height of triangle- ", HEIGHT
3Ø HYPOTENUSE = SQR(BASE^2 + HEIGHT^2)
4Ø PRINT "the hypotenuse equals---- " HYPOTENUSE
5Ø END
RUN
enter base of triangle--- 3
enter height of triangle- 4
the hypotenuse equals---- 5
Ok
```

This result tells you that the diagonal distance across a rectangle with the dimensions 3 by 4 equals 5. Notice that we also had the opportunity to use exponentiation in line 30.

EXP and LOG — The Number *e*, and Its Logarithm

There are some numbers in our universe that are very special, like the number pi, which crops up frequently whenever circles are involved in a problem. Another such number is called *e*; its value is 2.718283. It looks perfectly ordinary, but anyone who has taken a course in calculus knows that it appears quite "naturally" in many types of rather sophisticated calculations that we won't even bother to name! We can't explain its meaning here, but we don't really need to in order to show you the two BASIC functions that are related to it.

The EXP Function — Powers of e

The EXP function raises the number *e* to the power indicated by the operand. For example,

```
PRINT EXP(2)
 7.389Ø56          ← e raised to power 2 = e^2 = e²
Ok
```

tells us that the number *e* raised to the power 2 equals 7.389056. Or in the standard mathematical format

the BASIC expression $Y = EXP(2)$ means $y = e^2$

You might wish to use the following program to explore this function:

```
INPUT "enter exponent of e:   ", X
20 Y = EXP(X)
30 PRINT "e raised to the power " X "equals" Y
40 END
RUN
enter exponent of e:   1
e raised to the power  1 equals 2.718282
RUN
enter exponent of e:   -1
e raised to the power -1 equals .3678795
Ok
```

The second run gives the value of *e* raised to the -1 power, which is the same thing as $1/e^1$, or $1/e$.

The LOG Function — Taking the Natural Logarithm

The LOG function is the inverse of the EXP function: whereas EXP(X) raises *e* to the power X, LOG(Y) finds the exponent to which *e* must be raised in order to give the number Y. The mathematical notation for BASIC's LOG(Y) is ln(y). This form of the logarithm is the "natural" logarithm in contrast to the logarithm to the base 10. The relationship between raising *e* to a given power and the logarithm of a number is the following:

If $y = e^x$ then $x = \ln(y)$

or in BASIC's notation,

if Y = EXP(X)   then   X = LOG(Y)

You can familiarize yourself with the LOG function with the help of this program:

```
10 INPUT "enter a number:   ", X
20 X = LOG(Y)
30 PRINT "the natural logarithm of" X "equals" Y
40 END
RUN
enter a number:   1
the natural logarithm of 1 equals 0
Ok
RUN
enter a number    2.718282
the natural logarithm of 2.718282 equals 1
Ok
```

The result of the second run reflects the fact that e^1 equals e itself.

The functions EXP and LOG can be used to generate an interesting variety of graphics effects. As a simple illustration, we suggest that you modify our previous spiral program in the following manner to generate a beautifully shaped spiral that looks very similar to the seashell called the chambered nautilus: replace line 180 of the spiral program with

```
180    RADIUS = DOT*LOG(DOT)*20/NDOTS
```

Does the chambered nautilus know about logarithms?

RND and RANDOMIZE — Random Numbers

Most of the time we use our computer to produce very precise, predictable results. Computers excel at following instructions to the "bit"; they are not subject to the vagaries (well, not usually, anyway!) so characteristic of humankind. There are computer applications, however, that require the computer to do the very thing that it "likes" least: to produce random numbers. *Random numbers* are numbers that don't have any patterns in the way the digits appear. The applications of random numbers range from playing games of chance, like poker or similar games involving dice, to simulating the behavior of gas molecules, to graphic displays having some degree of randomness.

BASIC makes it easy for us to generate such random numbers. As a first experiment, enter the command

```
PRINT RND
 .6291626
Ok
```

The BASIC word RND is an abbreviation for "random." The output of RND is a seven-digit number that is always between 0 and 1. If you repeat the above direct command, you'll get a different number each time, which is certainly something we'd expect from a sequence of random numbers. RND selects and returns a number from a list of random numbers between 0 and 1. This list of random numbers is stored in the computer's memory.

The following program generates a list of five random numbers:

```
1Ø FOR J = 1 TO 5
2Ø     PRINT RND;
3Ø NEXT
4Ø END
RUN
 .6291626   .1948297   .63Ø5799   .8625749   .736353
Ok
```

Sure enough, RND generates a sequence of random numbers between 0 and 1. It's not obvious, by the way, that these numbers are truly random; that is, that there is no pattern in their digits, but they certainly appear to be random.

As an example of how we can make use of the computer's capability to generate a sequence of random numbers, let's write a program that "rolls" a die. Since a dice roll results in a random integer number from 1 to 6, we need to find a way to translate random decimal numbers between 0 and 1 into random integers between (and including) 1 and 6. The following program "throws the dice" 10 times:

```
1Ø FOR J = 1 TO 1Ø
2Ø     NDICE = INT(RND*6) + 1
3Ø     PRINT NDICE;
4Ø NEXT
5Ø END
Ok
RUN
 4  2  4  6  5  6  1  6  1  1
Ok
```

Great! Although there are a suspiciously large number of sixes in this list, groupings like that are perfectly natural to random numbers. The expression INT(RND*6) in line 20 produces integers between 0 and 5 (remember: INT truncates), so we just need to add a 1 to get numbers from 1 to 6.

Let's "throw the dice" again:

```
RUN
 4  2  4  6  5  6  1  6  1  1
Ok
RUN
 4  2  4  6  5  6  1  6  1  1
Ok
```

Hmm... We get the same sequence of "throws" every time we run this program! That's OK for many applications, but if your computer is rolling the dice for a poker game, you don't want its dice throws to be predictable. Fortunately for all you gamblers out there, BASIC gives us a way out — the RANDOMIZE statement.

RANDOMIZE — Reseeding Your Random Numbers

In order to cause your PC to select a different sequence of random numbers in a program like our previous example, use the RANDOMIZE statement before RND is executed. Insert RANDOMIZE at the beginning of the previous dice rolling program to give the following:

```
5  RANDOMIZE
1Ø FOR NDICE = 1 TO 1Ø
2Ø    NDICE = INT(RND*6) + 1
3Ø    PRINT NDICE;
4Ø NEXT
5Ø END
RUN
Random number seed (-32768 to 32767)? 4      ← Seed number = 4
 2  4  5  5  4  6  5  1  2  6
Ok
RUN
Random number seed (-32768 to 32767)? -345    ← Seed number = -345
 3  5  2  2  5  4  5  1  5  1
Ok
```

RANDOMIZE asks the user to enter a "seed" number. A particular seed number causes RND to return a sequence of random numbers that is unique to that particular seed number. A different seed number will result in a different sequence of random numbers.

That's a partial solution to our problem. Somebody still has to enter a seed number, although if you enter a new number every time, you'd be sure to get a different sequence of random numbers. But there's another, and perhaps, better way to handle the reseeding process. In effect, the seed number can also be written right into the RANDOMIZE statement like this:

```
5 RANDOMIZE 13
            |
            Seed number
```

If we can now find a way to "randomly" select the seed number, we should then be able to generate a *new* random list of numbers every time our program is run. We can come close to doing this by using some of the digits in the TIME$ output of your PC as seed values. We won't explain exactly how this statement works since it uses some statements that we'll cover in a later chapter, but here's one way to write it:

```
5 RANDOMIZE VAL(RIGHT$(TIME$,2))
```

The seed value returned by VAL( ) is equal to the number of seconds indicated by the internal clock of your PC; it changes every second, and stays in the range of 0 to 59. If you use this statement in our dice rolling program, we doubt if anyone would notice that there are only 60 different sequences of dice rolls!

Producing Random Numbers

The easiest way to produce random numbers is by means of the RND function:

RND returns a 7 digit random number between Ø and 1

In situations where you need to generate a different set of random numbers each time the program is run, you can "reseed" the random number generator by means of the statement

```
RANDOMIZE 6
          |
          Seed number
```

Changing the seed number will change the set of random numbers generated. If no seed number is indicated, BASIC will ask the user to enter a seed number when RANDOMIZE is executed.

A Graphics Example

Random numbers are also very useful in generating graphics displays. Images often are more interesting if they have a random element in them. The following program is a simple example that generates random radial lines (again, this program is designed to be used with a color display):

```
100 CLS
110 SCREEN 1                   'medium resol. graphics screen
120 COLOR 0,1                   'black bckgnd, palette 1
125 RANDOMIZE 40
130 FOR J = 1 TO 30             'draws 30 radial lines
140     X = 60 + RND*200        'random x between 60 and 260
150     Y = 20 + RND*160        'random y between 20 and 180
160     COL = FIX(RND*3) + 1    'random COL between 1 and 3
170     LINE (160,100)-(X,Y),COL
180 NEXT
190 END
Ok
```

You can change the pattern of the "explosion" by changing the seed number. Notice that RND also selects the color of the line to be drawn.

DEF FN and FN — Creating Your Own Functions

If BASIC doesn't have the function you need, you can make up your own. That's a very handy technique if you have to use a function or mathematical expression in several different parts of your program.

The first step is to define your function by means of the DEF FN statement. This statement must appear in your program before the function itself. The following statement defines a function that rounds off a number to the second place behind the decimal (very handy if you need to print out dollar amounts):

```
10 DEF FNROUND(X) = INT(X*100 + .5)/100
```

This statement "defines a function" having the name ROUND, a convenient abbreviation for "rounding off." The name of the function must always have the prefix FN. What follows can be any valid variable name. The variable *X* in FNROUND(*X*) is not a variable in the usual sense of the word: it's a *place-holder* for the actual variable that you'll insert in this position when you actually use the function. Sometimes such a variable is called a "dummy" variable (it's a dummy because it just sits there and takes up space).

The second step involves using the function. For example, you can write a statement like the following:

```
12Ø PRINT FNRND(CATFOOD)
```

⏝ ⏝
│   Variable CATFOOD replaces dummy variable
│
Function RND with FN prefix

The function is written just as we defined it in the DEF statement: it has the name ROUND and the prefix FN. The operand can be any variable — ours happens to be CATFOOD. If CATFOOD has the value 131.4598, FNROUND(CATFOOD) will return value 131.

As we mentioned earlier, BASIC doesn't supply us with the inverse sine and cosine functions. But we can easily define them ourselves if they are needed. The following example shows how to define and use the inverse sine function, also called the *arcsine*:

```
1Ø DEF FNARCSIN(X) = ATN(X/SQR(1 - X^2))
2Ø INPUT "enter a value between -1 and 1:  ", VALUE
3Ø PRINT "the arcsin of " VALUE "equals " FNARCSIN(VALUE) "radians
RUN
enter a value between -1 and 1:  .3Ø3
the arcsin of  .3Ø3 equals  .3Ø7839 radians
Ok
```

If you only need the arcsine once, there isn't any point in going through the trouble of defining the function in this way. However, if you need to use the arcsine over and over again within a program, this technique is very helpful in saving program space and giving order and clarity to your program.

Summary

Numeric functions are a powerful addition to your repertoire of BASIC commands. They are useful not only in solving scientific problems, but also in business and graphics applications. You may not fully understand the mathematical concepts behind some of these functions, but you can, nevertheless, experiment with them and in the process learn more about them.

The final program in this chapter is designed to show off some of the ways you can use numeric functions to generate interesting graphics. The possibilities are endless, and we invite you to try your own hand at it!

Exercise

Write an interesting program in the medium-resolution graphics mode using some of the numerical functions introduced in this chapter. We are purposely ambiguous in our instructions: this is your chance to use your imagination!

Solution

This is the way we went about it.

```
100 '----NAME: "BIGBANG.B15"-----------------------------------------
102 '
108 '----*************************************************
110 '----*                "THE BIGBANG"                  *-------------
120 '----* GRAPHICS PRGM TO ILLUSTRATE USE OF FUNCTIONS *-------------
130 '----*************************************************
140 CLS
150 SCREEN 1
160 PI = 3.141593: PI2 = 6.283185
170 COLOR 0,1
180 RANDOMIZE VAL(RIGHT$(TIME$,2))          'uses TIME$ to seed rnd # gen.
190 '
200 '----initializes arrays VX and VY for explosion SUBR-------------
210 '
220 NRAYS = 50
230 SPEED = 20
240 DIM VX(NRAYS), VY(NRAYS)
250 FOR RAY = 1 TO NRAYS
260     VX(RAY) = (RND-.5)*SPEED           'rnd speed in x direction
270     VY(RAY) = (RND-.5)*SPEED           'rnd speed in y direction
280 NEXT
290 '
300 '----MAIN PGRM calls SUBROUTINES----------------------------------
310 '
320 '==========
330 GOSUB 380                              'SUBR for spiral
340 '==========
350 GOSUB 520                              'SUBR for explosion
360 '==========
370 END
380 '
390 '====SUBR for spiral===============================================
400 '
410 FOR DOT = 100 TO 1 STEP -1
```

```
42Ø      FOR SPIRAL = 1 TO 2
43Ø          RADBEGIN = (SPIRAL - 1)*PI
44Ø          RAD = RADBEGIN + DOT/8
45Ø          RADIUS = DOT*LOG(DOT)/5
46Ø          X = 16Ø + RADIUS*COS(RAD)*1.6       'uses COS to find x coord
47Ø          Y = 1ØØ - RADIUS*SIN(RAD)           'uses SIN to find y coord
48Ø          PSET (X,Y),SPIRAL
49Ø      NEXT
5ØØ NEXT
51Ø RETURN
52Ø '
53Ø '====SUBR for explosion=========================================
54Ø '
55Ø FOR TIME = Ø TO 25
56Ø      FOR RAY = 1 TO NRAYS
57Ø          X = 16Ø + VX(RAY)*SQR(TIME*4)       'uses SQR to find x coord
58Ø          Y = 1ØØ - VY(RAY)*SQR(TIME*4)       'uses SQR to find y coord
59Ø          PSET(X,Y), TIME/1Ø + 1
6ØØ      NEXT RAY
61Ø NEXT TIME
62Ø RETURN
```

We encourage you to modify this program by using different functions
and adding new subroutines. In fact, we used subroutines to do different
parts of the graphics so that it would be easy to make such changes and
additions.

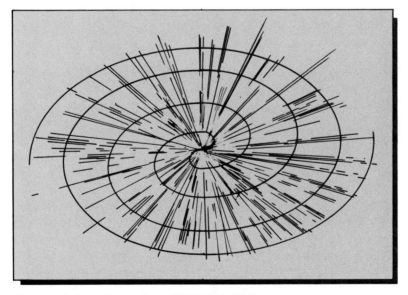

Figure 15-9.   Output from BIGBANG.B15

You may wonder why we put the part of the program that initializes the arrays VX and VY (lines 200 to 280) in the beginning of the program and not in the more appropriate position at the beginning of the explosion subroutine. The reason is that "loading" arrays takes time, and we wanted to minimize the delay between the first subroutine and the explosion produced by the second subroutine.

Making Development
Smoother

Concepts
Line numbering
Renumbering
Continuation of RUN
DOS-related functions

Instructions
AUTO, RENUM, CONT(F5), TRON(F7), TROFF(F8), FRE, CLEAR,
FILES, KILL, NAME, CHAIN, MERGE

Now that you have some programming experience under your belt,
we would like to share with you some BASIC commands which are
designed to make your life a little easier. These items fall into two
categories: one set will make your programming a little easier; the other
will help to simplify file management.

Programming Aids

In this section we'll cover a group of commands which, while not
essential to writing BASIC programs, will speed up programming,
program modification, and debugging.

Line Numbering with AUTO

Wouldn't it be nice to have a way of automatically placing the line
numbers before each line of a program, as you're typing the line in? The
AUTO command does just that. In its simplest form it starts the

numbering system with line 10 and increments the line numbers by 10 for each new line. For example:

```
AUTO        ← If you type this
1Ø PRINT "WHAT A CONVENIENCE"
|
```
... the line number 10 is printed automatically, and you enter the remaining BASIC statement

```
2Ø     ← The line number 2Ø is printed automatically
```

By including a number after AUTO, you can specify a starting number. For instance, if you were to type AUTO 100, you would get 100, 110, 120, and so on. You can also change the intervals between lines. If you typed AUTO 100,20 then 100, 120, 140, ... would be the resulting sequence of line numbers. If no line number is specified but the increment is given (say, 20) then 0, 20, 40, and so on would result. In this case the command must be followed by a comma before the increment: for example, AUTO ,20. The general form of the AUTO command is illustrated by the following:

```
AUTO  XXX, YYY
      ~~~  ~~~
       |    |
       |    Increment (by 10's, 20's, 100's etc.)
       Starting line number
```

Finally, if you started writing your program without the AUTO line generator and you wish to start automatic numbering from your current line, the command AUTO .,10 will start from the current position and increment by 10's, since the period (.) is used as a symbol for the current line number.

If you use the Auto line generator to generate a line number that already exists in the PC's memory, an asterisk (*) will be printed after the line number to indicate that, when you enter a new line, the new line will replace the old line of the same number. If you push the ENTER key immediately after the * position, the existing line will not be changed. To turn off the AUTO line function, merely depress the (Ctrl) (Break) keys.

Renumbering with RENUM

Even experienced programmers can sometimes find themselves with a chaotic, messed up bunch of line numbers in a program, especially after the program has undergone significant editing. BASIC comes to the rescue with the command RENUM, which will renumber a program for you, thus turning a hodgepodge of line numbers into a nice neat listing.

RENUM has the form:

```
RENUM XXX, YYY, ZZZ
         |    |    |  Increment
         |    |  Previous line number
         |  New line number
```

Following RENUM, you must type

1. The first line number to be used in the *new* renumbering system

2. The old line number where renumbering is to begin

3. The increment to be used in the new sequence.

Let's try renumbering the following program:

```
8  PRINT DATE$
1Ø PRINT "HAPPY BIRTHDAY -- ANNE"
23 PRINT
25 PRINT "FROM ALL YOUR FANS"
3Ø GOTO 1Ø
33 END
```

When we use the RENUM command without *old* or *new* line numbers or without an *interval*, RENUM starts by default with line 10 and has a spacing *interval* of 10. For example:

```
RENUM

1Ø PRINT DATE$
2Ø PRINT "HAPPY BIRTHDAY -- ANNE"
3Ø PRINT
4Ø PRINT "FROM ALL YOUR FANS"
5Ø GOTO 2Ø
6Ø END
```

Here's what happens if we specify the *interval* of 15:

```
RENUM , , 15

1Ø PRINT DATE$
25 PRINT "HAPPY BIRTHDAY -- ANNE"
4Ø PRINT
55 PRINT "FROM ALL YOUR FANS"
6Ø GOTO 25
75 END
```

Wow! In each instance the GOTO line number was changed to cause the program always to go to the line containing PRINT "HAPPY BIRTHDAY — ANNE". As you can see, all branching by line number is adjusted for with RENUM. Thus the branching line number references used in the commands GOTO, GOSUB, IF...THEN...ELSE, ON...GOTO, ON...GOSUB, and ON ERROR GOTO will all be changed by the RENUM command.

We'll give this another try. This time let's start with *old* line 40 and make it into *new* line 200, with an interval of 100.

```
RENUM 2ØØ,4Ø,1ØØ

1Ø PRINT DATE$
25 PRINT "HAPPY BIRTHDAY -- ANNE"
2ØØ PRINT
3ØØ PRINT "FROM ALL YOUR FANS"
4ØØ GOTO 25
5ØØ END
```

CONT — Resuming After Program Interruption

To resume the execution of a program after a (Ctrl) (Break), STOP, END, or after an error has occurred, the CONT (Soft Function Key (F5)) command may be used. In debugging a program, you may wish to insert stops at various parts of a program to see if your program is making it that far with the results that you expected. After the stop the CONT can be used to resume execution at the next line number. If the stop occurs at a point of input, the prompt will be repeated with the CONT command.

Suppose you have a program with a time-consuming loop such as the following:

```
1ØØ FOR N = 1 TO 1ØØØ
11Ø    PRINT N, N^2, N^3, N^4
12Ø NEXT N
```

Pressing the (Ctrl) (Break) will halt the program while it is running. Then if you press the (F5) key or if you type CONT, the computation will resume.

TRON and TROFF — Trace On and Off

When programs don't work, it would be nice to slow down the program so you can see what's happening. The TRON and TROFF commands let you do something very similar. BASIC's "trace" function is turned on by the command TRON (F7) and turned off by the command TROFF (F8). When the "trace" is on, the PC prints the line number that is currently being executed. To avoid confusion with a program's normal output, these line numbers are displayed within brackets (for example, [100]).

If the program becomes hopelessly caught in a loop, the line numbers will continually repeat themselves. In the following example, the problem is in the time counter in lines 160 through 180:

```
100 '----NAME: "TRONDEMO.B16"
110 '
120 '-----THIS PROGRAM IS A TIME WASTER -------------
130 '
140 FOR X = 1 TO 5
150   PRINT "I HAVEN'T GOT ALL DAY"
160     FOR N=1 TO 1600
170     PRINT ".";
180     NEXT N
190 NEXT X
200 END
```

Turn on the trace, either by entering TRON or by pressing the (F7) key. Then run the program. Here's the output:

```
Ok
RUN
[100] [110] [120] [130] [140] [150] I HAVEN'T GOT ALL DAY
[160] [170] . [180] [170] . [180] [170] . [180] [170] . [180] [170] . [180] [170] . [180] [170] . [18
0] [170] . [180] [170] . [180] [170] . [180] [170] . [180] [170] . [180] [170] . [180] [170] . [180] [
170] . [180] [170] . [180] [170] . [180] [170] . [180] [170] . [180] [170] . [180] [170] . [180] [170
] . [180] [170] . [180] [170] . [180] [170] . [180] [170] . [180] [170] . [180] [170] . [180] [170] . [
180] [170] . [180] [170] . [180] [170] . [180] [170] . [180] [170] . [180] [170] . [180] [170] . [180
] [170] . [180] [170] . [180] [170] . [180] [170] . [180] [170] . ^C
Break in 170
Ok
```

With this output we can see at a glance that the program cycles repeatedly between lines 170 and 180. We would then know where to begin to look for the problem.

The FRE Function — Checking Memory Space Available

The FRE function will return the number of unused bytes in memory. You must always include a dummy argument following FRE, as in FRE(0).

Without a program in your PC, type

```
Ok
NEW
Ok
PRINT FRE(Ø)
14542          ← Your value may differ depending upon your
Ok                version of DOS and the PC's memory size.
```

This will return all of the free space available for BASIC programs in your PC. After loading a program, again type FRE(0):

```
Ok
LOAD "LRGEPROG"
Ok
PRINT FRE(Ø)
  365
```

The difference between these returned values will give you the space taken up by your program.

The FRE function may also be used inside a program to keep track of space available and prevent the program from exceeding memory capacity. This is particularly important in machines with small memories or in programs that create very large arrays.

CLEAR — Resetting Variables

When you run a program the variables will change their values during execution. In program development it may be desirable to reset these variables from time to time. CLEAR is used to accomplish this. The CLEAR statement will set all the numeric variables in a program to the value zero (0) without erasing the program from the memory. In addition, all string variables are set to null (no characters).

CLEAR can also be used as a command to set a limit on the amount of memory BASIC can use. This is useful when you are using a machine-language program that must be loaded into memory above your BASIC program. To keep BASIC from writing over the machine-language program, you'd specify a value (for example, exp1 = 32768, as shown below), which is just below the lowest address used by the machine-language program. Note that a comma must *precede* exp1.

The general form of the CLEAR command is

```
CLEAR , exp1, exp2
```

Used for a large number of
GOSUB or FOR ... NEXT statements,
or complex PAINTING

Used for machine language program space

And here are some examples:

```
CLEAR , 32768, 1000
CLEAR , , 1000
CLEAR
```

The modifier "exp 2" is used to set aside stack space for BASIC. Normally this is the smaller of 512 bytes or 1/8th of maximum memory, but in rare circumstances you may need to modify these default values. This form of CLEAR is as follows:

```
CLEAR , , 2000
```

File Management Commands

In this section we'll discuss some BASIC commands that help you manage files. Some, like FILES, KILL, and NAME, let you do from BASIC what you can already do from DOS. Others, specifically MERGE and CHAIN, are useful when you want to combine two or more BASIC programs.

FILES — Displaying the Directory Within BASIC

You may display a list of all the files on the default disk drive with the command FILES, which is very much like the DOS command DIR. For instance, if we typed the command FILES, the following might appear on our screen:

```
COMMAND .COM FORMAT  .COM CHKDSK  .COM SYS     .COM DISKCOPY.COM DISKCOMP.COM
BASIC   .COM BASICA  .COM ART     .BAS SAMPLES .BAS MORTGAGE.BAS COLORBAR.BAS
BALL    .BAS COMM    .BAS AUTOEXEC.BAT ASTCLOCK.COM CHAPTER1.TXT CHAPTER2.TXT
CHAPTER1.BAK CHAPTER2.BAK INVOICE .SMC INVOICE .MAR PHONE-L .TXT
```

Like DIR, the command FILES may have a filespec, but it must be in quotation marks. In addition, the two wild card characters are available, as they are in DOS. The ? may be used in place of any single character, and the * may stand for any group of characters in the filename or file extension. Here are a few examples of using FILES (we assume that the programs shown above are on our disk):

```
Ok
FILES "*.BAS"
ART      .BAS SAMPLES .BAS MORTGAGE.BAS COLORBAR.BAS BALL     .BAS COMM      .BAS

Ok
FILES "CHAPTER?.TXT"


CHAPTER1.TXT CHAPTER2.TXT


Ok
FILES "INVOICE.*"


INVOICE .SMC INVOICE .MAR
```

KILL — Deleting Files

The KILL command is used to delete a file from the diskette. The command is used with a complete filespec (including extension), as follows:

```
Ok
KILL "BALL.BAS"
Ok
FILES
```

Now use FILES to be sure that BALL.BAS is really gone.

```
COMMAND .COM FORMAT   .COM CHKDSK  .COM SYS      .COM DISKCOPY.COM DISKCOMP.COM
BASIC   .COM BASICA   .COM ART      .BAS SAMPLES .BAS MORTGAGE.BAS COLORBAR.BAS
COMM    .BAS AUTOEXEC.BAT ASTCLOCK.COM CHAPTER1.TXT CHAPTER2.TXT CHAPTER1.BAK
CHAPTER2.BAK INVOICE .SMC INVOICE .MAR PHONE-L .TXT
```

NAME — Changing the Names of Files

NAME is the command used to change the name of a file, just as RENAME performs this function in DOS. The general form for the NAME command is

```
NAME filespec AS filename
```

The *filespec* must exist, and the *filename* must *not* exist. Here's an example:

```
Ok
NAME "SAMPLES.BAS" AS "EXAMPLES.BAS"
Ok
FILES

COMMAND .COM FORMAT  .COM CHKDSK  .COM SYS     .COM DISKCOPY.COM DISKCOMP.COM
BASIC   .COM BASICA  .COM ART      .BAS EXAMPLES.BAS MORTGAGE.BAS COLORBAR.BAS
COMM     .BAS AUTOEXEC.BAT ASTCLOCK.COM CHAPTER1.TXT CHAPTER2.TXT CHAPTER1.BAK
CHAPTER2.BAK INVOICE .SMC INVOICE .MAR PHONE-L .TXT
```

MERGE — Bringing Programs Together

Many people find it useful to write programs in small segments and later to put these segments together to make one large program. This technique allows the testing and debugging of smaller, more manageable programs.

The MERGE command allows you to bring together two small programs to form a larger program. Let's suppose that we have two such programs saved on the default disk drive. An important point here is that the programs *must be saved as ASCII files*. BASIC programs are normally saved in a special compressed binary format when the SAVE command is used. There is an option in the SAVE command that will save your program in ASCII (just as it appears on the screen). To save using the ASCII option, close the quotation marks after the filespec, and then type a comma and the letter *A*, which stands for ASCII. For example:

```
Ok
SAVE "PROGRAM1.BAS",A
```

The first of the two programs we want to merge is known as PROGRAM1.BAS and the second is PROGRAM2.BAS. We'll assume both these programs have been saved as ASCII files. First we type

```
Ok
LOAD "PROGRAM1.BAS"
```

This will load PROGRAM1.BAS into the PC's memory. Next we type

```
Ok
MERGE "PROGRAM2.BAS"
```

which will add PROGRAM2.BAS to what is already in memory.

Should any lines in PROGRAM2.BAS have the same line numbers as in PROGRAM1.BAS, the lines will be replaced by the PROGRAM2.BAS lines. If the programs are not saved in ASCII form, the error message "Bad file mode" will result.

CHAIN — Linking Programs

The CHAIN statement is used to call up a new program and at the same time pass variable values to it from the current program. This is a useful device when your program becomes very large and the PC's memory will not accommodate the total program at one time. The CHAIN statement can also be used to connect one program to another when both programs are relatively small and to pass variables from one program to the other. The general form of CHAIN is as follows:

```
CHAIN filespec
```

For example

```
2300 CHAIN "SECOND.PRG"
```

This command can be added to the end of the first program to pass control to the second.

There is unfortunately a problem: namely, that variable types definitions are not passed to the new program, nor are user-defined functions; that is, the DEFINT, DEFSNG, DEFDBL, and DEFFN statements must be restated in the new program. To solve this problem we may combine CHAIN and MERGE in this way:

```
CHAIN MERGE "SECOND.PRG"
```

As before, the merged program must have been stored as an ASCII file on the disk.

```
CHAIN MERGE "SECOND.PRG",ALL
```

This time with the ALL option, every variable in the current program is passed on to the invoked program.

We can also use CHAIN to link parts of programs:

```
CHAIN MERGE "THIRD.PRG",DELETE 1200-4600
```

In the above example, lines 1200 through 4600 would be deleted from the current program before THIRD.PRG is loaded.

Summary

In this chapter we've looked at some program development aids. The commands AUTO, CLEAR, and RENUM make program writing particularly convenient. The process of debugging is aided by CONT, TRON, and TROFF. The ability to execute DOS-like commands through FILES, FRE, KILL, and NAME from inside BASIC is helpful because it means that you don't have to exit from BASIC to manipulate files. Finally we looked at methods of connecting programs with the statements MERGE and CHAIN. The following list summarizes the instructions we've presented in this chapter.

AUTO *m,n* — Provides automatic line numbering starting with line number *m* and having interval of *n*.

RENUM *m,n,p* — Renumbers a program starting at *n* so that lines start with *m* and increment by *p*.

CONT — Resumes a halted program.

TRON or (F7) — Turns on trace.

TROFF or (F8) — Turns off trace.

FRE — Returns amount of free space in memory.

CLEAR — Sets variables to 0 and strings to null; also used to reserve memory for machine-language programs and to set aside memory for stack space.

FILES — Gives listing of files on diskette.

KILL — Removes file from diskette.

NAME — Changes the name of program on diskette.

MERGE — Combines two programs.

CHAIN — Calls a program from another program.

Exercises

1. Renumber the last program shown in Chapter 15 called BIGBANG.B15" so that (a) the first subroutine which in the original program begins with line 380 will now begin with line number 1000, and (b) that the second subroutine which originally begins with line 520 will begin with line number 2000.

2. Describe what the following BASIC program line does:

```
1000 CHAIN MERGE "ANOTHER", 2000, DELETE 2500 - 3000
```

Solutions

1. The required renumbering must be done in two steps. The first renumbers all program lines beginning with the original line 380. The required command is

```
RENUM 1000, 380
```

The second command renumbers the lines for the second subroutine, which now begins with line 1150. The required command is

```
RENUM 2000, 1150
```

The program "BIGBANG.B15" should now be renumbered with the first subroutine beginning with line number 1000, and the second with line number 2000.

2. The effects of the given CHAIN MERGE statement can be summarized by the following:

    a. The given statement deletes lines 2500 - 3000 of the current program.

    b. It also merges that part of the program "ANOTHER" that begins with line number 2000 with the current program.

    c. The next line to be executed is line 2000 of the merged programs.

17

String Functions

Concepts
Changing strings to numbers and vice versa
String generation
String length
String search
String manipulations

Instructions
SPACE$, SPC, VAL, STR$, STRING$, INPUT$, INKEY$, LEN,
LEFT$, RIGHT$, MID$, INSTR$

We've seen many interesting and powerful ways that numeric functions can be used to manipulate numbers. In this chapter we'll explore the use of *string functions*, which manipulate strings and characters. Although you can't take the square root or the sine of a string, we think you'll be rather amazed at the many different and interesting ways BASIC allows you to manipulate and transform strings.

In general, functions are rules by which an input determines an output. Numeric functions involve only numbers or numeric variables, whereas string functions always involve at least one string or string variable in the output or the input. Most string functions also include one or more numeric variables.

SPACE$ and SPC — Spacing Out

Let's begin with two of the very simple string functions: SPACE$ and SPC.

SPACE$ — String Space

The function SPACE$ returns a string consisting of nothing but spaces; the number of spaces is determined by the operand (the number in parentheses following STRING$) as shown in the following example:

```
10 SPACEOUT$ = "spaced" + SPACE$(5) + "out"
20 PRINT SPACEOUT$
RUN
spaced     out
Ok
         |
         5 spaces
```

SPACE$(5) is a string and consequently can be "added" or concatenated to other strings, as shown in the preceding example.

SPACE$ is useful if you need to insert a large number of spaces or if spaces are required repeatedly, as in the following example:

```
10 FOR J = 1 TO 10
20    X$ = X$ + SPACE$(5) + "+"
30 NEXT
40 PRINT X$
RUN
     +     +     +     +     +     +     +     +     +     +
Ok
```

Such a pattern of characters might be useful as markers or headings. Notice the "summing" procedure used to construct the string X$ by means of the FOR...NEXT loop — we've used it many times to find the totals of numbers. The operand of the STRING$ function (the number 5 in this example) can be a variable or a numeric expression. You might try to replace the number 5 in the preceding example with the variable J, and see what happens! The result might give you some ideas for ways to make interesting patterns on the text screen (SCREEN 0).

SPC — Spaces with PRINT

SPC is another way of producing spaces. For example, enter

```
PRINT "left" SPC(12) "right"
left            right
Ok
          |
          12 spaces
```

SPC(12) causes 12 spaces to be printed between "left" and "right". You can see that SPC is very similar to SPACE$. In fact, you can use SPACE$(12) in place of SPC(12) in the above example, but there is an important difference: SPC can only be used within a PRINT or PRINT-related statement, like LPRINT. The reason for this limitation is that, unlike SPACE$, SPC doesn't return a string; it can only do its job as part of PRINT or its relatives. You may be reminded of the TAB function here, since it also must be used as part of PRINT.

Speaking of the TAB function, how does it differ from the SPC function? The following example clarifies the difference:

```
10 FOR J = 0 TO 4
20     PRINT "*" SPC(J) "*" TAB(12) "tab"
30 NEXT
RUN
**          tab
* *         tab
*  *        tab
*   *       tab
*    *      tab
Ok
```

SPC(J) causes PRINT to print J number of spaces between what is in front of and behind SPC(J). TAB(12) causes PRINT to locate what follows in column number 12. If you want to control spaces in PRINT, use SPC; if you want to control absolute column position, use TAB.

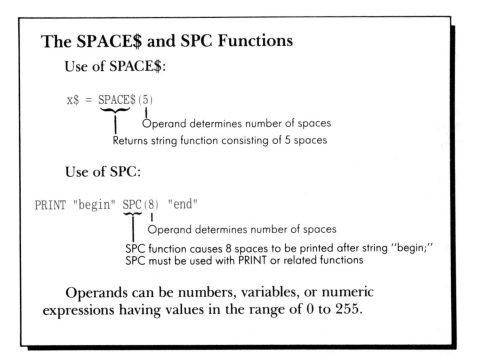

The SPACE$ and SPC Functions

Use of SPACE$:

```
x$ = SPACE$(5)
```
Operand determines number of spaces
Returns string function consisting of 5 spaces

Use of SPC:

```
PRINT "begin" SPC(8) "end"
```
Operand determines number of spaces
SPC function causes 8 spaces to be printed after string "begin;"
SPC must be used with PRINT or related functions

Operands can be numbers, variables, or numeric expressions having values in the range of 0 to 255.

VAL and STR$ — A Question of Values

The following sections describe efficient ways to convert strings into numbers or to turn numbers into strings.

VAL — Converting Strings to Numbers

The function VAL converts a string to a numerical value. Consider this example:

```
1Ø M$ = "5ØØØØ dollars"
2Ø PRINT M$
3Ø PRINT VAL(M$)
RUN
5ØØØØ dollars
 5ØØØØ
Ok
```

The difference between the two printed items is clear: M$ is a string, whereas VAL(M$) is a numeric value, which accounts for the space in front of the 50000 reserved for the sign of the number. Also, VAL ignored the word "dollars" — all it cares about are numbers. However, if the first character in the string is nonnumeric, VAL would return a 0, as in this example:

```
PRINT VAL("$5ØØØØ")
 Ø
Ok
```

A fast way to lose $50000!

Numbers within strings can't be manipulated mathematically the way real numbers can; for example, we can't multiply the strings "5" and "9". We can, however, convert them to numbers by means of the VAL function and *then* multiply them. The following example program converts time within a string in AM and PM notation to 24-hour time:

```
1Ø X$ = "6 PM is a good time for dinner"
2Ø TIME = VAL(X$) + 12
3Ø PRINT TIME "hrs. is a good time for dinner"
RUN
 18 hrs. is a good time for dinner
Ok
```

VAL(X$) in line 20 returns the number 6, which is then added arithmetically to 12 to give 18.

STR$ — Changing Numbers to Strings

The STR$ function is the complement of the VAL function: whereas VAL converts a string to a numeric value, STR$ converts a numeric value to a string. For example,

```
STR$(18) + "hrs"
 18hrs
Ok
```

STR$(18) returns the string " 18", which is concatenated to the string "hrs". Notice that the space in front of the number, which is always reserved for the sign of the number, is still present in the string. The space *after* the number, however, is absent in the string, which is why there's no space between 18 and hrs in the output.

The following program puts STR$ to use in playing all the notes possible on your IBM PC:

```
10 INPUT "enter interval:  ",INTERVAL
20 PLAY "L12"                  'sets length of following notes
30 FOR NOTE = 1 TO 84 STEP INTERVAL
40    NOTE$ = "N" + STR$(NOTE)   'constructs notes of form "N4",etc
50    PLAY NOTE$
60 NEXT
```

Go ahead and try it! By entering the number 1 in response to INPUT, you'll get a chromatic scale of 84 notes covering a range of 7 octaves! You might also enjoy trying other intervals; an interval of 2 (two half-steps, that is) gives you a whole note scale. You may never have heard such scales before!

The VAL and STR$ Functions

```
VAL("123")
```

returns the *numeric* value 123

```
STR$(123)
```

returns the *string* value "123"

The STRING$ Function — String Generation

Some applications require the use of strings that have many repetitions of a particular character. For example, a dashed, dotted, or solid line is made up of repetitions of the characters "-", ".", and ASCII character 196, respectively. The STRING$ function is a tool that makes it easy to construct strings that consist of such repetitions of a single character. There are two variations of this function.

STRING$ with ASCII Code

The first variation constructs a string made up of ASCII characters. We've already introduced this form of the STRING$ function in Chapter 10's discussion of character graphics, but we'll include a brief review here as a reminder.

The following statement generates a solid line:

```
1Ø PRINT STRING$(3Ø, 196)
Ok
```

_____

```
RUN
Ok
```

Notice that STRING$ has *two* operands that have the following meanings:

```
STRING$ (3Ø, 196)
```
ASCII code number for character to be used as building block

Number of repetitions of designated ASCII character

STRING$ with Keyboard Characters

The second variation of STRING$ allows us to generate a string made up of characters from the keyboard. Its form is identical to that of the first variation, except that you replace the ASCII code number with a string character. Consider the following example:

```
1Ø PERIODS$ = STRING$(3Ø, ".")
2Ø PRINT PERIODS$
RUN
```
. . . .
```
Ok
```

The function STRING$(30,".") returns a string of 30 periods — that is, a dotted line. Any keyboard character bracketed with quotation marks can be used as the second operand of STRING$. The following diagram summarizes the operands of STRING$:

```
STRING$ (3Ø, ".")
         |   |
         |   String character (in quotation marks) to be repeated
         |
         Number of repetitions of the specified string character
```

One surprising feature of this function is that the second operand in the STRING$ function — the string to be used as a building block — can actually have more than one character. Try the following program:

```
1Ø X$ = "$1.5Ø"
2Ø PRINT STRING(4Ø, X$)
RUN
$$$$$$$$$$$$$$$$$$$$$$$$$$$$$$$$$$$$$$$$$$
Ok
```

There are 40 repetitions (an easy way to make money?!), but only of the *first* character of X$! In general, this variation of STRING$ constructs a string out of the first character of the substring specified in the second operand.

Input from the Keyboard without ENTER

By this time you are certainly well acquainted with the INPUT statement, which we introduced in Chapter 7. For most purposes, it is the most convenient tool for allowing a user to input information into a running program. However, there are two other methods of inputting user information that may be more appropriate for certain types of applications. These are the functions INPUT$ and INKEY$. One very important difference between INPUT and these two new functions is that whereas INPUT requires the user to press ENTER to signal the computer to "read" the information that you typed in, INPUT$ and INKEY$ do not.

INPUT$ — INPUT without ENTER

Let's first take a look at the easier of the two functions — INPUT$.

The following example shows how INPUT$ can be used to enter keyboard characters without the need to press ENTER:

```
1Ø PRINT "press any two keys: "
2Ø RESPONSE$ = INPUT$(2)
3Ø PRINT "your input was " RESPONSE$
4Ø END
```

When this program is run, the following appears on your screen:

```
RUN
press any two keys:
```

That's all that happens; there's no question mark, not even a blinking cursor. The program is simply waiting for you to press two keys.

All right, let's press the keys *h* and *i*. The instant you've pressed *i*, the program responds with

```
your input was hi
Ok
```

Notice that you didn't have to press ENTER in order for the program to read and process your input. Also, note that as you typed the keys *h* and *i*, the letters *h* and *i* didn't immediately appear on the screen the way they would have had we used an INPUT statement in line 20. INPUT$ doesn't echo input information the way INPUT does.

Let's take a closer look at how INPUT$ works. When program execution reaches the BASIC word INPUT$(2) in line 20, it waits for the user to press two keys. If we wanted our program to wait for the user to press five keys, then we'd use INPUT(5)$. The number in parentheses between INPUT and the $ sign specifies the number of characters that need to be keyed in before program execution resumes. This number can be in the range of 1 to 255.

Once the required number of keys have been pressed — two in our example — the value of INPUT$(2) is assigned to the variable RESPONSE$. Whereas INPUT can be used all by itself in a BASIC line, INPUT$ cannot. INPUT$ is a *function* that returns a string value from the keyboard. As such, it must appear in conjunction with a BASIC statement that processes the value of the function. You could, for example, print its value with the statement

```
2Ø PRINT INPUT$(2)
```

although you'd lose the value of INPUT$(2) for later processing. In our example program, we assigned the value of INPUT$(2) to the variable RESPONSE$. Once the value of INPUT$ is captured in this manner, it can be printed and used in other ways later on in the program.

One application in which INPUT$ can be used very effectively is in a menu selection program, such as program MENU.B12 in Chapter 12. Line 230 of this program is a typical INPUT statement:

```
230 INPUT SELECTION
```

This statement requires the user to press ENTER to complete the selection entry. Previous PRINT statements have given the user information about the menu and instructions to enter a number from 1 through 4. If you wish to write this menu program in such a way that the user can make the selection by just pressing keys 1 through 4 without needing to press ENTER, replace the above line 230 with the following two lines:

```
230 SEL$ = INPUT$(1)
232 SELECTION = VAL(SEL$)
```

This new line 230 assigns the keyboard entry to the string variable SEL$. Line 232 converts the string value of SEL$ to a numeric value that can be used in the subsequent ON...GOSUB statement.

The INPUT function

INPUT$ is a string function that returns a string value containing a specified number of characters from the keyboard without requiring you to press ENTER. The number of characters returned is defined by a number in parentheses after INPUT$. All keyboard characters except `Ctrl` `Break` are accepted by INPUT$.

The value of INPUT$ is usually assigned to a string variable as in this example:

```
30 CODE$ = INPUT$(5)
                 |
```
Number of characters to be keyed in; value can range from 1 to 255

INPUT$(5) will return a string of five characters as soon as five keys have been pressed.

INKEY$ — An Input Function that Can't Wait

INKEY$ is a function similar to INPUT$. Both are string functions that return characters from the keyboard: neither requires the use of the ENTER key to input information, and neither echoes your keyboard entry.

There are, however, several important differences. The following program, which is very similar to the first program we used in our discussion of INPUT$, demonstrates one of these differences:

```
10 PRINT "press any key: "
20 RESPONSE$ = INKEY$
30 PRINT "your input was "  RESPONSE$
40 END
```

Run this program and be ready for a surprise:

```
RUN
your input was
Ok
```

Immediately after you enter RUN, your program prints "your input was" and the BASIC prompt appears. The program is finished before you have much of a chance to press a key (unless you're very fast)! The problem is that INKEY$ doesn't wait for user input the way INPUT$ does. When INKEY$ is executed, it checks to see if a key has been pressed. If you manage to press a key before INKEY$ is executed (which is very unlikely in our program above), INKEY$ will return the string value associated with the pressed key. You'll see that in our next example. Chances are, however, that you haven't yet pressed a key by the time INKEY$ is executed. In that case, it doesn't wait for you to make an entry, but instead returns a null string — that is, a string without any contents. That's what line 30 tells you: the value of RESPONSE$ was — well, nothing.

We can change our program so that it waits for user input by inserting a new line — line 25 — into the previous program:

```
10 PRINT "press any key"
20 RESPONSE$ = INKEY$
25 IF RESPONSE$ = ""  THEN 20      ← No spaces between quotes
30 PRINT "your input was " RESPONSE$
40 END
RUN
press any key
your input was h
Ok
```

This program *does* wait for user input. We pressed the H key. Notice that this entry is not echoed on your screen (as would be the case with INPUT$), although it is, of course, printed out by line 30.

The reason that this program waits for user input is that our new line 25 causes program execution to loop back to line 20 as long as INKEY$ returns a null string — that is, as long as no key has been pressed since the previous execution of INKEY$. However, the instant a key is pressed, the value of RESPONSE$ will cease to equal "" (the null string) and program execution will continue with line 30. The loop in lines 20 and 25 causes an effect very similar to that produced by a single statement which assigns INPUT$ to the variable RESPONSE$.

Another important difference between INKEY$ and INPUT$ is that INKEY$ reads only one character from the keyboard, whereas INPUT$ waits until a specified number of keys have been pressed.

INKEY$ is a useful tool to produce user-initiated program interrupts. As an example, consider the following program that simulates a stopwatch:

```
100 CLS
110 PRINT "press key "s" to stop count"
130 PRINT "press any key to restart count"
140 FOR J = 1 TO 1000
150    LOCATE 3, 5
160    PRINT J
170    N$ = INKEY$
180    IF N$ = "s" THEN GOSUB 300    'causes prgrm pause if "s" is pressed
190 NEXT
200 END
290 '
300 '----Subroutine causes pause until any key is pressed----
310 P$ = INKEY$
320 IF P$ = "" THEN 310
330 RETURN
```

When this program is run, line 160 prints out the value of the index J of the FOR...NEXT loop (lines 140 to 190). As soon as the user presses key S, line 180 interrupts the loop and redirects program execution to the pause subroutine beginning with line 300. This subroutine doesn't do anything except loop between lines 310 and 320 — as long as no key is pressed. The instant a key is pressed (almost any key will do, although there are several keys which won't work, including the familiar (Ctrl) (Break) combination which terminates program execution), the loop is broken and the RETURN statement is executed. Counting now resumes as the line 160 prints out the index of the FOR...NEXT loop.

There you have it — a stopwatch that you can start and stop at will. Of course our stopwatch doesn't measure time in seconds, but rather in units of the time it takes for one FOR...NEXT loop to be executed.

This function is very useful in games, where you often want to keep updating a picture on the video display (enemy spaceships getting closer and closer, for example), while at the same time you want your program to check for keyboard input (the user firing his lasers).

The INKEY$ Function

INKEY$ is a function that generally returns a single character from the keyboard. (Some special keys cause a two-character hexadecimal code to be returned.) Like INPUT$, INKEY$ does not require the user to press ENTER to complete the entry, nor does it automatically display the keyboard character on the screen. But unlike INPUT$, INKEY$ does not wait for user input. If no key is pressed, INKEY$ returns a null string, written as "".

The following statements are an example of how INKEY$ may be used:

```
*
*
3Ø VAL$ = INKEY$: IF VAL$ = "" THEN 3Ø
*
*
```

This line can be used to interrupt a program. The rest of the program is executed only after a key is pressed.

Manipulating Strings

In this section we'll introduce the most interesting and powerful of the string functions. Practically any kind of manipulation of a string you can think of can be done with these functions. Applications include word processing, games involving words and sentences, formatting text, reversing first and last names, and cryptography (coding and encoding).

LEN — The Length of a String

The function LEN returns the LENgth or number of characters in a string. The following example illustrates how it can be used:

```
10 JUSTAWORD$ = "supercalifragilisticexpialidocous"
20 PRINT LEN(JUSTAWORD$)
RUN
 33
Ok
```

The output shows that the operand of LEN, JUSTAWORD$, has 33 characters.

One of the many uses of this function is in automatic centering of text, such as a title. The way we've centered a title in the past is by counting the number of characters in the title, subtracting that number from the desired width of the page, and dividing by two; the resulting number gives us the number of spaces in front of the title. This formula may be summarized as follows:

# of spaces before title = (page width − title length)/2

Whereas before *we* had to determine the length of the title, we can now use the LEN function to find the length of the title for us. Given that our title has been assigned to the variable TITLE$, the following statement will PRINT the centered title with respect to a 65-character wide page:

```
PRINT SPC(((65 - LEN(TITLE$))/2) TITLE$
```

We could use TAB in place of SPC here, although for accurate centering we would then have to add the number 1 to its operand.

The following example illustrates how you might easily center text having more than one line (a two-part title, or even a poem!):

```
10 DATA "RECOLLECTIONS OF A TURTLE: "
20 DATA "the winter of 1642"
30 N = 2
40 FOR J = 1 TO N
50    READ TITLE$
60    PRINT SPC(((65 - LEN(TITLE$))/2) TITLE$
70 NEXT
RUN
                  RECOLLECTIONS OF A TURTLE:
                       the winter of 1642
Ok
```

LEFT$ — Extracting the Left Part of a String

The LEFT$ function is one of the three BASIC functions that extract a portion of a string. As the name of this function implies, LEFT$ returns the left part of a string as shown in the example below:

```
1Ø ACCT$ = "N234 Repairs"
15 '        123456789Ø12
2Ø NUMBER$ = LEFT$(ACCT$,4)
3Ø PRINT NUMBER$
RUN
N234
Ok
```

The function LEFT$ returns the first 4 characters of the string ACCT$, counting from the *left*. As you can see, this function has two operands with the following meaning:

```
LEFT$(ACCT$,  4)
```

Number of characters to return, counting from left

Parent string from which LEFT$ returns the 4 leftmost characters

If, in the preceding program, we replace the number 4 by 12 — the length of ACCT$ — or any number larger than 12, the whole string "N234 Repair" would be returned.

RIGHT$ — Extracting the Right Part of a String

A left side usually implies the existence of a right side. So it is in BASIC: the function RIGHT$ is identical to LEFT$, except that, as the name suggests, it returns the right part of a string.

To see how this works, substitute the word RIGHT$ for the word LEFT$ in line 20 of our last program:

```
1Ø ACCT$ = "N234 Repair"
2Ø DEPT$ = RIGHT$(ACCT$, 6)
3Ø PRINT DEPT$
RUN
Repair
Ok
```

The function RIGHT$(ACCT$, 6) returns the 6 *rightmost* characters of ACCT$. If you substitute the number 12 (equal to LEN(ACCT$)), for the number 6, RIGHT$ will return the whole string ACCT$. Here is a summary of the operands of RIGHT$:

```
RIGHT$ (ACCT$, 5)
```

Number of rightmost characters RIGHT$ returns

Parent string from which characters are extracted

Our example illustrates how RIGHT$ can be used to extract the right portion of a string. Such "extractions" are often very useful when dealing with information such as telephone numbers, inventory information, and addresses.

An application of RIGHT$ we've already used in Chapter 15 (in the discussion of numeric functions) is the following function:

```
10 RANDOMIZE VAL (RIGHT$ (TIME$, 2)
```

This is an interesting and sophisticated application of three functions squeezed into a single BASIC line. Let's analyze how this compound function works by starting from the innermost parenthesis. The TIME$ function returns the current time as determined by your PC in terms of a string value like "12:07:47". The first two digits are the hours in 24-hour time, the second two represent minutes, and the last two, seconds. Consequently, the function RIGHT$(TIME$,2) extracts the last two digits, the seconds, and VAL turns these seconds — a string value — into a numeric value. The net effect of this compound string function is to reseed the random number generator once every second with values ranging from 0 to 59. Pretty neat, huh? It wouldn't take much to also include the hour and minute values in order to get a larger range of seed values.

Our last example is for pure, unadulterated fun; as far as we can see, it has no practical application whatsoever. It does, however, use both LEFT$ and RIGHT$ functions. Here we go:

```
100 '---******************************************
110 '---*       METAMORPHOSIS by B.E.          *-------------
120 '---* (based on a cartoon by Louis Phillips) *-------------
130 '---******************************************
140 '
150 X1$ = "caterpillar"
```

```
160 X2$ = "butterfly"
170 FOR J = Ø TO 11
180    L$ = LEFT$(X2$,J)
190    R$ = RIGHT$(X1$,11 - J)
200    PRINT L$ + R$
210 NEXT
220 END
```

Go ahead and try this program — we won't spoil it by showing you the output here!

MID$ — Getting What You Want from a String

Now we come to our favorite string function: the MID$ function. It is perhaps the most versatile and most useful of all the string functions. As a relative of LEFT$ and RIGHT$, it can extract any part of a string, and in particular, the MIDdle of the string. Try the following example:

```
10 NAM$ = "Jerry Sylvester Snoddgrass"
11 '       1234567890123456          ← Scale for NAM$
20 MIDDLE$ = MID$(NAM$, 7, 9))
30 PRINT MIDDLE$
RUN
Sylvester
Ok
```

From the output it is evident that MID$ returns the middle portion of the string NAM$. Notice that MID$ has *three* operands. The first, of course, is the parent string from which the extraction is to be made (NAM$ in this case). The second and third are numeric values that determine exactly what part of the string is to be returned. Their specific function is explained by this diagram:

MID$ (NAME$, 7, 9)

Length of string to be returned

Starting position of string to be returned

Parent string from which MID$ extracts 9 characters starting at position 7

The example above printed out the word "Sylvester" rather than something else like "vester Sn" because the second operand, the number 7, is the position of the first letter of "Sylvester". The third operand gives the instruction to return a total of 9 characters — that's the length of the name "Sylvester". The function MID$ can return *any* part of a string; therein lies its versatility and power and, alas, its complexity.

We'd like to give you two examples that illustrate some of the possible applications of this function. The first example uses PLAY to play a harmonic minor scale:

```
10 MSCALE = "N37N39N40N42N44N45N48N49"
11 '         1  4  7  0  3  6  9  2
20 FOR NOTE = 1 TO 8
30     NOTE$ = MID$(MSCALE$, NOTE*3-2, 3)
40     PRINT NOTE$ + " ";
50     PLAY NOTE$
60 NEXT
RUN
N37 N39 N40 N42 N44 N45 N48 N49    ←— C minor harmonic scale plays as notes are printed
Ok
```

We inserted line 11 as a "scale" to identify the starting position of each note. For each value of the loop index NOTE, MID$ extracts the name of the note to be printed and played. For example, when NOTE equals 2, the second operand of MID$, which determines the starting position, has the value 4 (because 2*3-2 = 4); consequently, MID$ assigns the value "N39" to the variable NOTE$.

If you like playing with words, you'll enjoy our second example:

```
10 INPUT "enter some characters:  "; CHAR$
20 L = LEN(CHAR$)
30 DIM LETTER$(L)
35 '
40 FOR J = 1 TO L                  'loads array LETTER$
50     LETTER$(J) = MID$(CHAR$,J)
60 NEXT
65 '
70 FOR J = L TO 1 STEP -1          'PRINTs array LETTER$ backwards
80     PRINT LETTER$(J);
90 NEXT
100 END
RUN
enter some characters:  frankenstein
nietsneknarf
Ok
```

What? Read "frankenstein" backwards — yes, its the dreaded "nietsneknarf"! We can't resist at least one more run:

```
RUN
enter some characters: able was I ere I saw elba
able was I ere I saw elba
```

Hmm...a palindrome! (It reads the same from either end.) This one supposedly was uttered by Napoleon. Try some of your own words or phrases; you're bound to come up with some interesting surprises.

If you take a close look at the MID$ function in line 50, you'll notice that the third operand is missing. It turns out that the third operand, which specifies the number of characters to be returned from the parent string, is optional. If you omit it, as we have done, BASIC automatically assumes that MID$ should return only one character.

The technique of extracting letters from a string, as introduced in the previous problem, is useful whenever you need to manipulate individual letters. Another variation on this theme is the problem of turning lowercase letters into uppercase letters. Go ahead and try this on your own. First set up a loop in which you use MID$ to extract one letter at a time; then get its ASCII code number via ASC, subtract 32 to get the code number of the corresponding capital letter, and finally turn that code value back into a letter and print it.

INSTR — Positions of Characters Within a String

The three functions LEFT$, RIGHT$, and MID$ give us the tools to extract any part of a string. For some applications we also need to find the *position* of one or more characters within a given parent string. For example, if you wanted to use LEFT$ to extract the last name from the string "Frankenstein, Jerry", you'd need to know the number of characters in "Frankenstein". The INSTR function is designed to do just that job.

The following example shows how the INSTR function is used to find the position of the comma at the end of the last name "Frankenstein":

```
10 NAM$ = "Frankenstein, Josephine"
15 '      1234567890123456789Ø123
20 PRINT INSTR(NAM$, ",")
RUN
 13
Ok
```

The function INSTR returns the column *position* — in this case 13 — of the substring "," within the parent string NAM$. Notice that INSTR returns a numeric value, not a string. We could now easily extend this example to return the last name (written with a comma after it), no matter what length it is:

```
10 INPUT "enter 'last name, first name':  "; NAM$
20 COL = INSTR(NAM$, ",")
30 PRINT LEFT$(NAM$,COL)
RUN
enter 'last name, first name':  Jung, Karl
Jung
Ok
```

INSTR tells LEFT$ how many characters to return, starting at the left.

INSTR can search for more than just a one-character string as the following example illustrates:

```
10 INPUT "enter note as do, re, mi, etc.:  "; NOTE$
20 NOTENUMBER = INSTR("doremifasolatido", NOTE$)/2 + .5
30 PRINT NOTENUMBER
40 PLAY MID$("CDEFGABC", NOTENUMBER, 1)
RUN
enter note as do, re, mi, etc.:  so
 5    ← computer PLAYs note "so" or "G"
Ok
```

This example shows how to translate a word like "so" into a number, which later can be used for various purposes. In this case, INSTR tells us that "so" is the fifth note in the C major scale. That information is then used by MID$ in line 40 to PLAY the note corresponding to this number.

In all the examples above, INSTR always started its search at the beginning of the parent string. If we searched for the letter "u" in the Hawaiian word "humuhumunukunukuapuaa" (really, it's the name of a fish!), we'd get a number 2 — the position of the first "u". But what if you needed to find the position of the second, third, fourth, and possibly all the way up to the ninth "u"?

In cases like this it is important to be able to start the search for a particular character at a specified position. INSTR has an optional operand in the first position that specifies the starting position of the search. The following diagram summarizes the three operands of INSTR:

```
INSTR(3, WORD$, "u")
```

Sub-string that INSTR searches for

Parent string in which search takes place

Optional operand specifies starting position of search

If the value of WORD$ happens to be the previously named Hawaiian fish, the above function would return the number 4, which is the first position of letter "u" *after* the specified starting position, column 3.

One application that requires us to change the starting position of a search for a specified character is the word counting program below. This program also prints out the column position of each word:

```
1Ø WORDPOS = 1
2Ø SPACEPOS = 1                          'first test value for WHILE-WEND
3Ø INPUT "enter a phrase:  "; PHRASE$
4Ø WHILE SPACEPOS > Ø
5Ø     PRINT WORDPOS;
6Ø     SPACEPOS = INSTR(WORDPOS, PHRASE$, " ")
7Ø     WORDPOS = SPACEPOS + 1
8Ø     NWORDS = NWORDS + 1
9Ø WEND
1ØØ PRINT
11Ø PRINT "the number of words are" NWORDS
12Ø END
RUN
enter a phrase:  Halley's Comet returns in February 1986
 1  1Ø  16  24  27  36
the number of words are 6
Ok
```

You may wish to skip the explanation of this program, as it is one of the more difficult ones we've introduced and may take a bit of time to understand. Lines 10 and 20 simply initialize variables WORDPOS and SPACEPOS. The WHILE...WEND loop is executed as long as the variable SPACEPOS is larger than 0. SPACEPOS is the space position returned by INSTR in line 60. INSTR begins its search for the string " " at the beginning of a particular word, defined by the numeric variable WORDPOS. When INSTR finds the next space in PHRASE$, it returns the position of that space; line 70 assigns the sum of 1 and that space position to the next WORDPOSition. In this manner, the position of each word is printed out by line 30. This process continues until INSTR looks for spaces *after* the beginning of the last word. Since INSTR won't find any more spaces at this point, it returns a 0 — something we hadn't told you before. When WHILE notices the consequent zero value of SPACEPOS, it causes program execution to drop through the loop. By this time, all the WORDPOS variables have been printed out, and all that remains is to print out the word count, NWORDS. How did we get NWORDS? That part is simple: line 60 keeps a running total of the number of times the loop has been executed, which equals the number of words in PHRASE$. Phew! Counting words is hard work!

The LEFT$, RIGHT$, MID$, and INSTR Functions

`LEFT$("catnip",3)` ← Returns the string "cat", the leftmost 3 characters

`RIGHT$("catnip", 3)` ← Returns the string "nip", the rightmost 3 characters

`MID$("cathair", 4, 2)` ← Returns the string "ha", which starts in column 4 and is 2 characters long

`INSTR(3, "cathair", "a")` ← Returns the number 5, the column position of the first "a" after position number 3

Summary

We have to admit that string functions turned out to be much more interesting than we thought initially. In particular, the last group of functions LEFT$, RIGHT$, MID$, and INSTR provide us with some very sophisticated tools with which to manipulate strings in any way we might imagine. The other functions, SPACE$, SPC, VAL, STR$, STRINGS, and LEN, are easier to use and just as effective.

Exercise

Write a program that plays a note for each letter of a name (or any phrase); it should also print out the letters as it plays them.

Solution

Here is the program we wrote in response to this problem.

```
100 '----NAME: "PLAYNAME.B17"----by BE---------------------------------
102 '
108 '----*********************
110 '----* Prgm PLAYs a name *----------------------------------------
120 '----*********************
130 '
140 INPUT "enter name:  ",WORDS$
150 L = LEN(WORDS$)                      'finds LENgth of WORDS$
160 PLAY "T200 L12"                      'sets tempo
170 '
180 FOR J = 1 TO L
190     LETTER$ = MID$(WORDS$,J,1)       'extracts letters from WORDS$
200     PRINT LETTER$;
210     ACODE = ASC(LETTER$)             'finds ASCII code for LETTER$
220     NOTE$ = "n" + STR$(ACODE - 60)   'assembles NOTE$ from ASCII code
230     IF ACODE < 60 THEN NOTE$ = "N0"  'turns spaces into pauses
240     PLAY NOTE$
250 NEXT
260 END
RUN
enter name: Ursula Maria Beate Anna Susanna Enders Morwood
Ursula Maria Beate Anna Susanna Enders Morwood
Ok
```

This is a real name! Try your own, or a phrase, a poem... We won't explain the program as it is fairly "transparent"; you'll understand it by reading it.

Sequential Files — Your Disk as a Filing Cabinet

Concepts
  Data files
  Writing and reading data files to disk
  Records and fields
  Appending data files
  Changing data files

Instructions
  OPEN FOR OUTPUT, OPEN FOR INPUT, PRINT #, CLOSE,
  INPUT #, OPEN FOR APPEND, EOF, LINE INPUT #, WRITE #

We've seen how computers can be programmed to calculate and manipulate numbers and strings, and make decisions. Computers can also store information, such as mailing lists, tax records, inventories, manuscripts, recipes, and the physical properties of the planets. In short, computers can serve as electronic filing cabinets: instead of filing away sheets of paper with letters and symbols written on them, we can store bits or bytes in more or less permanent computer memory "filing cabinets." The temporary memory in your computer called *RAM* (which stands for random access memory) isn't much good for this job because it loses its memory every time you turn off your computer. However, the disks you've already been using to store your BASIC programs are well suited to serve as electronic filing cabinets: it's easy and convenient to store, retrieve, or change information on them, and the information remains on the disk even though your computer may be turned off. (You do have to treat your disks with care, though; don't get them close to magnets, or drop them into a mudpuddle!)

Any type of information stored on a disk, including your BASIC programs, can be referred to as a *file*. There are many different types of files that accommodate different needs. One general type of file with which you may already be familiar is the text file. It's used to store textlike information, such as letters, lists of names, and so on. Such files often require sophisticated word processing programs to manage the flow of information, and are therefore usually best obtained commercially.

BASIC's Data Files

Another type of file which is much simpler is called a *data file*. The word "data" refers to any kind of information that can be arranged in a list or as a table, such as a telephone directory.

We have already used the DATA statement to store data as part of some of our BASIC programs. The DATA statement is ideal for storing permanent information within a program. However, there are many applications in which such data needs to be entered or changed by the user of the program. For example, stock prices or telephone numbers need to be updated frequently. Making such additions or changes in DATA statements would be awkward at best (especially for users who are not programmers!). The best way to store this type of flexible information is by means of the data file.

Random and Sequential Files

There are two different techniques for setting up and managing a data file: the *sequential data file* and the *random data file*. The words "sequential" and "random" specify the way information is written into and read from the file. Sequential files are like music recorded on magnetic tape: to hear the music near the end of the tape, you have to search through the whole tape "sequentially" — that is, start at the beginning and keep searching until you find what you want. Random files, on the other hand, are more like LP records: you can put down the tone arm anywhere on the record to hear any musical segment of your choice without searching through the first part of the record. In other words, a random file, like a record player, can access musical information in any order you wish, even in a "random" manner.

Both types of data files have their advantages and disadvantages. Programs that manage sequential files are simpler than programs that manage random files. Also, sequential files generally require less memory space than random files. On the other hand, random files are better suited to applications such as electronic dictionaries, or large telephone directories — applications that would make a sequential search intolerably slow.

For most applications that a beginning programmer is likely to encounter, however, sequential files are preferable because they'll handle most of your data storage needs in a relatively straightforward and simple manner. This chapter is about such sequential files, how to "write" and "read" sequential files, and how to make changes in them.

Creating and Reading a Simple Sequential File

Files are created and read by computer programs. If you think of the disk files as filing cabinets, then the programs that create and read these files are the clerks who manage them. Before presenting and explaining all the new statements needed in such file management programs, we suggest that you enter the following complete program in order to get an overview of the whole process of creating and reading a file:

```
10  '---creates sequential file----------------------------
20  '
30   OPEN "a:test1" FOR OUTPUT AS #1
40  FOR J = 1 TO 5
45      SQUARE  = J * J
50      PRINT #1, SQUARE
60  NEXT
70  CLOSE #1
80  END
90  '
100 '---reads sequential file----------------------------
110 '
120 OPEN "a:test1" FOR INPUT AS #1
130 FOR J = 1 TO 5
140     INPUT #1, SQUARE
150     PRINT SQUARE
160 NEXT
170 CLOSE #1
180 END
```

The first part of this program up to line 80 creates a file called "test1", which contains the squares of the numbers 1 through 5. The second part of this program, beginning with line 100, reads this file. We've combined both of these functions into one program in order to be able to read the file right after we've created it, since this is a good way to find out what actually ended up in our file!

Now run this program. You'll hear your disk drive making some noises; then the "Ok" prompt will appear on your screen after the END statement in line 80 has been executed. At this point the data file "test1" has been created. To see what you've done, run the second half of this program by entering CONT (use the (F5) soft function key for convenience). CONT stands for "CONTinue", which tells your PC to continue running the program where it left off. You can also enter RUN 100 in its place.

The following should be the output on your screen:

```
RUN                    ←— Executes lines 1∅ through 8∅
Ok
CONT                   ←— Continues execution of lines 9∅ though 18∅
  1   4   9   16   25  ←— Contents of file "test1"
Ok
```

Sure enough, the second half of the program reads the SQUARE of the numbers 1 through 5. Let's take a look at some of the details of this program.

The OPEN Statement

Before you can put something into a filing cabinet, you need to open a file drawer. The OPEN statements in lines 30 and 120 fulfill an equivalent function in opening a data file on your PC. Until you've opened a file in this manner, you don't have access to what's inside. Let's see exactly what each part of the OPEN statement means.

The word "a:test1" in parentheses after OPEN is the *file specification*. It's the same thing as the file specification of a BASIC program: the letter in front of the colon specifies the disk to which the file is to be written (or read from) — in this case, the disk in drive "a". As always, the drive specification can be omitted if it is the default drive. The word after the colon is the name of the file ("test1" in our case). All the rules for naming program files that we discussed in Chapter 4 apply here, except for one minor variation: BASIC doesn't automatically add the .BAS extension to a sequential file name the way it does in the case of program file names. Extensions up to three characters are optional. Some examples of legitimate data file specifications are:

"b:test.32a"

"applepie"

"stock.IBM"

Note that file specifications must always appear within quotation marks.

The next part of the OPEN statement, FOR OUTPUT in line 30 and FOR INPUT in line 120, informs your PC of the purpose for opening the file. FOR OUTPUT means "for output *from* the program *to* the file"; that is, the line

```
3Ø OPEN "a:test1" FOR OUTPUT AS #1
```

instructs BASIC to OPEN a file in order to move or "output" information *from* the program *to* the file. This form of the OPEN statement *creates* a file.

The phrase FOR INPUT in line 120 means "for input *to* the program *from* the file." So the statement

```
12Ø OPEN "a:test1" FOR INPUT AS #1
```

instructs BASIC to open a file in order to move or "input" information *to* the program *from* the file. It does not create a file, but opens an existing data file in order to *read* it.

The last part of the OPEN statement, #1 in our example, specifies the file number. BASIC allows you to have up to three different files open at the same time. The file number is simply a convenient way of referring to a particular file in file-related statements that follow the OPEN statement. The phrase "AS #1" in our OPEN statements instructs BASIC that as long as the file is open, the file "test1" can be specified by #1. For example, the PRINT statement in line 50 includes #1 to instruct BASIC that information is to be printed to file #1 (equivalent to "test1"). This file number must be included in all file-related statements, even though only one file may be open.

Since up to three files can usually be open, the file numbers range from 1 to 3. If you need to have more than three files open simultaneously (a fairly rare requirement, we think), you can specify the required number by means of the /F option in the BASIC or BASICA command used to load BASIC into your RAM memory. For example, if you need to open 10 files in a specific BASIC program, load BASIC with the command

```
BASICA/F:1Ø
```

where the 10 specifies the maximum number of files that can be open simultaneously in subsequent programs. The maximum number you can specify is 15.

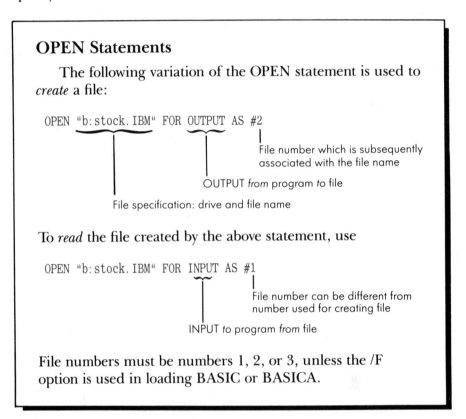

OPEN Statements

The following variation of the OPEN statement is used to *create* a file:

```
OPEN "b:stock.IBM" FOR OUTPUT AS #2
```

File number which is subsequently associated with the file name

OUTPUT *from program* to file

File specification: drive and file name

To *read* the file created by the above statement, use

```
OPEN "b:stock.IBM" FOR INPUT AS #1
```

File number can be different from number used for creating file

INPUT *to program* from file

File numbers must be numbers 1, 2, or 3, unless the /F option is used in loading BASIC or BASICA.

The PRINT # Statement

Once a file is OPENed FOR OUTPUT, information can be written to the specified file by means of the PRINT # statement. For example, line 50 in our program

```
5Ø PRINT #1, SQUARE
```

says "print the value of SQUARE into file #1." The number 1 in #1 is the same file number specified in the OPEN statement in line 30. The value that's written to the file is sometimes called a *record*.

Writing to a file with PRINT # creates a file "image" identical to what appears on the screen if you use PRINT. The only difference between the two is that PRINT sends information to the screen, whereas PRINT # sends information to a file. The way information is formatted, however, is the same in both instructions. Later in this chapter, we'll look at the implications of this formatting and at some of the difficulties that can arise. Figure 18-1 illustrates the relationship between PRINT and PRINT #.

We can also write strings to our file in the same way that we'd print a string onto the screen. For example, we can replace line 50 with

```
5Ø PRINT #1, "raspberries"
```

in order to write the word "raspberries" to the file. We can, however, run into a problem if the string contains a comma. We'll come back to this matter in a later section that deals with the LINE INPUT # and WRITE # instructions.

The CLOSE Statement

If you're finished with a particular file in a filing cabinet, it's customary to close the file drawer. That's what the CLOSE statement does in a BASIC data file. Line 70 in our program,

```
7Ø CLOSE #1
```

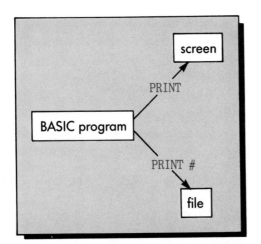

Figure 18-1. Relationship between PRINT and PRINT#

says "close the file opened under the file number 1." Notice that we used the same CLOSE statement in line 70 and 170: CLOSE doesn't care whether the file was originally opened FOR INPUT or FOR OUTPUT. A single CLOSE statement can also be used to close several files. For example,

```
CLOSE #1,#3
```

closes files associated with file numbers 1 and 3. If the file number is omitted altogether, CLOSE closes all files. Since our program had only one file open at a time, we could just as well have used CLOSE instead of CLOSE #1. Actually, we could have omitted the second CLOSE in line 170 altogether because END automatically closes all files. Nevertheless, it is good programming practice always to close files explicitly in order to clarify program flow and to prevent any chance of messing up or losing your data file.

Here's an important point: a file opened under a particular file number cannot be opened for both input and output at the same time. If you have OPENed a file FOR OUTPUT as we have done in our program, you must CLOSE it *before* opening the file FOR INPUT in order to read it.

The INPUT # Statement

We've seen that PRINT does the same thing as PRINT #, except that PRINT # writes information to a file rather than to the screen. The same relation exists between INPUT and INPUT #. INPUT # reads data from the specified file to the program. For example, line 140 of our program,

```
140 INPUT #1, SQUARE
```

inputs a number stored in the file opened under file number 1, and assigns this number to the variable SQUARE.

Figure 18-2 illustrates the relationship between INPUT and INPUT #.

Keeping Order in Reading and Writing

Numbers in the file are read and assigned to SQUARE in the same order that they were originally written into the file. For example, the second time INPUT # is executed (for J=2), it reads the second record in the file, which is 4. A sequential file must be read in the same order as it was originally written. We might imagine a sequential file to be like the storage bin shown in Figure 18-3 into which records are entered from above and retrieved from below.

This storage bin (the file) keeps strict order; records are kept in a linear format, a sequence without any mixing. The first record in is always the first record out. This is very much like a type of investment called "first in, first out," sometimes abbreviated FIFO.

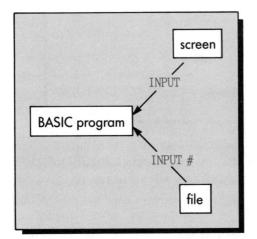

Figure 18-2. Relationship between INPUT and INPUT#

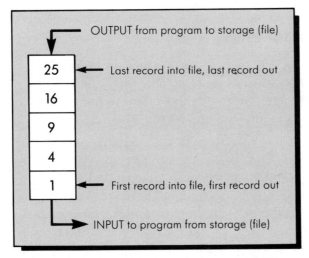

Figure 18-3. Data storage in a sequential file

These are the bare essentials of sequential data files. The particular example we've used illustrates how such files are set up and read, but it isn't a terribly useful one. At this point, you might wish to try your hand at writing your own program that creates and reads a data file, preferably a file that will be of interest and use to you. For example, based on the model presented here, it wouldn't be hard to set up a file containing daily or weekly stock prices, or musical notes of a composition that can be played.

The Finer Points of Sequential Files

In the following sections of this chapter, we'll take a closer look at sequential files. We'll learn how to write more complex files, how to append them, and how to change them — in short, how to increase our control over this type of information storage and retrieval.

Adding Data to a Sequential File

It is often necessary to be able to add data to an existing file. For example, if you wanted to maintain an up-to-date file of stock prices, you'd periodically need to add the most recent stock prices. Simple! Just use the OPEN statement to open the file FOR OUTPUT and start adding data, right?

Wrong. The problem is that as soon as you OPEN a sequential file FOR OUTPUT, you destroy its current contents. The solution is to use another variation of the OPEN statement specifically designed to append an existing file.

As an example, let's append some more data to the file "test1" we created in our original program in this chapter. For simplicity, we'll just append another copy of the same data that's already in the file. We'll do this by running the program again, but this time we'll substitute the statement

```
30 OPEN "a:test1" FOR APPEND AS #1
```

for 30 OPEN "a:test1" FOR OUTPUT AS #1. Whatever data is now read into the file with PRINT #1 will be added or "appended" to the end of the existing file.

Since the number of records in our file "test1" is now doubled, we also need to read twice as many records if we want to see the whole file (there's nothing illegal about reading a partial file, though). This means that we need to double the number of loops controlled by the FOR...NEXT statement in line 130; that is, substitute the number 10 for the number 5 in line 130 so that it reads

```
130 FOR J = 1 TO 10
```

Now we're ready to run our modified program. The result is the following:

```
RUN
Ok
CONT
  1   4   9   16   25   1   4   9   16   25
Ok
```

appended data

You can clearly see that a new set of numbers (the squares of 1 to 5) has been added to the existing file.

OPEN FOR APPEND can also be used to create a file if none existed previously. If you know you're going to append a file at some later time, you might as well use OPEN FOR APPEND to create the file in the first place.

The OPEN FOR APPEND Statement

Whenever you need to add data to a sequential file, use the following statement to open the file:

```
1ØØ OPEN "calories" FOR APPEND AS #3
```

Specifies that file is to be opened to add or APPEND new data

OPEN FOR APPEND adds new data to the end of the existing file, in contrast to OPEN FOR OUTPUT which writes over the named file.

The EOF Function — Knowing When to Stop

As we mentioned in the last section, it's perfectly OK not to read the whole file — no error messages, you just get what you ask for. However, it's *not* legal to attempt to read *more* than what's actually in a file. For example, if you try to read 11 records in our file "test1", which has only 10 records (change the loop index to 11 in line 130), you'll get the error message

```
Input past end in 13Ø
```

which means "Dummy, you tried to input more information from the file to the program than actually exists in the file!" OK, that makes sense: you can't get out what you haven't put in.

Wouldn't it be helpful to have a way of knowing when we get to the end of a file so we wouldn't have to be concerned with how many records we need to read? Such a feature would be especially helpful for the previously mentioned file of stock prices to which you would need to constantly add new data.

What we're looking for is the EOF function. EOF stands for "end of file," and informs the program that is reading a data file when the end of the file has been reached. One way to use this function is as a part of an

IF...THEN statement. For example, we could insert the following statement into our program:

```
135    IF EOF(1) THEN 170
```
|
Specifies file number

An English translation of this line is "IF the End Of the File #1 has been reached, THEN go to line 170." Line 170 closes the file. This statement will prevent us from ever again getting the error message "Input past end"! However, if you want to read the whole file, you'd better make sure that the maximum index of your FOR... NEXT loop is at least as large as the number of records in your file.

A somewhat better way to use EOF to help us read the whole file without worrying about or even knowing how much stuff is in your file is to use the WHILE...WEND statement as a test for the end of a file. For example, we can substitute the following lines for the FOR...NEXT statements in lines 130 and 160 of our program:

```
130 WHILE NOT EOF(1)
 *    *    *
 *    *    *
 *    *    *
160 WEND
```

This combination of statements means "while (or as long as) the end of the file #1 has not been reached, continue executing loops between the WHILE and the WEND statements." Perfect! This way we'll read exactly what's in the file, nothing more, nothing less! This is the way that we recommend you read *all* sequential files.

The following is the whole modified version of that part of our original program that reads the file "test1". We include it here to give you a complete model of our preferred method of reading sequential data files:

```
120 OPEN "a:test1" FOR INPUT AS #1
130 WHILE NOT EOF(1)
140     INPUT #1, SQUARE
150     PRINT SQUARE
160 WEND
170 CLOSE
```

This program will read and print the whole file "test1", no matter how many data records you've stored in it.

The BASIC statements that we've used with EOF read very much like English sentences. That's what makes them easy to use and to understand. However, you may be interested in the logical basis of EOF and its use in these statements. EOF returns the number -1 (the logical true) if the end of the file has been reached; if not, it returns a 0 (the logical false). Since NOT is actually a logical operator which turns true into false and vice versa, NOT EOF(1) returns a 0 if the end of the file has been reached, and a -1 if it hasn't. So the WHILE WEND loop operates as long as the logical value of NOT EOF(1) is -1, meaning "true"; execution drops through the loop whenever the logical value of NOT EOF(1) becomes the logical 0 — that is, "false." Whew! It's easier to stick to English!

The EOF Function

EOF is a function that signals the end of a file in the following manner:

if end of file,

> EOF(2) returns a logical false, or 0

if not yet the end of file,

> EOF(2) returns a logical true, or -1

An example of EOF is the following statement:

```
2ØØ WHILE NOT EOF(1)
 *    *    *
 *    *    * ◄── Statements to read and process file records
 *    *    *
26Ø WEND
```

This loop reads file records until it reaches the end of the file.

An Example Program — Storing Stock Prices

This is a good time to pull everything we've learned together into a single program that you might even find useful. The following barebones program stores and reads the daily (or weekly) closing prices of your favorite stock.

```
100 '---NAME: "STOCKPRC.B18"----------------------------------
105 '---PROGRAM WRITES STOCK PRICES TO FILE "stocks" ---------
110 '
120 PRINT "enter Ø when done": PRINT
130 OPEN "stocks" FOR APPEND AS #1
140 FOR J = 1 TO 50
150    INPUT "enter stock price:  ", PRICE
160    IF PRICE = Ø THEN GOTO 190
170    PRINT #1, PRICE
180 NEXT
190 CLOSE
200 END
210 '
220 '---PROGRAM READS FILE-------------------------------------
230 '
240 OPEN "stocks" FOR INPUT AS #1
250 WHILE NOT EOF(1)
260    INPUT #1, PRICE
270    PRINT PRICE
280 WHILE
290 CLOSE
300 END
```

The first part of the program allows you to add up to 50 new stock price values at a time. The second part reads all the records you've put into the file. You might wish to embellish the input and output to make this program more user-friendly.

LINE INPUT # — Dealing with Commas in Your Strings

We said earlier that strings can be written to files and read from files in the same way as numbers. This is true provided that the strings don't have any commas or semicolons in them. The problem is that INPUT # interprets a comma as a delimiter — as a signal to separate the phrases on either side of the comma (or semicolon) into two separate strings. For example, the statement

```
3Ø PRINT #1, "Donnerwetter, Dick"
```

creates the file image

```
Donnerwetter, Dick
```

without any quotation marks (just as PRINT would). When INPUT # reads this data, it interprets Donnerwetter and Dick as two separate strings. Unless you make a special effort to reconnect these two strings, your printed output is likely to look like this:

```
Donnerwetter
Dick
```

One way out of this problem is to use the LINE INPUT # statement to read your file. LINE INPUT # reads from a file the same way that LINE INPUT reads from the keyboard: both read and interpret an entire line, including commas and semicolons, as a single string. The end of the string is determined by a carriage return, not by a comma or semicolon as is the case for INPUT #.

The following program illustrates the use of LINE INPUT # in reading a file of names:

```
100 '---PROGRAM WRITES TO FILE-----------------------------
110 '
120 OPEN "friends" FOR APPEND AS #1
130 LINE INPUT "enter a name-- ", NAM$
140 PRINT #1, NAM$
150 CLOSE
160 END
170 '
180 '---PROGRAM READS FILE--------------------------------
190 '
200 OPEN "friends" FOR INPUT AS #1
210 WHILE NOT EOF(1)
220    LINE INPUT #1, NAM$
230    PRINT NAM$
240 WEND
250 CLOSE
260 END
RUN
enter a name-- Rodgers, Buck
Ok
CONT
Rodgers, Buck          ← Record in file "friends"
Ok
```

You can add a new name to the file "friends" each time you run this program. Notice that the name "Rodgers, Buck" is interpreted as a single string. If we had used INPUT # instead of LINE INPUT #, "Buck" would have been written underneath "Rodgers."

Another way to solve this comma/semicolon problem is by using the WRITE # statement in place of PRINT #, but we'll postpone the explanation of the WRITE # instruction until the next section which deals with multiple data items within a single record.

Records with Multiple Fields

In all past examples, we used PRINT # and (LINE) INPUT # to read one number or one string at a time. It is also possible, however, to write and read more than one data item with each PRINT # and INPUT # statement. This is very useful, for example, when you want to store names and phone numbers since each PRINT # and INPUT # statement can write and read both the name of the person and the phone number. In order to avoid potential comma difficulties, let's start with a simple numerical example.

The following program is based on the first program of this chapter. It stores and reads the numbers J and J*J:

```
10 '---creates sequential file-------------------------------------
20 '
30 OPEN "test2" FOR OUTPUT AS #1
40 FOR J = 1 TO 5
45     SQUARE = J * J
50     PRINT #1, J; SQUARE
60 NEXT
70 CLOSE
80 END
90 '
100 '---reads sequential file-------------------------------------
110 '
120 OPEN "test2" FOR INPUT AS #1
130 WHILE NOT EOF(1)
140     INPUT #1, NUMBER, SQUARE
150     PRINT NUMBER, SQUARE
160 WEND
170 CLOSE
180 END
RUN
Ok
CONT
 1          1
 2          4
 3          9
 4          16
 5          25
Ok
```

The output shows numbers 1 through 5 and their squares. Let's take a look at some of the details.

Line 50 writes *two* values to the file: J and SQUARE. This pair of values is called a *record*, whereas each data element (J and SQUARE, in this example) is called a *field*. Figure 18-4 identifies the records and fields in our PRINT # statement as well as in the file image:

Notice that we used a semicolon (;) to separate J and J*J. Its effect is identical to that of PRINT — it causes the two fields, the values J and J*J, to be written right next to each other without the insertion of any spaces (of course, the numbers themselves still have spaces attached to them). We certainly could have used a comma in place of the semicolon, but that would have resulted in wasted memory space since commas add spaces to each value to make them into fields having a width of 14 characters (remember? — that's also how commas work with PRINT).

Each record is read by the INPUT # statement in line 140:

```
14Ø      INPUT #1, NUMBER, SQUARE
```

The INPUT # statement here reads the record and assigns its first field to the variable NUMBER and its second field to the variable SQUARE. Numeric records are easy!

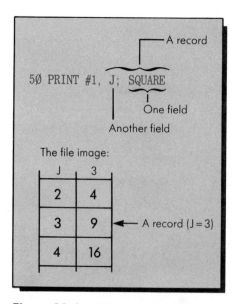

Figure 18-4. Records and fields in a sequential file

A Problem with Strings

Suppose that we want to create records consisting of a name and a phone number: that is, records with two separate string fields. To write to the file, we can use a statement like the following:

```
30 PRINT #1, "John Struvelpeter"; "456-1308"
```

The problem, however, is that PRINT # will write these two strings into the file right next to each other without any spaces, and without quotation marks; INPUT # will read this part of the file as

```
John Struvelpeter456-1308
```

The problem is even worse if there are commas present since, as before, they have the effect of dividing a string into separate strings. And LINE INPUT # can't come to the rescue as long as we want to deal with multiple fields within one record (LINE INPUT # reads a whole line into one record).

How do we get out of this difficulty? First, the hard way: you can insert additional commas (written as a string ",") as delimiters in the PRINT # statement so that each field in the file record is bracketed by quotation marks; INPUT # won't break up the contents of something bracketed by quotation marks. If you insist on doing it this way, you might check with your *IBM Personal Computer BASIC* manual under PRINT # for details.

By far the easiest way to deal with this problem (and most other delimiter problems) is to use the WRITE # statement in place of PRINT #.

WRITE # — The Easy Way To Write To a File

WRITE # and PRINT # are similar in that they both write to the specified file. However, they differ in the way they format the information passed to the file: whereas the format of PRINT #, which mimics that of PRINT, is best suited for output to the screen, WRITE # is tailor-made for writing to a file. For example, the statement

```
100 WRITE #2, "Struvelpeter, John", "456-1308"
```

creates the file image

```
"Struvelpeter, John", "456-1308"
```

which has quotation marks around both strings. INPUT # can now read this information as intended: that is, as two separate fields, without getting mixed up by the comma. We can then use PRINT to write the desired result to the screen:

```
Struvelpeter, John        456-1308
```

This example illustrates the following formatting features that make WRITE # so well suited to write to a file. First, WRITE # always brackets strings with quotation marks (PRINT # doesn't) so that INPUT # won't interpret commas and semicolons as delimiters between strings. And second, WRITE # always inserts commas between the various data items (or fields) in a record (PRINT # doesn't — that's why John and 456-1308 were concatenated). That's what INPUT # needs to recognize the different fields.

The second feature applies to both strings and numbers. Both WRITE # and PRINT # add a carriage return to the end of a record.

Making Changes in Your Files

We now know how to create a file, but how do you make changes in an existing file? You can't just pluck out one record from a sequential file and replace it with a new one (well, not using sequential records anyway). Remember, to access a record in a sequential file, you have to read *all* the records before the one you want to get to.

Well, the solution to our problem isn't hard. The basic idea can be summarized by the following steps:

1. OPEN the file FOR INPUT and read the whole file into one or more arrays (one array for each field). CLOSE the file.

2. Make the desired change in the array element.

3. OPEN the file FOR OUTPUT and read the corrected array back into the original file. CLOSE the file.

In many cases, it is convenient to combine steps 2 and 3.

The following program allows you to make changes in the file called "friends" which we set up in the section on LINE INPUT #. We've kept this example simple; you can use it as a model for other, perhaps more complex cases.

```
500 '---PROGRAM MAKES CHANGES IN FILE "friends"---------
510 '
520 DIM NAMES$(100)
530 OPEN "friends" FOR INPUT AS #1
540 FOR J = 1 TO 30
550     INPUT #1, NAMES$
560     NAMES$(J) = NAMES$
570 NEXT
580 CLOSE
590 '
600 INPUT "Enter record number to be changed:   ", JCHANGE
610 INPUT "Enter new name:                      ", NEWNAME$
620 '
630 OPEN "friends" FOR OUTPUT AS #1
640 FOR J = 1 TO 30
650     IF J = JCHANGE THEN NAME$(J) = NEWNAME$
660     WRITE #1, NAME$(J)
670 NEXT
680 CLOSE
690 END
```

The key statement is line 650; it exchanges the new name for the old one. This program makes the rather specific assumption that there are 30 names in the file "friends"; hence the index limit of 30 in line 540 and 640. It's not hard to add some statements to take care of this limitation, but we'll leave that up to you!

Summary

In this chapter we've delved into the world of sequential files. You can now store your recipes, telephone numbers, and inventories on disk!

The following statements summarize how to set up and read sequential files.

To set up or write a file:

1. OPEN the file FOR OUTPUT or FOR APPEND.

2. Write data to the file using PRINT # or WRITE #; the latter is generally easier to use because it avoids problems with delimiters.

3. CLOSE a file when you are done writing to it, especially when you subsequently want to read it.

To read a file:

1. OPEN the file FOR INPUT.

2. Read data from the file using INPUT # or LINE INPUT #; the latter is useful to read strings containing commas and semicolons, but it is limited to reading single field records.

3. CLOSE the file when done.

At this point, you're almost to the end of this book. So far, all the programs we've written require pretty smart users — users who have to know how to respond to computers, how to enter things in such a way that you don't get a bunch of error messages that often are indecipherable. Our last chapter deals with ways of "user-proofing" your programs so that someone besides yourself can use the programs you've written.

Exercise

Write a program that creates and reads a file containing records consisting of two fields: the name of a food, and the number of calories per ounce.

Solution

Here's the program we wrote:

```
100 '----NAME: "CAL-FILE.B18"-------------------------------------
102 '
108 '----*****************************************
110 '----* PRGRM CREATES AND READS FILE "CALORIES" *-------------
120 '----*****************************************
130 KEY OFF: CLS
140 '
150 '----PRGRM CREATES FILE "CALORIES"--------------------------
160 '
170 PRINT " This program stores a list of foods and their"
180 PRINT " calorie content per pound in a file CALORIES"
185 PRINT "If you just want to display file, enter RUN 500"
190 PRINT "---------------------------------------------"
200 PRINT
210 PRINT "Enter the word 'end' when finished"
220 PRINT "Use quoatation marks if food entry has commas"
230 PRINT: PRINT
240 '
250 OPEN "CALORIES" FOR APPEND AS #1     'OPENs file to add items
```

```
26Ø FOR J = 1 TO 1ØØ
27Ø PRINT
28Ø    INPUT "enter food--------------- ", FOOD$
29Ø    IF FOOD$ = "end" THEN GOTO 33Ø
3ØØ    INPUT "enter calories per pound-- ", CAL
31Ø    WRITE #1, FOOD$, CAL              'WRITEs data into record
32Ø NEXT
33Ø CLOSE
34Ø '
35Ø PRINT
36Ø PRINT "enter 'cont' to inspect file CALORIES"
37Ø END
38Ø '
5ØØ '----PRGRM READS FILE "CALORIES"----------------------------
51Ø '
52Ø CLS
53Ø PRINT SPC(2Ø) "CALORIES CONTENT OF FOODS"
54Ø PRINT: PRINT
55Ø PRINT "FOOD",,"CAL/LB.", " CAL/GRAM"
56Ø PRINT
57Ø '
58Ø OPEN "CALORIES" FOR INPUT AS #1      'OPENs file for reading
59Ø WHILE NOT EOF(1)
6ØØ    INPUT #1, FOOD$, CAL              'reads record
61Ø    PRINT FOOD$ TAB(28) CAL, CAL/453
62Ø WEND
63Ø CLOSE
64Ø END
```

After entering some foods and their calorie content, we got the following output:

```
                    CALORIE CONTENT OF FOODS


FOOD                      CAL/LB.        CAL/GRAM

Braunschweiger            1447           3.194261
Camembert                 1359           3
Cherry pie                1181           2.6Ø7Ø64
Tofu                      6Ø7            1.339956
Frog legs, fried          123Ø           2.715232
Gin                       1132           2.488896
Escargots                 1Ø56           2.331126
Ok
```

You might be interested in knowing that these are actual calorie values. Note that if an entry needs commas for any reason, INPUT requires you to use quotation marks around it.

19

Dealing with Errors Creatively

Concepts
   Error messages and error codes
   Error trapping
   Error-handling subroutines

Instructions
   ON ERROR GOTO, RESUME, ERR, ERL

Nobody likes to make mistakes, and if we do make them, we like even less to be reminded of them! However, given the fact that computers and computer programs tend to be extremely picky and obstinate (we have to do things *just* right), we might as well get all the help we can. BASIC's error messages, as aggravating as they may be at times, do help us to identify errors in our programs, and hence to correct them.

Some errors, however, are not caused by a flaw in the design of the program but are instead the result of inappropriate input by the user or some kind of simple problem with the system, like an open disk drive door. A programmer usually knows how to handle such errors, but if you're a computer novice, or if you're not familiar with BASIC, a message like "Illegal function call" can be worse than disconcerting. First of all, our novice user probably has no idea what this message means, nor what to do about it. And second, almost all error messages cause your program to "bomb" — that is, to return to the BASIC command mode without finishing program execution. This chapter is about BASIC instructions and methods that we, as programmers, can use to "user-proof" our programs for the benefit of users.

BASIC's Error Messages

Let's start with familiar territory, BASIC's error messages. This is your chance to make some errors *on purpose*! The following is a small sample of ways to make your PC cry "foul play":

```
Ok
lizt
Syntax error
Ok
GOTO 5Ø
Undefined line number
Ok
PRINT 5*
Missing operand
Ok
```

BASIC for your PC has a total of 53 such error messages. Notice that we used the Direct Mode to generate the preceding error messages; that's an efficient way to make a lot of errors quickly! Within a program, most such error messages also give you the line number in which the error occurred — an obvious aid to programmers. The following is an example:

```
1Ø DATA "03 G A B 04 C"
2Ø READ notes                    ← Notice missing dollar ($) sign
3Ø PLAY notes$
RUN
Type mismatch in 2Ø
Ok
```

Once you know where to look for the mistake, it's generally easy to identify and to correct the error.

Appendix G gives a summary of all the BASIC error messages (see the *IBM Personal Computer BASIC* manual for a complete description). Note that each error message is associated with an error code, ranging from 1 to 73. (Numbers 31 through 49 are missing — perhaps to leave room for future expansion.) For example, error message 2 is "Syntax error." These error codes will prove to be very useful later when we learn to write subroutines that handle specific user-related errors.

Error Trapping — User-Proofing Your Programs

As we've mentioned earlier, a correctly written program may still "bomb" or "crash." For example, consider the following simple program that prints the square root of a number:

```
1Ø INPUT "enter a number to find its square root: ", X
2Ø ROOT = SQR(X)
3Ø PRINT "the square root equals" ROOT
4Ø PRINT "finished"
5Ø END
```

There is no problem with running this program, unless the user enters a negative number:

```
RUN
enter a number to find its square root: 3
the square root equals 1.732Ø51
Ok
RUN
enter a number to find its square root: -3
Illegal function call
Ok
```

The problem is that you can't take the square root of a negative number (a number multiplied by itself cannot be negative, unless you're dealing with a special class of numbers called "imaginary numbers"). The error message "Illegal function call" tells you that a function has been used in an "illegal" manner. However, if you're not familiar with programming (or mathematics), such an error message may not be very helpful. Furthermore, although the program has bombed — that is, execution was terminated at line 40 before PRINT was able to print "finished," the user is given no further instructions as to how to proceed. If you're writing programs for your own use, that's OK, since you know how to handle such a situation. If your program is to be a professional product for the general public, however, you need to shield the user from such program behavior.

What's needed here is something called an *error trapping routine*, a collection of BASIC instructions that "traps" the error before it terminates program execution and that gives the user a chance to rectify the error. In the above example, you *could* use the following IF statement right after INPUT to redirect program execution back to the INPUT statement:

```
15 IF X < Ø THEN PRINT "negative numbers are a NO-NO!": GOTO 1Ø
```

This statement ensures that program execution will not proceed to the SQR function in line 20 until the user enters an acceptable number (positive or zero). It also gives the user explicit directions on what was wrong with the first entry and, by implication, how to do it right next time.

Error trapping, however, is a more generally applicable error handling technique that uses BASIC statements that are specially designed to handle and shield the user from virtually all possible errors. In the following section, we'll introduce you to the fundamentals of error trapping.

ON ERROR GOTO and RESUME — Trapping Errors

Let's rewrite the previous program to include a simple error trapping routine:

```
1Ø ON ERROR GOTO 1ØØ
2Ø INPUT "enter a number to find its square root: ", X
3Ø ROOT = SQR(X)
4Ø PRINT "the square root equals" ROOT
5Ø PRINT "finished"
6Ø END
7Ø '
1ØØ '---ERROR HANDLING SUBROUTINE--------------------------------
11Ø PRINT "no negative numbers, please; try again..."
12Ø RESUME 2Ø
```

Now if we enter a negative number, we'll get the following response:

```
RUN
enter a number to find its square root: -5
no negative numbers, please;  try again...
enter a number to find its square root: 5
the square root equals 2.236Ø68
finished
Ok
```

The advantage of this method of handling an INPUT error is clear: BASIC's error message "Illegal function call" is bypassed; instead, the user gets the explicit instruction "no negative numbers, please; try again" and a chance to enter another number without having to rerun the program.

The two new statements in this program are ON ERROR GOTO 100 in line 10 and RESUME 20 in line 120. The first of these,

```
1Ø ON ERROR GOTO 1ØØ
```

means "ON the occurrence of any type of error after this line, GOTO line 100 *without* invoking BASIC's error message." Line 100 is the beginning of an error-handling subroutine that does two things. First, it tells the user "no negative numbers; please try again;" that is, it explains what to do about the error. Second, it returns program execution to the desired point in the main program by means of the statement

```
12Ø RESUME 2Ø
```

which says "RESUME program execution at line 20." Since line 20 contains our INPUT statement, the user gets another chance to do it right.

If you happen to forget to include RESUME but you have an ON ERROR GOTO statement, your PC will respond with:

```
No RESUME in 11Ø
```

The message is clear: a RESUME statement is mandatory if you have an ON ERROR GOTO statement. The converse is also true: if you have a RESUME, you need an ON ERROR GOTO. The two statements form an inseparable pair. Another feature of BASIC, suggested by the "No RESUME in 110" error message, is that ON ERROR GOTO will not trap errors inside the error-trapping subroutine. That means that if you, the programmer, make a mistake inside the subroutine, you'll get the usual BASIC error messages.

Notice the similarity between the pair of instructions ON ERROR GOTO and RESUME, and ON GOSUB and RETURN. The first partner of each pair causes program execution to jump to a subroutine, and the second partner, RESUME or RETURN, causes program execution to return to the main program.

Dealing with System-Related Errors

It is also possible for an uninitiated user to get an error message like one of the following:

```
Out of paper in 22Ø
Disk not ready in 2Ø5Ø
```

The first message might appear in response to an LPRINT statement in line 220 if the printer isn't ready: either the printer is out of paper, or the printer isn't turned on. The second message might occur if you attempt in line 2050 to open a file on disk without closing the disk drive door, or if you forget to insert the disk altogether. To shield a user from such messages and the consequent program termination, you can use the following type of error-handling routine. This particular example relates to making sure that the printer is ready when an LPRINT statement is executed:

```
10 ON ERROR GOTO 100
20 LPRINT "hello, printer"
30 PRINT "printer is ready!"
40 END
50 '
100 '---ERROR HANDLING SUBROUTINE------------------
110 PRINT "printer isn't ready:  is it ON?  does it have paper?"
120 PRINT "press any key when printer is ready..."
130 A$ = INKEY$: IF A$ = "" THEN 130
140 RESUME
```

If you run this program with your printer ready to go, you'll get "hello, printer" on your printer, and "printer is ready" on your screen. However, if your printer is turned off or out of paper when you run this program, the following will appear on your screen:

```
RUN
printer isn't ready: is it ON? does it have paper?
press any key when printer is ready...
printer is ready!
Ok
```

Computer waits for you to press any key, presumably when you've prepared the printer

Message that appears immediately after line printer prints "hello, printer," assuming that you did turn it on and/or insert paper

In the meantime, of course, "hello, printer" will have also been written by the printer. Note the use of an endless loop in line 130 that can only be broken if "any key" is pressed (resulting in a string other than the null string ""). A similar error- handling subroutine would be useful for dealing with disk-related errors.

Note that we left off the line number after RESUME. The effect is equivalent to RESUME 120; that is, RESUME without any specified line number causes program execution to resume at the line in which the error was trapped originally. Another form of RESUME is

```
RESUME NEXT
```

which causes the program to return to the *next* line — that is, the line *following* the one in which the error occurred. In our last example, we could have used RESUME NEXT to bypass the printer if it wasn't turned on, and then just continue with the rest of the program.

The ON ERROR GOTO and RESUME Statements

The following statement initiates error trapping:

```
100 ON ERROR GOTO 1000
```

It means "ON the occurrence of any error, GOTO line 1000, which is the beginning of an error-handling subroutine." Error trapping can be turned off by the statement

```
1230 ON ERROR GOTO 0
```

One of the following statements must end an error-handling subroutine:

```
1100 RESUME          ← which returns program execution to the line in
                         which the error occurred
1100 RESUME NEXT     ← which returns program execution to the line
                         immediately following the line in which
                         the error occurred
1100 RESUME 20       ← which returns program execution to line 20
```

The Variables ERR and ERL — Becoming More Discriminating

The error-handling subroutines in our previous examples are very simple in that they anticipate the possible occurrence of only one type of error. But what if there are several errors that can occur? Or what if an altogether unanticipated error occurs? We might be advised to extend the adage "When something can go wrong, it will" with the corollary "When one thing can go wrong, a second is likely to go wrong as well!"

In order to ensure that we give the user correct error messages, we need to be able to identify precisely the nature of the error; and if we anticipate the occurrence of more than one error, we need to be able to discriminate between different types of errors. BASIC's tools for identifying errors are the ERR and ERL variables. If an error is trapped by ON ERROR GOTO, BASIC will assign the following values to ERR and ERL:

ERR is assigned the *code* number of the trapped error.

ERL is assigned the *line* number of the line in which the error occurred.

These variables can only be assigned values by BASIC itself; hence ERR and ERL are called *reserved variables*, meaning that you cannot use these variables for any purpose other than identifying errors in the way described above.

We can use ERR and ERL to make sure that an error handling subroutine will be engaged only if the error that occurred is really the one we anticipated. For example, let's add such an error-testing statement to our square root problem (look for line 105):

```
1Ø ON ERROR GOTO 1ØØ
2Ø INPUT "enter a number to find its square root:  ", X
3Ø ROOT = SQR(X)
4Ø PRINT "the square root equals" ROOT
5Ø PRINT "finished"
6Ø END
7Ø '
1ØØ '---ERROR HANDLING SUBROUTINE----------------------------------------
1Ø5 IF ERR <> 5 AND ERL <> 3Ø THEN ON ERROR GOTO Ø    'new statement
11Ø PRINT "no negative numbers please;  try again..."
12Ø RESUME 2Ø
```

Line 105 is the new statement; it says that "IF the trapped error does not have error code number 5, 'Illegal function call,' AND if the error did not occur in line 30, THEN GOTO line number 0, which has the effect of disabling the error trapping." The last part of this statement — ON ERROR GOTO 0 — is a use of the ON ERROR GOTO statement that we haven't told you about before (although we did sneak it into a summary!). Its effect is to cause BASIC to treat an error as if there were no error trapping routine, so that the usual BASIC error message is displayed and program execution comes to an immediate end. Thus the net effect of the IF...THEN statement in line 105 is to allow the subsequent error-handling statements (lines 110 and 120) to do their job *only if* the error really is the one that the subroutine is designed to handle. If the error is not the anticipated error, BASIC's built-in error handling mechanism takes over. For example, if you misspell INPUT as INPUTT in line 30, you'll get the usual "Syntax error."

It is usually a good idea to include in all your error-handling subroutines an error-checking statement, like the one in line 105, that returns BASIC to its own error-handling mode if an unanticipated error is encountered. The reason for this is clear: error-checking statements help ensure that you won't get an unintended, inappropriate, and misleading error message.

Preparing for More Than One Error

In the example problems used so far in this chapter, we've anticipated the occurrence of only one possible error. Chances are, however, that in most of the programs you'll write, several different errors might occur. For example, if we combine our program that uses LPRINT with the program that calculates the square root of a number, *two* possible BASIC errors can occur: the printer might not be ready, or a negative number might have been entered (or both!). The error-handling subroutine in such a program needs to discriminate between the different errors that might occur and to treat each in the appropriate manner.

The following program handles a printer error as well as an error caused by an attempt to find the square root of a negative number:

```
100 ON ERROR GOTO 500
110 INPUT "enter a number to find its square root:  ", X
120 ROOT = SQR(X)
130 LPRINT "square root of" X "equals" ROOT
140 END
150 '
500 '---ERROR HANDLING SUBROUTINE-----------------------------------
510 IF ERR <> 5 AND ERR <> 27 THEN ON ERROR GOTO 0
520 IF ERR = 5 THEN PRINT "Neg. numbers are a NO-NO; try again":
    RESUME 110
530 PRINT "Your printer isn't ready; is it ON?  does it have paper?"
540 A$ = INKEY$: IF A$ = "" THEN 540
555 RESUME 130
```

Any errors that are trapped by ON ERROR GOTO in line 100 are first checked to determine if the error is one of our anticipated errors: an "Illegal function call" (code number 5) or an "Out of paper" error (code number 27). If the error isn't one of these, BASIC's own error processing routine takes over. On the other hand, if the trapped error is either one of these two anticipated errors, then line 520 takes care of code 5 errors, and the remainder of the subroutine handles code 27 errors.

Notice that we neglected to use ERL to check for line number of error. We didn't need to use ERL because code 5 and 27 errors can only occur in lines 120 and 130, respectively. However, longer and more complex programs will frequently require the use of both ERR and ERL to identify errors unambiguously.

The ERR and ERL Variables

The reserved variables ERR and ERL have the following functions within an error-handling subroutine:

ERR   returns the error code number.

ERL   returns the line number where the error occurred.

For example, if the error is caused by an attempt in line 120 to use OPEN to open a disk file when the disk drive door isn't closed (error code 71), ERR returns 71 and ERL returns 120.

The ERROR Statement

Another very useful instruction that helps us to deal with errors is the ERROR statement. It is one of several BASIC instructions that has a dual purpose. First, it can be used to simulate an error; this is useful for testing your error-handling routines. Second, you can use it to define your own errors — a powerful and very useful technique to trap and handle errors that are not part of the BASIC error set (codes 1 to 73).

Making Errors on Purpose

The ERROR statement can be used to simulate an error. For example, enter the following command:

```
ERROR 67          ← Command
Too many files    ← Response of computer
Ok
```

If you look in Appendix G, you'll see that error code 67 does indeed correspond to the BASIC error message "Too many files." The command ERROR 67 causes your PC to act as if error number 67 had actually taken place.

ERROR 67 could also be included in your BASIC program. For example, if we inserted

```
125 ERROR 67
```

into our previous program that writes the square root to the printer, the program would bomb when execution reaches line 125, and BASIC would print out the error message "Too many files," despite the fact that you don't have too many files.

We work very hard at eliminating errors. Why would we want to create them on purpose? Well, to test our error-handling routines. Usually, using ERROR in this way is just a convenience; sometimes, though, it may be the only reasonable way to go about it. Take, for example, the above error "Too many files." What a nuisance it would be actually to assemble a disk with the maximum number of files on it if you don't happen to have such a disk already lying around! (In DOS 1.1 that would require 64 files for a single-sided disk and 112 for a double-sided disk!)

Often, the easiest way to use ERROR to test your error-handling routines is to run your program, and to press (Ctrl) (Break) before execution is finished. For example, run the last program (the one that writes the square root of a number to the printer) in the following manner:

```
RUN
enter a number of which you want the square root:        ← Press (Ctrl) (Break)
Break in 11Ø
ERROR 27                                                 ← Enter this
Your printer isn't ready; is it ON?  does it have paper?
press any key when printer is ready...
Ok      ← A key has been pressed and "square root of 0 equals 0" has been
           printed out on the printer
```

Instead of entering a number in response to the computer's request for input, we pressed (Ctrl) (Break) to break the program at line 110. Then we entered ERROR 27. As you can see from the output, the effect of this is to simulate an "Out of paper error" in the program that we just interrupted.

Using ERROR in this way is a fast, convenient way of checking your error-handling subroutines. However, we think that you'll find using ERROR to define your own errors even more valuable.

Defining Your Own Errors

We've seen how to trap and handle BASIC's errors. But suppose you're writing a program that requires the user to INPUT the month of a year: how would you prevent a user from entering numbers like 0 or 13 — that is, numbers that would result in erroneous output but that are perfectly legal as far as BASIC is concerned? That's where the second variation of ERROR comes in handy.

We can use ERROR to *define* a new error that would not otherwise be trapped by an ON ERROR GOTO statement. The following is a short program that ensures proper user input of the month number:

```
1Ø ON ERROR GOTO 1ØØ
2Ø INPUT "enter number of month:  ", MONTH
3Ø IF MONTH > 12 OR MONTH < 1 THEN ERROR 2ØØ
4Ø PRINT MONTH
5Ø END
6Ø '
7Ø '---ERROR HANDLING SUBROUTINE-----------------------
8Ø IF ERR <> 2ØØ THEN ON ERROR GOTO Ø
9Ø PRINT "try again; you must enter a number from 1 through 12"
1ØØ RESUME 2Ø
RUN
enter number of month:   13
try again; you must enter a number from 1 through 12
enter number of month:   3
 3
Ok
```

Since BASIC couldn't care less whether MONTH equals 13 (or 1013 for that matter), no error trapping would have occurred without our own definition of a new error in line 30. The statement

```
3Ø IF MONTH>12 OR MONTH<1 THEN ERROR 2ØØ
```
New error code defined by ERROR

means "if the value of MONTH is not in the range of 1 to 12, then cause an ERROR, which is to have an error code number 200." Line 80 makes sure that the trapped error really does have code number 200 before allowing the error to be handled by the subsequent error-handling instructions in lines 90 and 100.

What's special about error code number 200? Nothing, except that it isn't one of the error code numbers that BASIC reserves for itself. For the purpose of defining your own errors by means of ERROR, you can use any error number that isn't already used by BASIC. We used 200 because it's easy to remember and is definitely a safe number to use.

Handling Overflow and Division by Zero

Now here's a surprise for you. Although "Overflow" and "Division by zero" are perfectly standard BASIC errors (code numbers 6 and 11, respectively), you cannot trap and treat these errors in the way we've described. Try it and see for yourself! Run the following program with a 0 in response to INPUT:

```
10 ON ERROR GOTO 100
20 INPUT "enter a number ", X
30 RECIP = 1/X
40 PRINT RECIP
50 END
60 '
100 '---ERROR HANDLING SUBROUTINE------------------------------------
110 IF ERR <> 11 AND ERL <> 30 THEN ON ERROR GOTO 0
120 PRINT "tsk, tsk, no zeroes!  try again..."
130 RESUME 20
RUN
enter a number 0
Division by zero

 1.701412E+38
Ok
```

We've written a perfectly good error-handling subroutine, but it doesn't work! Instead we get what looks like the usual BASIC error message "Division by zero" and, of course, our program bombs. Notice also the answer we get for 1/0: it's the biggest number our computer can write, but it's not infinity. Similarly, the "Overflow" error cannot be trapped.

Most likely the answer to this mystery is that it isn't BASIC that responds to this "Division by zero" error, but DOS. That is, apparently DOS gets wind of the error and handles it in its own way before BASIC has a chance to do anything about it. This explanation makes sense in view of the fact that the error message printed out in our previous example does *not* include a line number, which would be typical of BASIC; and "Overflow" and "Division by zero" — without line numbers — are DOS error messages.

Is there a way to trap these errors anyway? Sure there is: the trick is to catch the error *before* DOS does by defining a new ERROR. For example, we can modify our previous program that finds the reciprocal of a number in the following manner:

```
1Ø ON ERROR GOTO 1ØØ
2Ø INPUT "enter a number: ", X
25 IF X = Ø THEN ERROR 2ØØ
3Ø RECIP = 1/X
4Ø PRINT RECIP
5Ø END
6Ø '
1ØØ '---ERROR HANDLING SUBROUTINE------------------------------------
11Ø IF ERR <> 2ØØ THEN ON ERROR GOTO Ø
12Ø PRINT "tsk, tsk, no zeroes!   try again..."
13Ø RESUME 2Ø
RUN
enter a number: Ø
tsk, tsk, no zeroes!   try again...
enter a number: 4
 .25
Ok
```

Now our error trap works! Line 25 causes an error identified by code number 200 if X equals 0. Notice that this statement is placed *before* the division is made in line 30, so that the program is never asked to divide by 0.

In a program like this, it might also be advisable to include some error protection against "Overflow". For example, if instead of printing 1/X, you printed 1/X^3, you could very well get an "Overflow" error if you entered a small enough, but nonzero, value for X.

The ERROR Statement

ERROR can be used in two different ways:

`ERROR 8` — Causes BASIC to respond *as if* error number 8 had occurred (code number 8 is "Undefined Line number").

`ERROR 200` — Defines a *new* error with code number 200; the requirement is that the code number is not part of the set of code numbers already defined by BASIC, i.e. numbers 1-30 and 50-73. This form of ERROR is usually used as part of an IF... THEN statement, as for example

```
IF LEN(WORD$) > 24 THEN ERROR 200
```

The error-handling subroutine can then discriminate the error defined in this manner from other errors by referring to the error code number.

Summary

A good error-trapping routine is often what distinguishes professional programming from casual, "Sunday" programming. There's nothing wrong with the latter; however, if you want your programs to be used by someone other than yourself or by people knowledgeable in BASIC, it is very important to shield users of your program from such frustrating, and perhaps catastrophic, messages like "Illegal function call" or worse yet, "Unprintable error" (we're not kidding — see error code number 21)!

Errors are trapped by the ON ERROR GOTO statement, which must be paired with a RESUME statement in order to return program execution to the main program. Errors can be precisely identified by means of the ERR and ERL variables so that each type of error can be handled in the appropriate manner. ERR identifies the error code and ERL identifies the line in which the error occurred. You can define your own errors (aside from the ones BASIC recognizes automatically) by using a statement like "IF *so and so* THEN ERROR 210", where 210 is the code number of the new error.

Exercise

Write a program that requests the user to input the month number, but add the following feature: usually, if a user enters "February" instead of "2," INPUT will respond with the message "Redo from start"; that's a bit ambiguous, so write the program in a way that replaces this message with your own crystal clear instruction!

Solution

The only way to bypass INPUT's "Redo from start" message is to use LINE INPUT, which accepts everything without complaint. Since the LINE INPUT variable is a string, we need to extract a number out of it by means of the VAL function. Here it goes:

```
80   '---NAME: "MO-INPUT.B19"-------------------------------------------
82   '
85   '---***************************************************
90   '---* Error Trapping INPUT Routine for Month of Year *---------------
95   '---***************************************************
98   '
100  ON ERROR GOTO 180    'sets error trap
110  LINE INPUT "Enter number of month (1 - 12):   "; N$
120  N = VAL(N$)
130  IF ASC(N$) > 57 OR ASC(N$) < 48 THEN ERROR 200   'error if
     letter
140  IF N > 12 OR N < 1 THEN ERROR 210      'error if out of range
150  PRINT "The month number equals" N
160  END
170  '
180  '---ERROR-HANDLING SUBROUTINE--------------------------------------
190  IF ERR = 200 THEN PRINT "Enter a number, not a word; try again...":
     RESUME 110
200  IF ERR = 210 THEN PRINT "Entry must be from 1 to 12; try again...":
     RESUME 110
210  ON ERROR GOTO 0
RUN
```

```
Enter number of month (1 - 12):   February
Enter a number, not a word; try again...
Enter number of month (1 - 12): 22
Entry must be from 1 to 12; try again...
Enter number of month (1 - 12):   2
The month number equals 2
Ok
```

User-proofing program input is a lot of work! But it goes quickly once you get the technique down. Notice that the errors the error-handling subroutine are designed to take care of are programmer-defined errors. Line 130 defines error number 200 to prevent someone from entering a word like "February" instead of a number; line 140 defines error number 210 to prevent out-of-range entries.

It's Time To Say Good-bye

We hope you've enjoyed reading this book as much as we enjoyed writing it and that you've learned even more about BASIC than you expected. This book covered a lot of ground. We've introduced most of the BASIC instructions available on your PC, and we've explained a lot of programming techniques that enable you to assemble these instructions into efficient, powerful, and coherent BASIC programs. In short, you have all the tools necessary to write first-class BASIC programs. We hope you're ready to seek fame and fortune in the wide world of programming! No matter what motivated you to learn BASIC on your PC, we hope this book has played a helpful role in achieving your goals.

Summary of Different BASICs

Statement/Command		Cassette BASIC or ROM BASIC	Disk BASIC	Advanced BASIC or BASICA
CHAIN		-	*	*
CIRCLE		-	-	*
COM(n)		-	-	*
COMMON		-	*	*
CVI, CVS, CVD		-	*	*
DATE$		-	*	*
DRAW		-	-	*
FILES	C	-	*	*
GET (files)		-	*	*
GET (graphics)		-	-	*
KEY(n)		-	-	*
KILL	C	-	*	*
LOC		-	*	*
LOF		-	*	*
LSET, RSET		-	*	*
MKI$, MKS$, MKD$		-		*
NAME	C	-	*	*
ON COM(n)		-	-	*
ON KEY(n)		-	-	*
ON PEN		-	-	*
ON STRIG(n)		-	-	*
OPEN "COM...		-	*	*
PAINT		-	-	*
PLAY		-	-	*
PUT (files)		-	*	*
PUT (graphics)		-	-	*
RESET		-	*	*
STRIG(n)		-	-	*
SYSTEM	C	-	*	*
TIMES		-	*	*
VARPTR$		-	*	*

C = command   * = implemented   - = not implemented

B

Switching Displays

IBM suggests you use the following BASIC program to switch
displays from the Color/Graphics Monitor Adapter and the IBM
Monochrome Display and Parallel Printer Adapter. Refer to *BASIC*, by
Microsoft (IBM Personal Computer Hardware Reference Library), page
1-8, for more information.

```
10 ' switch to monochrome adapter
20 DEF SEG = Ø
30 POKE &H41Ø, (PEEK(&H41Ø) OR &H3Ø)
40 SCREEN Ø
50 WIDTH 4Ø
60 WIDTH 8Ø
70 LOCATE ,,1,12,13

10 ' switch to color adapter
20 DEF SEG = Ø
30 POKE &H41Ø, (PEEK(&H41Ø) AND &HCF) OR &H1Ø
40 SCREEN 1,Ø,Ø,Ø
50 SCREEN Ø
60 WIDTH 4Ø
70 LOCATE ,,1,6,7
```

You can also use DOS 2.0 commands to switch displays as described
below. Refer to the *DOS Version 2.00* manual of the IBM Personal
Computer Language Series under "MODE" for complete information.

```
MODE MONO    ← Switches to IBM Monochrome Monitor
MODE CO8Ø    ← Switches to Color/Graphics Adapter, 8Ø-column screen
MODE CO4Ø    ← Switches to Color/Graphics Adapter, 4Ø-column screen
```

Reserved Words

Reserved words cannot be used as variable names. They are *reserved* by BASIC for use as, or part of, commands, statements, function names, and operator names.

Reserved Words in DOS 1.1

The following list includes all of the BASIC reserved words supported by DOS 1.1:

ABS	CVI
AND	CVS
ASC	DATA
ATN	DATE$
AUTO	DEF
BEEP	DEFDBL
BLOAD	DEFINT
BSAVE	DEFSNG
CALL	DEFSTR
CDBL	DELETE
CHAIN	DIM
CHRS	DRAW
CINT	EDIT
CIRCLE	ELSE
CLEAR	END
CLOSE	EOF
CLS	EQV
COLOR	ERASE
COM	ERL
COMMON	ERR
CONT	ERROR
COS	EXP
CSNG	FIELD
CSRLIN	FILES
CVD	FIX

FNxxxxxxxx	NOT
FOR	OCT$
FRE	OFF
GET	ON
GOSUB	OPEN
GOTO	OPTION
HEX$	OR
IF	OUT
IMP	PAINT
INKEY$	PEEK
INP	PEN
INPUT	PLAY
INPUT#	POINT
INPUT$	POKE
INSTR	POS
INT	PRESET
KEY	PRINT
KILL	PRINT#
LEFT$	PSET
LEN	PUT
LET	RANDOMIZE
LINE	READ
LIST	REM
LLIST	RENUM
LOAD	RESET
LOC	RESTORE
LOCATE	RESUME
LOF	RETURN
LOG	RIGHT$
LPOS	RND
LPRINT	RSET
LSET	RUN
MERGE	SAVE
MID$	SCREEN
MKD$	SGN
MKI$	SIN
MKS$	SOUND
MOD	SPACE$
MOTOR	SPC(
NAME	SQR
NEW	STEP
NEXT	STICK

STOP	USING
STR$	USR
STRIG	VAL
STRINGS	VARPTR
SWAP	VARPTR$
SYSTEM	WAIT
TAB(	WEND
TAN	WHILE
THEN	WIDTH
TIME$	WRITE
TO	WRITE#
TROFF	XOR
TRON	

Additional Reserved Words in DOS 2.0 Implementation

The following BASIC reserved words, in addition to those listed above for DOS 1.1, are supported by DOS 2.00:

CHDR	KEY$
ENVIRON	MKDIR
ENVIRON$	PMAP
ERDEV	RMDIR
ERDEV$	SHELL
INTER$	TIMER
IOCTL	VIEW
IOCTL$	WINDOW

D

ASCII and Numeric Conversions

Decimal (ASCII)	Character	Binary	Hexadecimal	Octal
0	(null)	00000000	00	000
1	☺	00000001	01	001
2	☻	00000010	02	002
3	♥	00000011	03	003
4	♦	00000100	04	004
5	♣	00000101	05	005
6	♠	00000110	06	006
7	(beep)	00000111	07	007
8	◘	00001000	08	010
9	(tab)	00001001	09	011
10	(line feed)	00001010	0A	012
11	(home)	00001011	0B	013
12	(form feed)	00001100	0C	014
13	(carriage return)	00001101	0D	015
14	♪	00001110	0E	016
15	☼	00001111	0F	017
16	►	00010000	10	020
17	◄	00010001	11	021
18	↕	00010010	12	022
19	‼	00010011	13	023
20	π	00010100	14	024
21	§	00010101	15	025
22	▬	00010110	16	026
23	↨	00010111	17	027
24	↑	00011000	18	030
25	↓	00011001	19	031
26	→	00011010	1A	032
27	←	00011011	1B	033
28	(cursor right)	00011100	1C	034
29	(cursor left)	00011101	1D	035
30	(cursor up)	00011110	1E	036
31	(cursor down)	00011111	1F	037
32	(space)	00100000	20	040
33	!	00100001	21	041

Decimal (ASCII)	Character	Binary	Hexadecimal	Octal
34	"	00100010	22	042
35	#	00100011	23	043
36	$	00100100	24	044
37	%	00100101	25	045
38	&	00100110	26	046
39	'	00100111	27	047
40	(	00101000	28	050
41	)	00101001	29	051
42	*	00101010	2A	052
43	+	00101011	2B	053
44	,	00101100	2C	054
45	-	00101101	2D	055
46	.	00101110	2E	056
47	/	00101111	2F	057
48	0	00110000	30	060
49	1	00110001	31	061
50	2	00110010	32	062
51	3	00110011	33	063
52	4	00110100	34	064
53	5	00110101	35	065
54	6	00110110	36	066
55	7	00110111	37	067
56	8	00111000	38	070
57	9	00111001	39	071
58	:	00111010	3A	072
59	;	00111011	3B	073
60	<	00111100	3C	074
61	=	00111101	3D	075
62	>	00111110	3E	076
63	?	00111111	3F	077
64	@	01000000	40	100
65	A	01000001	41	101
66	B	01000010	42	102
67	C	01000011	43	103
68	D	01000100	44	104
69	E	01000101	45	105
70	F	01000110	46	106
71	G	01000111	47	107
72	H	01001000	48	110
73	I	01001001	49	111
74	J	01001010	4A	112
75	K	01001011	4B	113
76	L	01001100	4C	114
77	M	01001101	4D	115
78	N	01001110	4E	116
79	O	01001111	4F	117

Decimal (ASCII)	Character	Binary	Hexadecimal	Octal
80	P	01010000	50	120
81	Q	01010001	51	121
82	R	01010010	52	122
83	S	01010011	53	123
84	T	01010100	54	124
85	U	01010101	55	125
86	V	01010110	56	126
87	W	01010111	57	127
88	X	01011000	58	130
89	Y	01011001	59	131
90	Z	01011010	5A	132
91	[	01011011	5B	133
92	\	01011100	5C	134
93	]	01011101	5D	135
94	∧	01011110	5E	136
95	—	01011111	5F	137
96	'	01100000	60	140
97	a	01100001	61	141
98	b	01100010	62	142
99	c	01100011	63	143
100	d	01100100	64	144
101	e	01100101	65	145
102	f	01100110	66	146
103	g	01100111	67	147
104	h	01101000	68	150
105	i	01101001	69	151
106	j	01101010	6A	152
107	k	01101011	6B	153
108	l	01101100	6C	154
109	m	01101101	6D	155
110	n	01101110	6E	156
111	o	01101111	6F	157
112	p	01110000	70	160
113	q	01110001	71	161
114	r	01110010	72	162
115	s	01110011	73	163
116	t	01110100	74	164
117	u	01110101	75	165
118	v	01110110	76	166
119	w	01110111	77	167
120	x	01111000	78	170
121	y	01111001	79	171
122	z	01111010	7A	172
123	{	01111011	7B	173
124	¦	01111100	7C	174
125	}	01111101	7D	175
126	~	01111110	7E	176

Decimal (ASCII)	Character	Binary	Hexadecimal	Octal
127	△	01111111	7F	177
128	Ç	10000000	80	200
129	ü	10000001	81	201
130	é	10000010	82	202
131	â	10000011	83	203
132	ä	10000100	84	204
133	à	10000101	85	205
134	å	10000110	86	206
135	ç	10000111	87	207
136	ê	10001000	88	210
137	ë	10001001	89	211
138	è	10001010	8A	212
139	ï	10001011	8B	213
140	î	10001100	8C	214
141	ì	10001101	8D	215
142	Ä	10001110	8E	216
143	Å	10001111	8F	217
144	É	10010000	90	220
145	æ	10010001	91	221
146	Æ	10010010	92	222
147	ô	10010011	93	223
148	ö	10010100	94	224
149	ò	10010101	95	225
150	û	10010110	96	226
151	ù	10010111	97	227
152	ÿ	10011000	98	230
153	Ö	10011001	99	231
154	Ü	10011010	9A	232
155	¢	10011011	9B	233
156	£	10011100	9C	234
157	¥	10011101	9D	235
158	Pt	10011110	9E	236
159	ƒ	10011111	9F	237
160	á	10100000	A0	240
161	í	10100001	A1	241
162	ó	10100010	A2	242
163	ú	10100011	A3	243
164	ñ	10100100	A4	244
165	Ñ	10100101	A5	245
166	ª	10100110	A6	246
167	º	10100111	A7	247
168	¿	10101000	A8	250
169	⌐	10101001	A9	251
170	¬	10101010	AA	252
171	½	10101011	AB	253
172	¼	10101100	AC	254
173	¡	10101101	AD	255

174	≪	10101110	AE	256
175	≫	10101111	AF	257
176		10110000	BO	260
177		10110001	B1	261
178		10110010	B2	262
179		10110011	B3	263
180		10110100	B4	264
181		10110101	B5	265
182		10110110	B6	266
183		10110111	B7	267
184		10111000	B8	270
185		10111001	B9	271
186		10111010	BA	272
187		10111011	BB	273
188		10111100	BC	274
189		10111101	BD	275
190		10111110	BE	276
191		10111111	BF	277
192		11000000	C0	300
193		11000001	C1	301
194		11000010	C2	302
195		11000011	C3	303
196	–	11000100	C4	304
197	+	11000101	C5	305
198		11000110	C6	306
199		11000111	C7	307
200		11001000	C8	310
201		11001001	C9	311
202		11001010	CA	312
203		11001011	CB	313
204		11001100	CC	314
205		11001101	CD	315
206		11001110	CE	316
207		11001111	CF	317
208		11010000	D0	320
209		11010001	D1	321
210		11010010	D2	322
211		11010011	D3	323
212		11010100	D4	324
213		11010101	D5	325
214		11010110	D6	326
215		11010111	D7	327
216		11011000	D8	330
217		11011001	D9	331
218		11011010	DA	332
219		11011011	DB	333
220		11011100	DC	334
221		11011101	DD	335
222		11011110	DE	336

223	▬	11011111	DF	337
224	α	11100000	E0	340
225	β	11100001	E1	341
226	γ	11100010	E2	342
227	π	11100011	E3	343
228	Σ	11100100	E4	344
229	σ	11100101	E5	345
230	μ	11100110	E6	346
231	τ	11100111	E7	347
232	Φ	11101000	E8	350
233	θ	11101001	E9	351
234	Ω	11101010	EA	352
235	δ	11101011	EB	353
236	∞	11101100	EC	354
237	Ø	11101101	ED	355
238	ε	11101110	EE	356
239	∩	11101111	EF	357
240	≡	11110000	F0	360
241	±	11110001	F1	361
242	≥	11110010	F2	362
243	≤	11110011	F3	363
244	∫	11110100	F4	364
245	∫	11110101	F5	365
246	÷	11110110	F6	366
247	≈	11110111	F7	367
248	°	11111000	F8	370
249	•	11111001	F9	371
250	·	11111010	FA	372
251	√	11111011	FB	373
252	ⁿ	11111100	FC	374
253	²	11111101	FD	375
254	■	11111110	FE	376
255	(blank 'FF')	11111111	FF	377

E

Character Attributes in the Text Mode

The COLOR statement can produce a variety of effects in the text mode. (The text mode is the default mode, or is implemented by typing the BASIC command SCREEN 0).

Desired effect	Statement	Foreground	Background
Invisible character	COLOR 0,0	0	0
Black on white	COLOR 0,7	0	7
Underlined	COLOR 1,0	1	0
White on black (normal display)	COLOR 7,0	7	0
High intensity underlined	COLOR 9,0	9	0
High intensity	COLOR 15,0	15	0
Blinking black on white	COLOR 16,7	16	7
Blinking	COLOR 20,0	20	0
Blinking underlined high intensity	COLOR 25,0	25	0
Blinking high intensity	COLOR 30,0	30	0

Derived Mathematical Functions

The mathematical functions listed in the left column below are calculated in BASIC using the formulas on the right.

Logarithm to base B	LOGB(X) = LOG(X)/LOG(B)
Secant	SEC(X) = 1/COS(X)
Cosecant	CSC(X) = 1/SIN(X)
Cotangent	COT(X) = 1/TAN(X)
Inverse sine	ARCSIN(X) = ATN(X/SQR(1-X*X))
Inverse cosine	ARCCOS(X) = 1.570796-ATN(X/SQR(1-X*X))
Inverse secant	ARCSEC(X) = ATN(SQR(X*X-1))+(X<0)*3.141593
Inverse cosecant	ARCCSC(X) = ATN(1/SQR(X*X-1))+(X<0)*3.141593
Inverse cotangent	ARCCOT(X) = 1.57096-ATN(X)
Hyperbolic sine	SINH(X) = (EXP(X)-EXP(-X))/2
Hyperbolic cosine	COSH(X) = (EXP(X)+EXP(-X))/2
Hyperbolic tangent	TANH(X) = (EXP(X)-EXP(-X))/(EXP(X)+EXP(-X))
Hyperbolic secant	SECH(X) = 2/(EXP(X)+EXP(-X))
Hyperbolic cosecant	CSCH(X) = 2/(EXP(X)-EXP(-X))
Hyperbolic cotangent	COTH(X) = (EXP(X)+EXP(-X))/(EXP(X)-EXP(-X))
Inverse hyperbolic sine	ARCSINH(X) = LOG(X+SQR(X*X+1))
Inverse hyperbolic cosine	ARCCOSH(X) = LOG(X+SQR(X*X+1))
Inverse hyperbolic tangent	ARCTANH(X) = LOG((1+X)/(1-X))/2
Inverse hyperbolic secant	ARCSECH(X) = LOG((1+SQR(1-X*X))/X)
Inverse hyperbolic cosecant	ARCCSCH(X) = LOG((1+SGN(X)*SQR(1+X*X))/X)
Inverse hyperbolic cotangent	ARCCOTH(X) = LOG((X+1)/(X-1))/2

A good way to use these formulas is to define these functions using the DEF FN statement. For example, the inverse sine function can be defined by

```
5Ø DEF FNARCSIN(X) = ATN(X/SQR(1-X*X))
```

and then used subsequently as

```
FNARCSIN(ANGLE)
```

whenever this function is needed.

G

BASIC Error Messages

Code Number	Error Message
1	NEXT without FOR
2	Syntax ERROR
3	RETURN without GOSUB
4	Out of DATA
5	Illegal function call
6	Overflow
7	Out of memory
8	Undefined Line number
9	Subscript out of range
10	Duplicate Definition
11	Division by zero
12	Illegal direct
13	Type mismatch
14	Out of string space
15	String too long
16	String formula too complex
17	Can't continue
18	Undefined user function
19	No RESUME
20	RESUME without ERROR
21	Unprintable error
22	Missing operand
23	Line buffer overflow
24	Device Timeout
25	Device Fault
26	FOR without NEXT
27	Out of Paper
29	WHILE without WEND
30	WEND without WHILE
50	FIELD overflow
51	Internal error
52	Bad file number
53	File not found
54	Bad file mode
55	File already open
57	Device I/O Error
58	File already exists
61	Disk full
62	Input past end

63	Bad record number
64	Bad file name
66	Direct statement in file
67	Too many files
68	Device unavailable
69	Communication buffer Overflow
70	Disk Write Protect
71	Disk not ready
72	Disk media error
73	Advanced feature
74	Rename across disks*
75	Path/file access error*
76	Path not found*
--	Unprintable error*
-	Incorrect DOS Version*

*= DOS 2.0 only

Index

Notes

℗

☐ **DOS PRIMER for the IBM® PC and XT**
by Mitchell Waite, John Angermeyer, and Mark Noble.
An easy-to-understand guide to IBM's disk operating-system, versions 1.1 and 2.0, which explains—from the ground up—what a DOS does and how to use it. Also covered are advanced topics such as the fixed disk, tree structured directories, and redirection.   (254949—$14.95)

☐ **PASCAL PRIMER for the IBM® PC**
by Michael Pardee.
An authoritative guide to this important structured language. Using sound and graphics examples, this book takes the reader from simple concepts to advanced topics such as files, linked lists, compilands, pointers, and the heap.   (254965—$17.95)

☐ **ASSEMBLY LANGUAGE PRIMER for the IBM® PC and XT**
by Robert Lafore.
This unusual book teaches assembly language to the beginner. The author's unique approach, using DEBUG and DOS functions, gets the reader programming fast without the usual confusion and overhead found in most books on this fundamental subject. Covers sound, graphics, and disk access.   (257115—$24.95)

☐ **BLUEBOOK OF ASSEMBLY ROUTINES for the IBM® PC and XT**
by Christopher L. Morgan.
A collection of expertly written "cookbook" routines that can be plugged in and used in any BASIC, Pascal, or assembly language program. Included are graphics, sound, and arithmetic conversions. Get the speed and power of assembly language in your program, even if you don't know the language!   (254981—$19.95)

All prices higher in Canada.

To order, use the convenient coupon on the next page.

Ⓟ

Computer Guides from PLUME

(0452)

☐ **THE COMPUTER PHONE BOOK by Mike Cane.**
The indispensable guide to personal computer networking. A complete annotated listing of names and numbers so you can go online with over 400 systems across the country. Includes information on: free software; electronic mail; computer games; consumer catalogs; medical data; stock market reports; dating services; and much, much more.
(254469—$9.95)

☐ **DATABASE PRIMER: AN EASY-TO-UNDERSTAND GUIDE TO DATABASE MANAGEMENT SYSTEMS by Rose Deakin.**
The future of information control is in database management systems —tools that help you organize and manipulate information or data. This essential guide tells you how a database works, what it can do for you, and what you should know when you go to buy one. (254922—$9.95)†

☐ **BEGINNING WITH BASIC: AN INTRODUCTION TO COMPUTER PROGRAMMING by Kent Porter.**
Now, at last, the new computer owner has a book that speaks in down-to-earth everyday language to explain clearly—and step-by-step—how to master BASIC, Beginner's All-Purpose Symbolic Instructional Code. And how to use it to program your computer to do exactly what you want it to do.
(254914—$10.95)

☐ **THE EASY-DOES-IT-GUIDE TO THE IBM® PCjr by Barbara Schwartz**
The guide no owner should be without includes information on learning BASIC, word processing, and home finance, choosing the right software, games and accessories and even how to connect the system and keep it going, plus tips on how to use the PCjr in conjunction with the PC.
(254892—$8.95)

All prices higher in Canada.   †Not available in Canada.

Buy them at your local bookstore or use this convenient
coupon for ordering.

NEW AMERICAN LIBRARY
P.O. Box 999, Bergenfield, New Jersey 07621

Please send me the PLUME BOOKS I have checked above. I am enclosing $_____(please add $1.50 to this order to cover postage and handling). Send check or money order—no cash or C.O.D.'s. Price and numbers are subject to change without notice.

Name _____

Address _____

City _____ State _____ Zip Code _____

Allow 4-6 weeks for delivery. This offer is subject to withdrawal without notice.